Assembly language subroutines for the 68000

L. A. LEVENTHAL
and
F. CORDES

McGRAW-HILL BOOK COMPANY

London · New York · St Louis · San Francisco · Auckland
Bogotá · Guatemala · Hamburg · Lisbon · Madrid · Mexico
Montreal · New Delhi · Panama · Paris · San Juan · São Paulo
Singapore · Sydney · Tokyo · Toronto

Published by
McGRAW-HILL Book Company (UK) Limited
MAIDENHEAD · BERKSHIRE · ENGLAND

British Library Cataloguing in Publication Data
Leventhal, Lance A, *1945–*
Assembly language subroutines for the 68000.
1. Motorola 68000 microprocessor systems.
Assembly languages
I. Title II. Cordes, F.
005.2'65

ISBN 0-07-707150-6

Library of Congress Cataloguing-in-Publication Data
Leventhal, Lance A, 1945–
Assembly language subroutines for the 68000 / L. A. Leventhal and F. Cordes
p. cm.
Includes index.
ISBN 0-07-707150-6
1. Motorola 68000 (Microprocessor) – Programming. 2. Assembler language (Computer program language) 3. Subroutines (Computer programs)
I. Cordes, F. II. Title.
QA76.8.M6895L48 1989
005.265--dc 19 88-39563

First published in Japanese

1234CUP8909
Typeset by Ponting-Green Publishing Services, London,
and printed and bound in Great Britain at the University Press, Cambridge

Contents

Preface

This book is intended as both a source and a reference for the 68000 assembly language programmer. It contains a collection of useful subroutines described in a standard format and accompanied by an extensive documentation package. All subroutines employ standard parameter passing techniques and follow the rules from Motorola's resident structured assembler. The documentation covers the procedure, parameters, results, execution time, and memory usage; it also includes at least one example. The routines will also run on related microprocessors such as the 68008, 68010, 68020, and 68030.

The collection emphasizes common tasks that occur in many applications. These tasks include code conversion, array manipulation, arithmetic, bit manipulation, shifting functions, string manipulation, data structure management, sorting, and searching. We have also provided examples of input/output (I/O) routines, interrupt service routines, and initialization routines for common family chips such as parallel interfaces, serial interfaces, and timers. You should be able to use these programs as subroutines in actual applications and as starting points for more complex programs.

This book is intended for the person who wants to use assembly language immediately, rather than just learn about it. The reader could be

- An engineer, technician, or programmer who must write assembly language programs for a design project.
- A microcomputer or personal computer user who wants to write an

I/O driver, a diagnostic program, a utility, or a systems program in assembly language.

- An experienced assembly language programmer who needs a quick review of techniques for the 68000 or related microprocessor.
- A system designer who needs a specific routine or technique for immediate use.
- A high-level language programmer who must debug or optimize programs at the assembly level, link a program written in a high-level language to one written in assembly language, or move the machine-dependent part of a program to a new computer.
- A maintenance programmer who must understand quickly how specific assembly language programs work.
- A microcomputer owner who wants to understand the operating system of a particular computer, or who wants to modify standard I/O routines or systems programs.
- A student, hobbyist, or teacher who wants to see examples of working assembly language programs.

This book should save the reader time and effort. He or she should not have to write, debug, test, or optimize standard routines, or search through a textbook for particular examples. The reader should instead be able to obtain easily the specific information, technique, or routine he or she needs.

Obviously, a book with such an aim demands feedback from its readers. We have, of course, tested all programs thoroughly and documented them carefully. If you find any errors, please inform the publisher. If you have suggestions for better methods or for additional topics, routines, or programming hints, please tell us about them. We have used our programming experience to develop this book, but we need your help to improve it. We would greatly appreciate your comments, criticisms, and suggestions.

Nomenclature

We have used the following nomenclature in this book to describe the architecture of the 68000 processor and to specify operands.

68000 Architecture

Figure N-1 shows the 68000's user registers. Figures N-2 and N-3 show the supervisor registers for the 68000 and 68010 processors, respectively. The address and data registers are all 32 bits long, the program counter is 24 bits long, and the status register is 16 bits long. We can describe the registers as follows:

- Data registers 0–7 (D0–D7) serve as accumulators or general-purpose registers. Parts of them are byte-addressable (bits 0–7 only) or word-addressable (bits 0–15 only).
- Address registers 0–6 (A0–A6) hold memory addresses. They are word-addressable (bits 0–15 only), but all quantities placed in them are extended automatically to 32 bits. The 68000 actually uses only the lower 24 bits to access memory.
- Address register 7 (A7 or SP) is the stack pointer. In fact, it may be one of two distinct registers, depending on the state of the supervisor/user mode bit. It is the user stack pointer (USP) in user mode, the supervisor stack pointer (SSP) in supervisor mode.
- The program counter (PC) holds a memory address.

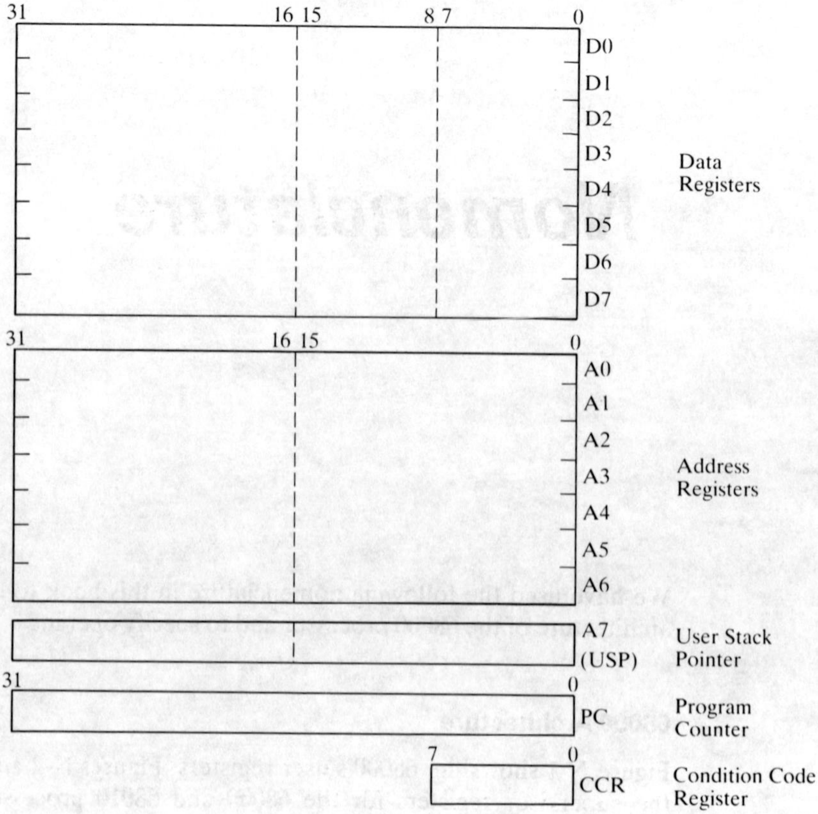

Figure N-1 68000 user registers.

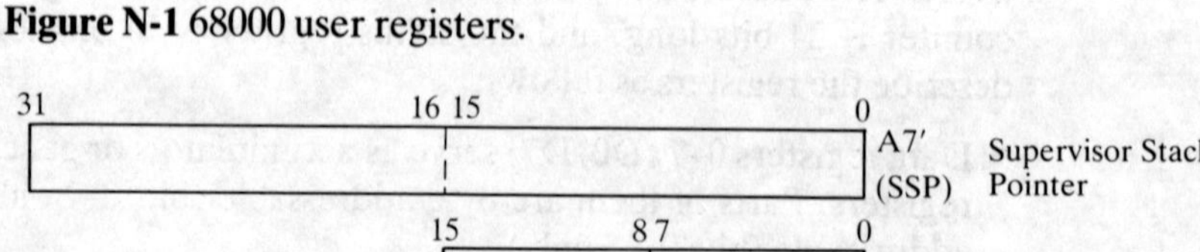

Figure N-2 68000 supervisor registers.

- The status register (SR) consists of two bytes, the system byte and the user byte (condition code register or CCR) as shown in Figure N-4.

We may describe its independent bits and fields more fully as follows:

C	Carry flag
I2, I1, I0	Interrupt mask (interrupt priority level or 0 for no interrupt request)

N	Negative (sign) flag
S	Supervisor/user mode select (1 = supervisor, 0 = user)
T	Trace mode select (1 = enable trace)
V	Overflow flag
X	Extend flag
Z	Zero flag

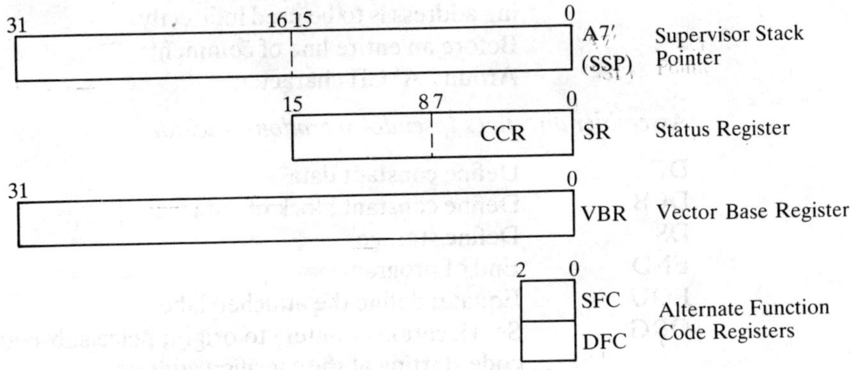

Figure N-3 68010 supervisor registers.

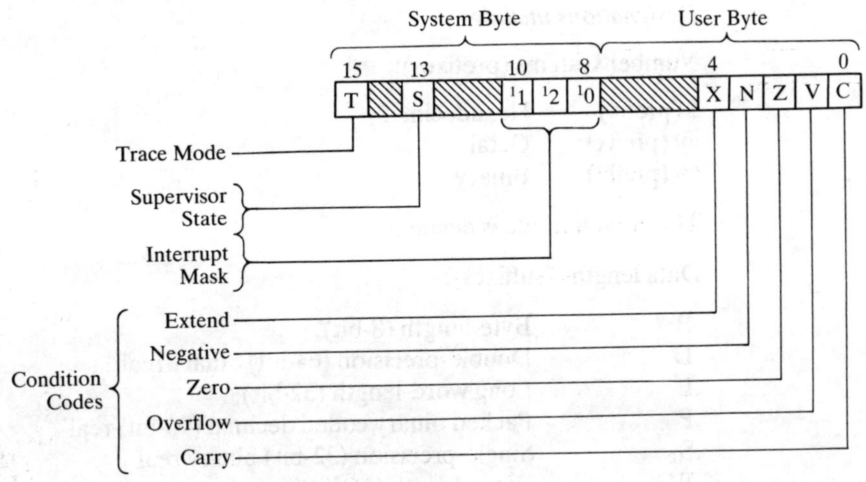

Figure N-4 68000 status register

68000 assembler

Delimiters include

space	After an operation code or a label that starts in column 1, before a comment on the same line as an instruction
, (comma)	Between entries in the operand (address) field
( )	Around addressing mode designations when the resulting address is to be used indirectly
*	Before an entire line of comments
' '	Around ASCII characters

Assembler directives (pseudo-operations) include

DC	Define constant data
DCB	Define constant block of data
DS	Define storage
END	End of program
EQU	Equate; define the attached label
ORG	Set (location counter) to origin; place subsequent object code starting at the specified address
REG	Define a register list

Designations include

Number systems (prefixes):

$ (prefix)	Hexadecimal
@ (prefix)	Octal
% (prefix)	Binary

The default mode is decimal.

Data lengths (suffixes):

.B	Byte-length (8-bit)
.D	Double-precision (64-bit) binary real
.L	Long word-length (32-bit)
.P	Packed binary coded decimal (96-bit) real
.S	Single-precision (32-bit) binary real
.W	Word-length (16-bit)
.X	Extended-precision (96-bit) binary real

The default value is generally .W (word-length).

Branch ranges:

.S (suffix)	Short (8-bit offset, range of −126 to +129 bytes)

.L (suffix) Long (16-bit offset, range of −32 765 to +32 770 bytes)

The default is .L (long branch).

Others:

★	Current value of location (program) counter
#	Immediate addressing
−	Before parentheses to indicate a predecrement
+	After parentheses to indicate a postincrement
/	Between register designations in a multiple register list to indicate 'and'
−	Between register designations in a multiple register list to indicate 'through'

Defaults include

- Unmarked values or expressions are taken to be addresses (not data).
- The default addressing mode is direct.
- Unmarked numbers are decimal.
- Undesignated instructions are generally assumed to be word-length.
- Undesignated branches are assumed to be long.

Introduction

Each description of an assembly language subroutine contains the following information:

- Purpose of the routine
- Procedure
- Entry conditions
- Exit conditions
- Examples
- Registers used
- Execution time
- Program size
- Data memory required
- Special cases

The program listing repeats this information and provides section-by-section comments.

We have made each routine as general as possible. This is difficult for the input/output (I/O) and interrupt service routines in Chapters 8 and 9 since they are always computer-dependent in practice. In such cases, we have limited the dependence to generalized input and output handlers and interrupt managers. We have drawn specific examples from the popular Atari 520ST computer, but the general principles apply to other 68000-based computers as well.

Almost all routines use the following parameter passing techniques (similar to those used in the Apple Macintosh; see pp. I-94 – I-95 of *Inside Macintosh*, Addison-Wesley, Reading, MA, 1985):

1. A single data parameter is passed in register D0. It may be 8, 16, or 32 bits long.

2. A single 32-bit address parameter is passed in register A0. The 68000 actually uses only the lower 24 bits to address memory.

3. Larger number of parameters are passed on the stack, either directly or indirectly. We assume that the subroutine entry is via a JSR instruction that places the return address at the top of the stack, and hence on top of the parameters.

Where trade-offs exist between execution time and memory usage, we have chosen to minimize execution time. We have also chosen the approach that minimizes repetitive calculations. For example, consider array indexing. The number of bytes between the starting addresses of elements differing only by one in a particular subscript (known as the *size* of that subscript) depends on the number of bytes per element and the array's bounds. We can, therefore, calculate the sizes of all subscripts and use them as parameters in indexing routines. We then need not recalculate them each time a particular array is indexed.

We have specified the execution times for most short routines. For long routines, we provide approximate execution times. The execution time of programs with many branches obviously depends on which path the computer follows in a particular case. Other complicating factors include memory management overhead, the dependence of branch execution times on whether a branch actually occurs, and the variation in execution times of the multiply and divide instructions. Thus, a precise execution time is often impossible to define. The documentation always contains at least one typical example showing an approximate or maximum execution time.

Our philosophy on error indicators and special cases has been the following:

1. Routines should provide an easily tested indicator (such as the Carry flag) of whether any errors or exceptions have occurred. An alternative for more complex situations is to return a status byte or result code. The common convention (established in UNIX and other operating systems) is for a zero value to indicate successful completion and for non-zero values to indicate types of errors.

2. Trivial cases, such as no elements in an array or strings of zero length, should result in immediate exits with minimal effect on the underlying data.

3. Misspecified data (such as a maximum string length of zero or an index beyond the end of an array) should result in immediate exits with minimal effect on the underlying data.

4. The documentation should include a summary of errors and exceptions (under the heading of 'Special cases').

5. Exceptions that are convenient for the user (such as deleting more characters than could possibly be left in a string rather than counting the precise number) should be handled reasonably, but should still be indicated as errors.

Obviously, no method of handling errors or exceptions can even be completely consistent or well-suited to all applications. Our approach is that a reasonable set of subroutines must deal with this issue, rather than ignoring it or assuming that the user will always provide properly formatted data.

1 Code conversion

1A Binary to BCD conversion (BN2BCD)

Converts one byte of binary data to two bytes of BCD data.

Procedure The program first divides the original data by 100 to obtain the hundreds digit, then divides the remainder by 10 to obtain the tens and ones digits, and finally shifts the higher digits left four bit positions and combines them with the lower digits.

Entry conditions

Binary data in low byte of D0

Exit conditions

BCD data in low word of D0

Examples

1. Data: (D0) = $6D_{16}$ (109 decimal)
   Result: (D0) = 0109_{16}

2. Data: (D0) = $B7_{16}$ (183 decimal)
Result: (D0) = 0183_{16}

Registers used CCR, D0, D1

Execution time 360 cycles maximum

Program size 30 bytes

Data memory required None

```
*
*
*
*
*       Title:                  Binary to BCD Conversion
*       Name:                   BN2BCD
*
*
*
*       Purpose:                Converts one byte of binary data to two
*                               bytes of BCD data
*
*       Entry:                  Low byte of register D0 = Binary data
*
*       Exit:                   Low word of register D0 = BCD data
*
*       Registers Used:         CCR,D0,D1
*
*       Time:                   360 cycles maximum
*
*       Size:                   Program 30 bytes
*
*

BN2BCD
        *
        *CALCULATE 100'S DIGIT
        *DIVIDE DATA BY 100
        *
        CLR.L     D1                EXTEND DATA TO 32 BITS
        MOVE.B    D0,D1
        DIVU      #100,D1           DIVIDE DATA BY 100
                                    *QUOTIENT (100'S DIGIT) ENDS UP
                                    * IN BITS 0-15, REMAINDER IN
                                    * BITS 16-31
        MOVE.W    D1,D0             SAVE QUOTIENT AS 100'S DIGIT
```

```
        *
        *CALCULATE TENS AND ONES DIGITS
        *DIVIDE REMAINDER BY 10
        *
        CLR.W    D1            EXTEND REMAINDER TO 32 BITS (HIGH
                               * BITS IN POSITIONS 0-15)
        SWAP     D1            NEW DIVIDEND = OLD REMAINDER
        DIVU     #10,D1        DIVIDE REMAINDER BY 10
                               *QUOTIENT (BITS 0-15) IS 10'S DIGIT,
                               *REMAINDER (BITS 16-31) IS 1'S DIGIT
        *
        *COMBINE DIGITS
        *SHIFT 100'S DIGIT LEFT 4 BITS, OR IN 10'S DIGIT
        *SHIFT 100'S AND 10'S DIGITS LEFT 4 BITS, OR IN 1'S DIGIT
        *
        ASL.W    #4,D0         MOVE 100'S DIGIT LEFT 1 DIGIT
        OR.W     D1,D0         COMBINE 10'S DIGIT WITH 100'S DIGIT
        ASL.W    #4,D0         MOVE 100'S, 10'S DIGITS LEFT
        SWAP     D1
        OR.W     D1,D0         COMBINE 1'S DIGIT WITH OTHER DIGITS
        RTS


*
*
*       SAMPLE EXECUTION
*
*

SC1A
        *CONVERT 0A HEXADECIMAL TO 10 BCD
        MOVE.B   #$0A,D0
        JSR      BN2BCD        D0 = 10 HEX

        *CONVERT FF HEXADECIMAL TO 255 BCD
        MOVE.B   #$FF,D0
        JSR      BN2BCD        D0 = 255 HEX

        *CONVERT 0 HEXADECIMAL TO 0 BCD
        CLR.B    D0
        JSR      BN2BCD        D0 = 0

        BRA.S    SC1A          REPEAT TEST

        END
```

1B BCD to binary conversion (BCD2BN)

Converts one byte of BCD data to one byte of binary data.

Procedure The program masks off the more significant digit and multiplies it by 10 using shifts. The program then adds the product to the less significant digit. We do not use MULU to multiply because of its long execution time (over 70 cycles).

Entry conditions

BCD data in low byte of D0

Exit conditions

Binary data in low byte of D0

Examples

1. Data: (D0) = 99_{16}
   Result: (D0) = $63_{16} = 99_{10}$

2. Data: (D0) = 23_{16}
   Result: (D0) = $17_{16} = 23_{10}$

Registers used CCR, D0, D1

Execution time 66 cycles

Program size 22 bytes

Data memory required None

```
*
*
*
*
*    Title:              BCD to Binary Conversion
*    Name:               BCD2BN
*
*
*
*    Purpose:            Converts one byte of BCD data to one
*                        byte of binary data
*
*    Entry:              Low byte of register D0 = BCD data
*
*    Exit:               Low byte of register D0 = Binary data
*
*    Registers Used:     CCR,D0,D1
*
*    Time:               66 cycles
*
*    Size:               Program 22 bytes
*
*

BCD2BN
        *
        *MULTIPLY UPPER DIGIT TIMES TEN BY SHIFTING
        *
        MOVE.B   D0,D1      SAVE ORIGINAL BCD VALUE
        ANDI.B   #$F0,D0    MASK OFF UPPER DIGIT
        LSR.B    #1,D0      CALCULATE UPPER DIGIT TIMES 8
                            *REMEMBER DIGIT IN UPPER 4 BITS
                            * IS EQUIVALENT TO DIGIT VALUE
                            * MULTIPLIED BY 16
        MOVE.B   D0,D2      SAVE UPPER DIGIT TIMES 8
        LSR.B    #2,D0      CALCULATE UPPER DIGIT TIMES 2
                            *THIS IS UPPER DIGIT TIMES 8
                            *  DIVIDED BY 4 (2 RIGHT SHIFTS)
        ADD.B    D2,D0      CALCULATE UPPER DIGIT TIMES 10
                            *  USING 10 = 8 + 2
        *
        *ADD PRODUCT TO LOWER DIGIT
        *
        ANDI.B   #$0F,D1    MASK OFF LOWER DIGIT
        ADD.B    D1,D0      ADD LOWER DIGIT TO PRODUCT
        RTS

*
*
*       SAMPLE EXECUTION
*
*

SC1B
        *CONVERT 0 BCD TO 0 HEXADECIMAL
        CLR.B    D0
```

```
JSR       BCD2BN          D0 = 00

*CONVERT 99 BCD TO 63 HEXADECIMAL
MOVE.B    #$99,D0
JSR       BCD2BN          D0 = 63 HEX

*CONVERT 23 BCD TO 17 HEXADECIMAL
MOVE.B    #$23,D0
JSR       BCD2BN          D0 = 17 HEX

BRA.S     SC1B            REPEAT TEST

END
```

1C Binary to hexadecimal ASCII conversion (BN2HEX)

Converts one byte of binary data to two hexadecimal digits represented as ASCII characters.

Procedure The program masks off each hexadecimal digit separately and converts it to its ASCII equivalent. This involves a simple addition of 30_{16} (ASCII 0) if the digit is decimal. If the digit is non-decimal, we must add an extra 7 to bridge the gap between ASCII 9 (39_{16}) and ASCII A (41_{16}).

Entry conditions

Binary data in low byte of D0

Exit conditions

ASCII version of hexadecimal digits in low word of D0

Examples

1. Data: (D0) = FB_{16}
   Result: (D0) = 4642_{16} (ASCII F, ASCII B)
2. Data: (D0) = 59_{16}
   Result: (D0) = 3539_{16} (ASCII 5, ASCII 9)

Registers used CCR, D0, D1

Execution time 124 cycles plus 2 cycles for each non-decimal digit

Program size 38 bytes

Data memory required None

```
 *
 *
 *
 *
 *   Title:              Binary to Hexadecimal ASCII
 *   Name:               BN2HEX
 *
 *
 *
 *   Purpose:            Converts one byte of binary data to two
 *                       ASCII characters
 *
 *   Entry:              Low byte of register D0 = Binary data
 *
 *   Exit:               Low word of register D0 = ASCII digits
 *
 *   Registers Used:     CCR,D0,D1
 *
 *   Time:               Approximately 124 cycles
 *
 *   Size:               Program 38 bytes
 *
 *

BN2HEX
         *
         *CONVERT MORE SIGNIFICANT DIGIT TO ASCII
         *
         MOVE.B   D0,D1              SAVE ORIGINAL BINARY VALUE
         LSR.B    #4,D0              MOVE HIGH DIGIT TO LOW DIGIT
         CMPI.B   #9,D0
         BLS.S    ADASCH             BRANCH IF HIGH DIGIT IS DECIMAL
         ADDQ.B   #7,D0              ELSE ADD 7 SO AFTER ADDING '0' THE
                                     * CHARACTER WILL BE IN 'A'..'F'
ADASCH   ADDI.B   '0',D0             ADD ASCII 0 TO MAKE A CHARACTER
         *
         *CONVERT LESS SIGNIFICANT DIGIT TO ASCII
         *
         ANDI.B   #$0F,D1            MASK OFF LOW DIGIT
         CMPI.B   #9,D1
         BLS.S    ADASCL             BRANCH IF LOW DIGIT IS DECIMAL
         ADDQ.B   #7,D1              ELSE ADD 7 SO AFTER ADDING '0' THE
                                     * CHARACTER WILL BE IN 'A'..'F'
ADASCL   ADDI.B   '0',D1             ADD ASCII 0 TO MAKE A CHARACTER
         ASL.W    #8,D0              SHIFT HIGH DIGIT LEFT
         ADD.B    D1,D0              COMBINE WITH LOW DIGIT
         RTS
 *
 *
 *       SAMPLE EXECUTION
 *
 *

SC1C
         *CONVERT 0 TO ASCII '00'
         CLR.B    D0
         JSR      BN2HEX             D0 = 3030 HEX = '00'
```

```
*CONVERT FF HEXADECIMAL TO ASCII 'FF'
MOVE.B      #$FF,D0
JSR         BN2HEX            D0 = 4646 HEX = 'FF'

*CONVERT 23 HEXADECIMAL TO ASCII '23'
MOVE.B      #$23,D0
JSR         BN2HEX            D0 = 3233 HEX = '23'

BRA.S       SC1C              REPEAT TEST

END
```

1D Hexadecimal ASCII to binary conversion (HEX2BN)

Converts two ASCII characters (representing two hexadecimal digits) to one byte of binary data.

Procedure The program converts each ASCII character separately to a hexadecimal digit. This involves a simple subtraction of 30_{16} (ASCII 0) if the digit is decimal. If the digit is non-decimal, the program must subtract another 7 to account for the gap between ASCII 9 (39_{16}) and ASCII A (41_{16}). The program then shifts the more significant digit left four bit positions and combines it with the less significant digit. The program does not check whether the ASCII characters represent valid hexadecimal digits.

Entry conditions

ASCII digits in low word of D0

Exit conditions

Binary data in low byte of D0

Examples

1. Data (D0) = 4437_{16} (ASCII D, ASCII 7)
   Result (D0) = $D7_{16}$
2. Data (D0) = 3142_{16} (ASCII 1, ASCII B)
   Result (D0) = $1B_{16}$

Registers used CCR, D0, D1

Execution time 112 cycles plus two cycles for each non-decimal digit

Program size 34 bytes

Data memory required None

```
*
*
*
*
*     Title:                 Hexadecimal ASCII to Binary
*     Name:                  HEX2BN
*
*
*
*     Purpose:               Converts two ASCII characters to one
*                            byte of binary data
*
*     Entry:                 Low word of register D0 = ASCII digits
*
*     Exit:                  Low byte of register D0 = Binary data
*
*     Registers Used:        CCR,D0,D1
*
*     Time:                  Approximately 112 cycles
*
*     Size:                  Program 34 bytes
*
*


*
*          CONVERT LESS SIGNIFICANT DIGIT TO BINARY
*
HEX2BN
           MOVE.W    D0,D1      SAVE ASCII DIGITS
           SUBI.B    #'0',D0    SUBTRACT ASCII OFFSET (ASCII 0)
           CMPI.B    #9,D0      CHECK IF DIGIT DECIMAL
           BLS.S     CNVTMS     BRANCH IF DIGIT IS DECIMAL
           SUBQ.B    #7,D0      ELSE SUBTRACT OFFSET FOR LETTERS
*
*          CONVERT MORE SIGNIFICANT DIGIT TO BINARY
*
CNVTMS
           LSR.W     #8,D1      MOVE MORE SIGNIFICANT DIGIT TO
                                * LESS SIGNIFICANT POSITION
           SUBI.B    #'0',D1    SUBTRACT ASCII OFFSET (ASCII 0)
           CMPI.B    #9,D1      CHECK IF DIGIT DECIMAL
           BLS.S     CMBDIG     BRANCH IF DIGIT IS DECIMAL
           SUBQ.B    #7,D1      ELSE SUBTRACT OFFSET FOR LETTERS
*
*          COMBINE LESS SIGNIFICANT, MORE SIGNIFICANT DIGITS
*
CMBDIG
           ASL.B     #4,D1      MOVE MORE SIGNIFICANT DIGIT LEFT
                                * TO MORE SIGNIFICANT POSITION
           OR.B      D1,D0      COMBINE HEXADECIMAL DIGITS
           RTS
*
*
*          SAMPLE EXECUTION
*
*
```

```
SC1D
        *CONVERT ASCII 'C7' TO C7 HEXADECIMAL
        MOVE.W   #'C7',D0
        JSR      HEX2BN    D0 = C7 HEX

        *CONVERT ASCII '2F' TO 2F HEXADECIMAL
        MOVE.W   #'2F',D0
        JSR      HEX2BN    D0 = 2F HEX

        *CONVERT ASCII '2A' TO 2A HEXADECIMAL
        MOVE.W   #'2A',D0
        JSR      HEX2BN    D0 = 2A HEX

        BRA.S    SC1D      REPEAT TEST

        END
```

1E Conversion of a binary number to decimal ASCII (BN2DEC)

Converts a 16-bit signed binary number into an ASCII string. The string consists of the length of the number in bytes, an ASCII minus sign (if needed), and the ASCII digits. Note that the length is in binary, not in ASCII.

Procedure If the number is negative, the program takes its absolute value and places an ASCII minus sign in the buffer. It then divides the absolute value by 10000. If the quotient is non-zero, the program converts it to ASCII (by adding ASCII zero) and saves it in the buffer. It continues through the rest of the digits, replacing the quotient with the remainder each time. It saves the ASCII version of each digit except for leading zeros. Finally, the program converts the remainder from the division by 10 to ASCII and saves it as the ones digit. This digit always appears in the buffer; i.e. it is not dropped even if its value is 0.

Entry conditions

Base address of output buffer in A0
Value to convert (between −32 767 and +32 767) in low word of D0

Exit conditions

Order in buffer:
Length of the string in bytes (a binary number)
ASCII − (if value to convert is negative)
ASCII digits (most significant digit first)

Examples

1. Data Value to convert = $3EB7_{16}$
   Result (in output buffer):
   05 (number of bytes in buffer)
   31 (ASCII 1)
   36 (ASCII 6)
   30 (ASCII 0)
   35 (ASCII 5)

35 (ASCII 5)
i.e. $3EB7_{16} = 16055_{10}$

2. Data Value to convert = $FFC8_{16}$
Result (in output buffer):
03 (number of bytes in buffer)
2D (ASCII −)
35 (ASCII 5)
36 (ASCII 6)
i.e. $FFC8_{16} = -56_{10}$, when considered as a signed two's complement number

Registers used A0, A1, CCR, D0, D1, D2

Execution time Approximately 1050 cycles

Program size 96 bytes

Data memory required None except for the output buffer, which should be 7 bytes long.

```
*
*
*
*
*       Title:              Binary to Decimal ASCII
*       Name:               BN2DEC
*
*
*
*       Purpose:            Converts a 16-bit signed binary number
*                           to ASCII data
*
*       Entry:              Low word of register D0 = Value to convert
*                           Register A0 = Output buffer address
*
*       Exit:               The first byte of the buffer is the
*                           length of the string in bytes, followed
*                           by the characters
*
*       Registers Used:     A0,A1,CCR,D0,D1,D2
*
*       Time:               Approximately 1050 cycles
*
*       Size:               Program  96 bytes
```

```
*
*
*
*
BN2DEC
*
*         SAVE ORIGINAL BUFFER POINTER FOR LATER USE
*           WHEN STORING LENGTH
*         SET BUFFER POINTER, NUMBER OF DIGITS, LEADING
*           NON-ZERO DIGIT FLAG
*
          MOVEM.W   D3-D4,-(SP) SAVE EXTRA DATA REGISTERS
          LEA       1(A0),A1    SAVE ORIGINAL BUFFER POINTER
                                * POINT BEYOND LENGTH BYTE
          CLR.W     D1          NUMBER OF DIGITS (D1) = 0
          CLR.B     D2          NO LEADING NON-ZERO DIGIT FOUND (D2=0)
*
*         TAKE ABSOLUTE VALUE AND STORE MINUS SIGN IN
*           BUFFER IF DATA NEGATIVE
*
          TST.W     D0          CHECK SIGN OF DATA
          BPL.S     CALCDG      BRANCH IF SIGN POSITIVE
          NEG.W     D0          DATA NEGATIVE, TAKE ABSOLUTE VALUE
          MOVE.B    '-',(A1)+   SAVE MINUS SIGN IN BUFFER
          ADDQ.B    #1,D1       ADD 1 TO STRING LENGTH FOR MINUS SIGN
*
*         DIVIDE BINARY DATA BY POWERS OF 10 TO GET DIGITS
*           STARTING WITH TEN THOUSAND
*         DO NOT SAVE LEADING ZEROS IN BUFFER
*
CALCDG
          MOVE.W    #10000,D3   DIVISOR = 10,000
          BSR       DIVS16      DIVIDE AND SAVE DIGIT IF NECESSARY
          MOVE.W    #1000,D3    DIVISOR = 1000
          BSR       DIVS16      DIVIDE AND SAVE DIGIT IF NECESSARY
          MOVE.W    #100,D3     DIVISOR = 100
          BSR       DIVS16      DIVIDE AND SAVE DIGIT IF NECESSARY
          MOVE.W    #10,D3      DIVISOR = 10
          BSR       DIVS16      DIVIDE AND SAVE DIGIT IF NECESSARY
          ADD.B     #'0',D0     CONVERT ONES DIGIT TO ASCII
          MOVE.B    D0,(A1)+    ALWAYS SAVE ONES DIGIT
          ADDQ.B    #1,D1       ADD 1 TO STRING LENGTH FOR ONES DIGIT
*
*         SAVE LENGTH OF STRING AT HEAD OF BUFFER AND EXIT
*
          MOVE.B    D1,(A0)   SAVE STRING LENGTH AT HEAD OF BUFFER
          MOVEM.W   (SP)+,D3-D4 RESTORE EXTRA DATA REGISTERS
          RTS

*********************************************************
*ROUTINE: DIVS16
*PURPOSE: DIVIDE 32-BIT DIVIDEND IN D0 BY 16-BIT DIVISOR IN LOW
*           WORD OF D3
*         SAVE ASCII QUOTIENT AT (A0) IF NON-ZERO OR NON-LEADING
*         FLAG LEADING NON-ZERO DIGIT WITH 1 IN REGISTER D2
```

```
*         MOVE BUFFER POINTER UP 1 IF DIGIT SAVED IN BUFFER
*ENTRY:   DO CONTAINS 32-BIT DIVIDEND, D3 16-BIT DIVISOR
*EXIT:    REMAINDER IN DO (EXTENDED TO 32 BITS)
*REGISTERS USED: A1,CCR,DO,D1,D2,D3,D4
*******************************************************

DIVS16
          DIVU      D3,D0      UNSIGNED DIVISION OF 32-BIT DIVIDEND IN
                               * D3 BY 16-BIT DIVISOR IN D3
                               * QUOTIENT ENDS UP IN BITS 0-15 OF
                               * D0, REMAINDER IN BITS 16-31 OF D0
          MOVE.W    D0,D4      SAVE QUOTIENT
          CLR.W     D0         EXTEND REMAINDER TO 32 BITS (LOW BITS
                               * IN POSITIONS 16-31, HIGH IN 0-15)
          SWAP      D0         ROTATE REMAINDER SO IT CAN BE USED
                               * AS DIVIDEND LATER
          TST.B     D2         TEST LEADING ZERO FLAG
          BNE.S     SVDIG      IF NON-ZERO DIGIT ALREADY FOUND, SAVE
                               * CURRENT DIGIT
          TST.B     D4         NO NON-ZERO DIGIT FOUND (FLAG IS 0), SO
                               * CHECK CURRENT DIGIT
          BEQ.S     ENDDIV     IF CURRENT DIGIT ALSO ZERO, DO NOT SAVE IT
          ADDQ.B    #1,D2      CURRENT DIGIT NONZERO, SO INDICATE LEADING
                               * NONZERO DIGIT FOUND BY SETTING FLAG
SVDIG     ADD.B     #'0',D4    CONVERT DIGIT TO ASCII BY ADDING ASCII 0
          ADDQ.B    #1,D1      ADD 1 TO STRING LENGTH
          MOVE.B    D4,(A1)+   SAVE ASCII DIGIT IN STRING
ENDDIV
          RTS

    *
    *
    *     SAMPLE EXECUTION
    *
    *

SC1E
          *CONVERT 0 TO ASCII '0'
          CLR.W     D0              DATA VALUE = 0
          MOVEA.L   #BUFFER,A0      GET BASE ADDRESS OF BUFFER
          JSR       BN2DEC          CONVERT TO ASCII
                                    *BUFFER SHOULD CONTAIN
                                    * BINARY 1 (LENGTH)
                                    * ASCII 0 (STRING)
          *CONVERT 32767 TO ASCII '32767'
          MOVE.W    #32767,D0       DATA VALUE = 32767
          MOVEA.L   #BUFFER,A0      GET BASE ADDRESS OF BUFFER
          JSR       BN2DEC          CONVERT TO ASCII
                                    *BUFFER SHOULD CONTAIN
                                    * BINARY 5 (LENGTH)
                                    * ASCII 32767 (STRING)
          *CONVERT -32767 TO ASCII '-32767'
          MOVE.W    #-32767,D0      DATA VALUE = -32767
          MOVEA.L   #BUFFER,A0      GET BASE ADDRESS OF BUFFER
          JSR       BN2DEC          CONVERT TO ASCII
                                    *BUFFER SHOULD CONTAIN
```

```
                                 * BINARY 6 (LENGTH)
                                 * ASCII - (SIGN)
                                 * ASCII 32767 (STRING)
        BRA.S      SC1E          REPEAT TEST
*
*       DATA
*
BUFFER  DS.B       7             7-BYTE BUFFER
        END
```

1F Conversion of ASCII decimal to binary (DEC2BN)

Converts an ASCII string consisting of the length of the number (in bytes), a possible ASCII + or − sign, and a series of ASCII digits to two bytes of binary data. Note that the length is in binary, not in ASCII. This is a Pascal-style string with an initial length byte, rather than a C language-style string with a terminating character.

Procedure The program checks whether the first byte is a sign and skips over it if it is. The program then uses the length of the string to determine the leftmost digit position. Moving left to right, it converts each digit to decimal (by subtracting ASCII 0), validates it, multiplies it by the corresponding power of 10, and adds the product to the running total. Finally, the program subtracts the binary value from zero if the string started with a minus sign. The program exits immediately, setting the Carry flag, if it finds something other than a leading sign or a decimal digit in the string.

Entry conditions

Base address of string in A0

Exit conditions

Binary value in low word of D0
The Carry flag is 0 if the string is valid, and 1 otherwise.
Note that the result is a signed two's complement 16-bit number.

Examples

1. Data String consists of
   04 (number of bytes in string)
   31 (ASCII 1)
   32 (ASCII 2)
   33 (ASCII 3)
   34 (ASCII 4)
   i.e. the number is $+1234_{10}$

   Result (D0) = $04D2_{16}$ (binary data)

i.e. $+1234_{10} = 04D2_{16}$

2. Data String consists of
06 (number of bytes in string)
2D (ASCII −)
33 (ASCII 3)
32 (ASCII 2)
37 (ASCII 7)
35 (ASCII 5)
30 (ASCII 0)
i.e. the number is $-32\,750_{10}$

Result (D0) = 8016_{16} (binary data)
i.e. $-32\,750_{10} = 8012_{16}$

Registers used A0, A1, CCR, D0, D1, D2

Execution time Approximately 180 cycles per ASCII digit plus 175 cycles overhead

Program size 186 bytes

Data memory required None

Special cases

1. If the string contains something other than a leading sign or a decimal digit, the program returns with the Carry flag set to 1. The result in D0 is invalid.

2. If the string contains only a leading sign (ASCII + or ASCII −), the program returns with the Carry flag set to 1 and a result of 0.

```
*
*
*
*
*       Title:                  Decimal ASCII to Binary
*       Name:                   DEC2BN
*
*
*
```

```
*       Purpose:            Converts ASCII characters to two bytes
*                           of binary data
*
*       Entry:              Register A0 = Input buffer address
*
*       Exit:               Low word of register D0 = Binary data
*                           If no errors then
*                             Carry = 0
*                           else
*                             Carry = 1
*
*       Registers Used:     A0,A1,CCR,D0,D1,D2
*
*       Time:               Approximately 180 cycles per ASCII digit
*                           plus 175 cycles overhead
*
*       Size:               Program 186 bytes
*
*
*
*           SAVE BUFFER POINTER, INITIALIZE BINARY VALUE TO ZERO
*
DEC2BN
            MOVEM.W   D3,-(SP)  SAVE EXTRA DATA REGISTER
            MOVEA.L   A0,A1     STRING POINTER = BUFFER POINTER
            CLR.W     D0        INITIALIZE BINARY VALUE TO ZERO
            MOVE.B    (A0)+,D2  GET NUMBER OF BYTES IN STRING
            CLR.B     D3        INDICATE THERE IS A SIGN IN BUFFER
*
*           CHECK IF FIRST BYTE OF ACTUAL STRING IS SIGN
*           IF SO, INDICATOR IN D3 IS CORRECT AND DIGIT COUNTS
*             ARE CORRECT SINCE THEY ASSSUME A SIGN BYTE
*
            MOVE.B    (A0)+,D1  GET FIRST BYTE OF ACTUAL STRING
            CMPI.B    '-',D1    CHECK IF IT IS ASCII -
            BEQ.S     STMSD     BRANCH IF IT IS
            CMPI.B    '+',D1    CHECK IF IT IS ASCII +
            BEQ.S     STMSD     BRANCH IF IT IS
*
*           FIRST BYTE IS NOT A SIGN
*           SET A FLAG, MOVE POINTER BACK TO START AT FIRST DIGIT
*           INCREASE BYTE COUNT BY 1 SINCE NO SIGN INCLUDED
*
            ADDQ.B    #1,D3     NO SIGN IN BUFFER (D3=1)
            SUBQ.L    #1,A0     MOVE POINTER BACK TO FIRST DIGIT
            ADDQ.B    #1,D2     ADD 1 TO BYTE COUNT
*
*           START CONVERSION AT MOST SIGNIFICANT DIGIT IN BUFFER
*           COULD BE UP TO SIX BYTES INCLUDING SIGN
*
STMSD
            CMPI.B    #6,D2     LOOK FOR 10000'S DIGIT
            BEQ.S     TENKD     BRANCH IF FOUND
            CMPI.B    #5,D2     LOOK FOR 1000'S DIGIT
            BEQ.S     ONEKD     BRANCH IF FOUND
            CMPI.B    #4,D2     LOOK FOR 100'S DIGIT
```

```
        BEQ.S     HUNDD       BRANCH IF FOUND
        CMPI.B    #3,D2       LOOK FOR TENS DIGIT
        BEQ.S     TENSD       BRANCH IF FOUND
        CMPI.B    #2,D2       LOOK FOR ONES DIGIT
        BEQ.S     ONESD       BRANCH IF FOUND
        BRA.S     ERREXIT     NO DIGITS, INDICATE ERROR
*
*       CONVERT 10000'S DIGIT TO BINARY
*
TENKD
        MOVE.B    (A0)+,D1    GET 10000'S ASCII DIGIT
        BSR       ASCDEC      CONVERT TO BINARY, CHECK VALIDITY
        BCS.S     ERREXIT     JUMP IF ERROR RETURN
        CMPI.B    #3,D1       CHECK IF DIGIT TOO LARGE
        BHI.S     ERREXIT     TAKE ERROR EXIT IF IT IS
        MULU      #10000,D1   MULTIPLY TIMES 10,000
        MOVE.W    D1,D0       SAVE PRODUCT
        CLR.W     D1          CLEAR HIGH BYTE OF NEXT DIGIT
*
*       CONVERT 1000'S DIGIT TO BINARY
*
ONEKD
        MOVE.B    (A0)+,D1    GET 1000'S ASCII DIGIT
        BSR       ASCDEC      CONVERT TO BINARY, CHECK VALIDITY
        BCS.S     ERREXIT     JUMP IF ERROR RETURN
        MULU      #1000,D1    MULTIPLY TIMES 1000
        ADD.W     D1,D0       ADD PRODUCT TO PREVIOUS DIGITS
        CLR.W     D1          CLEAR HIGH BYTE OF NEXT DIGIT
*
*       CONVERT 100'S DIGIT TO BINARY
*
HUNDD
        MOVE.B    (A0)+,D1    GET 100'S ASCII DIGIT
        BSR       ASCDEC      CONVERT TO BINARY, CHECK VALIDITY
        BCS.S     ERREXIT     JUMP IF ERROR RETURN
        MULU      #100,D1     MULTIPLY TIMES 100
        ADD.W     D1,D0       ADD PRODUCT TO PREVIOUS DIGITS
        CLR.W     D1          CLEAR HIGH BYTE OF NEXT DIGIT
*
*       CONVERT TENS DIGIT TO BINARY
*
TENSD
        MOVE.B    (A0)+,D1    GET 10'S ASCII DIGIT
        BSR       ASCDEC      CONVERT TO BINARY, CHECK VALIDITY
        BCS.S     ERREXIT     JUMP IF ERROR RETURN
        MULU      #10,D1      MULTIPLY TIMES 10
        ADD.W     D1,D0       ADD PRODUCT TO PREVIOUS DIGITS
        CLR.W     D1          CLEAR HIGH BYTE OF NEXT DIGIT
*
*       CONVERT ONES DIGIT TO BINARY
*
ONESD
        MOVE.B    (A0)+,D1    GET 1'S ASCII DIGIT
        BSR       ASCDEC      CONVERT TO BINARY, CHECK VALIDITY
        BCS.S     ERREXIT     JUMP IF ERROR RETURN
        ADD.W     D1,D0       ADD TO PREVIOUS DIGITS
```

```
*
*         CHECK FOR MINUS SIGN
*
          TST.B     D3        WAS THERE A SIGN BYTE?
          BNE.S     VALEXIT   BRANCH IF NO SIGN
          CMP.B     #'-',(A1) CHECK IF IT IS ASCII -
          BNE.S     VALEXIT   BRANCH IF IT ISN'T
*
*         NEGATIVE NUMBER, SO SUBTRACT VALUE FROM ZERO
*
          NEG.W     D0        SUBTRACT VALUE FROM ZERO
*
*         CLEAR CARRY, INDICATING NO ERRORS
*
VALEXIT
          ANDI      #$FE,CCR  CLEAR CARRY, INDICATING NO ERRORS
          BRA.S     ASCEXIT
*
*         ERROR EXIT - SET CARRY FLAG TO RETURN ERROR CONDITION
*
ERREXIT
          ORI       #1,CCR    SET CARRY TO INDICATE ERROR
ASCEXIT
          MOVEM.W   (SP)+,D3  RESTORE EXTRA DATA REGISTER (NOTE THAT
                              * MOVEM DOES NOT AFFECT CARRY)
          RTS
************************************************************
*ROUTINE: ASCDEC
*PURPOSE: CONVERTS ASCII TO DECIMAL, CHECKS VALIDITY OF DIGITS
*ENTRY: ASCII DIGIT IN LOW BYTE OF D1
*EXIT: DECIMAL DIGIT IN LOW BYTE OF D1
*      CARRY = 0 IF DIGIT VALID, 1 IF NOT VALID
*REGISTERS USED: CCR,D1
************************************************************
ASCDEC    SUBI.B    #'0',D1   CONVERT TO DECIMAL BY SUBTRACTING ASCII 0
          BCS.S     EREXIT    BRANCH IF ERROR (VALUE TOO SMALL)
          CMPI.B    #9,D1     CHECK IF RESULT IS DECIMAL DIGIT
          BHI.S     EREXIT    BRANCH IF ERROR (VALUE TOO LARGE)
          ANDI      #$FE,CCR  ELSE RETURN DECIMAL DIGIT AND CLEAR
                              * CARRY TO INDICATE VALID RESULT
          RTS
EREXIT    ORI       #1,CCR    SET CARRY TO INDICATE INVALID RESULT
          RTS

*
*
*    SAMPLE EXECUTION
*
*

SC1F
          *CONVERT ASCII '1234' TO 04D2 HEX
          MOVEA.L   #S1,A0    GET BASE ADDRESS OF STRING 1
          JSR       DEC2BN    LOW WORD OF D0=04D2 HEX
```

```
        *CONVERT ASCII '+32767' TO 7FFF HEX
        MOVEA.L   #S2,A0    GET BASE ADDRESS OF STRING 2
        JSR       DEC2BN    LOW WORD OF D0=7FFF HEX

        *CONVERT ASCII '-32768' TO 8000 HEX
        MOVEA.L   #S3,A0    GET BASE ADDRESS OF STRING 3
        JSR       DEC2BN    LOW WORD OF D0=8000 HEX

        BRA.S     SC1F      REPEAT TEST

*
*       DATA
*

S1      DC.B      4         STRING 1
        DC.B      '1234'
S2      DC.B      6         STRING 2
        DC.B      '+32767'
S3      DC.B      6         STRING 3
        DC.B      '-32768'
        END
```

2 Array manipulation and indexing

2A Two-dimensional byte array indexing (D2BYTE)

Calculates the address of an element of a two-dimensional byte-length array, given the array's base address, the element's two subscripts, and the size of a row (i.e. the number of columns). The array is assumed to be stored in row major order (i.e. by rows), and both subscripts are assumed to begin at 0.

Procedure The program multiplies the row size (number of columns in a row) times the row subscript (since the elements are stored by rows) and adds the product to the column subscript. It then adds the sum to the base address.

Entry conditions

Order in stack (starting from the top)

High word of return address
Low word of return address

High byte of column subscript
Low byte of column subscript

High byte of the size of a row (in bytes)

Low byte of the size of a row (in bytes)

High byte of row subscript
Low byte of row subscript

High word of base address of array
Low word of base address of array

Exit conditions

Address of element in A0

Examples

1. Data: Base address = $1D3C00_{16}$
Column subscript = 0004_{16}
Size of row (number of columns) = 0018_{16}
Row subscript = 0003_{16}
Result: Element address = $1D3C00_{16} + 0003_{16} \times 0018_{16} + 0004_{16}$
$= 1D3C00_{16} + 0048_{16} + 0004_{16}$
$= 1D3C4C_{16}$
i.e. the address of ARRAY(3,4) is $1D3C4C_{16}$.

2. Data: Base address = $2E6A4A_{16}$
Column subscript = 0037_{16}
Size of row (number of columns) = 0050_{16}
Row subscript = 0002_{16}
Result: Element address = $2E6A4A_{16} + 0002_{16} \times 0050_{16} + 0037_{16}$
$= 2E6A4A_{16} + 00A0_{16} + 0037_{16}$
$= 2E6B21_{16}$
i.e. the address of ARRAY(2,35) is $2E6B21_{16}$.

Note that all subscripts are hexadecimal (e.g. $37_{16} = 55_{10}$). The general formula is

ELEMENT ADDRESS = ARRAY BASE ADDRESS + ROW SUBSCRIPT × ROW SIZE + COLUMN SUBSCRIPT

Note that we refer to the *size* of the row subscript; this is the number of consecutive memory addresses for which the subscript has the same value. It is also the distance in bytes from the address of an element to the address of the element with the same column subscript but a row subscript one larger.

Registers used A0, A1, CCR, D0, D1, D2

Execution time Approximately 138 cycles

Program size 18 bytes

Data memory required None

```
*
*
*
*
*       Title:                  Two-Dimensional Byte Array Indexing
*       Name:                   D2BYTE
*
*
*
*       Purpose:                Given the base address of a byte array,
*                               two subscripts 'I' and 'J', and the size
*                               of the first subscript in bytes, calculate
*                               the address of A[I,J].  The array is assumed
*                               to be stored in row major order (A[0,0],
*                               A[0,1],...,A[K,L]), and both dimensions
*                               are assumed to begin at zero as in the
*                               C language or in the following Pascal
*                               declaration:
*                                 A:ARRAY[0..2,0..7] OF BYTE;
*
*       Entry:                  TOP OF STACK
*                                 High word of return address
*                                 Low word of return address
*                                 High byte of second subscript (column number)
*                                 Low byte of second subscript (column number)
*                                 High byte of first subscript size, in bytes
*                                 Low byte of first subscript size, in bytes
*                                 High byte of first subscript (row number)
*                                 Low byte of first subscript (row number)
*                                 High word of array base address
*                                 Low word of array base address
*                               NOTE:
*                                 The first subscript size is the length of
*                                 a row in bytes (number of columns).
*
*       Exit:                   Register A0 = Element address
*
*       Registers Used:         A0,A1,CCR,D0,D1,D2
*
*       Time:                   Approximately 138 cycles
*
*       Size:                   Program 18 bytes
```

```
*
*
*

D2BYTE
        *
        *SAVE RETURN ADDRESS, GET PARAMETERS FROM STACK
        *
        MOVEA.L   (SP)+,A1        SAVE RETURN ADDRESS
        CLR.L     D0              CLEAR MORE SIGNIFICANT WORD OF
                                  * OFFSET (A 32-BIT QUANTITY)
        MOVEM.W   (SP)+,D0-D2     GET COLUMN NUMBER (D0), ROW SIZE (D1),
                                  * ROW SUBSCRIPT (D2)
        MOVEA.L   (SP)+,A0        GET BASE ADDRESS OF ARRAY
        *
        *ELEMENT ADDRESS = ROW SIZE X ROW SUBSCRIPT + COLUMN
        *  SUBSCRIPT + BASE ADDRESS
        *
        MULU      D2,D1           ROW SIZE X ROW SUBSCRIPT
                                  *THIS IS A 16-BIT BY 16-BIT MULTIPLY
                                  * YIELDING A 32-BIT RESULT
        ADD.L     D1,D0           ADD PRODUCT TO COLUMN SUBSCRIPT
                                  * TO GET 32-BIT OFFSET
        ADDA.L    D0,A0           ADD OFFSET TO BASE ADDRESS OF ARRAY
        *
        *EXIT TO RETURN ADDRESS
        *
        JMP       (A1)            EXIT TO RETURN ADDRESS


*
*
*       SAMPLE EXECUTION
*
*

SC2A
        PEA       ARY             PUSH BASE ADDRESS OF ARRAY ONTO STACK
        MOVE.W    SUBS1,D2        GET FIRST (ROW) SUBSCRIPT
        MOVE.W    SSUBS1,D1       GET SIZE OF FIRST SUBSCRIPT
        MOVE.W    SUBS2,D0        GET SECOND (COLUMN) SUBSCRIPT
        MOVEM.W   D0-D2,-(SP)     PUT DATA PARAMETERS IN STACK
        JSR       D2BYTE          CALCULATE ADDRESS OF ELEMENT
                                  *FOR THE INITIAL TEST DATA
                                  *A0 = ADDRESS OF ARY(2,4)
                                  *   = ARY + (2 X 8) + 4
                                  *   = ARY + 20 (CONTENTS ARE 21)
                                  *NOTE BOTH SUBSCRIPTS START AT 0
        BRA.S     SC2A            REPEAT TEST
*
*DATA
*
SUBS1   DC.W      2               SUBSCRIPT 1 (ROW NUMBER)
SSUBS1  DC.W      8               SIZE OF SUBSCRIPT 1 (NUMBER OF BYTES
                                  * PER ROW)
SUBS2   DC.W      4               SUBSCRIPT 2 (COLUMN NUMBER)
```

```
*THE ARRAY (3 ROWS OF 8 COLUMNS)
ARY     DC.B    1,2,3,4,5,6,7,8
        DC.B    9,10,11,12,13,14,15,16
        DC.B    17,18,19,20,21,22,23,24

        END
```

2B Two-dimensional word array indexing (D2WORD)

Calculates the address of an element of a two-dimensional word-length (16-bit) array, given the array's base address, the element's two subscripts, and the size of a row (i.e. the number of columns). The array is assumed to be stored in row major order (i.e. by rows), and both subscripts are assumed to begin at 0.

Procedure The program multiplies the row size (number of bytes in a row) times the row subscript (since the elements are stored by rows), adds the product to the doubled column subscript (doubled because each element occupies 2 bytes), and adds the sum to the base address.

Entry conditions

Order in stack (starting from the top)

High word of return address
Low word of return address

High byte of column subscript
Low byte of column subscript

High byte of the size of a row (in bytes)
Low byte of the size of a row (in bytes)

High byte of row subscript
Low byte of row subscript

High word of base address of array
Low word of base address of array

Exit conditions

Base address of element in A0
The element occupies the address in A0 and the next higher address.

Examples

1. Data: Base address = $A45E14_{16}$

Column subscript = 0008_{16}
Size of row (in bytes) = $001C_{16}$ (i.e. each row has 0014_{10} or $000E_{16}$ word-length elements)
Row subscript = 0005_{16}

Result: Element base address = $A45E14_{16} + 0005_{16} \times 001C_{16} + 0008_{16} \times 2$
$= A45E14_{16} + 008C_{16} + 0010_{16}$
$= A45EB0_{16}$
i.e. the base address of ARRAY(5,8) is $A45EB0_{16}$ and the element occupies addresses $A45EB0_{16}$ and $A45EB1_{16}$.

2. Data: Base address = $2FB100_{16}$
Column subscript = 0002_{16}
Size of row (in bytes) = 0008_{16} (i.e. each row has four word-length elements)
Row subscript = 0006_{16}

Result: Element's base address = $2FB100_{16} + 0006_{16} \times 0008_{16} + 0002_{16} \times 2$
$= 2FB100_{16} + 0030_{16} + 0004_{16}$
$= 2FB134_{16}$
i.e. the base address of ARRAY(6,2) is $2FB134_{16}$ and the element occupies addresses $2FB134_{16}$ and $2FB135_{16}$.

The general formula is

ELEMENT'S BASE ADDRESS = ARRAY BASE ADDRESS + ROW SUBSCRIPT × ROW SIZE + COLUMN SUBSCRIPT × 2

Note that one parameter of this routine is the size of a row in bytes. The size for word-length elements is the number of columns per row times 2 (the size of an element in bytes). The reason for choosing this parameter rather than the number of columns or the maximum column index is that it can be calculated once (when the array bounds are determined) and used whenever the array is accessed. The alternative parameters (number of columns or maximum column index) would require extra calculations during each indexing operation.

Registers used A0, A1, CCR, D0, D1, D2

Execution time Approximately 142 cycles

Program size 20 bytes

Data memory required None

```
*
*
*
*
*   Title:                  Two-Dimensional Word Array Indexing
*   Name:                   D2WORD
*
*
*
*   Purpose:                Given the base address of a word array,
*                           two subscripts 'I' and 'J', and the size
*                           of the first subscript in bytes, calculate
*                           the address of A[I,J].  The array is assumed
*                           to be stored in row major order (A[0,0],
*                           A[0,1],...,A[K,L]), and both dimensions
*                           are assumed to begin at zero as in the C
*                           language or the following Pascal declaration:
*                             A:ARRAY[0..2,0..7] OF WORD;
*
*   Entry:                  TOP OF STACK
*                             High word of return address
*                             Low word of return address
*                             High byte of second subscript (column element)
*                             Low byte of second subscript (column element)
*                             High byte of first subscript size, in bytes
*                             Low byte of first subscript size, in bytes
*                             High byte of first subscript (row element)
*                             Low byte of first subscript (row element)
*                             High word of array base address
*                             Low word of array base address
*                           NOTE:
*                             The first subscript's size is the length of
*                             a row in words times 2.
*
*   Exit:                   Register A0 = Element's base address
*
*   Registers Used:         A0,A1,CCR,D0,D1,D2
*
*   Time:                   Approximately 142 cycles
*
*   Size:                   Program 20 bytes
*
*
*

D2WORD
        *
        *SAVE RETURN ADDRESS, GET PARAMETERS FROM STACK
```

```
        *
        MOVEA.L   (SP)+,A1        SAVE RETURN ADDRESS
        CLR.L     D0              CLEAR MORE SIGNIFICANT WORD OF
                                  * OFFSET (A 32-BIT QUANTITY)
        MOVEM.W   (SP)+,D0-D2     GET COLUMN NUMBER (D0), ROW SIZE (D1),
                                  * ROW SUBSCRIPT (D2)
        MOVEA.L   (SP)+,A0        GET BASE ADDRESS OF ARRAY
        *
        *ELEMENT ADDRESS = ROW SIZE X ROW SUBSCRIPT + COLUMN
        *  SUBSCRIPT + BASE ADDRESS
        *
        MULU      D2,D1           ROW SIZE X ROW SUBSCRIPT
                                  *THIS IS A 16-BIT BY 16-BIT MULTIPLY
                                  * YIELDING A 32-BIT RESULT
        ADD.L     D0,D0           DOUBLE COLUMN SUBSCRIPT SINCE
                                  * ELEMENTS EACH OCCUPY 2 BYTES
        ADD.L     D1,D0           ADD PRODUCT TO DOUBLED COLUMN
                                  * TO GET 32-BIT OFFSET
        ADDA.L    D0,A0           ADD OFFSET TO BASE ADDRESS OF ARRAY
        *
        *EXIT TO RETURN ADDRESS
        *
        JMP       (A1)            EXIT TO RETURN ADDRESS


*
*
*       SAMPLE EXECUTION
*
*
SC2B
        PEA       ARY             PUSH BASE ADDRESS OF ARRAY ONTO STACK
        MOVE.W    SUBS1,D2        GET FIRST (ROW) SUBSCRIPT
        MOVE.W    SSUBS1,D1       GET SIZE OF FIRST SUBSCRIPT
        MOVE.W    SUBS2,D0        GET SECOND (COLUMN) SUBSCRIPT
        MOVEM.W   D0-D2,-(SP)     PUT DATA PARAMETERS IN STACK
        JSR       D2WORD          CALCULATE ADDRESS OF ELEMENT
                                  *FOR THE INITIAL TEST DATA
                                  *A0 = ADDRESS OF ARY(2,4)
                                  *   = ARY + (2 X 16) + 4 X 2
                                  *   = ARY + 40 (CONTENTS ARE 2100H)
                                  *NOTE BOTH SUBSCRIPTS START AT 0
        BRA.S     SC2B            REPEAT TEST
*
*DATA
*
SUBS1   DC.W      2               SUBSCRIPT 1 (ROW NUMBER)
SSUBS1  DC.W      16              SIZE OF SUBSCRIPT 1 (NUMBER OF BYTES
                                  * PER ROW)
SUBS2   DC.W      4               SUBSCRIPT 2 (COLUMN NUMBER)

*THE ARRAY (3 ROWS OF 8 COLUMNS)
```

```
ARY     DC.W    0100H,0200H,0300H,0400H,0500H,0600H,0700H,0800H
        DC.W    0900H,1000H,1100H,1200H,1300H,1400H,1500H,1600H
        DC.W    1700H,1800H,1900H,2000H,2100H,2200H,2300H,2400H

        END
```

2C Two-dimensional array indexing with a dope vector (CRDVEC, D2BYDV)

Calculates the address of an element of a two-dimensional byte-length (8-bit) array, given the array's base address, the element's two subscripts, and the size of a row (i.e. the number of columns). The array is assumed to be stored in row major order (i.e. by rows), and both subscripts are assumed to begin at 0.

Consists of two subroutines: CRDVEC, which creates a 'dope vector' consisting of the addresses of the zeroth elements of each row; and D2BYDV, which calculates the address of an element using the dope vector. This approach saves indexing time (since no multiplications are necessary); the cost is the extra storage required for the dope vector.

Procedure Subroutine CRDVEC creates the dope vector by starting with the base address and adding the row size repeatedly to determine the remaining elements. Subroutine D2BYDV calculates the address of a particular byte-length element by adding the column subscript to the selected element of the dope vector. This routine can be modified easily to handle elements of different sizes. Note that the dope vector's elements are 32-bit addresses.

Entry conditions

Order in stack (starting from the top)

1. CRDVEC

High word of return address
Low word of return address

High byte of the size of a row (in bytes)
Low byte of the size of a row (in bytes)

High byte of number of rows in array
Low byte of number of rows in array

High word of base address of dope vector
Low word of base address of dope vector

High word of base address of array
Low word of base address of array

2. D2BYDV

High word of return address

Low word of return address

High byte of column subscript
Low byte of column subscript

High byte of row subscript
Low byte of row subscript

High word of base address of dope vector
Low word of base address of dope vector

Exit conditions

1. CRDVEC
Dope vector stored in memory

2. D2BYDV
Base address of element in A0

Examples

1. Creating a dope vector:
   Base address = $B15E14_{16}$
   Size of row (in bytes) = $001C_{16}$
   Number of rows = 0005_{16}
   Result: Dope vector has the following elements:
   $B15E14_{16}$ (address of element in row 0, column 0)
   $B15E30_{16}$ (address of element in row 1, column 0)
   $B15E4C_{16}$ (address of element in row 2, column 0)
   $B15E68_{16}$ (address of element in row 3, column 0)
   $B15E84_{16}$ (address of element in row 4, column 0)

2. Using a dope vector (created in part 1) with byte-length elements:
   Column subscript = $0B_{16}$
   Row subscript = 2
   Result: Element's address = Element 2 of dope vector + column subscript = $B15E4C_{16}$ + 0B = $B15E57_{16}$
   i.e. ARRAY(2,11) is in address $B15E57_{16}$.

The general formula is

ELEMENT'S ADDRESS = DOPE VECTOR (ROW SUBSCRIPT) + COLUMN SUBSCRIPT

Note that one parameter of CRDVEC is the size of a row in bytes. For example, the size for word-length elements would be the number of columns per row times 2 (the size of an element in bytes). However, D2BYDV assumes byte-length elements; you would have to adjust either the routine or the column subscript to handle elements of other sizes.

Registers used

1. CRDVEC: A0, A1, CCR, D0, D1
2. D2BYDV: A0, A1, CCR, D0, D1

Execution time

1. CRDVEC: 96 cycles overhead plus 32 cycles per row
2. D2BYDV: 116 cycles

Program size

1. CRDVEC: 34 bytes
2. D2BYDV: 28 bytes

Data memory required

1. CRDVEC: None
2. D2BYDV: None

```
*
*
*
*
*       Title:              Two-Dimensional Array Indexing
*                           with a Dope Vector
*       Name:               CRDVEC, D2BYDV
*
*
*
*       Purpose:            Given the base address of an array,
*                           and two subscripts 'I' and 'J', calculate
*                           the address of A[I,J], using a dope
*                           vector containing the addresses of the
*                           first element in each row.
*                           The array is assumed to be stored
```

```
*                      in row major order (A[0,0], A[0,1],
*                      A[0,2],...,A[K,L]), and both dimensions
*                      are assumed to begin at zero as in the C
*                      language or the following Pascal declaration:
*                        A:ARRAY[0..2,0..7] OF BYTE;
*
*                      D2BYDV assumes that the array consists of
*                      byte-length elements
*
*    Entry:            TOP OF STACK
*
*                        1) CRDVEC
*                        High word of return address
*                        Low word of return address
*                        High byte of row size, in bytes
*                        Low byte of row size, in bytes
*                        High byte of number of rows
*                        Low byte of number of rows
*                        High word of base address of dope vector
*                        Low word of base address of dope vector
*                        High word of array base address
*                        Low word of array base address
*
*                        2) D2BYDV
*                        High word of return address
*                        Low word of return address
*                        High byte of column subscript
*                        Low byte of column subscript
*                        High byte of row subscript
*                        Low byte of row subscript
*                        High word of base address of dope vector
*                        Low word of base address of dope vector
*
*    Exit:             CRDVEC - Dope vector in memory
*                      D2BYDV - Base address of element in A0
*
*    Registers Used:   CRDVEC - A0,A1,CCR,D0,D1
*                      D2BYDV - A0,A1,CCR,D0,D1
*
*    Time:             CRDVEC - 96 cycles overhead plus 32
*                        cycles per row
*                      D2BYDV - Approximately 116 cycles
*
*    Size:             CRDVEC - Program 34 bytes
*                      D2BYDV - Program 28 bytes
*
*
*

*
*CREATE A DOPE VECTOR IN MEMORY
*IT CONTAINS THE ADDRESSES OF THE ZEROTH ELEMENT
*  OF EACH ROW OF THE ARRAY
*
CRDVEC
        CLR.L     D0                    CLEAR UPPER WORD OF SUBSCRIPT
```

```
                                          * SIZE
        MOVEM.W   4(SP),D0-D1             GET SUBSCRIPT SIZE, NUMBER OF
                                          * ROWS
        MOVEM.L   8(SP),A0-A1             GET DOPE VECTOR BASE ADDRESS,
                                          * ARRAY BASE ADDRESS
        *
        *BUILD DOPE VECTOR STARTING WITH ARRAY BASE ADDRESS
        *  AND ADDING ROW SIZE FOR EACH SUCCESSIVE ELEMENT
        *
        SUBQ.W    #1,D1                   REDUCE ROW COUNT TO EXIT LOOP
                                          * ON -1
STVEC   MOVEA.L   A1,(A0)+                SAVE 32-BIT ELEMENT OF VECTOR
                                          * IN MEMORY
        ADDA.L    D0,A1                   ADD ROW SIZE TO GET NEXT ELEMENT
        DBRA      D1,STVEC                CONTINUE THROUGH NUMBER
                                          * OF ROWS
        *
        *REMOVE PARAMETERS FROM STACK AND EXIT
        *
        MOVEA.L   (SP),A1                 GET RETURN ADDRESS
        ADDA.L    #16,SP                  UPDATE STACK POINTER TO REMOVE
                                          * PARAMETERS
        JMP       (A1)                    EXIT TO RETURN ADDRESS
*
*
*ACCESS AN ELEMENT GIVEN ITS ROW AND COLUMN SUBSCRIPTS AND
*  THE DOPE VECTOR
*THIS ROUTINE ASSUMES BYTE-LENGTH ELEMENTS
*
D2BYDV
        *
        *GET ELEMENT OF DOPE VECTOR BASED ON ROW SUBSCRIPT
        *
        CLR.L     D0                      CLEAR UPPER WORD OF SUBSCRIPT
                                          * SIZE
        MOVEM.W   4(SP),D0-D1             GET ROW SUBSCRIPT, COLUMN
                                          * SUBSCRIPT
        MOVEA.L   8(SP),A1                GET DOPE VECTOR BASE ADDRESS
        ASL.L     #2,D0                   MULTIPLY ROW SUBSCRIPT TIMES
                                          * 4 SINCE VECTOR ELEMENTS ARE
                                          * 32-BIT ADDRESSES
        MOVEA.L   (A1,D0.L),A0            GET ELEMENT FROM DOPE VECTOR
                                          *THIS IS THE ADDRESS OF THE
                                          * FIRST ELEMENT IN THE GIVEN ROW
        *
        *ADD COLUMN SUBSCRIPT TO ELEMENT OF DOPE VECTOR
        *
        ADDA.L    D1,A0                   ADD COLUMN SUBSCRIPT
        *
        *REMOVE PARAMETERS FROM STACK AND EXIT
        *
        MOVEA.L   (SP),A1                 GET RETURN ADDRESS
        ADDA.L    #12,SP                  UPDATE STACK POINTER TO REMOVE
                                          * PARAMETERS FROM STACK
        JMP       (A1)                    EXIT TO RETURN ADDRESS
```

```
*
*       SAMPLE EXECUTION
*
*
SC2C
        PEA       ARY             PUT BASE ADDRESS OF ARRAY
                                  * ONTO STACK
        PEA       DPVECT          PUT BASE ADDRESS OF DOPE VECTOR
                                  * ONTO STACK
        MOVE.W    SIZEROW,D0      GET SIZE OF ROW IN BYTES
        MOVE.W    NROWS,D1        GET NUMBER OF ROWS
        MOVEM.W   D0-D1,-(SP)     PUSH PARAMETERS ONTO STACK
        JSR       CRDVEC          CREATE DOPE VECTOR
                                  *IT CONTAINS THE ADDRESSES
                                  * OF THE FIRST ELEMENTS OF
                                  * EACH ROW
        PEA       DPVECT          PUT BASE ADDRESS OF DOPE VECTOR
                                  * ONTO STACK
        MOVE.W    ROWNO,D0        GET ROW SUBSCRIPT
        MOVE.W    COLNO,D1        GET COLUMN SUBSCRIPT
        MOVEM.W   D0-D1,-(SP)     PUSH PARAMETERS ONTO STACK
        JSR       D2BYDV          CALCULATE ADDRESS FOR TEST
                                  * DATA
                                  *A0 = ADDRESS OF ARY(2,4)
                                  *    = ARY + (2 X 16) + 4
                                  *    = ARY + 36
                                  *CONTENTS ARE 37
        BRA.S     SC2C            REPEAT TEST

*
*DATA
*
COLNO     DC.W    4         COLUMN SUBSCRIPT (COLUMN NUMBER)
NROWS     DC.W    5         NUMBER OF ROWS IN ARRAY
ROWNO     DC.W    2         ROW SUBSCRIPT (ROW NUMBER)
SIZEROW   DC.W    16        SIZE OF A ROW IN BYTES

DPVECT    DS.L    5         DOPE VECTOR (ADDRESSES OF FIRST
                            * ELEMENT IN EACH ROW)

*THE ARRAY (5 ROWS OF 16 COLUMNS) - ONE BYTE PER ELEMENT
ARY       DC.B    1,2,3,4,5,6,7,8,9,10,11,12,13,14,15,16
          DC.B    17,18,19,20,21,22,23,24,25,26,27,28,29,30,31,32
          DC.B    33,34,35,36,37,38,39,40,41,42,43,44,45,46,47,48
          DC.B    49,50,51,52,53,54,55,56,57,58,59,60,61,62,63,64
          DC.B    65,66,67,68,69,70,71,72,73,74,75,76,77,78,79,80
          END
```

2D N-dimensional array indexing (NDIM)

Calculates the base address of an element of an *N*-dimensional array, given the array's base address and *N* pairs of sizes and subscripts. The size of a dimension is the number of bytes from the base address of an element to the base address of the element with an index one larger in the dimension but the same in all other dimensions. The array is assumed to be stored in row major order (i.e. organized so that subscripts to the right change before ones to the left). All subscripts are assumed to begin at 0.

Note that the size of the rightmost subscript is simply the size of an element in bytes; the size of the next subscript is the size of an element times the maximum value of the rightmost subscript plus 1, and so on. All subscripts are assumed to begin at 0. Otherwise, the user must normalize them (see the second example at the end of the listing).

Procedure The program loops on each dimension, calculating the offset in it as the subscript times the size. After calculating the overall offset, the program adds it to the array's base address to obtain the element's base address.

Entry conditions

Order in stack (starting from the top)

High word of return address
Low word of return address

Number of dimensions

Size of rightmost dimension

Rightmost subscript

.

.

.

Size of leftmost dimension

Leftmost subscript

High word of base address of array
Low word of base address of array

Note that the number of parameters in the stack depends on the number of dimensions.

Exit conditions

Base address of element in A0
The element occupies memory addresses START through START + SIZE − 1, where START is the calculated address and SIZE is the size of an element in bytes.

Example

Data: Base address = $E13C00_{16}$
Number of dimensions = 0003_{16}
Rightmost subscript = 0005_{16}
Rightmost size = 0003_{16} (3-byte entries)
Middle subscript = 0003_{16}
Middle size = 0012_{16} (six 3-byte entries)
Leftmost subscript = 0004_{16}
Leftmost size = $007E_{16}$ (seven sets of six 3-byte entries)

Result: Element base address = $E13C00_{16} + 0005_{16} \times 0003_{16} + 0003_{16} \times 0012_{16} + 0004_{16} \times 007E_{16} =$
$E13C00_{16} + 000F_{16} + 0036_{16} + 01F8_{16} = E13E3D_{16}$
i.e. the element is ARRAY(4,3,5); it occupies addresses $E13E3D_{16}$ through $E13E3F_{16}$. (The maximum values of the various subscripts are 6 (leftmost) and 5 (middle), with each element occupying three bytes.)

The general formula is

$$\text{ELEMENT BASE ADDRESS} = \text{ARRAY BASE ADDRESS} + \sum_{i=0}^{N-1} \text{SUBSCRIPT}_i \times \text{SIZE}_i$$

where:

N is the number of dimensions
SUBSCRIPT_i is the ith subscript
SIZE_i is the size of the ith dimension

Note that we use the size of each dimension as a parameter to reduce the number of repetitive multiplications and to generalize the procedure. The sizes can be calculated and saved as soon as the bounds of the array are known. Those sizes can then be used whenever indexing is performed on the array. Obviously, the sizes do not change if the bounds are fixed, and they should not be recalculated as part of each indexing operation. The sizes are also general, since the elements can themselves consist of any number of bytes.

Registers used A0, A1, CCR, D0, D1, D2

Execution time Approximately 108 cycles per dimension plus 122 cycles overhead

Program size 46 bytes

Data memory required None

Special case If the number of dimensions is 0, the program returns with the base address in A0.

```
*
*
*
*
*       Title:                N-Dimensional Array Indexing
*       Name:                 NDIM
*
*
*
*       Purpose:              Calculate the address of an element in an
*                             N-dimensional array given the base address,
*                             N pairs of size in bytes and subscript, and
*                             the number of dimensions of the array.  The
*                             array is assumed to be stored in row major
*                             order (e.g., A[0,0,0],A[0,0,1],...,A[0,1,0],
*                             A[0,1,1],...).  Also, it is assumed that all
*                             dimensions begin at 0 as in the C language or
*                             in the following Pascal declaration:
*                               A:ARRAY[0..10,0..3,0..5] OF SOMETHING
*
*       Entry:                TOP OF STACK
*                               High word of return address
*                               Low word of return address
*                               Number of dimensions
*                               Dimension N-1 size
*                               Dimension N-1 subscript
*                               Dimension N-2 size
```

```
*                          Dimension N-2 subscript
*                            .
*                            .
*                            .
*                          High word of array base address
*                          Low word of array base address
*                        NOTE:
*                          All sizes are in bytes.
*
*    Exit:               Register A0 = Element's base address
*
*    Registers Used:     A0,A1,CCR,D0,D1,D2
*
*    Time:               Approximately 108 cycles per dimension plus
*                        122 cycles overhead
*
*    Size:               Program 46 bytes
*
*
*

*
*        EXIT IMMEDIATELY IF NUMBER OF DIMENSIONS IS ZERO
*        GET BASE ADDRESS OF ARRAY IN CASE EXIT IS TAKEN
*
NDIM
        LEA       4(SP),A1              GET BASE ADDRESS OF PARAMETERS
        MOVE.W    (A1)+,D2              GET NUMBER OF DIMENSIONS
        MOVEA.L   (A1)+,A0              GET BASE ADDRESS IF ZERO
                                        * DIMENSIONS (FOR PROPER EXIT)
                                        *NOTE: IF NUMBER OF DIMENSIONS
                                        * IS NOT ZERO, THIS ISN'T THE
                                        * BASE ADDRESS AND MUST SIMPLY
                                        * BE DISCARDED
        TST.W     D2
        BEQ.S     EXITND                BRANCH IF NUMBER OF DIMENSIONS
                                        * IS ZERO
        SUBQ.L    #4,A1                 OTHERWISE, BACK UP POINTER TO
                                        * DISCARD BASE ADDRESS
        *
        *ELEMENT ADDRESS = BASE ADDRESS + SIZE(I) X SUBSCRIPT(I) FOR
        *  I = 0 TO N-1
        *
        CLR.L     D1                    START ELEMENT ADDRESS AT ZERO
        MOVEA.L   D1,A0                 NOTE THAT WE CANNOT APPLY CLR
                                        * OR MOVEQ TO AN ADDRESS
                                        * REGISTER
        *
        *MULTIPLY ROW SUBSCRIPT X ROW SIZE AND ADD TO PREVIOUS
        *  ACCUMULATION
        *
        SUBQ.W    #1,D2                 ADJUST NUMBER OF DIMENSIONS
                                        * FOR DBCC LOOP
NXTDIM  MOVEM.W   (A1)+,D0-D1           GET NEXT SIZE, SUBSCRIPT
        MULU      D1,D0                 SIZE X SUBSCRIPT
                                        *NOTE: SUBSCRIPTS ARE ALWAYS
```

```
                                         * POSITIVE - THE CALLING
                                         * ROUTINE MUST NORMALIZE THEM
        ADDA.L    D0,A0                  ADD TO ACCUMULATED ELEMENT
                                         * ADDRESS
        DBRA      D2,NXTDIM              COUNT DIMENSIONS
        *
        *ADD TOTAL OFFSET TO BASE ADDRESS OF ARRAY
        *
        ADDA.L    (A1)+,A0               ADD BASE ADDRESS OF ARRAY
        *
        *EXIT
        *
EXITND  MOVEA.L   (SP)+,A1               GET RETURN ADDRESS FROM STACK
        MOVE.W    (SP)+,D2               GET NUMBER OF DIMENSIONS
        ASL.W     #2,D2                  DEPTH OF SIZE-SUBSCRIPT
                                         * PARAMETERS IN STACK IS
                                         * NUMBER OF DIMENSIONS X 4
        ADDQ      #4,D2                  DEPTH OF PARAMETERS IS FOUR
                                         * BYTES MORE BECAUSE OF BASE
                                         * ADDRESS OF ARRAY
        ADDA.W    D2,SP                  ADJUST STACK POINTER TO REMOVE
                                         * PARAMETERS FROM STACK
        JMP       (A1)                   EXIT TO RETURN ADDRESS

*
*       SAMPLE EXECUTION
*
*

SC2D
        *
        *CALCULATE ADDRESS OF AY1[1,3,0]
        *SINCE LOWER BOUNDS OF ARRAY 1 ARE ALL ZERO, IT IS
        *  NOT NECESSARY TO NORMALIZE THEM
        *
        PEA       AY1                    PUSH BASE ADDRESS OF ARRAY
                                         * ONTO STACK
        MOVE.W    #1,D6                  FIRST SUBSCRIPT
        MOVE.W    #A1SZ1,D5              SIZE OF FIRST SUBSCRIPT
        MOVE.W    #3,D4                  SECOND SUBSCRIPT
        MOVE.W    #A1SZ2,D3              SIZE OF SECOND SUBSCRIPT
        CLR.W     D2                     THIRD SUBSCRIPT = 0
        MOVE.W    #A1SZ3,D1              SIZE OF THIRD SUBSCRIPT
        MOVE.W    #A1DIM,D0              NUMBER OF DIMENSIONS
        MOVEM.W   D0-D6,-(SP)            PUSH PARAMETERS ONTO STACK
        JSR       NDIM              CALCULATE ADDRESS OF ELEMENT
                                    *A0 = STARTING ADDRESS OF AY1(1,3,0)
                                    *    = AY1 + (1 X 126) + (3 X 21) + (0 X 3)
                                    *    = AY1 + 189
        *
        *CALCULATE ADDRESS OF AY2[-1,6]
        * SINCE LOWER BOUNDS OF ARRAY 2 DO NOT START AT 0, SUBSCRIPTS
        * MUST BE NORMALIZED
        *
        PEA       AY2                    PUSH BASE ADDRESS OF ARRAY
                                         * ONTO STACK
```

```
        MOVE.W   #-1,D4                UNNORMALIZED FIRST SUBSCRIPT
        SUB.W    #A2D1L,D4             NORMALIZE FIRST SUBSCRIPT BY
                                       * SUBTRACTING LOWER BOUND
        MOVE.W   #A2SZ1,D3             SIZE OF FIRST SUBSCRIPT
        MOVE.W   #6,D2                 UNNORMALIZED SECOND SUBSCRIPT
        SUB.W    #A2D2L,D2             NORMALIZE SECOND SUBSCRIPT BY
                                       * SUBTRACTING LOWER BOUND
        MOVE.W   #A2SZ2,D1             SIZE OF SECOND SUBSCRIPT
        MOVE.W   #A2DIM,D0             NUMBER OF DIMENSIONS
        MOVEM.W  D0-D4,-(SP)           PUSH PARAMETERS ONTO STACK
        JSR      NDIM        CALCULATE ADDRESS
                             *A0 = STARTING ADDRESS OF AY2(-1,6)
                             *   = AY2+(((-1)-(-5)) X 18)+((6-2) X 2)
                             *   = AY2+80
        BRA      SC2D        REPEAT TEST
*DATA
*AY1 ARRAY[A1D1L..A1D1H,A1D2L..A1D2H,A1D3L..A1D3H] 3-BYTE ELEMENTS
*         [ 0  . .  3  ,  0  . . 5  ,  0  . . 6  ]
A1DIM    EQU      3          NUMBER OF DIMENSIONS
A1D1L    EQU      0          LOW BOUND OF DIMENSION 1
A1D1H    EQU      3          HIGH BOUND OF DIMENSION 1
A1D2L    EQU      0          LOW BOUND OF DIMENSION 2
A1D2H    EQU      5          HIGH BOUND OF DIMENSION 2
A1D3L    EQU      0          LOW BOUND OF DIMENSION 3
A1D3H    EQU      6          HIGH BOUND OF DIMENSION 3
A1SZ3    EQU      3          SIZE OF ELEMENT IN DIMENSION 3
A1SZ2    EQU      ((A1D3H-A1D3L)+1)*A1SZ3  SIZE OF ELEMENT IN D2
A1SZ1    EQU      ((A1D2H-A1D2L)+1)*A1SZ2  SIZE OF ELEMENT IN D1
AY1      DS.B     ((A1D1H-A1D1L)+1)*A1SZ1  ARRAY

*AY2 ARRAY [A2D1L..A2D1H,A2D2L..A2D2H] OF WORD
*         [  -5 ..  -1  ,  2  .. 10  ]
A2DIM    EQU      2          NUMBER OF DIMENSIONS
A2D1L    EQU      -5         LOW BOUND OF DIMENSION 1
A2D1H    EQU      -1         HIGH BOUND OF DIMENSION 1
A2D2L    EQU      2          LOW BOUND OF DIMENSION 2
A2D2H    EQU      10         HIGH BOUND OF DIMENSION 2
A2SZ2    EQU      2                        SIZE OF ELEMENT IN D2
A2SZ1    EQU      ((A2D2H-A2D2L)+1)*A2SZ2  SIZE OF ELEMENT IN D1
AY2      DS.B     ((A2D1H-A2D1L)+1)*A2SZ1  ARRAY
         END
```

3 Arithmetic

3A Multiple-precision binary addition (MPBADD)

Adds two multi-byte unsigned binary numbers. Both are stored with their most significant bytes at the lowest address. The sum replaces the number with the base address lower in the stack.

Procedure The program clears the Extend flag initially and adds the operands a byte at a time, starting with the least significant bytes. The final Extend flag indicates whether the overall addition produced a carry. A length of zero causes an immediate exit with no addition.

Entry conditions

Order in stack (starting from the top)

High word of return address
Low word of return address

Length of operands in bytes

High word of base address of second operand (address containing the most significant byte of array 2)
Low word of base address of second operand (address containing the most significant byte of array 2)

High word of base address of first operand and sum (address containing the most significant byte of array 1)
Low word of base address of first operand and sum (address containing the most significant byte of array 1)

Exit conditions

First operand (array 1) replaced by first operand (array 1) plus second operand (array 2)

Example

Data: Length of operands (in bytes) = 6
Top operand (array 2) = $19D028A193EA_{16}$
Bottom operand (array 1) = $293EABF059C7_{16}$
Result: Bottom operand (array 1) = Bottom operand (array 1) + Top operand (array 2) = $430ED491EDB1_{16}$
Extend (X) flag = 0 (no carry)

Registers used A0, A1, CCR, D0

Execution time 29 cycles per byte plus 120 cycles overhead. For example, adding two 6-byte operands takes

$29 \times 6 + 120 = 294$ cycles

Program size 36 bytes

Data memory required None

Special case A length of 0 causes an immediate exit with the sum equal to the bottom operand (i.e. array 1 is unchanged). The Extend flag is cleared.

```
*
*
*
*
*    Title:                  Multiple-Precision Binary Addition
*    Name:                   MPBADD
*
*
*
*    Purpose:                Add 2 arrays of binary bytes
*                            Array1 := Array 1 + Array 2
*
*    Entry:                  TOP OF STACK
*                              High word of return address
*                              Low word of return address
*                              Array length in bytes
*                              High word of array 2 address
*                              Low word of array 2 address
*                              High word of array 1 address
*                              Low word of array 1 address
*
*                              The arrays are unsigned binary numbers
*                              with a maximum length of 65,535 bytes,
*                              ARRAY[0] is the most significant
*                              byte, and ARRAY[LENGTH-1] is the
*                              least significant byte.
*
*    Exit:                   Array1 := Array1 + Array2
*
*    Registers Used:         A0,A1,CCR,D0
*
*    Time:                   29 cycles per byte plus 120 cycles overhead
*
*    Size:                   Program 36 bytes
*
*
*

MPBADD
        *
        *CHECK IF LENGTH OF OPERANDS IS ZERO
        *EXIT WITH EXTEND FLAG CLEARED (0) IF IT IS
        *
        MOVE      #0,CCR     NO CARRY INITIALLY (EXTEND FLAG = 0)
        MOVEM.L   6(SP),A0-A1     GET BASE ADDRESSES OF OPERANDS
                                * ARRAY 1 IN A1, ARRAY 2 IN A0
        MOVE.W    4(SP),D0   GET LENGTH OF OPERANDS
        BEQ.S     ADEXIT     BRANCH (EXIT) IF OPERAND LENGTH IS ZERO
        *
        *ADD ARRAYS ONE BYTE AT A TIME
        *
```

```
        ADDA.W    D0,A1     GET ADDRESS JUST BEYOND LSB OF ARRAY 1
        ADDA.W    D0,A0     GET ADDRESS JUST BEYOND LSB OF ARRAY 2
                            *ADDRESSES ARE 1 TOO HIGH TO ALLOW
                            *  FOR INITIAL PREDECREMENT
        SUBQ.W    #1,D0     ADJUST COUNT FOR LOOP EXIT ON -1
ADDBYT
        ADDX.B    -(A0),-(A1)    ADD BYTE FROM ARRAY 2 TO ARRAY 1
        DBRA      D0,ADDBYT CONTINUE UNTIL ALL BYTES SUMMED
        *
        *REMOVE PARAMETERS FROM STACK AND EXIT
        *
ADEXIT
        MOVEA.L   (SP)+,A0  GET RETURN ADDRESS
                            *NOTE: REPLACING THIS INSTRUCTION WITH
                            * MOVEA.L (SP),A0 LEAVES THE BASE ADDRESS
                            * OF THE SUM AT THE TOP OF THE STACK (AS
                            * MANY COMPILERS DO)
        LEA       10(SP),SP REMOVE PARAMETERS FROM STACK
        JMP       (A0)      EXIT TO RETURN ADDRESS
*
*
*       SAMPLE EXECUTION
*
*


SC3A
        MOVEA.L   AY1ADR,A1      GET POINTER TO FIRST OPERAND
        MOVEA.L   AY2ADR,A0      GET POINTER TO SECOND OPERAND
        MOVEM.L   A0-A1,-(SP)    PUSH OPERAND ADDRESSES ONTO STACK
        MOVE.W    #SZAYS,-(SP)   PUSH LENGTH OF ARRAYS ONTO STACK
        JSR       MPBADD    MULTIPLE-PRECISION BINARY ADDITION
                            *RESULT OF $12345678 + $9ABCDEF0
                            *  = $ACF13568
                            * IN MEMORY AY1      = $00
                            *            AY1+1   = $00
                            *            AY1+2   = $00
                            *            AY1+3   = $AC
                            *            AY1+4   = $F1
                            *            AY1+5   = $35
                            *            AY1+6   = $68
        BRA.S     SC3A      REPEAT TEST
*
*  DATA
*
SZAYS   EQU       7         LENGTH OF ARRAYS IN BYTES


AY1ADR  DC.L      AY1       BASE ADDRESS OF FIRST OPERAND
AY2ADR  DC.L      AY2       BASE ADDRESS OF SECOND OPERAND
```

```
AY1     DC.B    0,0,0,$12,$34,$56,$78       FIRST OPERAND
AY2     DC.B    0,0,0,$9A,$BC,$DE,$F0       SECOND OPERAND

        END
```

3B Multiple-precision binary subtraction (MPBSUB)

Subtracts two multi-byte unsigned binary numbers. Both are stored with their most significant bytes at the lowest address. The subtrahend (number to be subtracted) is stored on top of the minuend (number from which it is subtracted). The difference replaces the minuend.

Procedure The program clears the Extend flag initially and subtracts the subtrahend from the minuend one byte at a time, starting with the least significant bytes. The final Extend flag indicates whether the overall subtraction required a borrow. A length of 0 causes an immediate exit with no subtraction.

Entry conditions

Order in stack (starting from the top)

High word of return address
Low word of return address

Operand length in bytes

High word of base address of subtrahend
Low word of base address of subtrahend

High word of base address of minuend
Low word of base address of minuend

Exit conditions

Minuend replaced by minuend minus subtrahend

Example

Data: Length of operands (in bytes) = 4
Minuend = $2F5BA7C3_{16}$
Subtrahend = $14DF35B8_{16}$
Result: t Minuend = $1A7C720B_{16}$
Extend (X) flag = 0, since no borrow is necessary.

Registers used A0, A1, CCR, D0

Execution time 29 cycles per byte plus 120 cycles overhead. For example, subtracting two 10-byte operands takes

$29 \times 10 + 120 = 410$ cycles.

Program size 36 bytes

Data memory required None

Special case A length of 0 causes an immediate exit with the minuend unchanged (i.e. the difference is equal to the minuend). The Extend flag is cleared.

```
*
*
*
*
*       Title:              Multiple-Precision Binary Subtraction
*       Name:               MPBSUB
*
*
*
*       Purpose:            Subtract 2 arrays of binary bytes
*                           Minuend := Minuend - Subtrahend
*
*       Entry:              TOP OF STACK
*                             High word of return address
*                             Low word of return address
*                             Array length in bytes
*                             High word of subtrahend address
*                             Low word of subtrahend address
*                             High word of minuend address
*                             Low word of minuend address
*
*                             The arrays are unsigned binary numbers,
*                             ARRAY[0] is the most significant
*                             byte, and ARRAY[LENGTH-1] is the
*                             least significant byte.
*
*       Exit:               Minuend := Minuend - Subtrahend
*
*       Registers Used:     A0,A1,CCR,D0
*
*       Time:               29 cycles per byte plus 120 cycles overhead
*
```

```
*     Size:                 Program 36 bytes
*
*
*

MPBSUB
        *
        *CHECK IF LENGTH OF OPERANDS IS ZERO
        *EXIT WITH EXTEND FLAG CLEARED (0) IF IT IS
        *
        MOVE       #0,CCR     NO BORROW INITIALLY (EXTEND FLAG = 0)
        MOVEM.L    6(SP),A0-A1  GET BASE ADDRESSES OF SUBTRAHEND (A0),
                              * MINUEND (A1)
        MOVE.W     4(SP),D0   GET LENGTH OF OPERANDS
        BEQ.S      SBEXIT     BRANCH (EXIT) IF LENGTH IS ZERO
        *
        *SUBTRACT ARRAYS ONE BYTE AT A TIME
        *
        ADDA.W     D0,A1      GET ADDRESS JUST BEYOND LSB OF MINUEND
        ADDA.W     D0,A0      GET ADDRESS JUST BEYOND LSB OF SUBTRAHEND
                              *ADDRESSES ARE 1 TOO HIGH TO ALLOW
                              * FOR INITIAL PREDECREMENT
        SUBQ.W     #1,D0      REDUCE COUNT FOR LOOP EXIT ON -1
SUBBYT
        SUBX.B     -(A1),-(A0)     SUBTRACT BYTE OF SUBTRAHEND FROM
                                   * MINUEND
        DBRA       D0,SUBBYT  CONTINUE UNTIL ALL BYTES SUBTRACTED
        *
        *REMOVE PARAMETERS FROM STACK AND EXIT
        *
SBEXIT
        MOVE.L     (SP)+,A0   GET RETURN ADDRESS
                              *NOTE: REPLACING THIS INSTRUCTION WITH
                              * MOVEA.L (SP),A0 LEAVES THE BASE ADDRESS
                              * OF THE DIFFERENCE AT THE TOP OF THE
                              * STACK (AS MANY COMPILERS DO)
        LEA        10(SP),SP  REMOVE PARAMETERS FROM STACK
        JMP        (A0)       EXIT TO RETURN ADDRESS
*
*
*       SAMPLE EXECUTION
*
*

SC3B
        MOVE.L     AY1ADR,A1       GET BASE ADDRESS OF MINUEND
        MOVE.L     AY2ADR,A0       GET BASE ADDRESS OF SUBTRAHEND
        MOVEM.L    A0-A1,-(SP)     PUSH OPERAND ADDRESSES ONTO STACK
        MOVE.W     #SZAYS,-(SP)    PUSH LENGTH OF ARRAYS ONTO STACK
        JSR        MPBSUB     MULTIPLE-PRECISION BINARY SUBTRACTION
                              *RESULT OF $2F3E4D5C-$175E809F
                              *  = $17DFCCBD
                              * IN MEMORY AY1       = $00
                              *           AY1+1     = $00
                              *           AY1+2     = $00
                              *           AY1+3     = $17
```

```
                                *          AY1+4     = $DF
                                *          AY1+5     = $CC
                                *          AY1+6     = $BD
          BRA.S     SC3B        REPEAT TEST

*
*  DATA
*
SZAYS     EQU       7           LENGTH OF OPERANDS IN BYTES

AY1ADR    DC.L      AY1         BASE ADDRESS OF MINUEND
AY2ADR    DC.L      AY2         BASE ADDRESS OF SUBTRAHEND

AY1       DC.B      0,0,0,$2F,$3E,$4D,$5C   MINUEND
AY2       DC.B      0,0,0,$17,$5E,$80,$9F   SUBTRAHEND

          END
```

3C Multiple-precision binary multiplication (MPBMUL)

Multiplies two multi-byte unsigned binary numbers. Both are stored with their most significant bytes at the lowest address. The product replaces the multiplicand. The length of the numbers (in bytes) is 255 or less. Only the less significant bytes of the product are returned for compatibility with other multiple-precision binary operations.

Procedure The program multiplies the numbers one byte at a time, starting with the least significant bytes. It keeps a full double-length unsigned partial product in memory locations starting at PROD (more significant bytes) and in the multiplicand (less significant bytes). The less significant bytes of the product replace the multiplicand as it is shifted. A zero length causes an exit with no multiplication.

Entry conditions

Order in stack (starting from the top)

High word of return address
Low word of return address

Length of operands in bytes

High word of base address of multiplier
Low word of base address of multiplier

High word of base address of multiplicand
Low word of base address of multiplicand

Exit conditions

Multiplicand replaced by multiplicand times multiplier

Example

Data: Length of operands (in bytes) = 4
Multiplicand = $0005D1F7_{16} = 381\,431_{10}$
Multiplier = $00000AB1_{16} = 2737_{10}$
Result: Multiplicand = $3E39D1C7_{16} = 1\,043\,976\,647_{10}$

Note that MPBMUL returns only the product's less significant bytes (i.e. the number of bytes in the multiplicand and multiplier) to be compatible with other multiple-precision binary arithmetic operations. The product's more significant bytes are available starting with their most significant byte at address PROD. The user may need to check them for overflow.

Registers used A0, A1, CCR, D0, D1, D2

Execution time Depends on the length of the operands and on the number of non-zero bytes in the multiplicand. If all the multiplicand's bytes are non-zero, the execution time is approximately

$$227 \times \text{LENGTH}^2 + 98 \times \text{LENGTH} + 291$$

If, for example, the operands are 4 bytes (32 bits) long, the execution time is approximately

$$227 \times 16 + 98 \times 4 + 291 = 4315 \text{ cycles}$$

There is a saving of 202 × LENGTH cycles for each multiplicand byte that is 0.

Program size 128 bytes

Data memory required 256 bytes anywhere in RAM for the more significant bytes of the partial product (starting at address PROD). This includes an overflow byte. Also 24 stack bytes.

Special case A length of 0 causes an immediate exit with the product equal to the multiplicand.

```
*
*
*
*
*       Title:              Multiple-Precision Binary Multiplication
*       Name:               MPBMUL
*
*
```

```
*
*    Purpose:                Multiply 2 arrays of binary bytes
*                            Multiplicand := Multiplicand X Multiplier
*
*    Entry:                  TOP OF STACK
*                              High word of return address
*                              Low word of return address
*                              Array length in bytes
*                              High word of multiplier address
*                              Low word of multiplier address
*                              High word of multiplicand address
*                              Low word of multiplicand address
*
*                              The arrays are unsigned binary numbers
*                              with a maximum length of 255 bytes,
*                              ARRAY[0] is the most significant
*                              byte, and ARRAY[LENGTH-1] is the
*                              least significant byte.
*
*    Exit:                   Multiplicand := Multiplicand X Multiplier
*
*    Registers Used:         A0,A1,CCR,D0,D1,D2
*
*    Time:                   Assuming all multiplicand bytes are non-zero,
*                            the time is approximately
*                             (227 X length^2) + (98 X length) + 291 cycles
*
*    Size                    Program  128 bytes
*                            Data     256 bytes plus 24 stack bytes
*
*

MPBMUL
*
*       CHECK LENGTH OF OPERANDS
*       EXIT IF LENGTH IS ZERO, PRODUCT = MULTIPLICAND
*
        MOVE.W   4(SP),D0         GET LENGTH OF ARRAYS IN BYTES
        BEQ.S    EXITML           EXIT IF LENGTH IS ZERO
                                  * PRODUCT = MULTIPLICAND IN THIS CASE
*
*       SET POINTERS JUST BEYOND ENDS OF ARRAYS
*       ADDRESSES ARE ONE TOO HIGH TO ALLOW FOR INITIAL PREDECREMENT
*
        MOVEM.L  6(SP),A0-A1      GET BASE ADDRESSES OF MULTIPLIER
                                  * (A0), MULTIPLICAND (A1)
        MOVEM.L  A2-A5/D3-D4,-(SP)   SAVE EXTRA REGISTERS IN STACK
        ADDA.W   D0,A0            POINT JUST BEYOND END OF MULTIPLIER
        ADDA.W   D0,A1            POINT JUST BEYOND END OF MULTIPLICAND
        LEA      PROD+1,A2        POINT JUST BEYOND END OF PARTIAL
        ADDA.W   D0,A2              PRODUCT PLUS OVERFLOW BYTE
*
*       CLEAR PARTIAL PRODUCT AREA PLUS OVERFLOW BYTE
*
        MOVE.W   D0,D1            COUNT = ARRAY LENGTH IN BYTES
                                  *NOTE THIS ADDS 1 BYTE FOR OVERFLOW
```

```
                                        * BECAUSE LOOP EXITS ON -1
        MOVEA.L   A2,A3                 GET POINTER TO PARTIAL PRODUCT
        CLR.B     D2                    GET ZERO FOR CLEARING
CLEAR
        MOVE.B    D2,-(A3)              CLEAR A BYTE
        DBRA      D1,CLEAR              CONTINUE THROUGH ALL BYTES
*
*       LOOP OVER ALL MULTIPLICAND BYTES
*       MULTIPLYING EACH ONE BY ALL MULTIPLIER BYTES
*
        SUBQ.W    #1,D0                 ADJUST ARRAY LENGTH TO EXIT ON -1
        MOVE.W    D0,D2                 OUTER COUNT = MULTIPLICAND LENGTH - 1
MCNDLP
        MOVEQ     #0,D3                 GET MULTIPLICAND BYTE, EXTENDED
        MOVE.B    -(A1),D3               TO 32 BITS
        BEQ.S     SKIP                  SKIP OVER A ZERO BYTE
        MOVEA.L   A0,A3                 GET MULTIPLIER ADDRESS
        MOVEA.L   A2,A4                 GET PARTIAL PRODUCT ADDRESS
        MOVE.W    D0,D1                 GET ARRAY LENGTH IN BYTES - 1
*
*       MULTIPLY BYTE OF MULTIPLICAND TIMES EACH BYTE OF
*        MULTIPLIER
*
MPLRLP
        MOVEQ     #0,D4                 EXTEND MULTIPLIER BYTE TO 32 BITS
        MOVEA.L   A4,A5                 SAVE CURRENT PARTIAL PRODUCT POINTER
                                        * SO WE CAN EXTEND ADDITION THROUGH
                                        * HIGHER BYTES WITHOUT MOVING IT
        MOVE.B    -(A3),D4              GET MULTIPLIER BYTE
        BEQ.S     GETPTR                BRANCH WITHOUT MULTIPLYING IF BYTE
                                        * IS ZERO
        MULU      D3,D4                 MULTIPLY TIMES MULTIPLICAND BYTE
                                        * (16-BIT OPERATION)
        ADD.B     D4,-(A4)              ADD LOW BYTE OF PRODUCT TO PARTIAL
                                        * PRODUCT
        BCC       HIBYTE                BRANCH IF CARRY CLEAR AND PROCESS
                                        * HIGH BYTE
ADCRY1
        ADDQ.B    #1,-(A4)              ADD CARRY TO NEXT BYTE OF PARTIAL
                                        * PRODUCT
        BCS.S     ADCRY1                LOOP AS LONG AS CARRY PROPAGATES
HIBYTE
        LSR.W     #8,D4                 SHIFT ANSWER RIGHT 1 BYTE
        BEQ.S     GETPTR                SKIP IF BYTE IS ZERO
        LEA       -1(A5),A4             RESTORE CURRENT PRODUCT POINTER
                                        * THEN MOVE IT LEFT ONE BYTE
        ADD.B     D4,-(A4)              ADD UPPER BYTE OF RESULT TO PARTIAL
                                        * PRODUCT
        BCC       GETPTR                BRANCH (CONTINUE) IF NO CARRY
ADCRY2
        ADDQ.B    #1,-(A4)              OTHERWISE, ADD CARRY TO NEXT BYTE
        BCS       ADCRY2                CONTINUE AS LONG AS CARRY PROPAGATES
GETPTR
        LEA       -1(A5),A4             RESTORE CURRENT PRODUCT POINTER
                                        * THEN MOVE IT LEFT ONE BYTE
        DBRA      D1,MPLRLP             LOOP THROUGH ALL MULTIPLIER BYTES
```

```
*
*         MOVE LOW BYTE OF PARTIAL PRODUCT INTO RESULT AREA
*         THIS OVERWRITES THE MULTIPLICAND BYTE USED IN THE
*           LATEST MULTIPLICATION LOOP
*
SKIP
          MOVEA.L   A2,A4             GET PARTIAL PRODUCT POINTER
          MOVE.B    -(A4),(A1)        MOVE LOW BYTE OF PARTIAL PRODUCT TO
                                      * CURRENT BYTE OF MULTIPLICAND
          MOVEA.L   A2,A3             GET ANOTHER COPY OF PARTIAL PRODUCT
                                      * POINTER FOR SHIFTING
*
*         SHIFT PARTIAL PRODUCT RIGHT ONE BYTE
*
          MOVE.W    D0,D1             GET NUMBER OF BYTES TO SHIFT
PRODRT
          MOVE.B    -(A4),-(A3)       SHIFT ONE BYTE RIGHT
          DBRA      D1,PRODRT         CONTINUE THROUGH ALL BYTES
*
*         COUNT MULTIPLICAND BYTES
*
          DBRA      D2,MCNDLP         LOOP UNTIL ALL BYTES MULTIPLIED
*
*         REMOVE PARAMETERS FROM STACK AND EXIT
*
          MOVEM.L   (SP)+,A2-A5/D3-D4   RESTORE EXTRA REGISTERS
EXITML
          MOVEA.L   (SP)+,A0          GET RETURN ADDRESS
                                      *NOTE: REPLACING THIS INSTRUCTION
                                      * WITH MOVEA.L (SP),A0 LEAVES THE
                                      * BASE ADDRESS OF THE PRODUCT AT
                                      * THE TOP OF THE STACK (AS MANY
                                      * COMPILERS DO)
          LEA       10(SP),SP         REMOVE PARAMETERS FROM STACK
          JMP       (A0)              EXIT TO RETURN ADDRESS
*
*         DATA
*
PROD      DS.B      256          PARTIAL PRODUCT BUFFER WITH OVERFLOW BYTE
*
*
*         SAMPLE EXECUTION
*
*

SC3C
          MOVEA.L   AY1ADR,A1         GET BASE ADDRESS OF MULTIPLICAND
          MOVEA.L   AY2ADR,A0         GET BASE ADDRESS OF MULTIPLIER
          MOVEM.L   A0-A1,-(SP)       PUSH OPERAND ADDRESSES INTO STACK
          MOVE.W    #SZAYS,-(SP)      PUSH LENGTH OF OPERANDS INTO STACK
          JSR       MPBMUL       MULTIPLE-PRECISION BINARY MULTIPLICATION
                                 *RESULT OF $12345 X $1234 = $14B60404
                                 * IN MEMORY AY1      = $00
                                 *           AY1+1    = $00
                                 *           AY1+2    = $00
                                 *           AY1+3    = $00
```

```
                                 *            AY1+4     = $14
                                 *            AY1+5     = $B6
                                 *            AY1+6     = $04
                                 *            AY1+7     = $04
         BRA.S     SC3C          REPEAT TEST
*
*  DATA
*
SZAYS    EQU       8             LENGTH OF OPERANDS IN BYTES

AY1ADR   DC.L      AY1           BASE ADDRESS OF MULTIPLICAND
AY2ADR   DC.L      AY2           BASE ADDRESS OF MULTIPLIER

AY1      DC.B      0,0,0,0,0,1,$23,$45       MULTIPLICAND
AY2      DC.B      0,0,0,0,0,0,$12,$34       MULTIPLIER

         END
```

3D Multiple-precision binary division (MPBDIV)

Divides two multi-byte unsigned binary numbers. Both are stored with their most significant bytes at the lowest address. The quotient replaces the dividend, and the address of the most significant byte of the remainder ends up in register A0. The length of the numbers (in bytes) is 255 or less. The Carry flag is cleared if no errors occur; if a divide by 0 is attempted, the Carry flag is set to 1, the dividend is left unchanged, and the remainder is set to 0.

Procedure The program divides using the standard shift-and-subtract algorithm, shifting quotient and dividend and placing a 1 bit in the quotient each time a trial subtraction succeeds. An extra buffer holds the result of the trial subtraction; that buffer is simply switched with the buffer holding the dividend if the subtraction succeeds. The program sets the Carry flag if the divisor is 0 and clears Carry otherwise.

Entry conditions

Order in stack (starting from the top)

High word of return address
Low word of return address

Operand length in bytes

High word of base address of divisor
Low word of base address of divisor

High word of base address of dividend
Low word of base address of dividend

Exit conditions

Dividend replaced by quotient (dividend divided by divisor)
If the divisor is non-zero, Carry = 0 and the result is normal.
If the divisor is 0, Carry = 1, the dividend is unchanged, and the remainder is 0.
The remainder is stored starting with its most significant byte at the address in A0.

Example

Data: Length of operands (in bytes) = 3
Top operand (array 2 or divisor) = $000F45_{16} = 3909_{10}$
Bottom operand (array 1 or dividend) = $35A2F7_{16}$ = $3\,515\,127_{10}$

Result: Bottom operand (array 1) = Bottom operand (array 1)/Top operand (array 2) = $000383_{16} = 899_{10}$
Remainder (starting at address in A0) = $0003A8_{16} = 936_{10}$
Carry flag = 0 to indicate no divide by zero error

Registers used A0, A1, CCR, D0, D1, D2

Execution time Depends on the length of the operands and on the number of 1 bits in the quotient (requiring a replacement of the dividend by the remainder). If the average number of 1 bits in the quotient is four per byte, the execution time is approximately

$$976 \times \text{LENGTH}^2 + 838 \times \text{LENGTH} + 490$$

cycles where LENGTH is the length of the operands in bytes. If, for example, LENGTH = 4 (32-bit division), the approximate execution time is

$$976 \times 4^2 + 838 \times 4 + 490 = 19\,458 \text{ cycles}$$

Program size 166 bytes

Data memory required 510 bytes anywhere in RAM for the buffers holding either the high dividend or the result of the trial subtraction (255 bytes starting at addresses HIDE1 and HIDE2, respectively). Also 24 stack bytes.

Special cases

1. A length of 0 causes an immediate exit with the Carry flag cleared, the quotient equal to the original dividend, and the remainder equal to the original divisor.

2. A divisor of 0 causes an exit with the Carry flag set to 1, the quotient equal to the original dividend, and the remainder equal to 0.

```
*
*
*
*
*     Title:                  Multiple-Precision Binary Division
*     Name:                   MPBDIV
*
*
*
*     Purpose:                Divide 2 arrays of binary bytes
*                             Array1 := Array 1 / Array 2
*
*     Entry:                  TOP OF STACK
*                               High word of return address
*                               Low word of return address
*                               Array length in bytes
*                               High word of divisor address
*                               Low word of divisor address
*                               High word of dividend address
*                               Low word of dividend address
*
*                               The arrays are unsigned binary numbers
*                               with a maximum length of 255 bytes,
*                               ARRAY[0] is the most significant
*                               byte, and ARRAY[LENGTH-1] is the
*                               least significant byte.
*
*     Exit:                   Array1 := Array1 / Array2
*                             Register A0 := Base address of remainder
*                             If no errors then
*                               Carry := 0
*                             else
*                               divide-by-zero error
*                               Carry := 1
*                               quotient := array 1 unchanged
*                               remainder := 0
*
*     Registers Used:         A0,A1,CCR,D0,D1,D2
*
*     Time:                   Assuming there are length/2 1 bits in the
*                             quotient, then the time is approximately
*                               (976 X length^2) + (838 X length) +
*                                490 cycles
*
*     Size:                   Program   166 bytes
*                             Data      510 bytes plus 24 stack bytes
*
*

MPBDIV
*
*        EXIT INDICATING NO ERROR IF LENGTH OF OPERANDS IS ZERO
*        QUOTIENT = DIVIDEND, REMIANDER = DIVISOR IF LENGTH IS ZERO
```

```
*
        MOVEM.L   6(SP),A0-A1      GET BASE ADDRESSES OF DIVISOR (A0),
                                   * DIVIDEND (A1)
        MOVE.W    4(SP),D0         GET LENGTH OF OPERANDS, CLEAR CARRY
        BEQ       EXITDV           BRANCH IF LENGTH IS ZERO
                                   * NOTE: MOVE CLEARS CARRY SO EXIT
                                   * IS GOOD (NO ERRORS) - REMAINDER
                                   * = DIVISOR, QUOTIENT = DIVIDEND
                                   * IN THIS CASE
        MOVEM.L   A2-A6/D3,-(SP)   SAVE EXTRA REGISTERS
*
*       CHECK FOR ZERO DIVISOR BY TESTING DIVISOR FOR NONZERO BYTES
*       EXIT WITH CARRY SET IF ENTIRE DIVISOR IS ZERO
*
        MOVE.W    D0,D1            GET LENGTH - 1 FOR LOOP CONTROL
        SUBQ.W    #1,D1
        MOVEA.L   A0,A2            GET DIVISOR POINTER
ZEROCHK
        TST.B     (A2)+            IS NEXT BYTE OF DIVISOR ZERO?
        DBNE      D1,ZEROCHK       CONTINUE UNTIL NONZERO BYTE FOUND
                                   * OR ALL BYTES EXAMINED
        BNE.S     INITDV           BRANCH IF NONZERO BYTE FOUND
        ORI.B     #1,CCR           ALL BYTES ARE ZERO - INDICATE
                                   * ERROR BY SETTING CARRY
                                   * REMAINDER = DIVISOR = ZERO
                                   * QUOTIENT = DIVIDEND
        BRA       EXITRS           EXIT, DIVISOR IS ZERO
*
*       SET POINTERS JUST BEYOND ENDS OF ARRAYS
*       ADDRESSES ARE ONE TOO HIGH TO ALLOW FOR INITIAL PREDECREMENT
*
INITDV
        ADDA.W    D0,A0            POINT JUST BEYOND END OF DIVISOR
        ADDA.W    D0,A1            POINT JUST BEYOND END OF DIVIDEND
        LEA       HIDE1,A2         DIVIDEND POINTER = ARRAY 1
        LEA       HIDE2,A3         DIFFERENCE POINTER = ARRAY 2
        ADDA.W    D0,A2            POINT JUST BEYOND END OF HIGH
                                   * DIVIDEND
        ADDA.W    D0,A3            POINT JUST BEYOND END OF DIFFERENCE
*
*       BIT COUNT = 8 X ARRAY LENGTH + 1
*       ONE EXTRA SHIFT NEEDED TO ALIGN QUOTIENT PROPERLY
*
        MOVE.W    D0,D1            GET ARRAY LENGTH
        ASL.W     #3,D1            BIT COUNT = 8 X ARRAY LENGTH + 1
        ADDQ.W    #1,D1
*
*       CLEAR HIGH DIVIDEND AND DIFFERENCE ARRAYS
*       ARRAYS 1 AND 2 ARE USED INTERCHANGEABLY FOR THESE TWO
*         PURPOSES.  THE POINTERS ARE SWITCHED WHENEVER A TRIAL
*         SUBTRACTION SUCCEEDS
*
        SUBQ.W    #1,D0            COUNT = ARRAY LENGTH - 1
        MOVE.W    D0,D2            GET ARRAY LENGTH - 1
        MOVEQ     #0,D3            GET ZERO FOR CLEARING ARRAYS
        MOVEA.L   A2,A4            GET POINTERS TO ARRAYS
```

```
        MOVEA.L   A3,A5
CLRHI
        MOVE.B    D3,-(A4)        CLEAR BYTE OF ARRAY 1
        MOVE.B    D3,-(A5)        CLEAR BYTE OF ARRAY 2
        DBRA      D2,CLRHI        CONTINUE THROUGH ALL BYTES
*
*       DIVIDE USING TRIAL SUBTRACTIONS
*
*
*       SHIFT QUOTIENT/DIVIDEND ARRAY LEFT 1 BIT
*       CARRY IN (EXTEND FLAG) IS RESULT OF PREVIOUS TRIAL SUBTRACTION
*
        CLR.B     D2              START WITH LATEST BIT OF QUOTIENT = 0
DIVLOOP
        MOVE.W    D0,D3           GET ARRAY LENGTH - 1
        MOVEA.L   A1,A4           GET DIVIDEND POINTER
        ROXL.B    #1,D2           SET CARRY IN (EXTEND FLAG) FROM
                                  * LATEST BIT OF QUOTIENT
SHFTQT
        MOVE.B    -(A4),D2        GET BYTE OF DIVIDEND/QUOTIENT
        ROXL.B    #1,D2           SHIFT LEFT 1 BIT WITH CARRY
        MOVE.B    D2,(A4)         SAVE SHIFTED BYTE
        DBRA      D3,SHFTQT       CONTINUE THROUGH ALL BYTES
*
*       SHIFT UPPER DIVIDEND LEFT WITH CARRY FROM LOWER
*         DIVIDEND.
*
        MOVE.W    D0,D3           GET ARRAY LENGTH - 1
        MOVEA.L   A2,A5           GET HIGH DIVIDEND POINTER
SHFTDV
        MOVE.B    -(A5),D2        GET BYTE OF HIGH DIVIDEND
        ROXL.B    #1,D2           SHIFT LEFT 1 BIT WITH CARRY
        MOVE.B    D2,(A5)         SAVE SHIFTED BYTE
        DBRA      D3,SHFTDV       CONTINUE THROUGH ALL BYTES
*
*       CHECK IF FINAL SHIFT OF QUOTIENT HAS BEEN MADE
*       EXIT WITH QUOTIENT IF SO, ELSE DO NEXT SUBTRACTION
*
        SUBQ.W    #1,D1           COUNT BITS
        BEQ       GDEXIT          BRANCH (EXIT) IF ALL BITS DONE,
                                  * INDICATE NO ERRORS
*
*       TRIAL SUBTRACTION OF DIVISOR FROM DIVIDEND
*       SAVE DIFFERENCE IN CASE IT IS NEEDED LATER
*
        MOVE.W    D0,D3           GET ARRAY LENGTH - 1
        MOVEA.L   A0,A4           GET DIVISOR POINTER
        MOVEA.L   A2,A5           GET HIGH DIVIDEND POINTER
        MOVEA.L   A3,A6           GET DIFFERENCE POINTER
SUBDVS
        MOVE.B    -(A5),-1(A6)    MOVE HIGH DIVIDEND BYTE TO DIFFERENCE
        SUBX.B    -(A4),-(A6)     SUBTRACT BYTE OF DIVISOR
        DBRA      D3,SUBDVS       CONTINUE THROUGH ALL BYTES
*
*       NEXT BIT OF QUOTIENT IS 1 IF SUBTRACTION WAS SUCCESSFUL,
*         0 IF IT WAS NOT
```

```
*          THIS IS COMPLEMENT OF FINAL BORROW FROM SUBTRACTION
*
           SCC       D2            NEXT BIT OF QUOTIENT = COMPLEMENT
                                   * OF FINAL BORROW FROM SUBTRACTION
           BCS.S     DIVLOOP       DO NEXT SHIFT IF TRIAL SUBTRACTION
                                   * FAILED
*
*          TRIAL SUBTRACTION SUCCEEDED, SO REPLACE UPPER DIVIDEND
*            WITH DIFFERENCE BY SWITCHING POINTERS
*
           EXG       A2,A3         SWITCH HIGH DIVIDEND, DIFFERENCE
                                   * POINTERS
           BRA.S     DIVLOOP       DO NEXT SHIFT
*
*          CLEAR CARRY TO INDICATE NO ERRORS
*
GDEXIT
           ANDI.B    #$FE,CCR      CLEAR CARRY - NO DIVIDE-BY-ZERO ERROR
           MOVEA.L   A2,A0         GET ADDRESS JUST BEYOND LSB OF
                                   * REMAINDER
           SUBA.W    D0,A0         CALCULATE BASE ADDRESS OF REMAINDER
           SUBQ.L    #1,A0         (ADDRESS OF MSB)
*
*          REMOVE PARAMETERS FROM STACK AND EXIT
*
EXITRS
           MOVEM.L   (SP)+,A2-A6/D3 RESTORE EXTRA REGISTERS
EXITDV
           MOVEA.L   (SP)+,A1      GET RETURN ADDRESS
                                   *NOTE: REPLACING THIS INSTRUCTION
                                   * WITH MOVEA.L (SP),A1 LEAVES THE
                                   * BASE ADDRESS OF THE QUOTIENT AT
                                   * THE TOP OF THE STACK (AS MANY
                                   * COMPILERS DO)
           LEA       10(SP),SP     REMOVE PARAMETERS FROM STACK
           JMP       (A1)          EXIT TO RETURN ADDRESS
*
*          DATA
*
HIDE1      DS.B      255           HIGH DIVIDEND BUFFER 1
HIDE2      DS.B      255           HIGH DIVIDEND BUFFER 2
*
*          SAMPLE EXECUTION
*
*

SC3D
           MOVE.L    AY1ADR,-(SP)  PUSH DIVIDEND ONTO STACK
           MOVE.L    AY2ADR,-(SP)  PUSH DIVISOR ONTO STACK
           MOVE.W    #SZAYS,-(SP)  PUSH LENGTH OF OPERANDS ONTO STACK
           JSR       MPBDIV     MULTIPLE-PRECISION BINARY DIVISION
                                *RESULT OF $14B60404 / $1234 = $12345
                                * IN MEMORY AY1        = $00
                                *           AY1+1      = $00
                                *           AY1+2      = $00
                                *           AY1+3      = $00
```

```
                                *              AY1+4     = $01
                                *              AY1+5     = $23
                                *              AY1+6     = $45
        BRA.S       SC3D        REPEAT TEST

*
*  DATA
*
SZAYS   EQU         7           LENGTH OF OPERANDS IN BYTES

AY1ADR  DC.L        AY1         BASE ADDRESS OF ARRAY 1 (DIVIDEND)
AY2ADR  DC.L        AY2         BASE ADDRESS OF ARRAY 2 (DIVISOR)

AY1     DC.B        0,0,0,$14,$B6,$04,$04          DIVIDEND
AY2     DC.B        0,0,0,0,0,$12,$34              DIVISOR
        END
```

3E Multiple-precision binary comparison (MPBCMP)

Compares two multi-byte unsigned binary numbers and sets the Carry and Zero flags. Both numbers are stored with their most significant bytes at the lowest address. Sets the Zero flag to 1 if the operands are equal and to 0 otherwise. Sets the Carry flag to 1 if the subtrahend (the number stored higher in the stack) is larger than the minuend and to 0 otherwise. Thus, it sets the flags as if it had subtracted the subtrahend from the minuend.

Procedure The program compares the operands one byte at a time, starting with the most significant bytes and continuing until it finds corresponding bytes that are not equal. If all the bytes are equal, it exits with the Zero flag set to 1. Note that comparison starts with the operands' most significant bytes, whereas subtraction (Subroutine 3B) starts with the least significant bytes.

Entry conditions

Order in stack (starting from the top)

High word of return address
Low word of return address

Operand length in bytes

High word of base address of subtrahend
Low word of base address of subtrahend

High word of base address of minuend
Low word of base address of minuend

Exit conditions

Flags set as if subtrahend had been subtracted from minuend

Zero flag = 1 if subtrahend and minuend are equal, 0 if they are not equal

Carry flag = 1 if subtrahend is larger than minuend in the unsigned sense, 0 if it less than or equal to the minuend

Examples

1. Data: Length of operands (in bytes) = 6
   Top operand (subtrahend) = $19D028A193EA_{16}$
   Bottom operand (minuend) = $4E67BC15A266_{16}$
   Result: Zero flag = 0 (operands are not equal)
   Carry flag = 0 (subtrahend is not larger than minuend)

2. Data: Length of operands (in bytes) = 6
   Top operand (subtrahend) = $19D028A193EA_{16}$
   Bottom operand (minuend) = $19D028A193EA_{16}$
   Result: Zero flag = 1 (operands are equal)
   Carry flag = 0 (subtrahend is not larger than minuend)

3. Data: Length of operands (in bytes) = 6
   Top operand (subtrahend) = $19D028A193EA_{16}$
   Bottom operand (minuend) = $0F37E5991D7C_{16}$
   Result: Zero flag = 0 (operands are not equal)
   Carry flag = 1 (subtrahend is larger than minuend)

Registers used A0, A1, CCR, D0

Execution time 22 cycles per byte that must be examined plus approximately 108 cycles overhead. That is, the program continues until it finds corresponding bytes that are not the same; each pair of bytes it must examine requires 22 cycles.

Examples

1. Comparing two 6-byte numbers that are equal takes

$$22 \times 6 + 108 = 240 \text{ cycles.}$$

2. Comparing two 8-byte numbers that differ in the next to most significant bytes takes

$$22 \times 2 + 108 = 152 \text{ cycles.}$$

Program Size 32 bytes

Data memory required None

Special case A length of 0 causes an immediate exit with both the Carry flag and the Zero flag set to 1.

```
*
*
*
*       Title:                  Multiple-Precision Binary Comparison
*       Name:                   MPBCMP
*
*
*
*       Purpose:                Compare 2 arrays of binary bytes and
*                               return the Carry and Zero flags set or
*                               cleared
*
*       Entry:                  TOP OF STACK
*                                 High word of return address
*                                 Low word of return address
*                                 Operand length in bytes
*                                 High word of subtrahend address
*                                 Low word of subtrahend address
*                                 High word of minuend address
*                                 Low word of minuend address
*
*                                 The arrays are unsigned binary numbers,
*                                 ARRAY[0] is the most significant
*                                 byte, and ARRAY[LENGTH-1] is the
*                                 least significant byte.
*
*       Exit:                   IF minuend = subtrahend THEN
*                                 C=0,Z=1
*                               IF minuend > subtrahend THEN
*                                 C=0,Z=0
*                               IF minuend < subtrahend THEN
*                                 C=1,Z=0
*                               IF array length = 0 THEN
*                                 C=1,Z=1
*
*       Registers Used:         A0,A1,CCR,D0
*
*       Time:                   22 cycles per byte that must be examined plus
*                                 108 cycles overhead
*
*       Size:                   Program  32 bytes
*

*
*          CHECK IF LENGTH OF ARRAYS IS ZERO
*          EXIT WITH SPECIAL FLAG SETTING (C=1, Z=1) IF IT IS
*
MPBCMP
           MOVEM.L    6(SP),A0-A1     GET BASE ADDRESSES OF SUBTRAHEND (A0)
                                      * AND MINUEND (A1)
           MOVE.W     4(SP),D0     GET LENGTH OF OPERANDS
           ORI.B      #1,CCR       SET CARRY IN CASE LENGTH IS 0
           BEQ.S      CPEXIT       BRANCH (EXIT) IF LENGTH IS ZERO
```

```
                                * C=1,Z=1 IN THIS CASE
*
*         COMPARE ARRAYS ONE BYTE AT A TIME UNTIL UNEQUAL BYTES
*          ARE ENCOUNTERED
*
          SUBQ.W     #1,D0      ADJUST COUNT FOR LOOP EXIT ON -1
CMPBYT
          CMPM.B     (A0)+,(A1)+  COMPARE BYTES OF MINUEND, SUBTRAHEND
          DBNE       D0,CMPBYT THROUGH ALL BYTES OR UNTIL UNEQUAL BYTES
                                *  ARE FOUND
*
*         REMOVE PARAMETERS FROM STACK AND EXIT
*
EXITCP
          MOVEA.L    (SP)+,A0   GET RETURN ADDRESS
          LEA        10(SP),SP REMOVE PARAMETERS FROM STACK
                                * NOTE: MOVEA, ADDA DO NOT AFFECT FLAGS
          JMP        (A0)       EXIT TO RETURN ADDRESS
*
*
*         SAMPLE EXECUTION
*
*

SC3E
          MOVEA.L    AY1ADR,A1       GET BASE ADDRESS OF MINUEND
          MOVEA.L    AY2ADR,A0       GET BASE ADDRESS OF SUBTRAHEND
          MOVEM.L    A0-A1,-(SP)     PUSH OPERAND ADDRESSES ONTO STACK
          MOVE.W     #SZAYS,-(SP)    PUSH LENGTH OF OPERANDS ONTO STACK
          JSR        MPBCMP     MULTIPLE-PRECISION BINARY COMPARISON
                                *RESULT OF COMPARE ($2F3E4D5C,$175E809F)
                                *  IS C=0,Z=0
          BRA.S      SC3E       REPEAT TEST
*
*  DATA
*
SZAYS     EQU        7          LENGTH OF OPERANDS IN BYTES

AY1ADR    DC.L       AY1        BASE ADDRESS OF MINUEND
AY2ADR    DC.L       AY2        BASE ADDRESS OF SUBTRAHEND

AY1       DC.B       0,0,0,$2F,$3E,$4D,$5C     MINUEND
AY2       DC.B       0,0,0,$17,$5E,$80,$9F     SUBTRAHEND

          END
```

3F Multiple-precision decimal addition (MPDADD)

Adds two multi-byte unsigned decimal (BCD) numbers. Both are stored with their most significant digits at the lowest address. The sum replaces the number with the base address lower in the stack.

Procedure The program clears the Extend flag initially and then adds the operands a byte (two digits) at a time, starting with the least significant digits. The final Extend flag indicates whether the overall addition produced a carry. A length of 0 causes an immediate exit with no addition.

Entry conditions

Order in stack (starting from the top)

High word of return address
Low word of return address

Length of operands in bytes

High word of base address of second operand (address containing the most significant byte of array 2)
Low word of base address of second operand (address containing the most significant byte of array 2)

High word of base address of first operand and sum (address containing the most significant byte of array 1)
Low word of base address of first operand and sum (address containing the most significant byte of array 1)

Exit conditions

First operand (array 1) replaced by first operand (array 1) plus second operand (array 2)

Example

Data: Length of operands (in bytes) = 6
Top operand (array 2) = 196028819315_{16}

Bottom operand (array 1) = 293471605987_{16}

Result: Bottom operand (array 1) = Bottom operand (array 1) + Top operand (array 2) = 489500425302_{16}
Extend (X) flag = 0 (no carry)

Registers used A0, A1, CCR, D0

Execution time 29 cycles per byte plus 120 cycles overhead. For example, adding two 8-byte operands takes

$$29 \times 8 + 120 = 352 \text{ cycles.}$$

Program size 36 bytes

Data memory required None

Special case A length of 0 causes an immediate exit with the sum equal to the bottom operand (i.e. array 1 is unchanged). The Extend flag is cleared.

```
*
*
*
*
*       Title:                  Multiple-Precision Decimal Addition
*       Name:                   MPDADD
*
*
*
*       Purpose:                Add 2 arrays of BCD bytes
*                               Array1 := Array 1 + Array 2
*
*
*       Entry:                  TOP OF STACK
*                                 High word of return address
*                                 Low word of return address
*                                 Array length in bytes
*                                 High word of array 2 address
*                                 Low word of array 2 address
*                                 High word of array 1 address
*                                 Low word of array 1 address
*
*                                 The arrays are unsigned BCD numbers,
*                                 ARRAY[0] is the most significant
```

```
*                               byte, and ARRAY[LENGTH-1] is the
*                               least significant byte
*
*       Exit:                 Array1 := Array1 + Array2
*
*       Registers Used:       A0,A1,CCR,D0
*
*       Time:                 29 cycles per byte plus 120 cycles overhead
*
*       Size:                 Program  36 bytes
*
*
*
MPDADD
        *
        *CHECK IF LENGTH OF OPERANDS IS ZERO
        *EXIT WITH EXTEND FLAG CLEARED (0) IF IT IS
        *
        MOVEM.L   6(SP),A0-A1 GET BASE ADDRESSES OF OPERANDS
                                * ARRAY 1 IN A1, ARRAY 2 IN A0
        MOVE      #0,CCR      NO CARRY INITIALLY (EXTEND FLAG = 0)
        MOVE.W    4(SP),D0    GET LENGTH OF OPERANDS
        BEQ.S     ADEXIT      BRANCH (EXIT) IF OPERAND LENGTH IS ZERO
        *
        *ADD OPERANDS 2 DIGITS AT A TIME
        *
        ADDA.W    D0,A1       GET ADDRESS JUST BEYOND LSB OF ARRAY 1
        ADDA.W    D0,A0       GET ADDRESS JUST BEYOND LSB OF ARRAY 2
                              *ADDRESSES ARE 1 TOO HIGH TO ALLOW
                              *  FOR INITIAL PREDECREMENT
        SUBQ.W    #1,D0       REDUCE COUNT FOR LOOP EXIT ON -1
ADDBYT
        ABCD      -(A0),-(A1)     ADD 2 DIGITS FROM ARRAY 2 TO ARRAY 1
        DBRA      D0,ADDBYT CONTINUE UNTIL ALL DIGITS SUMMED
        *
        *REMOVE PARAMETERS FROM STACK AND EXIT
        *
ADEXIT
        MOVE.L    (SP)+,A0    GET RETURN ADDRESS
                              *NOTE: REPLACING THIS INSTRUCTION WITH
                              * MOVEA.L (SP),A0 LEAVES THE BASE ADDRESS
                              * OF THE SUM AT THE TOP OF THE STACK (AS
                              * MANY COMPILERS DO)
        LEA       10(SP),SP REMOVE PARAMETERS FROM STACK
        JMP       (A0)        EXIT TO RETURN ADDRESS

*
*
*       SAMPLE EXECUTION
*
*

SC3F
        MOVEA.L   AY1ADR,A1       GET POINTER TO FIRST OPERAND
        MOVEA.L   AY2ADR,A0       GET POINTER TO SECOND OPERAND
```

```
        MOVEM.L   A0-A1,-(SP)     PUSH OPERAND ADDRESSES ONTO STACK
        MOVE.W    #SZAYS,-(SP)    PUSH LENGTH OF OPERANDS ONTO STACK
        JSR       MPDADD      MULTIPLE-PRECISION BCD ADDITION
                              *RESULT OF $12345678 + $35914028
                              *  = $48259706
                              * IN MEMORY AY1        = $00
                              *           AY1+1      = $00
                              *           AY1+2      = $00
                              *           AY1+3      = $48
                              *           AY1+4      = $25
                              *           AY1+5      = $97
                              *           AY1+6      = $06
        BRA.S     SC3F        REPEAT TEST
*
*  DATA
*
SZAYS   EQU       7           LENGTH OF OPERANDS IN BYTES

AY1ADR  DC.L      AY1         BASE ADDRESS OF FIRST OPERAND
AY2ADR  DC.L      AY2         BASE ADDRESS OF SECOND OPERAND

AY1     DC.B      0,0,0,$12,$34,$56,$78     FIRST OPERAND
AY2     DC.B      0,0,0,$35,$91,$40,$28     SECOND OPERAND

        END
```

3G Multiple-precision decimal subtraction (MPDSUB)

Subtracts two multi-byte unsigned decimal (BCD) numbers. Both are stored with their most significant digits at the lowest address. The subtrahend (number to be subtracted) is stored on top of the minuend (number from which it is subtracted). The difference replaces the minuend.

Procedure The program clears the Extend flag initially and then subtracts the subtrahend from the minuend one byte (two digits) at a time, starting with the least significant digits. The final Extend flag indicates whether the overall subtraction required a borrow. A length of 0 causes an immediate exit with no subtraction.

Entry conditions

Order in stack (starting from the top)

High word of return address
Low word of return address

Operand length in bytes

High word of base address of subtrahend
Low word of base address of subtrahend

High word of base address of minuend
Low word of base address of minuend

Exit conditions

Minuend replaced by minuend minus subtrahend

Example

Data: Length of operands (in bytes) = 6
Minuend = 293471605987_{16}
Subtrahend = 196028819315_{16}
Result: Minuend = 097442786672_{16}
Extend (X) flag = 1, since no borrow is necessary

Registers used A0, A1, CCR, D0

Execution time 29 cycles per byte plus 120 cycles overhead. For example, subtracting two 8-byte operands takes

$$29 \times 8 + 120 = 352 \text{ cycles}$$

Program size 36 bytes

Data memory required None

Special case A length of 0 causes an immediate exit with the minuend unchanged (i.e. the difference is equal to the minuend). The Extend flag is cleared.

```
*
*
*
*
*       Title:                  Multiple-Precision Decimal Subtraction
*       Name:                   MPDSUB
*
*
*
*       Purpose:                Subtract 2 arrays of BCD bytes
*                               Minuend := Minuend - Subtrahend
*
*       Entry:                  TOP OF STACK
*                                 High word of return address
*                                 Low word of return address
*                                 Array length in bytes
*                                 High word of subtrahend address
*                                 Low word of subtrahend address
*                                 High word of minuend address
*                                 Low word of minuend address
*
*                                 The arrays are unsigned BCD numbers,
*                                 ARRAY[0] is the most significant byte, and
*                                 ARRAY[LENGTH-1] is the least significant byte.
*
*       Exit:                   Minuend := Minuend - Subtrahend
*
*       Registers Used:         A0,A1,CCR,D0
*
*       Time:                   29 cycles per byte plus 120 cycles overhead
*
*       Size:                   Program 36 bytes
```

```
*
*
*

MPDSUB
        *
        *CHECK IF LENGTH OF OPERANDS IS ZERO
        *EXIT WITH EXTEND FLAG CLEARED (0) IF IT IS
        *
        MOVE      #0,CCR     NO BORROW INITIALLY (EXTEND FLAG = 0)
        MOVEM.L   6(SP),A0-A1  GET BASE ADDRESSES OF SUBTRAHEND (A0),
                             * MINUEND (A1)
        MOVE.W    4(SP),D0   GET LENGTH OF OPERANDS
        BEQ       SBEXIT     BRANCH (EXIT) IF OPERAND LENGTH IS ZERO
        *
        *SUBTRACT OPERANDS 2 DIGITS AT A TIME
        *
        ADDA.W    D0,A1      GET ADDRESS JUST BEYOND LSB OF MINUEND
        ADDA.W    D0,A0      GET ADDRESS JUST BEYOND LSB OF SUBTRAHEND
                             *ADDRESSES ARE 1 TOO HIGH TO ALLOW
                             *  FOR INITIAL PREDECREMENT
        SUBQ.W    #1,D0      REDUCE COUNT FOR LOOP EXIT ON -1
SUBBYT
        SBCD      -(A0),-(A1)    SUBTRACT 2 DIGITS OF SUBTRAHEND FROM
                             * 2 DIGITS OF MINUEND IN DECIMAL
        DBRA      D0,SUBBYT CONTINUE UNTIL ALL DIGITS SUBTRACTED
        *
        *REMOVE PARAMETERS FROM STACK AND EXIT
        *
SBEXIT
        MOVE.L    (SP)+,A0   GET RETURN ADDRESS
                             *NOTE: REPLACING THIS INSTRUCTION WITH
                             * MOVEA.L (SP),A0 LEAVES THE BASE ADDRESS
                             * OF THE DIFFERENCE AT THE TOP OF THE
                             * STACK (AS MANY COMPILERS DO)
        LEA       10(SP),SP REMOVE PARAMETERS FROM STACK
        JMP       (A0)       EXIT TO RETURN ADDRESS

*
*
*       SAMPLE EXECUTION
*
*

SC3G
        MOVEA.L   AY1ADR,A1      GET BASE ADDRESS OF MINUEND
        MOVEA.L   AY2ADR,A0      GET BASE ADDRESS OF SUBTRAHEND
        MOVEM.L   A0-A1,-(SP)    PUSH OPERAND ADDRESSES ONTO STACK
        MOVE.W    #SZAYS,-(SP)   PUSH LENGTH OF ARRAYS INTO STACK
        JSR       MPDSUB     MULTIPLE-PRECISION DECIMAL SUBTRACTION
                             *RESULT OF $28364150-$17598093
                             *  = $10766057
                             * IN MEMORY AY1       = $00
                             *           AY1+1     = $00
                             *           AY1+2     = $00
                             *           AY1+3     = $10
```

```
                                 *         AY1+4      = $76
                                 *         AY1+5      = $60
                                 *         AY1+6      = $57
         BRA.S      SC3G         REPEAT TEST
*
*  DATA
*
SZAYS    EQU        7            LENGTH OF OPERANDS IN BYTES

AY1ADR   DC.L       AY1          BASE ADDRESS OF MINUEND
AY2ADR   DC.L       AY2          BASE ADDRESS OF SUBTRAHEND

AY1      DC.B       0,0,0,$28,$36,$41,$50         MINUEND
AY2      DC.B       0,0,0,$17,$59,$80,$93         SUBTRAHEND

         END
```

3H Multiple-precision decimal multiplication (MPDMUL)

Multiplies two multi-byte unsigned decimal (BCD) numbers. Both numbers are stored with their most significant digits at the lowest address. The product replaces the multiplicand. The length of the numbers (in bytes) is 255 or less. Only the less significant bytes of the product are returned to be compatible with other multiple-precision decimal operations.

Procedure The program handles each digit of the multiplicand separately. It masks the digit off, shifts it (if it is the upper digit of a byte), and then uses it to determine how many times to add the multiplier to the partial product. The least significant digit of the partial product is saved as the next digit of the full product, and the partial product is shifted right four bits. The program uses a flag to determine whether it is currently working with the upper or lower digit of a byte. A length of 0 causes an exit with no multiplication.

Entry conditions

Order in stack (starting from the top)

High word of return address
Low word of return address

Length of operands in bytes

High word of base address of multiplier
Low word of base address of multiplier

High word of base address of multiplicand
Low word of base address of multiplicand

Exit conditions

Multiplicand replaced by multiplicand times multiplier

Example

Data: Length of operands (in bytes) = 4
Multiplicand = 0003518_{16}
Multiplier = 00006294_{16}
Result: Multiplicand = 221422826_{16}

Note that MPDMUL returns only the less significant bytes (i.e. the number of bytes in the multiplicand and multiplier) of the product to be compatible with other multiple-precision decimal arithmetic operations. The more significant bytes of the product are available starting with their most significant byte at address PROD. The user may need to check those bytes for overflow or extend the operands with additional zeros.

Registers used A0, A1, CCR, D0, D1, D2

Execution time Depends on the length of the operands and on the size of the digits in the multiplicand (since they control how many times the multiplier is added to the partial product). If the average digit in the multiplicand is 5, the execution time is approximately

$$562 \times \text{LENGTH}^2 + 411 \times \text{LENGTH} + 331 \text{ cycles}$$

where LENGTH is the number of bytes in the operands. If, for example, LENGTH = 6 (12 digits), the approximate execution time is

$$\begin{aligned} 562 \times 6^2 + 411 \times 6 + 312 &= 562 \times 36 + 2466 + 331 \\ &= 20\,232 + 2797 = 23\,029 \text{ cycles} \end{aligned}$$

Program size 168 bytes

Data memory required 256 bytes anywhere in RAM. This is temporary storage for the high bytes of the partial product plus an overflow byte (starting at address PROD). Also 28 stack bytes.

Special case A length of 0 causes an immediate exit with the multiplicand unchanged. The more significant bytes of the product (starting at address PROD) are undefined.

```
*
*    Title:               Multiple-Precision Decimal Multiplication
*    Name:                MPDMUL
*
*
*    Purpose:             Multiply 2 arrays of BCD bytes
*                         Multiplicand := Multiplicand X Multiplier
*
*    Entry:               TOP OF STACK
*                           High word of return address
*                           Low word of return address
*                           Length of arrays in bytes
*                           High word of multiplier address
*                           Low word of multiplier address
*                           High word of multiplicand address
*                           Low word of multiplicand address
*
*                           The arrays are unsigned BCD numbers
*                           with a maximum length of 255 bytes,
*                           ARRAY[0] is the most significant
*                           byte, and ARRAY[LENGTH-1] is the
*                           least significant byte.
*
*    Exit:                Multiplicand := Multiplicand X Multiplier
*
*    Registers Used:      A0,A1,CCR,D0,D1,D2
*
*    Time:                Assuming average digit value in multiplicand
*                         is 5, the time is approximately
*                          (562 X length^2)+ (411 X length) + 331 cycles
*
*    Size:                Program  168 bytes
*                         Data     256 bytes plus 28 stack bytes
*
*


*
*         CHECK LENGTH OF OPERANDS
*         EXIT IF LENGTH IS ZERO, PRODUCT = MULTIPLICAND
*
MPDMUL
          MOVE.W    4(SP),D0         GET LENGTH OF OPERANDS
          BEQ       EXITML           EXIT IF LENGTH IS ZERO
                                     * PRODUCT = MULTIPLICAND IN THIS CASE
*
*         SET POINTERS TO ENDS OF ARRAYS
*         ADDRESSES OF MULTIPLIER, PARTIAL PRODUCT ARE ONE TOO
*           HIGH TO ALLOW FOR INITIAL PREDECREMENT
*         ADDRESS OF MULTIPLICAND IS AT END OF ARRAY AS IT IS
*           NOT PREDECREMENTED
*
          MOVEM.L   6(SP),A0-A1      GET BASE ADDRESSES OF OPERANDS
                                     * MULTIPLIER IN A0, MULTIPLICAND
                                     * IN A1
          MOVEM.L   A2-A4/D3-D6,-(SP)   SAVE EXTRA REGISTERS IN STACK
          ADDA.W    D0,A0            POINT JUST BEYOND END OF MULTIPLIER
```

```
        ADDA.W   D0,A1          POINT JUST BEYOND END OF MULTIPLICAND
        SUBQ.L   #1,A1          POINT TO LSB OF MULTIPLICAND
        LEA      PROD+1,A2      POINT JUST BEYOND END OF PARTIAL
        ADDA.W   D0,A2           PRODUCT PLUS OVERFLOW BYTE
*
*       CLEAR PARTIAL PRODUCT AREA PLUS OVERFLOW BYTE
*
        MOVE.W   D0,D1          COUNT = ARRAY LENGTH IN BYTES
                                *NOTE THIS ADDS 1 BYTE FOR OVERFLOW
                                * BECAUSE LOOP EXITS ON -1
        MOVEA.L  A2,A3          GET POINTER TO PARTIAL PRODUCT
        CLR.B    D2             GET ZERO FOR CLEARING
CLEAR
        MOVE.B   D2,-(A3)       CLEAR A BYTE
        DBRA     D1,CLEAR       CONTINUE THROUGH ALL BYTES
                                *D2 ALSO CONTAINS INITIAL VALUE
                                * OF DIGIT FLAG (0=LOW,FF=HIGH)
*
*       LOOP THROUGH ALL BYTES OF MULTIPLICAND
*       USE EACH DIGIT TO DETERMINE HOW MANY TIMES TO ADD
*        MULTIPLIER TO PARTIAL PRODUCT
*
*       LOOP THROUGH 2 DIGITS PER BYTE
*       DURING LOWER DIGIT, DIGIT FLAG = 0
*       DURING UPPER DIGIT, DIGIT FLAG = FF HEX
*
        MOVE.W   D0,D1          DIGIT COUNT = 2 X ARRAY LENGTH
        ADD.W    D1,D1
        SUBQ.W   #1,D1          SUBTRACT 1 FROM DIGIT COUNT FOR DBRA
        MOVE.W   D0,D3          SAVE ARRAY LENGTH FOR USE WITH
                                * PARTIAL PRODUCT ARRAY (INCLUDING
                                * OVERFLOW BYTE)
        SUBQ.W   #1,D0          REDUCE ARRAY LENGTH TO EXIT ON -1
MCNDLP
        CLR.W    D4             GET MULTIPLICAND BYTE, EXTEND
        MOVE.B   (A1),D4         TO 16-BIT COUNT
        TST.B    D2             TEST DIGIT FLAG (0=LOW,FF=HIGH)
        BEQ.S    LOWDGT         JUMP IF WORKING ON LOW DIGIT
        LSR.B    #4,D4          SHIFT HIGH DIGIT TO LOW NIBBLE
LOWDGT
        ANDI.B   #$0F,D4        MASK OFF LOW NIBBLE
        BEQ.S    STRDGT         SKIP MULTIPLY IF MULTIPLICAND DIGIT
                                * IS ZERO
*
*       ADD MULTIPLIER TO PRODUCT NUMBER OF TIMES GIVEN BY
*        DIGIT OF MULTIPLICAND
*
        SUBQ.W   #1,D4          REDUCE DIGIT BY 1 FOR DBRA USE
MPLRLP
        MOVEA.L  A0,A3          GET MULTIPLIER ADDRESS
        MOVEA.L  A2,A4          GET PARTIAL PRODUCT ADDRESS
        MOVE.W   D0,D5          GET NUMBER OF BYTES
ADDLP
        ABCD     -(A3),-(A4)    ADD BCD MULTIPLIER TO PARTIAL PRODUCT
        DBRA     D5,ADDLP
        CLR.B    D6             ADD CARRY (EXTEND FLAG) TO OVERFLOW
```

```
        ROXL.B    #1,D6            BYTE.  NO DECIMAL OPERATION NEEDED
        ADD.B     D6,-(A4)         HERE SINCE HIGH BYTE NEVER EXCEEDS
                                   * 9
        DBRA      D4,MPLRLP        DECREMENT MULTIPLICAND DIGIT
STRDGT
        MOVEA.L   A2,A4            GET PARTIAL PRODUCT ADDRESS
        MOVE.B    -1(A2),D5        GET LSB OF PARTIAL PRODUCT
        ANDI.B    #$0F,D5          MASK OFF LOWER FOUR BITS
        TST.B     D2               TEST DIGIT FLAG (0=LOW,FF=HIGH)
        BNE.S     HIGHDGT          BRANCH IF HIGH DIGIT
        ANDI.B    #$F0,(A1)        MASK OFF HIGH DIGIT OF MULTIPLICAND
                                   * LSB
        OR.B      D5,(A1)          OR MULTIPLICAND AND PARTIAL PRODUCT
                                   * LSB'S
        BRA.S     SETSHFT
HIGHDGT
        ANDI.B    #$0F,(A1)        MASK OFF LOW DIGIT OF MULTIPLICAND
                                   * LSB
        ASL.B     #4,D5            SHIFT LSB OF PARTIAL PRODUCT TO
                                   * UPPER DIGIT
        OR.B      D5,(A1)          OR MULTIPLICAND AND PARTIAL PRODUCT
                                   * LSB'S
        SUBQ.L    #1,A1            MOVE MULTIPLICAND POINTER TO NEXT
                                   * DIGIT PAIR
*
*       SHIFT PARTIAL PRODUCT RIGHT 1 DIGIT (4 BITS), INCLUDING
*         OVERFLOW BYTE
*
SETSHFT
        MOVE.W    D0,D4            SET LENGTH COUNTER
        MOVEA.L   A2,A3            GET PRODUCT POINTER
SHRDGT
        MOVE.B    -(A3),D5         GET A BYTE OF PARTIAL PRODUCT
        ROR.W     #8,D5            ROTATE RIGHT 1 BYTE
        MOVE.B    -(A3),D5         GET NEXT BYTE
        ROL.W     #4,D5            ROTATE LEFT ONE DIGIT
        ADDQ.L    #1,A3            MOVE POINTER BACK 1 BYTE
        MOVE.B    D5,(A3)          PUT SHIFTED BYTE BACK IN MEMORY
        DBRA      D4,SHRDGT
        LSR.B     #8,D5            PROCESS OVERFLOW BYTE - SHIFT IN
                                   * 0 DIGIT FOR UPPER NIBBLE
        MOVE.B    D5,-(A3)         STORE SHIFTED OVERFLOW BYTE
*
*       CHECK IF MORE MULTIPLICAND DIGITS LEFT
*
        NOT.B     D2               INVERT DIGIT FLAG
        DBRA      D1,MCNDLP        CONTINUE THROUGH ALL DIGITS
*
*       REMOVE PARAMETERS FROM STACK AND EXIT
*
        MOVEM.L   (SP)+,A2-A4/D3-D6   RESTORE EXTRA REGISTERS
EXITML
        MOVEA.L   (SP)+,A0         GET RETURN ADDRESS
                                   *NOTE: REPLACING THIS INSTRUCTION
                                   * WITH MOVEA.L (SP),A0 LEAVES THE
                                   * BASE ADDRESS OF THE PRODUCT AT
```

```
                                   * THE TOP OF THE STACK (AS MANY
                                   * COMPILERS DO)
        LEA       10(SP),SP        REMOVE PARAMETERS FROM STACK
        JMP       (A0)             EXIT TO RETURN ADDRESS
*
*       DATA
*
PROD    DS.B      256              PRODUCT BUFFER WITH OVERFLOW BYTE

*
*
*       SAMPLE EXECUTION
*
*

SC3H
        MOVEA.L   AY1ADR,A1        GET MULTIPLICAND
        MOVEA.L   AY2ADR,A0        GET MULTIPLIER
        MOVEM.L   A0-A1,-(SP)      PUSH OPERAND ADDRESSES ONTO STACK
        MOVE.W    #SZAYS,-(SP)     PUSH LENGTH OF OPERANDS ONTO STACK
        JSR       MPDMUL      MULTIPLE-PRECISION DECIMAL MULTIPLICATION
                              *RESULT OF $1234 X $5718 = $7056012
                              * IN MEMORY AY1      = $00
                              *           AY1+1    = $00
                              *           AY1+2    = $00
                              *           AY1+3    = $07
                              *           AY1+4    = $05
                              *           AY1+5    = $60
                              *           AY1+6    = $12
        BRA.S     SC3H        REPEAT TEST

SZAYS   EQU       7           LENGTH OF ARRAYS IN BYTES

AY1ADR  DC.L      AY1         BASE ADDRESS OF MULTIPLICAND
AY2ADR  DC.L      AY2         BASE ADDRESS OF MULTIPLIER

AY1     DC.B      0,0,0,0,0,$12,$34         MULTIPLICAND
AY2     DC.B      0,0,0,0,0,$57,$18         MULTIPLIER

        END
```

3I Multiple-precision decimal division (MPDDIV)

Divides two multi-byte unsigned decimal (BCD) numbers. Both numbers are stored with their most significant digits at the lowest address. The quotient replaces the dividend; the base address of the remainder is also returned. The length of the numbers (in bytes) is 255 or less. The Carry flag is cleared if no errors occur; if a divide by 0 is attempted, the Carry flag is set to 1, the dividend is unchanged, and the remainder is set to 0.

Procedure The program divides by determining how many times the divisor can be subtracted from the dividend. It saves that number in the quotient, makes the remainder into the new dividend, and rotates the dividend and the quotient left one digit.

Entry conditions

Order in stack (starting from the top)

High word of return address
Low word of return address

Length of operands in bytes

High word of base address of divisor
Low word of base address of divisor

High word of base address of dividend
Low word of base address of dividend

Exit conditions

Dividend replaced by dividend divided by divisor
If the divisor is non-zero, Carry = 0 and the result is normal
If the divisor is zero, Carry = 1, the dividend is unchanged, and the remainder is zero
The base address of the remainder (i.e. the address of its most significant digits) is in register A0

Example

Data: Length of operands (in bytes) = 4
Dividend = 22142298_{16}
Divisor = 00006294_{16}

Result: Dividend = 00003518_{16}
Remainder (base address in A0) = 00000006_{16}
Carry = 0, indicating no divide-by-0 error

Registers used A0, A1, CCR, D0, D1, D2

Execution time Depends on the length of the operands and on the size of the digits in the quotient (determining how many times the divisor must be subtracted from the dividend). If the average digit in the quotient is 5, the execution time is approximately

$804 \times \text{LENGTH}^2 + 1094 \times \text{LENGTH} + 724$ cycles

where LENGTH is the length of the operands in bytes. If, for example, LENGTH = 6 (12 digits), the approximate execution time is

$$804 \times 6^2 + 1094 \times 6 + 724 = 804 \times 36 + 6564 + 724$$
$$= 28944 + 7288 = 36\,232 \text{ cycles}$$

Program size 172 bytes

Data memory required 510 bytes anywhere in RAM for the buffers holding either the high dividend or the result of the trial subtraction (255 bytes each starting at addresses HIDE1 and HIDE2, respectively). Also 24 stack bytes.

Special cases

1. A length of 0 causes an immediate exit with the Carry flag cleared, the quotient equal to the original dividend, and the remainder equal to the original divisor.

2. A divisor of 0 causes an exit with the Carry flag set to 1, the quotient equal to the original dividend, and the remainder equal to 0.

```
*
*
*
*
*    Title:                  Multiple-Precision Decimal Division
*    Name:                   MPDDIV
*
*
*
*    Purpose:                Divide 2 arrays of BCD bytes
*                            Quotient := Dividend / Divisor
*
*    Entry:                  TOP OF STACK
*                              High word of return address
*                              Low word of return address
*                              Operand length in bytes
*                              High word of divisor address
*                              Low word of divisor address
*                              High word of dividend address
*                              Low word of dividend address
*
*                              The arrays are unsigned BCD numbers
*                              with a maximum length of 255 bytes,
*                              ARRAY[0] is the most significant
*                              byte, and ARRAY[LENGTH-1] is the
*                              least significant byte.
*
*    Exit:                   Dividend := Dividend / Divisor
*                            If no errors then
*                              Carry := 0
*                              Dividend unchanged
*                              Remainder := 0
*
*    Registers Used:         A0,A1,CCR,D0,D1,D2
*
*    Time:                   Assuming the average digit value in the
*                            quotient is 5, then the time is approximately
*                              (804 X length^2) + (1094 X length) +
*                              724 cycles
*
*    Size:                   Program  172 bytes
*                            Data     510 bytes plus 24 stack bytes
*
*


*
*        CHECK LENGTH OF OPERANDS
*        EXIT INDICATING NO ERRORS IF LENGTH IS ZERO
*        QUOTIENT = DIVIDEND, REMAINDER = DIVISOR IF LENGTH IS ZERO
*
MPDDIV
         MOVEM.L   6(SP),A0-A1       GET BASE ADDRESSES OF OPERANDS
                                     * DIVISOR IN A0, DIVIDEND IN A1
         MOVE.W    4(SP),D0          GET LENGTH OF OPERANDS, CLEAR CARRY
         BEQ       EXITDV            BRANCH (EXIT) IF LENGTH OF OPERANDS
                                     * IS ZERO
```

```
                                     * NOTE: MOVE CLEARS CARRY SO EXIT
                                     * IS GOOD (NO ERRORS) - REMAINDER
                                     * = DIVISOR, QUOTIENT = DIVIDEND
                                     * IN THIS CASE
        MOVEM.L   A2-A6/D3,-(SP) SAVE EXTRA REGISTERS
*
*       CHECK FOR ZERO DIVISOR BY TESTING DIVISOR FOR NONZERO BYTES
*       EXIT WITH CARRY SET IF DIVISOR IS ZERO
*
        MOVE.W    D0,D1          GET LENGTH - 1 FOR LOOP CONTROL
        SUBQ.W    #1,D1
        MOVEA.L   A0,A2          GET DIVISOR POINTER
ZEROCHK
        TST.B     (A2)+          IS NEXT BYTE OF DIVISOR ZERO?
        DBNE      D1,ZEROCHK     CONTINUE UNTIL NONZERO BYTE FOUND OR
                                 * ALL BYTES EXAMINED
        BNE.S     INITDV         BRANCH IF NONZERO BYTE FOUND
        ORI.B     #1,CCR         ALL BYTES ARE ZERO - INDICATE
                                 * ERROR BY SETTING CARRY
                                 * REMAINDER = DIVISOR = ZERO
                                 * QUOTIENT = DIVIDEND
        BRA       EXITRS         EXIT, DIVISOR IS ZERO
*
*       SET POINTERS JUST BEYOND ENDS OF ARRAYS
*       ADDRESSES ARE ONE TOO HIGH TO ALLOW FOR INITIAL PREDECREMENT
*
INITDV
        ADDA.W    D0,A0          POINT JUST BEYOND END OF DIVISOR
        ADDA.W    D0,A1          POINT JUST BEYOND END OF DIVIDEND
        LEA       HIDE1,A2       DIVIDEND POINTER = ARRAY 1
        LEA       HIDE2,A3       DIFFERENCE POINTER = ARRAY 2
        ADDA.W    D0,A2          POINT JUST BEYOND END OF HIGH
                                 * DIVIDEND
        ADDA.W    D0,A3          POINT JUST BEYOND END OF DIFFERENCE
*
*       DIGIT COUNT = 2 X ARRAY LENGTH + 1
*       ONE EXTRA OPERATION NEEDED TO ALIGN QUOTIENT PROPERLY
*
        MOVE.W    D0,D1          GET ARRAY LENGTH
        ADD.W     D1,D1          DIGIT COUNT = 2 X ARRAY LENGTH + 1
        ADDQ.W    #1,D1
        SUBQ.W    #1,D0          COUNT = ARRAY LENGTH - 1
*
*       CLEAR HIGH DIVIDEND AND DIFFERENCE ARRAYS
*       ARRAYS 1 AND 2 ARE USED INTERCHANGEABLY FOR THESE TWO
*         PURPOSES. THE POINTERS ARE SWITCHED WHENEVER A
*         TRIAL SUBTRACTION SUCCEEDS
*
        MOVE.W    D0,D2          GET ARRAY LENGTH
        MOVEQ     #0,D3          GET ZERO FOR CLEARING ARRAYS
        MOVEA.L   A2,A4          GET POINTERS TO ARRAYS
        MOVEA.L   A3,A5
CLRHI
        MOVE.B    D3,-(A4)       CLEAR BYTE OF ARRAY 1
        MOVE.B    D3,-(A5)       CLEAR BYTE OF ARRAY 2
        DBRA      D2,CLRHI       CONTINUE THROUGH ALL BYTES
```

```
*
*       SHIFT QUOTIENT/DIVIDEND ARRAY AND UPPER DIVIDEND LEFT 1 DIGIT
*       SHIFT RESULT VALUE INTO THE LOW NIBBLE OF THE DIVIDEND
*       SHIFT UPPER DIGIT OF DIVIDEND INTO THE LOW NIBBLE OF THE
*         UPPER DIVIDEND
*
        CLR.W     D2             START WITH LATEST DIGIT OF QUOTIENT
                                 * = 0
DIVLOOP
        MOVE.W    D0,D3          GET ARRAY LENGTH
        MOVEA.L   A1,A4          GET DIVIDEND POINTER
        ROL.W     #8,D2          ROTATE UPPER DIGIT OF LSB LEFT 1 BYTE
SHFTQT
        MOVE.B    -(A4),D2       GET BYTE OF DIVIDEND/QUOTIENT
        ROL.W     #4,D2          SHIFT LEFT 1 DIGIT
        MOVE.B    D2,(A4)        RETURN BYTE TO DIVIDEND/QUOTIENT
        ROL.W     #4,D2          SHIFT LEFT 1 DIGIT
        DBRA      D3,SHFTQT      CONTINUE THROUGH ALL BYTES
*
*       SHIFT UPPER DIVIDEND LEFT WITH DIGIT CARRY FROM LOWER
*         DIVIDEND
*
        MOVE.W    D0,D3          GET ARRAY LENGTH
        MOVEA.L   A2,A5          GET HIGH DIVIDEND POINTER
SHFTDV
        MOVE.B    -(A5),D2       GET BYTE OF HIGH DIVIDEND
        ROL.W     #4,D2          SHIFT LEFT 1 DIGIT
        MOVE.B    D2,(A5)        RETURN BYTE TO HIGH DIVIDEND
        ROL.W     #4,D2          SHIFT LEFT 1 DIGIT
        DBRA      D3,SHFTDV      CONTINUE THROUGH ALL BYTES
*
*       CHECK IF QUOTIENT HAS BEEN SHIFTED ENOUGH TIMES
*       EXIT WITH QUOTIENT IF SO, ELSE DO NEXT SUBTRACTION
*
        SUBQ.W    #1,D1          COUNT DIGITS
        BEQ       GDEXIT         BRANCH (EXIT) IF ALL DIGITS DONE,
                                 * INDICATE NO ERRORS
*
*       TRIAL SUBTRACTION OF DIVISOR FROM DIVIDEND
*       SAVE DIFFERENCE IN CASE IT IS NEEDED LATER
*
        CLR.W     D2             START WITH DIGIT = 0
SUBSET
        MOVE.W    D0,D3          GET ARRAY LENGTH
        MOVEA.L   A0,A4          GET DIVISOR POINTER
        MOVEA.L   A2,A5          GET HIGH DIVIDEND POINTER
        MOVEA.L   A3,A6          GET DIFFERENCE POINTER
SUBDVS
        MOVE.B    -(A5),-1(A6)   MOVE HIGH DIVIDEND BYTE TO DIFFERENCE
        SBCD      -(A4),-(A6)    SUBTRACT BYTE OF DIVISOR
        DBRA      D3,SUBDVS      CONTINUE THROUGH ALL BYTES
        BCS       DIVLOOP        PROCEED TO NEXT DIGIT IF TRIAL
                                 * SUBTRACTION FAILS
*
*       TRIAL SUBTRACTION SUCCEEDED, SO REPLACE UPPER DIVIDEND
*         WITH DIFFERENCE BY SWITCHING POINTERS.  ADD 1 TO UPPER
```

```
*           DIGIT FOR EVENTUAL SHIFTING INTO DIVIDEND/QUOTIENT
*           ARRAY FROM THE RIGHT
*
SUCSES
        ADDQ.B   #$10,D2         ADD 1 TO UPPER DIGIT
        EXG      A2,A3           SWAP POINTERS
        BRA.S    SUBSET          TRY SUBTRACTION AGAIN
*
*       CLEAR CARRY TO INDICATE NO ERRORS
*
GDEXIT
        ANDI.B   #$FE,CCR        CLEAR CARRY - NO DIVIDE-BY-ZERO ERROR
        MOVEA.L  A2,A0           GET ADDRESS JUST BEYOND LSB OF
                                 * REMAINDER
        SUBA.W   D0,A0           CALCULATE BASE ADDRESS OF REMAINDER
        SUBQ.W   #1,A0           (ADDRESS OF MSB)
*
*       REMOVE PARAMETERS FROM STACK AND EXIT
*
EXITRS
        MOVEM.L  (SP)+,A2-A6/D3 RESTORE EXTRA REGISTERS
EXITDV
        MOVEA.L  (SP)+,A1        GET RETURN ADDRESS
                                 *NOTE: REPLACING THIS INSTRUCTION
                                 * WITH MOVEA.L (SP),A2 LEAVES THE
                                 * BASE ADDRESS OF THE QUOTIENT AT
                                 * THE TOP OF THE STACK (AS MANY
                                 * COMPILERS DO)
        LEA      10(SP),SP       REMOVE PARAMETERS FROM STACK
        JMP      (A1)            EXIT TO RETURN ADDRESS

*
*       DATA
*
HIDE1   DS.B     255             HIGH DIVIDEND BUFFER 1
HIDE2   DS.B     255             HIGH DIVIDEND BUFFER 2

*
*
*       SAMPLE EXECUTION
*
*

SC3I
        MOVEA.L  AY1ADR,A1       GET DIVIDEND
        MOVEA.L  AY2ADR,A0       GET DIVISOR
        MOVEM.L  A0-A1,-(SP)     PUSH OPERAND ADDRESSES ONTO STACK
        MOVE.W   #SZAYS,-(SP)    PUSH LENGTH OF OPERANDS ONTO STACK
        JSR      MPDDIV    MULTIPLE-PRECISION DECIMAL DIVISION
                           *RESULT OF 3822756 / 1234 = 3097
                           * IN MEMORY AY1     = $00
                           *           AY1+1   = $00
                           *           AY1+2   = $00
                           *           AY1+3   = $00
                           *           AY1+4   = $00
                           *           AY1+5   = $30
```

```
                                * AY1+6        = $97
         BRA       SC3I         REPEAT TEST

SZAYS    EQU       7            LENGTH OF ARRAYS IN BYTES

AY1ADR   DC.L      AY1          BASE ADDRESS OF ARRAY 1 (DIVIDEND)
AY2ADR   DC.L      AY2          BASE ADDRESS OF ARRAY 2 (DIVISOR)

AY1      DC.B      0,0,0,$03,$82,$27,$56          DIVIDEND
AY2      DC.B      0,0,0,0,0,$12,$34              DIVISOR

         END
```

3J Multiple-precision decimal comparison

Compares two multi-byte unsigned decimal (BCD) numbers, setting the Carry and Zero flags. Both numbers are stored with their most significant bytes at the lowest address. Sets the Zero flag to 1 if the operands are equal and to 0 otherwise. Sets the Carry flag to 1 if the subtrahend is larger than the minuend and to 0 otherwise. Thus, it sets the flags as if it had subtracted the subtrahend from the minuend.

Note

This program is exactly the same as Subroutine 3E, the multiple-precision binary comparison, since the form of the operands does not matter if they are only being compared. See Subroutine 3E for a listing and other details.

4 Bit manipulation and shifts

4A Bit field extraction (BFE)

Extracts a field of bits from a word and returns it in the least significant bit positions. The width of the field and its lowest bit position are specified. This operation is useful in graphics, compilation, database management, and other applications where bit fields contain attributes such as colour, printed appearance (e.g. bold-face, italics, or double-width), record type, or identifier type. The 68020 microprocessor has two instructions (BFEXTS and BFEXTU) for this operation; BFEXTS produces a signed result, BFEXTU an unsigned result.

Procedure The program obtains a mask consisting of right-justified 1 bits covering the field's width. It shifts the mask left to align it with the specified lowest bit position and obtains the field by logically ANDing the mask with the data. It then normalizes the bit field by shifting it right until it starts in bit 0.

Entry conditions

Order in stack (starting from the top)

High word of return address
Low word of return address

Starting (lowest) bit position in the field (0–15)

Width of the field in bits (0–15)

Data

Exit conditions

Bit field in low word of register D0 (normalized to bit 0)

Examples

1. Data: Value = $F67C_{16} = 1111011001111100_2$
   Lowest bit position = 4
   Width of field in bits = 8
   Result: Bit field = $0067_{16} = 0000000001100111_2$
   We have extracted 8 bits from the original data, starting with bit 4 (i.e. bits 4–11)

2. Data: Value = $A2D4_{16} = 1010001011010100_2$
   Lowest bit position = 6
   Width of field in bits = 5
   Result: Bit field = $000B_{16} = 0000000000001011_2$
   We have extracted 5 bits from the original data, starting with bit 6 (i.e. bits 6–10)

Registers used A0, CCR, D0, D1, D2

Execution time 4 × LOWEST BIT POSITION plus 148 cycles overhead. The lowest bit position determines how many times the program must shift the mask left and the bit field right. For example, if the field starts in bit 6, the execution time is

$$4 \times 6 + 148 = 24 + 148 = 172 \text{ cycles}$$

Program size 82 bytes (including the table of masks)

Data memory required None

Special cases

1. Requesting a field that would extend beyond the end of the word causes the program to return with only the bits through bit 15. That is, no wraparound is provided. If, for example, the user asks for a 10-bit field starting at bit 8, the program will return only 8 bits (bits 8–15).

2. Both the lowest bit position and the number of bits in the field are interpreted mod 16. For example, bit position 17 is equivalent to bit position 1 and a field of 20 bits is equivalent to a field of 4 bits.

3. Requesting a field of 0 width causes a return with a result of 0.

```
*
*
*
*
*       Title:                  Bit Field Extraction
*       Name:                   BFE
*
*
*
*       Purpose:                Extract a field of bits from a 16-bit
*                               word and return the field normalized
*                               to bit 0.
*                               NOTE: IF THE REQUESTED FIELD IS TOO
*                                     LONG, THEN ONLY THE BITS THROUGH
*                                     BIT 15 WILL BE RETURNED.  FOR
*                                     EXAMPLE, IF A 4 BIT FIELD IS
*                                     REQUESTED STARTING AT BIT 15,
*                                     ONLY 1 BIT (BIT 15) WILL BE
*                                     RETURNED.
*
*       Entry:                  TOP OF STACK
*                                 High word of return address
*                                 Low word of return address
*                                 Width of field in bits (0..15)
*                                 Lowest (starting) bit position in
*                                   the field (0..15)
*                                 Data
*
*       Exit:                   Low word of register D0 = Field (normalized
*                                 to bit 0)
*
*       Registers Used:         A0,CCR,D0,D1,D2
*
*       Time:                   148 cycles overhead plus
*                                 (4 X lowest bit position) cycles
*
*       Size:                   Program  82 bytes (including the table
*                                 of masks)
*
*
*
```

```
BFE
*
*         EXIT WITH ZERO RESULT IF WIDTH OF FIELD IS ZERO
*
          CLR.W     D0                 INITIALIZE RESULT TO ZERO
          MOVEM.W   4(SP),D1-D2        GET FIELD WIDTH IN BITS,
                                       * STARTING BIT POSITION
          ANDI.W    #$0F,D1            BE SURE FIELD WIDTH IS 0..15
          TST.B     D1                 TEST FIELD WIDTH
          BEQ.S     EXITBF             BRANCH (EXIT) IF FIELD WIDTH
                                       * IS ZERO
                                       *NOTE: RESULT IN D0 IS ZERO
*
*         USE FIELD WIDTH TO OBTAIN EXTRACTION MASK FROM ARRAY
*         MASK CONSISTS OF A 16-BIT RIGHT-JUSTIFIED SEQUENCE OF 1 BITS
*           WITH LENGTH GIVEN BY THE FIELD WIDTH
*
          ASL.W     #1,D1              DOUBLE FIELD WIDTH TO ACCESS TABLE
                                       * OF 16-BIT MASKS
          LEAL      MSKARY-2,A0        GET BASE ADDRESS OF MASK TABLE
                                       * REMEMBER WIDTH IS 1 TO 15 SINCE
                                       * ZERO WIDTH WOULD CAUSE EXIT
          MOVE.W    (A0,D1.W),D1       GET EXTRACTION MASK FROM TABLE
*
*         SHIFT MASK LEFT LOGICALLY TO ALIGN IT WITH LOWEST BIT
*           POSITION IN FIELD
*
          ANDI.W    #$0F,D2            BE SURE LOWEST BIT POSITION IS 0..15
          ASL.W     D2,D1              SHIFT MASK LEFT LOGICALLY
*
*         OBTAIN FIELD BY LOGICALLY ANDING SHIFTED MASK WITH VALUE
*
          MOVE.W    8(SP),D0           GET DATA FROM STACK
          AND.W     D1,D0              AND SHIFTED MASK WITH DATA
*
*         NORMALIZE FIELD TO BIT 0 BY SHIFTING RIGHT LOGICALLY FROM
*           LOWEST BIT POSITION
*
          LSR.W     D2,D0              SHIFT RESULT RIGHT LOGICALLY
*
*         REMOVE PARAMETERS FROM STACK AND EXIT
*
EXITBF
          MOVEA.L   (SP)+,A0           GET RETURN ADDRESS
          ADDA.W    #6,SP              REMOVE PARAMETERS FROM STACK
          JMP       (A0)               EXIT TO RETURN ADDRESS
*
*         ARRAY OF MASKS WITH 1 TO 15 ONE BITS RIGHT-JUSTIFIED
*
MSKARY
          DC.W      %0000000000000001
          DC.W      %0000000000000011
          DC.W      %0000000000000111
          DC.W      %0000000000001111
          DC.W      %0000000000011111
          DC.W      %0000000000111111
```

```
        DC.W    %0000000001111111
        DC.W    %0000000011111111
        DC.W    %0000000111111111
        DC.W    %0000001111111111
        DC.W    %0000011111111111
        DC.W    %0000111111111111
        DC.W    %0001111111111111
        DC.W    %0011111111111111
        DC.W    %0111111111111111

*
*       SAMPLE EXECUTION
*
SC4A
        MOVE.W  VAL,D2          GET DATA
        MOVE.W  POS,D1          GET LOWEST BIT POSITION
        MOVE.W  NBITS,D0        GET FIELD WIDTH IN BITS
        MOVEM.W D0-D2,-(SP)     PUSH PARAMETERS INTO STACK
        JSR     BFE             EXTRACT BIT FIELD
                                *RESULT FOR VAL=$1234, NBITS=4,
                                *  POS=4 IS D0 = $0003
                                *THIS OPERATION EXTRACTS 4 BITS
                                *  STARTING AT BIT POSITION 4
                                *  (THAT IS, BITS 4 THROUGH 7)
        BRA.S   SC4A            REPEAT TEST
*
*DATA
*
VAL     DC.W    $1234           DATA
NBITS   DC.W    4               FIELD WIDTH IN BITS
POS     DC.W    4               LOWEST BIT POSITION

        END
```

4B Bit field insertion (BFI)

Inserts a field of bits into a word. The width of the field and its lowest (starting) bit position are the parameters. This operation is useful in graphics, compilation, database management, and other applications where bit fields contain attributes such as colour, printed appearance (e.g. bold-face, italics, or double-width), record type, or identifier type. The 68020 microprocessor has an instruction (BFINS) for this operation.

Procedure The program obtains a mask consisting of right-justified 0 bits covering the field's width. It shifts the mask left to align it with the specified lowest bit position. It then logically ANDs the mask and the original data word, thus clearing the required bit positions. It also shifts the bit field left to align it properly and ORs it logically with the result of the AND.

Entry conditions

Order in stack (starting from the top)

High word of return address
Low word of return address

Starting (lowest) bit position in the field (0–15)

Width of the field in bits (0–15)

Bit field (value to insert)

Data

Exit conditions

Result in low word of register D0

The result is the original data value with the bit field inserted, starting at the specified lowest bit position.

Examples

1. Data: Value = $F67C_{16}$ = 1111011001111100_2
Lowest bit position = 4
Number of bits in the field = 8
Bit field = $008B_{16}$ = 0000000010001011_2
Result: Value with bit field inserted = $F8BC_{16}$
= 1111100010111100_2
The 8-bit field has been inserted into the original value starting at bit 4 (that is, into bits 4 through 11).

2. Data: Value = $A2D4_{16}$ = 1010001011010100_2
Lowest bit position = 6
Number of bits in the field = 5
Bit field = 0015_{16} = 0000000000010101_2
Result: Value with bit field inserted = $A554_{16}$
= 1010010101010100_2
The 5-bit field has been inserted into the original value starting at bit 6 (i.e. into bits 6–10). Those five bits were 01011_2 ($0B_{16}$) and are now 10101_2 (15_{16}).

Registers used A0, CCR, D0, D1, D2

Execution time 4 × LOWEST BIT POSITION plus 160 cycles overhead. The lowest bit position of the field determines how many times the program must shift the mask and the field left. For example, if the starting position is bit 10, the execution time is

$$4 \times 10 + 160 = 40 + 160 = 200 \text{ cycles}$$

Program size 84 bytes (including the table of masks)

Data memory required None

Special cases

1. Attempting to insert a field that would extend beyond the end of the word causes the program to insert only the bits through bit 15. That is, no wraparound is provided. If, for example, the user attempts to insert a 6-bit field starting at bit 14, only 2 bits (bits 14 and 15) are actually replaced.

2. Both the lowest bit position and the length of the bit field are interpreted mod 16. For example, bit position 17 is the same as bit position 1 and a 20-bit field is the same as a 4-bit field.

3. Attempting to insert a field of 0 width causes a return with a result equal to the initial data.

```
*
*
*
*
*       Title:                  Bit Field Insertion
*       Name:                   BFI
*
*
*
*       Purpose:                Inserts a field of bits which is
*                               normalized to bit 0 into a 16-bit word.
*                               NOTE: IF THE REQUESTED FIELD IS TOO LONG, THEN
*                                     ONLY THE BITS THROUGH BIT 15 WILL BE
*                                     INSERTED.  FOR EXAMPLE, IF A 4-BIT FIELD
*                                     IS TO BE INSERTED STARTING AT BIT 15,
*                                     THEN ONLY THE FIRST BIT WILL BE INSERTED
*                                     AT BIT 15.
*
*       Entry:                  TOP OF STACK
*                                 High word of return address
*                                 Low word of return address
*                                 Bit position at which inserted field
*                                   will start (0..15)
*                                 Width of field in bits (0..15)
*                                 Value to insert
*                                 Data
*
*       Exit:                   Low word of register DO = Value with field
*                                 inserted
*
*       Registers Used:         AO,CCR,DO,D1,D2
*
*       Time:                   160 cycles overhead plus
*                                 (4 X lowest bit position) cycles
*
*       Size:                   Program  84 bytes (including the table
*                                 of masks)
*
*
*

BFI
*
*       EXIT WITH DATA AS RESULT IF FIELD WIDTH IS ZERO
*
        MOVE.W    10(SP),DO       GET DATA
```

```
        MOVEM.W   4(SP),D1-D2      GET NUMBER OF BITS IN FIELD, LOWEST
                                   *  BIT POSITION
        ANDI.W    #$0F,D1          BE SURE FIELD WIDTH IS 0..15
        TST.B     D1               TEST NUMBER OF BITS IN FIELD
        BEQ.S     EXITBF           BRANCH (EXIT) IF FIELD WIDTH IS ZERO
                                   *  RESULT IN D0 IS ORIGINAL DATA
*
*       USE FIELD WIDTH TO OBTAIN MASK FROM ARRAY
*       16-BIT MASK HAS A NUMBER OF RIGHT-JUSTIFIED 0 BITS GIVEN
*         BY FIELD WIDTH
*
        ASL.W     #1,D1            DOUBLE FIELD WIDTH TO ACCESS INTO
                                   *  TABLE OF 16-BIT MASKS
        LEA       MSKARY-2,A0      GET BASE ADDRESS OF MASK TABLE
                                   *NOTE FIELD WIDTH IS 1..15 ONLY SINCE
                                   *  ZERO WIDTH CAUSES EARLIER EXIT
        MOVE.W    (A0,D1.W),D1     GET MASK FROM MASK TABLE
*
*       SHIFT MASK LEFT TO ALIGN IT WITH THE FIELD'S LOWEST BIT
*         POSITION, THEN LOGICALLY AND SHIFTED MASK WITH DATA
*         TO CLEAR FIELD POSITIONS
*
        ANDI.W    #$0F,D2          BE SURE LOWEST BIT POSITION IS 0..15
        ROL.W     D2,D1            ROTATE MASK LEFT TO ALIGN IT,
                                   *  FILLING EMPTY POSITIONS WITH 1S
        AND.W     D1,D0            AND DATA VALUE WITH SHIFTED MASK
*
*       SHIFT FIELD TO BE INSERTED LEFT TO ALIGN IT WITH THE
*         SPECIFIED LOWEST BIT POSITION, THEN OR IT WITH DATA
*
        MOVE.W    8(SP),D1         GET FIELD TO INSERT
        ASL.W     D2,D1            SHIFT FIELD LEFT TO ALIGN IT, FILL
                                   *  EMPTY POSITIONS WITH ZEROS
        OR.W      D1,D0            OR FIELD WITH DATA AFTER MASKING
*
*       REMOVE PARAMETERS FROM STACK AND EXIT
*
EXITBF
        MOVEA.L   (SP)+,A0         GET RETURN ADDRESS
        ADDA.W    #8,SP            REMOVE PARAMETERS FROM STACK
        JMP       (A0)             EXIT TO RETURN ADDRESS
*
*       MASK ARRAY USED TO CLEAR THE BIT FIELD INITIALLY
*       HAS 0 BITS RIGHT-JUSTIFIED IN 1 TO 15 BIT POSITIONS
*
MSKARY
        DC.W      %1111111111111110
        DC.W      %1111111111111100
        DC.W      %1111111111111000
        DC.W      %1111111111110000
        DC.W      %1111111111100000
        DC.W      %1111111111000000
        DC.W      %1111111110000000
        DC.W      %1111111100000000
        DC.W      %1111111000000000
        DC.W      %1111110000000000
```

```
        DC.W      %1111100000000000
        DC.W      %1111000000000000
        DC.W      %1110000000000000
        DC.W      %1100000000000000
        DC.W      %1000000000000000

*
*
*       SAMPLE EXECUTION
*
*
SC4B
        MOVE.W    VAL,D3             GET VALUE
        MOVE.W    VALINS,D2          GET VALUE TO INSERT
        MOVE.W    POS,D1             GET LOWEST BIT POSITION OF FIELD
        MOVE.W    NBITS,D0           GET FIELD WIDTH IN BITS
        MOVEM.W   D0-D2,-(SP)        PUSH PARAMETERS INTO STACK
        JSR       BFI                INSERT BIT FIELD
                                     *RESULT FOR VAL=$1234, VALINS=$0E,
                                     *  NBITS = 4, POS = $0C IS
                                     *  REGISTER D0 = $E234
                                     *THIS OPERATION INSERTS 4 BITS (1110)
                                     *  STARTING IN BIT POSITION 12 (THAT
                                     *  IS, INTO BITS 12 THROUGH 15)
        BRA.S     SC4B               REPEAT TEST

*
*DATA SECTION
*
VAL     DC.W      $1234              DATA VALUE
VALINS  DC.W      $0E                VALUE TO INSERT
NBITS   DC.W      4                  FIELD WIDTH IN BITS
POS     DC.W      $0C                LOWEST BIT POSITION IN FIELD

        END
```

4C Multiple-precision arithmetic shift right (MPASR)

Shifts a multi-byte operand right arithmetically by a specified number of bit positions. Sets the Carry and Extend flags from the last bit shifted out of the rightmost bit position. The operand is stored with its most significant byte at the lowest address.

Procedure The program obtains the sign bit from the most significant byte and saves it in the Extend flag. It then rotates all the full words in the operand right one bit through the Extend flag, starting with the most significant word. If the operand has an odd number of bytes, the program next performs a byte-length rotate of the least significant byte. It repeats the operation for the specified number of shifts.

Entry conditions

Order in stack (starting from the top)

High word of return address
Low word of return address

Number of shifts (bit positions)

Length of the operand in bytes

High word of base address of operand (address of its most significant byte)
Low word of base address of operand (address of its most significant byte)

Exit conditions

Operand shifted right arithmetically by the specified number of bit positions. The original sign bit is extended to the right.
The Carry and Extend flags are set from the last bit shifted out of the rightmost bit position. The Carry flag is cleared if either the number of shifts or the length of the operand is 0.

Examples

1. Data: Length of operand (in bytes) = 8
   Operand = $85A4C719FE06741E_{16}$
   Number of shifts = 4

   Result: Shifted operand = $F85A4C719FE06741_{16}$.
   This is the original operand shifted right four bits arithmetically. The four most significant bits thus all take on the value of the original sign bit (1).
   Carry = Extend = 1, since the last bit shifted from the rightmost bit position was 1.

2. Data: Length of operand (in bytes) = 4
   Operand = $3F6A42D3_{16}$
   Number of shifts = 3

   Result: Shifted operand = $07ED485A_{16}$.
   This is the original operand shifted right three bits arithmetically. The three most significant bits thus all take on the value of the original sign bit (0).
   Carry = Extend = 0, since the last bit shifted from the rightmost bit position was 0.

Registers used A0, A1, CCR, D0, D1, D2

Execution time NUMBER OF SHIFTS × (54 + 23 × LENGTH OF OPERAND IN BYTES/2) + 135 cycles.

If, for example, NUMBER OF SHIFTS = 6 and LENGTH OF OPERAND IN BYTES = 8, the execution time is

$$6 \times (54 + 23 \times 4) + 135 = 6 \times 146 + 135 = 1011 \text{ cycles}$$

Program size 68 bytes

Data memory required 2 stack bytes

Special cases

1. If the length of the operand is 0, the program exits immediately with the operand unchanged and the Carry flag cleared.

2. If the number of shifts is 0, the program exits immediately with the operand unchanged and the Carry flag cleared.

```
*
*
*
*
*       Title:                  Multiple-Precision Arithmetic Shift Right
*       Name:                   MPASR
*
*
*
*       Purpose:                Arithmetic shift right a multi-byte operand
*                               N bits.
*
*       Entry:                  TOP OF STACK
*                                 High word of return address
*                                 Low word of return address
*                                 Number of bits to shift
*                                 Length of the operand in bytes
*                                 High word of operand base address
*                                 Low word of operand base address
*
*                                 The operand is stored with ARRAY[0] as its
*                                 most significant byte and ARRAY[LENGTH-1]
*                                 as its least significant byte
*
*       Exit:                   Operand shifted right with the most
*                               significant bit propagated.
*                               Carry := Extend := Last bit shifted from least
*                                         significant position.
*
*       Registers Used:         A0,A1,CCR,D0,D1,D2
*
*       Time:                   135 cycles overhead plus
*                                 ((23 X length/2) + 54) cycles per shift
*
*       Size:                   Program  68 bytes
*                               Data      2 stack bytes
*
*

MPASR
*
*       EXIT IF LENGTH OF OPERAND OR NUMBER OF BITS TO SHIFT
*         IS ZERO.  CARRY IS CLEARED (BY TST) IN EITHER CASE
*
        MOVEM.W   4(SP),D0-D1  GET NUMBER OF BITS TO SHIFT,
                               *  OPERAND LENGTH IN BYTES
        TST.B     D0           TEST NUMBER OF BITS TO SHIFT
        BEQ.S     EXITAS       EXIT IF NUMBER OF BITS TO SHIFT IS ZERO
        TST.B     D1           TEST OPERAND LENGTH
        BEQ.S     EXITAS       EXIT IF LENGTH OF OPERAND IS ZERO
*
*       SET UP POINTER AND COUNTERS
```

```
*         WORD COUNT = NUMBER OF FULL WORDS IN OPERAND
*         BOTH WORD COUNT AND SHIFT COUNT REDUCED BY 1 BECAUSE DBRA
*           EXITS ON -1, NOT 0
*
          SUBQ.W    #1,D0       REDUCE SHIFT COUNT TO EXIT ON -1
          MOVE.W    D1,D2       GET OPERAND LENGTH IN BYTES
          LSR.W     #1,D2       DIVIDE BY 2 TO GET LENGTH IN WORDS
          SUBQ.W    #1,D2       REDUCE WORD COUNT TO EXIT ON -1
          MOVEA.L   8(SP),A0    GET BASE ADDRESS OF OPERAND (ADDRESS
                                * OF MSB)
          MOVE.W    D3,-(SP)    SAVE EXTRA DATA REGISTER IN STACK
*
*         SHIFT ENTIRE OPERAND RIGHT ONE BIT ARITHMETICALLY
*         SIGN BIT FROM MOST SIGNIFICANT BYTE IS INITIAL
*           SERIAL INPUT (THROUGH EXTEND FLAG)
*         IF LENGTH IS ODD, SHIFT LEAST SIGNIFICANT BYTE AFTER SHIFTING
*           ALL FULL WORDS
*
ASRLP
          MOVEA.L   A0,A1       GET ADDRESS OF MOST SIGNIFICANT BYTE
          MOVE.B    (A1),D3     GET MOST SIGNIFICANT BYTE
          ASL.B     #1,D3       MOVE SIGN BIT TO EXTEND FLAG FOR USE
                                * IN SIGN EXTENSION
          MOVE.W    D2,D3       GET NUMBER OF FULL WORDS IN OPERAND
*
*         SHIFT EACH FULL WORD OF OPERAND RIGHT ONE BIT
*         START WITH MOST SIGNIFICANT WORD
*
ASRLP1
          ROXR      (A1)+       ROTATE NEXT WORD RIGHT
          DBRA      D3,ASRLP1   CONTINUE THROUGH ALL WORDS
*
*         IF OPERAND LENGTH IS ODD, SHIFT LEAST SIGNIFICANT BYTE RIGHT
*           ONE BIT
*
          BTST      #0,D1       CHECK IF OPERAND LENGTH IS EVEN OR ODD
          BEQ.S     BITCNT      BRANCH IF LENGTH IS EVEN
          MOVE.B    (A1),D3     LENGTH IS ODD, SO GET LEAST SIGNIFICANT
                                * BYTE
          ROXR.B    #1,D3       SHIFT LEAST SIGNIFICANT BYTE RIGHT
                                * NOTE: THIS CANNOT BE DONE IN MEMORY
                                * SINCE ONLY WORD-LENGTH MEMORY SHIFTS
                                * ARE ALLOWED
          MOVE.B    D3,(A1)     SAVE SHIFTED LEAST SIGNIFICANT BYTE
*
*         COUNT NUMBER OF SHIFTS
*
BITCNT
          DBRA      D0,ASRLP    COUNT NUMBER OF SHIFTS
          MOVE.W    (SP)+,D3    RESTORE EXTRA DATA REGISTER
*
*         REMOVE PARAMETERS FROM STACK AND EXIT
*
EXITAS
          MOVEA.L   (SP)+,A0    GET RETURN ADDRESS
          ADDA.W    #8,SP       REMOVE PARAMETERS FROM STACK
```

```
        JMP       (A0)      EXIT TO RETURN ADDRESS
*
*       SAMPLE EXECUTION
*
*
SC4C
        MOVEA.L   AYADR,A0       GET BASE ADDRESS OF OPERAND
        MOVE.L    A0,-(SP)       PUSH BASE ADDRESS INTO STACK
        MOVE.W    #SZAY,D1       GET LENGTH OF OPERAND IN BYTES
        MOVE.W    SHIFTS,D0      GET NUMBER OF SHIFTS
        MOVEM.W   D0-D1,-(SP)    PUSH PARAMETERS INTO STACK
        JSR       MPASR          ARITHMETIC SHIFT RIGHT
                            *RESULT OF SHIFTING AY=$EDCBA987654321
                            *4 BITS IS AY=$FEDCBA98765432, C=0
                            *  IN MEMORY AY   = $FE
                            *            AY+1 = $DC
                            *            AY+2 = $BA
                            *            AY+3 = $98
                            *            AY+4 = $76
                            *            AY+5 = $54
                            *            AY+6 = $32
        BRA.S     SC4C      REPEAT TEST

*
*DATA SECTION
*
SZAY    EQU       7         LENGTH OF OPERAND IN BYTES
SHIFTS  DC.W      4         NUMBER OF SHIFTS
AYADR   DC.L      AY        BASE ADDRESS OF OPERAND
AY      DC.B      $ED,$BC,$A9,$87,$65,$43,$21   OPERAND
        END
```

4D Multiple-precision logical shift left (MPLSL)

Shifts a multi-byte operand left logically by a specified number of bit positions. Sets the Carry and Extend flags from the last bit shifted out of the leftmost bit position. The operand is stored with its most significant byte at the lowest address.

Procedure The program clears the Extend flag initially to fill with a 0 bit. If the operand has an odd number of bytes, the program first shifts the least significant byte left logically. It then rotates all remaining words left one bit through the Extend flag, starting with the least significant remaining word. It repeats the operation for the specified number of shifts.

Entry conditions

Order in stack (starting from the top)

High word of return address
Low word of return address

Number of shifts (bit positions)

Length of the operand in bytes

High word of base address of operand (address of its most significant byte)
Low word of base address of operand (address of its most significant byte)

Exit conditions

Operand shifted left logically by the specified number of bit positions.
The least significant bit positions are filled with 0s.
The Carry and Extend flags are set from the last bit shifted out of the leftmost bit position. The Carry flag is cleared if either the number of shifts or the length of the operand is 0.

Examples

1. Data: Length of operand (in bytes) = 8

Operand = $85A4C719FE06741E_{16}$
Number of shifts = 4

Result: Shifted operand = $5A4C719FE06741E0_{16}$.
This is the original operand shifted left four bits logically.
The four least significant bits are all cleared.
Carry = Extend = 0, since the last bit shifted from the leftmost bit position was 0.

2. Data: Length of operand (in bytes) = 4
Operand = $3F6A42D3_{16}$
Number of shifts = 3

Result: Shifted operand = $FB521698_{16}$.
This is the original operand shifted left three bits logically.
The three least significant bits are all cleared.
Carry = Extend = 1, since the last bit shifted from the leftmost bit position was 1.

Registers used A0, A1, CCR, D0, D1, D2

Execution time NUMBER OF SHIFTS × (50 + 25 × LENGTH OF OPERAND IN BYTES/2) + 143 cycles.

If, for example, NUMBER OF SHIFTS = 6 and LENGTH OF OPERAND IN BYTES = 8, the execution time is

$$6 \times (50 + 25 \times 4) + 143 = 6 \times 150 + 143 = 1043 \text{ cycles}$$

Program size 70 bytes

Data memory required 2 stack bytes

Special cases

1. If the length of the operand is 0, the program exits immediately with the operand unchanged and the Carry flag cleared.

2. If the number of shifts is 0, the program exits immediately with the operand unchanged and the Carry flag cleared.

```
*
*
*
*
*
*
*    Title:              Multiple-Precision Logical Shift Left
*    Name:               MPLSL
*
*
*
*
*    Purpose:            Logical shift left a multi-byte operand
*                        N bits.
*
*
*    Entry:              TOP OF STACK
*                          High word of return address
*                          Low word of return address
*                          Number of bits to shift
*                          Length of the operand in bytes
*                          High word of operand base address
*                          Low word of operand base address
*
*                          The operand is stored with ARRAY[0] as its
*                          most significant byte and ARRAY[LENGTH-1]
*                          as its least significant byte
*
*    Exit:               Operand shifted left filling the least
*                        significant bits with zeros.
*                        Carry := Extend: = Last bit shifted from most
*                                 significant position
*
*
*    Registers Used:     A0,A1,CCR,D0,D1,D2
*
*
*    Time:               143 cycles overhead plus
*                          ((25 X length/2) + 50) cycles per shift
*
*
*    Size:               Program  70 bytes
*                        Data      2 stack bytes
*
*
*
*

MPLSL
*
*         EXIT IF LENGTH OF OPERAND OR NUMBER OF BITS TO SHIFT
```

```
*          IS ZERO.  CARRY IS CLEARED BY TST IN EITHER CASE
*
*
        MOVEM.W   4(SP),D0-D1  GET NUMBER OF BITS TO SHIFT,
                           *  OPERAND LENGTH IN BYTES
        TST.B     D0       TEST NUMBER OF BITS TO SHIFT
        BEQ.S     EXITLS   EXIT IF NUMBER OF BITS TO SHIFT IS ZERO
        TST.B     D1       TEST OPERAND LENGTH
        BEQ.S     EXITLS   EXIT IF OPERAND LENGTH IS ZERO
*
*
*       SET UP POINTER AND COUNTERS
*       WORD COUNT = NUMBER OF FULL WORDS IN OPERAND
*       BOTH WORD COUNT AND SHIFT COUNT REDUCED BY 1 BECAUSE DBRA
*         EXITS ON -1, NOT 0
*       SET ARRAY POINTER BEYOND LEAST SIGNIFICANT BYTE
*
*
        SUBQ.W    #1,D0    REDUCE SHIFT COUNT TO EXIT ON -1
        MOVE.W    D1,D2    GET OPERAND LENGTH IN BYTES
        LSR.W     #1,D2    DIVIDE BY 2 TO GET LENGTH IN WORDS
        SUBQ.W    #1,D2    REDUCE WORD COUNT TO EXIT ON -1
        MOVEA.L   8(SP),A0 GET BASE ADDRESS OF OPERAND (ADDRESS
                           * OF MSB)
        ADDA.W    D1,A0    POINT BEYOND END OF OPERAND (ADDRESS
                           * OF LSB)
        MOVE.W    D3,-(SP) SAVE EXTRA DATA REGISTER IN STACK
*
*
*       SHIFT ENTIRE OPERAND LEFT ONE BIT LOGICALLY
*       MAKE INITIAL EXTEND INPUT ZERO TO PRODUCE LOGICAL SHIFT
*       IF LENGTH IS ODD, DO A BYTE-LENGTH LOGICAL SHIFT
*         OF LEAST SIGNIFICANT BYTE FIRST
*
*
LSLLP
        MOVEA.L   A0,A1    GET ADDRESS BEYOND LEAST SIGNIFICANT BYTE
        MOVE      #0,CCR   CLEAR EXTEND FLAG TO PRODUCE LOGICAL SHIFT
        BTST      #0,D1    CHECK IF OPERAND LENGTH IS ODD OR EVEN
        BEQ.S     WDSHFT   BRANCH IF OPERAND LENGTH IS EVEN
        MOVE.B    -(A1),D3 LENGTH IS ODD, SO GET LEAST SIGNIFICANT
                           * BYTE.  NOTE: THIS SHIFT CANNOT BE DONE
                           * IN MEMORY SINCE ONLY WORD-LENGTH MEMORY
                           * SHIFTS ARE ALLOWED
        ASL.B     #1,D3    SHIFT LEAST SIGNIFICANT BYTE LEFT
        MOVE.B    D3,(A1)  RETURN SHIFTED LSB TO MEMORY
*
*
*       ROTATE EACH WORD OF OPERAND LEFT ONE BIT THROUGH EXTEND FLAG
*       START WITH LEAST SIGNIFICANT WORD IF LENGTH IS EVEN
*       START WITH WORD AFTER LEAST SIGNIFICANT BYTE IF LENGTH IS ODD
*
```

```
*
WDSHFT
        MOVE.W    D2,D3      GET NUMBER OF FULL WORDS IN OPERAND
LSLLP1
        ROXL      -(A1)      ROTATE NEXT WORD LEFT
        DBRA      D3,LSLLP1  CONTINUE THROUGH ALL WORDS
*
*
*       COUNT NUMBER OF SHIFTS
*
*
        DBRA      D0,LSLLP   COUNT NUMBER OF SHIFTS
        MOVE.W    (SP)+,D3   RESTORE EXTRA DATA REGISTER
*
*
*       REMOVE PARAMETERS FROM STACK AND EXIT
*
*
EXITLS
        MOVEA.L   (SP)+,A0   GET RETURN ADDRESS
        ADDA.W    #8,SP      REMOVE PARAMETERS FROM STACK
        JMP       (A0)       EXIT TO RETURN ADDRESS
*
*
*
*       SAMPLE EXECUTION
*
*
*


SC4D
        MOVEA.L   AYADR,A0   GET BASE ADDRESS OF OPERAND
        MOVE.L    A0,-(SP)   PUSH BASE ADDRESS INTO STACK
        MOVE.W    #SZAY,D1   GET LENGTH OF OPERAND IN BYTES
        MOVE.W    SHIFTS,D0  GET NUMBER OF SHIFTS
        MOVEM.W   D0-D1,-(SP)  PUSH PARAMETERS INTO STACK
        JSR       MPLSL      LOGICAL SHIFT LEFT
                             *RESULT OF SHIFTING AY=$EDCBA987654321
                             *4 BITS IS AY=$DCBA9876543210, C=0
                             *  IN MEMORY AY    = $DC
                             *            AY+1  = $BA
                             *            AY+2  = $98
                             *            AY+3  = $76
                             *            AY+4  = $54
                             *            AY+5  = $32
                             *            AY+6  = $10
        BRA.S     SC4D       REPEAT TEST


*
*
```

```
*DATA SECTION
*
SZAY      EQU     7          LENGTH OF OPERAND IN BYTES
SHIFTS    DC.W    4          NUMBER OF SHIFTS
AYADR     DC.L    AY         BASE ADDRESS OF OPERAND
AY        DC.B    $ED,$CB,$A9,$87,$65,$43,$21  OPERAND

          END
```

4E Multiple-precision logical shift right (MPLSR)

Shifts a multi-byte operand right logically by a specified number of bit positions. Sets the Carry and Extend flags from the last bit shifted out of the rightmost bit position. The operand is stored with its most significant byte at the lowest address.

Procedure The program clears the Extend flag (to fill with a 0 bit). It then rotates all the full words in the operand right one bit through the Extend flag, starting with the most significant word. If the operand has an odd number of bytes, the program next performs a byte-length rotate of the least significant byte. It repeats the operation for the specified number of shifts.

Entry conditions

Order in stack (starting from the top)

High word of return address
Low word of return address

Number of shifts (bit positions)

Length of the operand in bytes

High word of base address of operand (address of its most significant byte)
Low word of base address of operand (address of its most significant byte)

Exit conditions

Operand shifted right logically by the specified number of bit positions.
The most significant bit positions are filled with 0s.
The Carry and Extend flags are set from the last bit shifted out of the rightmost bit position. The Carry flag is cleared if either the number of shifts or the length of the operand is 0.

Examples

1. Data: Length of operand (in bytes) = 8

Operand = $85A4C719FE06741E_{16}$
Number of shifts = 4

Result: Shifted operand = $085A4C719FE06741_{16}$.
This is the original operand shifted right four bits logically. The four most significant bits are all cleared.
Carry = Extend = 1, since the last bit shifted from the rightmost bit position was 1.

2. Data: Length of operand (in bytes) = 4
Operand = $3F6A42D3_{16}$
Number of shifts = 3

Result: Shifted operand = $07ED485A_{16}$.
This is the original operand shifted right three bits logically. The three most significant bits are all cleared.
Carry = Extend = 0, since the last bit shifted from the rightmost bit position was 0.

Registers used A0, A1, CCR, D0, D1, D2

Execution time NUMBER OF SHIFTS × (54 + 23 × LENGTH OF OPERAND IN BYTES/2) + 135 cycles.

If, for example, NUMBER OF SHIFTS = 6 and LENGTH OF OPERAND IN BYTES = 8, the execution time is

$$6 \times (54 + 23 \times 4) + 135 = 6 \times 146 + 135 = 1011 \text{ cycles}$$

Program size 68 bytes

Data memory required 2 stack bytes

Special cases

1. If the length of the operand is 0, the program exits immediately with the operand unchanged and the Carry flag cleared.

2. If the number of shifts is 0, the program exits immediately with the operand unchanged and the Carry flag cleared.

```
*
*
*
*
*       Title:                  Multiple-Precision Logical Shift Right
*       Name:                   MPLSR
*
*
*
*       Purpose:                Logical shift right a multi-byte operand
*                               N bits.
*
*       Entry:                  TOP OF STACK
*                                 High word of return address
*                                 Low word of return address
*                                 Number of bits to shift
*                                 Length of the operand in bytes
*                                 High word of operand base address
*                                 Low word of operand base address
*
*                                 The operand is stored with ARRAY[0] as its
*                                 most significant byte and ARRAY[LENGTH-1]
*                                 as its least significant byte
*
*       Exit:                   Operand shifted right filling the most
*                               significant bits with zeros.
*                               Carry := Extend := Last bit shifted from least
*                                        significant position.
*
*       Registers Used:         A0,A1,CCR,D0,D1,D2
*
*       Time:                   135 cycles overhead plus
*                                 ((23 X length/2) + 54) cycles per shift
*
*       Size:                   Program  68 bytes
*                               Data      2 stack bytes
*
*
*

MPLSR
*
*       EXIT IF LENGTH OF OPERAND OR NUMBER OF BITS TO SHIFT
*         IS ZERO.  CARRY IS CLEARED BY TEST IN EITHER CASE
*
        MOVEM.W   4(SP),D0-D1  GET NUMBER OF BITS TO SHIFT,
                               *  OPERAND LENGTH IN BYTES
        TST.B     D0           TEST NUMBER OF BITS TO SHIFT
        BEQ.S     EXITLS       EXIT IF NUMBER OF BITS TO SHIFT IS ZERO
        TST.B     D1           TEST OPERAND LENGTH
        BEQ.S     EXITLS       EXIT IF LENGTH OF OPERAND IS ZERO
*
*       SET UP POINTERS AND COUNTERS
*       WORD COUNT = NUMBER OF FULL WORDS IN OPERAND
*       BOTH WORD, SHIFT COUNT REDUCED BY 1 BECAUSE DBRA EXITS
*         ON -1, NOT 0
*
```

```
        SUBQ.W    #1,D0      REDUCE SHIFT COUNT TO EXIT ON -1
        MOVE.W    D1,D2      GET OPERAND LENGTH IN BYTES
        LSR.W     #1,D2      DIVIDE BY 2 TO GET LENGTH IN WORDS
        SUBQ.W    #1,D2      REDUCE WORD COUNT TO EXIT ON -1
        MOVEA.L   8(SP),A0   GET BASE ADDRESS OF OPERAND (ADDRESS
                             * OF MSB)
        MOVE.W    D3,-(SP)   SAVE EXTRA DATA REGISTER IN STACK
*
*       SHIFT ENTIRE OPERAND RIGHT ONE BIT LOGICALLY
*       INITIAL SERIAL INPUT (THROUGH EXTEND FLAG) IS 0 TO FILL
*         WITH 0 BITS
*       IF LENGTH IS ODD, SHIFT LEAST SIGNIFICANT BYTE AFTER SHIFTING
*         ALL FULL WORDS RIGHT LOGICALLY
*
LSRLP
        MOVEA.L   A0,A1      GET ADDRESS OF MOST SIGNIFICANT BYTE
        MOVE      #0,CCR     EXTEND FLAG = 0 TO FILL WITH ZEROS
        MOVE.W    D2,D3      GET NUMBER OF FULL WORDS IN OPERAND
*
*       SHIFT EACH WORD OF OPERAND RIGHT ONE BIT
*       START WITH MOST SIGNIFICANT WORD
*
LSRLP1
        ROXR      (A1)+      ROTATE NEXT WORD RIGHT
        DBRA      D3,LSRLP1  CONTINUE THROUGH ALL WORDS
*
*       IF OPERAND LENGTH IS ODD, SHIFT LEAST SIGNIFICANT BYTE
*         RIGHT ONE BIT
*
        BTST      #0,D1      CHECK IF OPERAND LENGTH IS ODD OR EVEN
        BEQ.S     BITCNT     BRANCH IF LENGTH IS EVEN
        MOVE.B    (A1),D3    LENGTH IS ODD, SO GET LEAST SIGNIFICANT
                             * BYTE
        ROXR.B    #1,D3      SHIFT LEAST SIGNIFICANT BYTE RIGHT
                             * NOTE: THIS CANNOT BE DONE IN MEMORY
                             * SINCE ONLY WORD-LENGTH MEMORY SHIFTS
                             * ARE ALLOWED
        MOVE.B    D3,(A1)    RETURN SHIFTED LEAST SIGNIFICANT BYTE
                             * TO MEMORY
*
*       COUNT NUMBER OF SHIFTS
*
BITCNT
        DBRA      D0,LSRLP   COUNT NUMBER OF SHIFTS
        MOVE.W    (SP)+,D3   RESTORE EXTRA DATA REGISTER
*
*       REMOVE PARAMETERS FROM STACK AND EXIT
*
EXITLS
        MOVEA.L   (SP)+,A0   GET RETURN ADDRESS
        ADDA.W    #8,SP      REMOVE PARAMETERS FROM STACK
        JMP       (A0)       EXIT TO RETURN ADDRESS

*
*
*       SAMPLE EXECUTION
```

```
*
*

SC4E
          MOVEA.L   AYADR,A0   GET BASE ADDRESS OF OPERAND
          MOVE.L    A0,-(SP)   PUSH BASE ADDRESS INTO STACK
          MOVE.W    #SZAY,D1   GET LENGTH OF OPERANDS IN BYTES
          MOVE.W    SHIFTS,D0  GET NUMBER OF SHIFTS
          MOVEM.W   D0-D1,-(SP)  PUSH PARAMETERS INTO STACK
          JSR       MPLSR      LOGICAL SHIFT LEFT
                               *RESULT OF SHIFTING AY=$EDCBA987654321
                               *4 BITS IS AY=$0EDCBA98765432, C=0
                               *  IN MEMORY AY    = $0E
                               *            AY+1 = $DC
                               *            AY+2 = $BA
                               *            AY+3 = $98
                               *            AY+4 = $76
                               *            AY+5 = $54
                               *            AY+6 = $32
          BRA.S     SC4E       REPEAT TEST

*
*DATA SECTION
*
SZAY      EQU       7          LENGTH OF OPERAND IN BYTES
SHIFTS    DC.W      4          NUMBER OF SHIFTS
AYADR     DC.L      AY         BASE ADDRESS OF OPERAND
AY        DC.B      $ED,$CB,$A9,$87,$65,$43,$21   OPERAND

          END
```

4F Multiple-precision rotate right (MPRR)

Rotates a multi-byte operand right by a specified number of bit positions as if the most significant bit and least significant bit were connected. Sets the Carry and Extend flags from the last bit shifted out of the rightmost bit position. The operand is stored with its most significant byte at the lowest address.

Procedure The program shifts bit 0 of the least significant byte of the operand to the Extend flag. It then rotates all the full words in the operand right one bit through the Extend flag, starting with the most significant word. If the operand has an odd number of bytes, the program next performs a byte-length rotate of the least significant byte. It repeats the operation for the specified number of rotates.

Entry conditions

Order in stack (starting from the top)

High word of return address
Low word of return address

Number of rotates (bit positions)

Length of the operand in bytes

High word of base address of operand (address of its most significant byte)
Low word of base address of operand (address of its most significant byte)

Exit conditions

Operand rotated right by the specified number of bit positions. The most significant bit positions are filled from the least significant bit positions.
The Carry and Extend flags are set from the last bit shifted out of the rightmost bit position. The Carry flag is cleared if either the number of shifts or the length of the operand is 0).

Examples

1. Data: Length of operand (in bytes) = 8
   Operand = $85A4C719FE06741E_{16}$
   Number of rotates = 4

   Result: Shifted operand = $E85A4C719FE06741_{16}$
   This is the original operand rotated right four bits. The four most significant bits are equivalent to the original four least significant bits.
   Carry = Extend = 1, since the last bit shifted from the rightmost bit position was 1.

2. Data: Length of operand (in bytes) = 4
   Operand = $3F6A42D3_{16}$
   Number of rotates = 3

   Result: Shifted operand = $67ED485A_{16}$
   This is the original operand rotated right three bits. The three most significant bits (011) are equivalent to the original three least significant bits.
   Carry = Extend = 0, since the last bit shifted from the rightmost bit position was 0.

Registers used A0, A1, CCR, D0, D1, D2

Execution time NUMBER OF ROTATES × (58 + 23 × LENGTH OF OPERAND IN BYTES/2) + 153 cycles.

If, for example, NUMBER OF ROTATES = 6 and LENGTH OF OPERAND IN BYTES = 8, the execution time is

$$6 \times (58 + 23 \times 4) + 153 = 6 \times 150 + 153 = 1053 \text{ cycles}$$

Program size 74 bytes

Data memory required 2 stack bytes

Special cases

1. If the length of the operand is 0, the program exits immediately with the operand unchanged and the Carry flag cleared.

2. If the number of rotates is 0, the program exits immediately with the operand unchanged and the Carry flag cleared.

```
*
*
*
*
*       Title:                  Multiple-Precision Rotate Right
*       Name:                   MPRR
*
*
*
*       Purpose:                Rotate right a multi-byte operand
*                               N bits.
*
*       Entry:                  TOP OF STACK
*                                 High word of return address
*                                 Low word of return address
*                                 Number of bits to rotate
*                                 Length of the operand in bytes
*                                 High word of operand base address
*                                 Low word of operand base address
*
*                                 The operand is stored with ARRAY[0] as its
*                                 most significant byte and ARRAY[LENGTH-1]
*                                 as its least significant byte
*
*                               Operand rotated right
*                               Carry := Extend := Last bit shifted from least
*                                         significant position.
*
*       Registers Used:         A0,A1,CCR,D0,D1,D2
*
*       Time:                   153 cycles overhead plus
*                                 ((23 X length/2) + 58) cycles per rotate
*
*       Size:                   Program  74 bytes
*                               Data      2 stack bytes
*
*

MPRR
*
*       EXIT IF LENGTH OF OPERAND OR NUMBER OF BITS TO ROTATE
*         IS ZERO.  CARRY IS CLEARED BY TST IN EITHER CASE
*
        MOVEM.W   4(SP),D0-D1  GET NUMBER OF BITS TO ROTATE,
                               *  OPERAND LENGTH IN BYTES
        TST.B     D0           TEST NUMBER OF BITS TO ROTATE
        BEQ.S     EXITRR       EXIT IF NUMBER OF BITS TO ROTATE IS ZERO
        TST.B     D1           TEST OPERAND LENGTH
        BEQ.S     EXITRR       EXIT IF LENGTH OF OPERAND IS ZERO
*
*       SET UP POINTER AND COUNTERS
*       WORD COUNT = NUMBER OF FULL WORDS IN OPERAND
```

```
*         BOTH WORD COUNT AND SHIFT COUNT REDUCED BY 1 BECAUSE DBRA
*           EXITS ON -1, NOT 0
*
          SUBQ.W    #1,D0     REDUCE SHIFT COUNT TO EXIT ON -1
          MOVE.W    D1,D2     GET OPERAND LENGTH IN BYTES
          LSR.W     #1,D2     DIVIDE BY 2 TO GET LENGTH IN WORDS
          SUBQ.W    #1,D2     REDUCE WORD COUNT TO EXIT ON -1
          MOVEA.L   8(SP),A0  GET BASE ADDRESS OF OPERAND (ADDRESS
                              * OF MSB)
          MOVE.W    D3,-(SP)  SAVE EXTRA DATA REGISTER IN STACK
*
*         ROTATE ENTIRE OPERAND RIGHT ONE BIT
*         USE PREVIOUS LEAST SIGNIFICANT BIT AS INITIAL SERIAL INPUT
*           (THROUGH EXTEND FLAG) TO PRODUCE ROTATION
*         IF LENGTH OF OPERAND IS ODD, ROTATE LEAST SIGNIFICANT BYTE
*           AFTER ROTATING ALL FULL WORDS
*
          MOVEA.L   A0,A1     GET ADDRESS OF MOST SIGNIFICANT BYTE
          ADDA.W    D1,A1     POINT BEYOND LEAST SIGNIFICANT BYTE
          SUBQ.L    #1,A1     POINT TO LEAST SIGNIFICANT BYTE
RRLP
          MOVE.B    (A1),D3   GET LEAST SIGNIFICANT BYTE
          LSR.B     #1,D3     EXTEND FLAG = BIT 0 OF LEAST
                              * SIGNIFICANT BYTE TO PRODUCE ROTATION
          MOVEA.L   A0,A1     GET ADDRESS OF MOST SIGNIFICANT BYTE
          MOVE.W    D2,D3     GET NUMBER OF FULL WORDS IN OPERAND
*
*         SHIFT EACH WORD OF OPERAND RIGHT ONE BIT
*         START WITH MOST SIGNIFICANT WORD
*
RRLP1
          ROXR      (A1)+     SHIFT NEXT WORD RIGHT
          DBRA      D3,RRLP1  CONTINUE THROUGH ALL WORDS
*
*         IF OPERAND LENGTH IS ODD, SHIFT LEAST SIGNIFICANT BYTE
*           RIGHT ONE BIT
*
          BTST      #0,D1     CHECK IF OPERAND LENGTH IS EVEN OR ODD
          BEQ.S     BITCNT    BRANCH IF LENGTH IS EVEN
          MOVE.B    (A1),D3   LENGTH IS ODD, SO GET LEAST SIGNIFICANT
                              * BYTE
          ROXR.B    #1,D3     SHIFT LEAST SIGNIFICANT BYTE RIGHT
                              * NOTE: THIS CANNOT BE DONE IN MEMORY
                              * SINCE ONLY WORD-LENGTH MEMORY SHIFTS
                              * ARE ALLOWED
          MOVE.B    D3,(A1)   RETURN SHIFTED LEAST SIGNIFICANT BYTE
                              * TO MEMORY
*
*         COUNT NUMBER OF ROTATES
*
BITCNT
          DBRA      D0,RRLP   COUNT NUMBER OF ROTATES
          MOVE.W    (SP)+,D3  RESTORE EXTRA DATA REGISTER
*
*         REMOVE PARAMETERS FROM STACK AND EXIT
*
```

```
EXITRR
        MOVEA.L   (SP)+,A0   GET RETURN ADDRESS
        ADDA.W    #8,SP      REMOVE PARAMETERS FROM STACK
        JMP       (A0)       EXIT TO RETURN ADDRESS

*
*
*       SAMPLE EXECUTION
*
*

SC4F
        MOVEA.L   AYADR,A0   GET BASE ADDRESS OF OPERAND
        MOVE.L    A0,-(SP)   PUSH BASE ADDRESS INTO STACK
        MOVE.W    #SZAY,D1   GET LENGTH OF OPERAND IN BYTES
        MOVE.W    ROTATS,D0  GET NUMBER OF SHIFTS
        MOVEM.W   D0-D1,-(SP)  PUSH PARAMETERS INTO STACK
        JSR       MPRR       ROTATE RIGHT
                             *RESULT OF ROTATING AY=$EDCBA987654321
                             *4 BITS IS AY=$1EDCBA98765432, C=0
                             *  IN MEMORY AY   = $1E
                             *          AY+1 = $DC
                             *          AY+2 = $BA
                             *          AY+3 = $98
                             *          AY+4 = $76
                             *          AY+5 = $54
                             *          AY+6 = $32
        BRA.S     SC4F       REPEAT TEST

*
*DATA SECTION
*
SZAY    EQU       7          LENGTH OF OPERAND IN BYTES
ROTATS  DC.W      4          NUMBER OF ROTATES
AYADR   DC.L      AY         BASE ADDRESS OF OPERAND
AY      DC.B      $ED,$CB,$A9,$87,$65,$43,$21  OPERAND
        END
```

4G Multiple-precision rotate left (MPRL)

Rotates a multi-byte operand left by a specified number of bit positions as if the most significant bit and least significant bit were connected. Sets the Carry and Extend flags from the last bit shifted out of the leftmost bit position. The operand is stored with its most significant byte at the lowest address.

Procedure The program first shifts bit 7 of the operand's most significant byte to the Extend flag to produce a complete rotation. If the operand has an odd number of bytes, the program rotates the least significant byte through the Extend flag. It then rotates all remaining words left one bit through the Extend flag, starting with the least significant word. It repeats the operation for the specified number of rotates.

Entry conditions

Order in stack (starting from the top)

High word of return address
Low word of return address

Number of rotates (bit positions)

Length of the operand in bytes

High word of base address of operand (address of its most significant byte)
Low word of base address of operand (address of its most significant byte)

Exit conditions

Operand rotated left by the specified number of bit positions. The least significant bit positions are filled from the most significant bit positions. The Carry and Extend flags are set from the last bit shifted out of the leftmost bit position. The Carry flag is cleared if either the number of shifts or the length of the operand is 0.

Examples

1. Data: Length of operand (in bytes) = 8
Operand = $85A4C719FE06741E_{16}$
Number of rotates = 4

Result: Shifted operand = $5A4C719FE06741E8_{16}$
This is the original operand rotated left four bits. The four least significant bits are equivalent to the original four most significant bits.
Carry = Extend = 0, since the last bit shifted from the leftmost bit position was 0.

2. Data: Length of operand (in bytes) = 4
Operand = $3F6A42D3_{16}$
Number of rotates = 3

Result: Shifted operand = $FB521699_{16}$
This is the original operand rotated left three bits. The three least significant bits (001) are equivalent to the original three most significant bits.
Carry = Extend = 1, since the last bit shifted from the leftmost bit position was 0.

Registers used A0, A1, CCR, D0, D1, D2

Execution time NUMBER OF ROTATES × (58 + 25 × LENGTH OF OPERAND IN BYTES/2) + 151 cycles.

If, for example, NUMBER OF ROTATES = 6 and LENGTH OF OPERAND IN BYTES = 8, the execution time is

$$6 \times (58 + 25 \times 4) + 151 = 6 \times 158 + 151 = 1099 \text{ cycles}$$

Program size 72 bytes

Data memory required 2 stack bytes

Special cases

1. If the length of the operand is 0, the program exits immediately with the operand unchanged and the Carry flag cleared.

2. If the number of rotates is 0, the program exits immediately with the operand unchanged and the Carry flag cleared.

```
*
*
*
*
*       Title:                  Multiple-Precision Rotate Left
*       Name:                   MPRL
*
*
*
*       Purpose:                Rotate left a multi-byte operand
*                               N bits.
*
*       Entry:                  TOP OF STACK
*                                 High word of return address
*                                 Low word of return address
*                                 Number of bits to rotate
*                                 Length of the operand in bytes
*                                 High word of operand base address
*                                 Low word of operand base address
*
*                                 The operand is stored with ARRAY[0] as its
*                                 most significant byte and ARRAY[LENGTH-1]
*                                 as its least significant byte
*
*       Exit:                   Number rotated left
*                               Carry := Extend := Last bit shifted from the
*                                         most significant position.
*
*       Registers Used:         A0,A1,CCR,D0,D1,D2
*
*       Time:                   151 cycles overhead plus
*                                 ((25 X length/2) + 58) cycles per rotate
*
*       Size:                   Program  72 bytes
*                               Data       2 stack bytes
*
*

MPRL
*
*          EXIT IF LENGTH OF OPERAND OR NUMBER OF BITS TO ROTATE
*            IS ZERO.  CARRY IS CLEARED BY TST IN EITHER CASE
*
           MOVEM.W    4(SP),D0-D1  GET NUMBER OF BITS TO ROTATE
                                   * OPERAND LENGTH IN BYTES
           TST.B      D0         TEST NUMBER OF BITS TO ROTATE
           BEQ.S      EXITRL     EXIT IF NUMBER OF BITS TO ROTATE IS ZERO
           TST.B      D1         TEST OPERAND LENGTH
           BEQ.S      EXITRL     EXIT IF OPERAND LENGTH IS ZERO
*
*          SET UP POINTERS AND COUNTERS
*          WORD COUNT = NUMBER OF FULL WORDS IN OPERAND
```

```
*         WORD COUNT AND SHIFT COUNT BOTH REDUCED BY 1 BECAUSE DBRA
*           EXITS ON -1, NOT 0
*         SET ARRAY POINTER BEYOND LEAST SIGNIFICANT BYTE
*
          SUBQ.W    #1,D0       REDUCE SHIFT COUNT TO EXIT ON -1
          MOVE.W    D1,D2       GET OPERAND LENGTH IN BYTES
          LSR.W     #1,D2       DIVIDE BY 2 TO GET LENGTH IN WORDS
          SUBQ.W    #1,D2       REDUCE WORD COUNT BY 1 TO EXIT ON -1
          MOVEA.L   8(SP),A0    GET BASE ADDRESS OF OPERAND (ADDRESS
                                * OF MSB)
          MOVEA.L   A0,A1       SAVE POINTER TO MSB
          ADDA.W    D1,A0       POINT BEYOND END OF OPERAND (ADDRESS
                                * OF LSB)
          MOVE.W    D3,-(SP)    SAVE EXTRA DATA REGISTER IN STACK
*
*
*         ROTATE ALL FULL WORDS IN OPERAND LEFT ONE BIT
*         USE PREVIOUS MOST SIGNIFICANT BIT AS INITIAL SERIAL INPUT
*           (THROUGH EXTEND FLAG) TO PRODUCE ROTATION
*         IF LENGTH OF OPERAND IS ODD, ROTATE LEAST SIGNIFICANT BYTE
*           BEFORE ROTATING ALL FULL WORDS
*
RLLP
          MOVE.B    (A1),D3     GET MOST SIGNIFICANT BYTE
          ASL.B     #1,D3       EXTEND FLAG = BIT 7 OF MOST SIGNIFICANT
                                * BYTE TO PRODUCE ROTATION
          MOVEA.L   A0,A1       GET ADDRESS BEYOND LEAST SIGNIFICANT BYTE
          BTST      #0,D1       CHECK IF OPERAND LENGTH IS ODD OR EVEN
          BEQ.S     WDSHFT      BRANCH IF OPERAND LENGTH IS EVEN
          MOVE.B    -(A1),D3    LENGTH IS ODD, SO GET LEAST SIGNIFICANT
                                * BYTE.  NOTE: THIS SHIFT CANNOT BE DONE
                                * IN MEMORY SINCE ONLY WORD-LENGTH MEMORY
                                * SHIFTS ARE ALLOWED
          ROXL.B    #1,D3       ROTATE LEAST SIGNIFICANT BYTE LEFT
          MOVE.B    D3,(A1)     RETURN SHIFTED BYTE TO MEMORY
*
*         ROTATE EACH WORD OF OPERAND LEFT ONE BIT THROUGH EXTEND FLAG
*         START WITH LEAST SIGNIFICANT WORD IF LENGTH IS EVEN
*         START WITH WORD AFTER LEAST SIGNIFICANT BYTE IF LENGTH IS ODD
*
WDSHFT
          MOVE.W    D2,D3       GET NUMBER OF FULL WORDS IN OPERAND
RLLP1
          ROXL      -(A1)       ROTATE NEXT WORD LEFT
          DBRA      D3,RLLP1    CONTINUE THROUGH ALL FULL WORDS
*
*         COUNT NUMBER OF ROTATES
*
          DBRA      D0,RLLP     COUNT NUMBER OF ROTATES
          MOVE.W    (SP)+,D3    RESTORE EXTRA DATA REGISTER
*
*         REMOVE PARAMETERS FROM STACK AND EXIT
*
EXITRL
          MOVEA.L   (SP)+,A0    GET RETURN ADDRESS
          ADDA.W    #8,SP       REMOVE PARAMETERS FROM STACK
```

```
        JMP       (A0)       EXIT TO RETURN ADDRESS

*
*
*       SAMPLE EXECUTION
*
*

SC4G
        MOVEA.L   AYADR,A0   GET BASE ADDRESS OF OPERAND
        MOVE.L    A0,-(SP)   PUSH BASE ADDRESS INTO STACK
        MOVE.W    #SZAY,D1   GET LENGTH OF OPERAND IN BYTES
        MOVE.W    ROTATS,D0  GET NUMBER OF SHIFTS
        MOVEM.W   D0-D1,-(SP)  PUSH PARAMETERS INTO STACK
        JSR       MPRL       ROTATE LEFT
                             *RESULT OF ROTATING AY=$EDCBA987654321
                             *4 BITS IS AY=$DCBA987654321E, C=0
                             *  IN MEMORY AY   = $DC
                             *           AY+1  = $BA
                             *           AY+2  = $98
                             *           AY+3  = $76
                             *           AY+4  = $54
                             *           AY+5  = $32
                             *           AY+6  = $1E
        BRA.S     SC4G       REPEAT TEST

*
*DATA SECTION
*
SZAY    EQU       7          LENGTH OF OPERAND IN BYTES
ROTATS  DC.W      4          NUMBER OF ROTATES
AYADR   DC.L      AY         BASE ADDRESS OF OPERAND
AY      DC.B      $ED,$CB,$A9,$87,$65,$43,$21   OPERAND

        END
```

5 String manipulation

5A String compare (STRCMP)

Compares two strings. Sets the Zero flag to 1 if they are identical and to 0 otherwise. Sets the Carry flag to 1 if the string with the base address higher in the stack (string 2) is larger than the other string (string 1), and to 0 otherwise. Each string consists of at most 256 bytes, including an initial byte containing the length. That is, these are Pascal-style strings with a length byte, rather than C language-style strings with a terminating character. If the two strings are identical through the length of the shorter, the longer string is considered to be larger.

Procedure The program first determines which string is shorter. It then compares the strings a byte at a time through the length of the shorter. It exits with the flags set if it finds corresponding bytes that differ. If there are no differences, the program sets the flags by comparing the lengths.

Entry conditions

Order in stack (starting from the top)

High word of return address
Low word of return address

High word of base address of string 2
Low word of base address of string 2

High word of base address of string 1
Low word of base address of string 1

Exit conditions

Flags set as if string 2 had been subtracted from string 1. If the strings are the same through the length of the shorter, the flags are set as if the length of string 2 had been subtracted from the length of string 1.

Zero flag = 1 if the strings are identical, 0 if they are not identical.

Carry flag = 1 if string 2 is larger than string 1, 0 if they are identical or string 1 is larger. If the strings are the same through the length of the shorter one, the longer one is considered to be larger.

Examples

1. Data: String 1 = 05'PRINT' (05 is the length of the string)
String 2 = 03'END' (03 is the length of the string)
Result: Zero flag = 0 (strings are not identical)
Carry flag = 0 (string 2 is not larger than string 1)

2. Data: String 1 = 05'PRINT' (05 is the length of the string)
String 2 = 02'PR' (02 is the length of the string)
Result: Zero flag = 0 (strings are not identical)
Carry flag = 0 (string 2 is not larger than string 1)

The longer string (string 1) is considered to be larger. To determine whether string 2 is an abbreviation of string 1, use Subroutine 5C (Find the Position of a Substring). String 2 is an abbreviation if it is part of string 1 and starts at the first character.

3. Data: String 1 = 05'PRINT' (05 is the length of the string)
String 2 = 06'SYSTEM' (06 is the length of the string)
Result: Zero flag = 0 (strings are not identical)
Carry flag = 1 (string 2 is larger than string 1)

We are assuming here that the strings consist of ASCII characters. Note that the initial length byte is a hexadecimal number, not a character. We have represented this byte as two hexadecimal digits in front of the string; the string itself is surrounded by single quotation marks.

This routine treats spaces like other characters. Assuming ASCII strings, the routine will, for example, find that SPRINGMAID is larger than SPRING MAID, since an ASCII M ($4D_{16}$) is larger than an ASCII space (20_{16}).

Note that this routine does not order strings alphabetically as defined in common uses such as indexes and telephone directories. Instead, it uses the ASCII character order shown in Appendix 3. Note, in particular, that:

1. Spaces precede all printing characters.
2. Periods, commas, and dashes (hyphens) precede numbers.
3. Numbers precede letters.
4. Capital letters precede lower-case letters.

This ordering produces such non-standard results as the following:

1. 9TH AVENUE SCHOOL comes before CAPITAL CITY SCHOOL (or, in fact, any string starting with a letter). 9TH AVENUE is not treated as if it started with the letter N.

2. EZ8 Motel comes before East Street Motel since a capital Z precedes a lower-case a.

3. NEW YORK comes before NEWARK or NEWCASTLE since a space precedes any letter.

Registers used A0, A1, CCR, D0, D1, D2

Execution time

1. If the strings are not identical through the length of the shorter one, the execution time is approximately

$$98 + 30 \times \text{NUMBER OF CHARACTERS COMPARED}$$

If, for example, the routine compares five characters before finding a disparity, the execution time is approximately

$$98 + 30 \times 5 = 98 + 150 = 248 \text{ cycles}$$

2. If the strings are identical through the length of the shorter one, the execution time is approximately

$$110 + 30 \times \text{LENGTH OF SHORTER STRING}$$

If, for example, the shorter string is eight bytes long, the execution time is

$$110 + 30 \times 8 = 110 + 240 = 350 \text{ cycles}$$

Program size 38 bytes

Data memory required None

Special case If either string (but not both) has a 0 length, the program returns with the flags set as though the other string were larger. If both strings have 0 length, they are considered to be equal.

```
*       Title               String Compare
*       Name:               STRCMP
*
*       Purpose:            Compare 2 strings and return C and Z flags set
*                           or cleared.
*
*       Entry:              TOP OF STACK
*                             High word of return address
*                             Low word of return address
*                             High word of string 2 address
*                             Low word of string 2 address
*                             High word of string 1 address
*                             Low word of string 1 address
*
*                             Each string consists of a length byte
*                             followed by a maximum of 255 characters.
*
*       Exit:               IF string 1 = string 2 THEN
*                             Z=1,C=0
*                           IF string 1 > string 2 THEN
*                             Z=0,C=0
*                           IF string 1 < string 2 THEN
*                             Z=0,C=1
*
*       Registers Used: A0,A1,CCR,D0,D1,D2
*
*       Time:               98 cycles overhead plus 30 cycles per byte
*                           plus 12 cycles if the strings are identical
*                           through the length of the shorter one.
*
*       Size:               Program 38 bytes
*
*
STRCMP
          *
```

```
        *REMOVE PARAMETERS FROM STACK
        *
        MOVEM.L   4(SP),A0-A1     GET BASE ADDRESSES OF STRINGS
                                  * STRING 2 IN A0, STRING 1 IN A1
        *
        *DETERMINE WHICH STRING IS SHORTER
        *LENGTH OF SHORTER = NUMBER OF BYTES TO COMPARE
        *
        CLR.W     D2              CLEAR 16-BIT CHARACTER COUNT
        MOVE.B    (A1)+,D1        GET LENGTH OF STRING 1
        MOVE.B    (A0)+,D0        GET LENGTH OF STRING 2
        MOVE.B    D1,D2           SAVE LENGTH OF STRING 1 AS BYTE COUNT
        CMP.B     D1,D0           COMPARE STRING LENGTHS
        BCC.S     BEGCMP          BRANCH IF STRING 1 IS SHORTER THAN
                                  * STRING 2 OR THE SAME LENGTH
        MOVE.B    D0,D2           OTHERWISE, STRING 2 IS SHORTER SO
                                  * ITS LENGTH IS NUMBER OF BYTES TO
                                  * COMPARE
        *
        *JUST COMPARE LENGTHS IF SHORTER STRING HAS ZERO LENGTH
        *
BEGCMP
        TST.B     D2              TEST LENGTH OF SHORTER STRING
        BEQ.S     CMPLEN          BRANCH AND COMPARE LENGTHS IF NO
                                  * CHARACTERS TO COMPARE

        *
        *COMPARE STRINGS THROUGH LENGTH OF SHORTER
        *EXIT AS SOON AS CORRESPONDING CHARACTERS DIFFER
        *
        SUBQ.W    #1,D2           ADJUST COUNT FOR LOOP EXIT ON -1
CMPCHR
        CMPM.B    (A0)+,(A1)+     COMPARE CHARACTERS ONE AT A TIME
                                  * AND INCREMENT BOTH POINTERS
        BNE.S     EXITSC          BRANCH IF UNEQUAL CHARACTERS FOUND
                                  * Z,C WILL BE PROPERLY SET OR
                                  * CLEARED
        DBRA      D2,CMPCHR       CONTINUE UNTIL ALL CHARACTERS
                                  * COMPARED
        *
        *STRINGS SAME THROUGH LENGTH OF SHORTER
        *SO USE LENGTHS TO SET FLAGS
        *
CMPLEN
        CMP.B     D0,D1           COMPARE STRING LENGTHS
        *
        *EXIT TO RETURN ADDRESS
        *
EXITSC
        RTS                       EXIT TO RETURN ADDRESS

*
*       SAMPLE EXECUTION:
*
```

```
SC5A
        PEA     S1        PUSH ADDRESS OF STRING 1 ONTO STACK
        PEA     S2        PUSH ADDRESS OF STRING 2 ONTO STACK
        JSR     STRCMP    COMPARE STRINGS
                          *COMPARING "STRING 1" AND "STRING 2"
                          *  RESULTS IN STRING 1 LESS THAN
                          *  STRING 2, SO Z=0,C=1
        BRA.S   SC5A      LOOP THROUGH TEST
*
*       TEST DATA
*
S1      DC.B    $20       LENGTH OF STRING 1 IN BYTES
        DC.B    'STRING 1                          '
S2      DC.B    $20       LENGTH OF STRING 2 IN BYTES
        DC.B    'STRING 2                          '

        END
```

5B String concatenation (CONCAT)

Combines (concatenates) two strings, placing the second immediately after the first in memory. If the concatenation would produce a string longer than a specified maximum, the program uses only enough of string 2 to give the combined string its maximum length. The Carry flag is cleared if all of string 2 can be concatenated. It is set to 1 if part of string 2 must be dropped. Each string consists of at most 256 bytes, including an initial byte containing the length. The strings are thus Pascal-style, rather than C language-style with a terminating character.

Procedure The program uses the length of string 1 to determine where to start adding characters, and the length of string 2 to determine how many characters to add. If the sum of the lengths exceeds the maximum, the program indicates an overflow. It then reduces the number of characters it must add to the maximum length minus the length of string 1. Finally, it moves the characters from string 2 to the end of string 1, updates the length of string 1, and sets the Carry flag to indicate whether characters were discarded.

Entry conditions

Order in stack (starting from the top)

High word of return address
Low word of return address

Maximum length of string 1 (less than 256)

High word of base address of string 2
Low word of base address of string 2

High word of base address of string 1
Low word of base address of string 1

Exit conditions

String 2 concatenated at the end of string 1 and the length of string 1 increased accordingly. If the combined string would exceed the maximum length, only the part of string 2 that would give string 1 its maximum length is concatenated. If any part of string 2 must be dropped, the Carry flag is set to 1. Otherwise, the Carry flag is cleared.

Examples

1. Data: Maximum length of string 1 = $0E_{16} = 14_{10}$
   String 1 = 07'JOHNSON' (07 is the length of the string)
   String 2 = 05', DON' (05 is the length of the string)

   Result: String 1 = 0C'JOHNSON, DON' ($0C_{16} = 12_{10}$ is the length of the combined string with string 2 placed after string 1).
   Carry = 0, since no characters were dropped.

2. Data: String 1 = 07'JOHNSON' (07 is the length of the string)
   String 2 = 09', RICHARD' (09 is the length of the string)

   Result: String 1 = 0E'JOHNSON, RICHA' ($0E_{16} = 14_{10}$ is the maximum length allowed, so the last two characters of string 2 have been dropped).
   Carry = 1, since characters had to be dropped.

Note that we are representing the initial byte (containing the string's length) as two hexadecimal digits in both examples.

Registers used A0, A1, CCR, D0, D1, D2

Execution time Approximately

23 × NUMBER OF CHARACTERS CONCATENATED plus 197 cycles overhead

NUMBER OF CHARACTERS CONCATENATED is usually the length of string 2, but will be the maximum length of string 1 minus its current length if the combined string would be too long. If, for example, NUMBER OF CHARACTERS CONCATENATED is 14_{16} (20_{10}), the execution time is

$$20 \times 23 + 197 = 460 + 197 = 657 \text{ cycles}$$

The overhead is an extra 22 cycles if the string must be truncated.

Program size 70 bytes

Data memory required 4 stack bytes

Special cases

1. If the concatenation would make the string exceed its specified maximum length, the program concatenates only enough of string 2 to reach the maximum. If any of string 2 must be truncated, the Carry flag is set to 1.

2. If string 2 has a length of 0, the program exits with the Carry flag cleared (no errors) and string 1 unchanged. That is, a length of 0 for either string is interpreted as 0, not as 256.

3. If the original length of string 1 exceeds the specified maximum, the program exits with the Carry flag set to 1 (indicating an error) and string 1 unchanged.

```
*
*       Title               String Concatenation
*       Name:               CONCAT
*
*       Purpose:            Concatenate 2 strings into one string.
*
*       Entry:              TOP OF STACK
*                             High word of return address
*                             Low word of return address
*                             Maximum length of string 1
*                             High word of string 2 address
*                             Low word of string 2 address
*                             High word of string 1 address
*                             Low word of string 1 address
*
*                            Each string consists of a length byte
*                             followed by a maximum of 255 characters.
*
*       Exit:               String 1 := string 1 concatenated with string 2
*                           If no errors then
*                             Carry := 0
*                           else
*                             begin
*                               Carry := 1
*                               if the concatenation makes string 1 too
*                               long, concatenate only the part of string 2
*                               that results in string 1 having its maximum
*                               length
*                               if length(string1) > maximum length then
*                                 no concatenation is done
*                             end
*
*       Registers Used: A0,A1,CCR,D0,D1,D2
*
```

```
*       Time:           Approximately 23 X (length of string 2) cycles
*                       plus 197 cycles overhead
*
*       Size:           Program 70 bytes
*                       Data     4 stack bytes
*

CONCAT
        *
        *REMOVE PARAMETERS FROM STACK
        *SET MARKER TO INDICATE NO TRUNCATION NECESSARY
        *
        MOVE.W   4(SP),D0         GET MAXIMUM LENGTH OF STRING 1
        MOVEM.L  6(SP),A0-A1      GET BASE ADDRESSES OF STRINGS
                                  * STRING 2 IN A0, STRING 1 IN A1
        CLR.B    D1               INDICATE NO TRUNCATION NECESSARY
                                  * TRUNCATION FLAG IN D1
        *
        *GET STRING LENGTHS AND EXTEND THEM TO 16 BITS
        *NO CONCATENATION NECESSARY IF STRING 2 HAS ZERO LENGTH
        *
        MOVEM.W  D3-D4,-(SP)      SAVE EXTRA DATA REGISTERS IN STACK
        CLR.W    D2               CLEAR UPPER BYTES OF STRING LENGTHS
        CLR.W    D3
        MOVE.B   (A1),D2          GET LENGTH OF STRING 1
        MOVE.B   (A0)+,D3         GET LENGTH OF STRING 2 AND POINT TO
                                  * FIRST ACTUAL CHARACTER
        BEQ.S    SETTRN           BRANCH (EXIT) IF STRING 2 HAS ZERO
                                  * LENGTH - NO ERROR IN THIS CASE
        *
        *DETERMINE HOW MANY CHARACTERS TO CONCATENATE
        *THIS IS LENGTH OF STRING 2 IF COMBINED STRING WOULD
        *  NOT EXCEED MAXIMUM LENGTH
        *OTHERWISE, IT IS THE NUMBER THAT WOULD BRING COMBINED
        *  STRING TO ITS MAXIMUM LENGTH - THAT IS, MAXIMUM LENGTH
        *  MINUS LENGTH OF STRING 1
        *
        MOVE.W   D3,D4            SAVE STRING 2'S LENGTH
        ADD.W    D2,D4            COMPUTE LENGTH OF COMBINED STRING
        CMP.W    D4,D0            COMPARE LENGTH TO MAXIMUM LENGTH
        BCC.S    DOCAT            BRANCH IF LENGTH DOES NOT EXCEED
                                  * MAXIMUM
        NOT.B    D1               INDICATE TRUNCATION NECESSARY BY
                                  * SETTING TRUNCATION FLAG
        MOVE.W   D0,D4            LIMIT COMBINED STRING TO MAXIMUM
                                  * LENGTH
        SUB.W    D2,D0            COMPUTE MAXIMUM LENGTH MINUS LENGTH
                                  * OF STRING 1
        BHI.S    RPLEN            BRANCH IF STRING 1 IS NOT ALREADY
                                  * LONGER THAN ITS MAXIMUM LENGTH
        CLR.W    D0               NUMBER OF CHARACTERS TO CONCATENATE
                                  * IS ZERO SINCE STRING IS TOO LONG
RPLEN
        MOVE.W   D0,D3            NUMBER OF CHARACTERS TO CONCATENATE
                                  * IS MAXIMUM LENGTH MINUS STRING 1'S
                                  * LENGTH
```

```
        *
        *CONCATENATE STRINGS BY MOVING CHARACTERS FROM STRING 2
        * TO THE AREA FOLLOWING STRING 1
        *END OF STRING 1 = BASE 1 + LENGTH 1 + 1, WHERE THE EXTRA 1
        * IS FOR THE LENGTH BYTE
        *NEW CHARACTERS COME FROM STRING 2, STARTING AT BASE2+1
        * (SKIPPING OVER LENGTH BYTE)
        *
DOCAT
        TST.B    D3              TEST NUMBER OF CHARACTERS TO
                                 * CONCATENATE
        BEQ.S    SETTRN          BRANCH (EXIT) IF NOTHING TO
                                 * CONCATENATE
        MOVE.B   D4,(A1)+        SET LENGTH OF COMBINED STRING AND
                                 * POINT TO ITS FIRST CHARACTER
        ADDA.W   D3,A1           POINT BEYOND LAST BYTE OF STRING 1
        SUBQ.W   #1,D3           ADJUST COUNT FOR LOOP EXIT ON -1
MVCHAR
        MOVE.B   (A0)+,(A1)+     MOVE CHARACTER FROM STRING 2 TO END
                                 * OF STRING 1
        DBRA     D3,MVCHAR       CONTINUE THROUGH ALL CHARACTERS
        *
        *EXIT, SETTING CARRY FROM TRUNCATION FLAG
        *CARRY = 1 IF CHARACTERS HAD TO BE TRUNCATED, 0 OTHERWISE
        *
SETTRN
        MOVEM.W  (SP)+,D3-D4     RESTORE EXTRA DATA REGISTERS
        LSR.B    #1,D1           CARRY = 1 IF TRUNCATION, 0 IF NOT
        RTS                      EXIT TO RETURN ADDRESS


*
*       SAMPLE EXECUTION:
*


SC5B
        PEA      S1         PUSH ADDRESS OF STRING 1 ONTO STACK
        PEA      S2         PUSH ADDRESS OF STRING 2 ONTO STACK
        MOVE.W   #$20,-(SP) PUSH MAXIMUM LENGTH OF STRING 1 ONTO
                            * STACK
        JSR      CONCAT     CONCATENATE STRINGS
                            *RESULT OF CONCATENATING
                            * "LASTNAME" AND ", FIRSTNAME"
                            * IS S1 = $13,"LASTNAME, FIRSTNAME"
        BRA.S    SC5B       LOOP THROUGH TEST
*
*TEST DATA
*
S1      DC.B     8               LENGTH OF S1 IN BYTES
        DC.B     'LASTNAME                        ' *32 BYTE MAX LENGTH
S2      DC.B            $0B                         LENGTH OF S2 IN BYTES
        DC.B     ', FIRSTNAME                     ' *32 BYTE MAX LENGTH

        END
```

5C Find the position of a substring (POS)

Searches for the first occurrence of a substring within a string. Returns the index at which the substring starts if it is found and 0 otherwise. The string and the substring each consist of at most 256 bytes, including an initial byte containing the length. Thus, if the substring is found, its starting index cannot be less than 1 or more than 255. These are Pascal-style strings with a length byte, rather than C language-style strings with a terminating character.

Procedure The program moves through the string searching for the substring. It continues until it finds a match or until the remaining part of the string is shorter than the substring and hence cannot possibly contain it. If the substring does not appear in the string, the program clears register D0; otherwise, the program places the substring's starting index in register D0.

Entry conditions

Order in stack (starting from the top)

High word of return address
Low word of return address

High word of base address of substring
Low word of base address of substring

High word of base address of string
Low word of base address of string

Exit conditions

Low byte of register D0 contains index at which first occurrence of substring starts if it is found; low byte of register D0 contains 0 if substring is not found.

Examples

1. Data: String = 1D'ENTER SPEED IN MILES PER HOUR' ($1D_{16} = 29_{10}$ is the length of the string)

Substring = 05'MILES' (05 is the length of the substring)

Result: Register D0 contains 10_{16} (16_{10}), the index at which the substring 'MILES' starts

2. Data: String = 1B'SALES FIGURES FOR JUNE 1981' ($1B_{16}$ = 27_{10} is the length of the string)

Substring = 04'JUNE' (04 is the length of the substring)

Result: Register D0 contains 13_{16} (19_{10}), the index at which the substring 'JUNE' starts.

3. Data: String = 10'LET Y1 = X1 + R7' (10_{16} = 16_{10} is the length of the string)

Substring = 02'R4' (02 is the length of the substring)

Result: Register D0 contains 0, since the substring 'R4' does not appear in the string LET Y1 = X1 + R7

4. Data: String = 07'RESTORE' (07 is the length of the string).

Substring = 03'RES' (03 is the length of the substring)

Result: Register D0 contains 1, the index at which the substring 'RES' starts. An index of 1 indicates that the substring could be an abbreviation of the string. Interactive programs, such as BASIC interpreters and word processors, often use abbreviations to save on typing and storage.

Registers used A0, A1, CCR, D0, D1, D2

Execution time Data-dependent, but the overhead is approximately 198 cycles, each successful match of 1 character takes 30 cycles, and each unsuccessful match of 1 character takes 48 cycles. The worst case is when the string and substring always match except for the last character in the substring, such as

String = 'AAAAAAAAB'
Substring = 'AAB'

The execution time in that case is

(STRING LENGTH − SUBSTRING LENGTH + 1) × [30 × (SUBSTRING LENGTH − 1) + 48] + 198

If, for example, STRING LENGTH = 9 and SUBSTRING LENGTH = 3 (as in the example above), the execution time is

$$(9 - 3 + 1) \times (30 \times (3 - 1) + 48) + 198 = 7 \times 108 + 198$$

$$= 756 + 198$$
$$= 954 \text{ cycles}$$

Program size 72 bytes

Data memory required 12 stack bytes

Special cases

1. If either the string or the substring has a length of 0, the program exits with 0 in register D0, indicating that it did not find the substring.

2. If the substring is longer than the string, the program exits with 0 in register D0, indicating that it did not find the substring.

3. If the program returns an index of 1, the substring may be regarded as an abbreviation of the string. That is, the substring occurs in the string, starting at the first character. A typical example would be a string PRINT and a substring PR.

4. If the substring occurs more than once in the string, the program will return only the index to the first occurrence (the one with the smallest starting index).

```
*       Title           Find the Position of a Substring
*       Name:           POS
*
*       Purpose:        Search for the first occurrence of a substring
*                       in a string and return its starting index.
*                       If the substring is not found, 0 is returned.
*
*       Entry:          TOP OF STACK
*                         High word of return address
*                         Low word of return address
*                         High word of substring address
*                         Low word of substring address
*                         High word of string address
*                         Low word of string address
*
*                         Each string consists of a length byte
*                         followed by a maximum of 255 characters.
*
*       Exit:           If the substring is found then
*                         Low byte of register D0 = its starting index
*                       else
*                         Low byte of register D0 = 0
```

```
*
*       Registers Used: A0,A1,CCR,D0,D1,D2
*
*
*       Time:           Since the algorithm is so data dependent
*                       a simple formula is impossible but the
*                       following statements are true and a
*                       worst case is given below:
*
*                       198 cycles overhead.
*                       Each match of 1 character takes 30 cycles
*                       A mismatch takes 48 cycles
*
*                       Worst case timing occurs when the
*                       string and substring always match
*                       except for the last character of the
*                       substring, such as:
*                           string = 'AAAAAAAAAB'
*                           substring = 'AAB'
*
*       Size:           Program 72 bytes
*                       Data    12 stack bytes
*

POS
        *
        *OBTAIN PARAMETERS FROM STACK
        *
        MOVEM.L   4(SP),A0-A1     GET BASE ADDRESSES OF SUBSTRING (A0)
                                  * AND STRING (A1)
        *
        *EXIT, INDICATING SUBSTRING NOT FOUND, IF STRING OR SUBSTRING
        *  HAS ZERO LENGTH OR IF SUBSTRING IS LONGER THAN STRING
        *
        CLR.B     D0              STARTING INDEX IS ZERO
                                  * THIS INDICATES SUBSTRING NOT FOUND
        CLR.W     D1              EXTEND LENGTHS TO 16 BITS
        CLR.W     D2
        MOVE.B    (A1)+,D1        GET STRING LENGTH
        BEQ.S     EXITPO          BRANCH (EXIT) IF STRING LENGTH
                                  * IS ZERO
        MOVE.B    (A0)+,D2        GET SUBSTRING LENGTH
        BEQ.S     EXITPO          BRANCH (EXIT) IF SUBSTRING LENGTH
                                  * IS ZERO
        SUB.W     D2,D1           COMPARE STRING, SUBSTRING LENGTH
        BCS.S     EXITPO          BRANCH (EXIT) IF SUBSTRING IS LONGER
                                  * THAN STRING
        *
        *SET UP PARAMETERS FOR SEARCH
        *
        MOVEM.L   A2-A3/D3,-(SP)  SAVE EXTRA REGISTERS IN STACK
        SUBQ.W    #1,D2           GET SUBSTRING LENGTH - 1 FOR USE
                                  * IN LOOP EXITING ON -1
        MOVE.W    D2,D3           SAVE SUBSTRING LENGTH - 1
        MOVE.W    D1,D0           SAVE LENGTH OF PART THAT MUST BE
                                  * EXAMINED
```

```
                                  *LENGTH OF PART IS STRING LENGTH -
                                  * SUBSTRING LENGTH + 1.  REMAINDER
                                  * IS TOO SHORT TO CONTAIN SUBSTRING
                                  * +1 IS BALANCED BY -1 FOR DBRA EXIT
        MOVEA.L   A0,A3           SAVE ADDRESS OF FIRST CHARACTER IN
                                  * SUBSTRING
        MOVEA.L   A1,A2           SAVE CURRENT STARTING POSITION IN
                                  * STRING
        *
        *SEARCH FOR SUBSTRING IN STRING
        *START SEARCH AT BASE OF STRING
        *CONTINUE UNTIL REMAINING STRING SHORTER THAN SUBSTRING
        *
CMPPOS
        MOVEA.L   A2,A1           GET CURRENT STARTING POSITION IN
                                  * STRING
        ADDQ.W    #1,A2           MOVE CURRENT STARTING POSITION IN
                                  * STRING UP ONE CHARACTER
        MOVEA.L   A3,A0           GET ADDRESS OF FIRST CHARACTER IN
                                  * SUBSTRING
        MOVE.W    D3,D2           GET SUBSTRING LENGTH - 1 AS COUNTER
                                  * FOR NEXT COMPARISON
        *
        *COMPARE BYTES OF SUBSTRING WITH BYTES OF STRING,
        * STARTING AT CURRENT POSITION IN STRING
        *
FNDSTR
        CMPM.B    (A0)+,(A1)+     COMPARE CHARACTERS ONE AT A TIME
                                  * AND INCREMENT BOTH STRING AND
                                  * SUBSTRING POINTERS
        BNE.S     NOTFND          BRANCH IF UNEQUAL CHARACTERS FOUND -
                                  * SUBSTRING NOT FOUND
        DBRA      D2,FNDSTR       CONTINUE UNTIL ALL CHARACTERS IN
                                  * SUBSTRING COMPARED
        *
        *SUBSTRING FOUND - CALCULATE INDEX AT WHICH IT STARTS IN
        * STRING (LENGTH OF PART THAT MUST BE EXAMINED - NUMBER
        * OF COMPARISONS REMAINING + 1)

        *
        SUB.B     D1,D0           LENGTH OF PART THAT MUST BE EXAMINED
                                  * MINUS NUMBER OF COMPARISONS LEFT
        ADDQ.B    #1,D0           ADD 1 TO CALCULATE INDEX
        BRA.S     REMTMP          *EXIT AND CLEAN STACK
        *
        *ARRIVE HERE IF SUBSTRING NOT FOUND
        *COUNT NUMBER OF COMPARISONS
        *
NOTFND
        DBRA      D1,CMPPOS       SEARCH THROUGH SECTION OF STRING
                                  *  THAT COULD CONTAIN SUBSTRING
        CLR.B     D0              SUBSTRING NOT FOUND AT ALL - MAKE
                                  *  STARTING INDEX ZERO
        *
        *REMOVE TEMPORARY STORAGE AND EXIT
        *
```

```
REMTMP
        MOVEM.L   (SP)+,A2-A3/D3   RESTORE EXTRA REGISTERS FROM STACK
EXITPO
        RTS                        EXIT TO RETURN ADDRESS

*
*       SAMPLE EXECUTION:
*

SC5C
        PEA       STG         PUSH STRING ADDRESS ONTO STACK
        PEA       SSTG        PUSH SUBSTRING ADDRESS ONTO STACK
        JSR       POS         FIND POSITION OF SUBSTRING
                              * SEARCHING "AAAAAAAAAB" FOR "AAB"
                              * RESULTS IN REGISTER D0=8
        BRA.S     SC5C        LOOP THROUGH TEST
*
*       TEST DATA
*
STG     DC.B      $0A         LENGTH OF STRING
        DC.B      'AAAAAAAAAB                       ' 32 BYTE MAX
SSTG    DC.B      3           LENGTH OF SUBSTRING
        DC.B      'AAB                              ' 32 BYTE MAX

        END
```

5D Copy a substring from a string (COPY)

Copies a substring from a string, given a starting index and the number of bytes to copy. Each string consists of at most 256 bytes, including an initial byte containing the length. If the starting index of the substring is 0 (i.e. the substring would start in the length byte) or is beyond the end of the string, the substring is given a length of 0 and the Carry flag is set to 1. If the substring would exceed its maximum length or would extend beyond the end of the string, then only the maximum number or the available number of characters (up to the end of the string) are placed in the substring, and the Carry flag is set to 1. If the substring can be formed as specified, the Carry flag is cleared. The strings are Pascal-style with a length byte, rather than C language-style with a terminating character.

Procedure The program exits immediately if the number of bytes to copy, the maximum length of the substring, or the starting index is 0. It also exits immediately if the starting index exceeds the length of the string. If none of these conditions holds, the program checks whether the number of bytes to copy exceeds either the maximum length of the substring or the number of characters available in the string. If either is exceeded, the program reduces the number of bytes to copy accordingly. It then copies the bytes from the string to the substring. The program clears the Carry flag if the substring can be formed as specified and sets the Carry flag if it cannot.

Entry conditions

Order in stack (starting from the top)

High word of return address
Low word of return address

Number of bytes to copy (less than 256)

Starting index to copy from (less than 256)

Maximum length of substring (less than 256)

High word of base address of substring
Low word of base address of substring

High word of base address of string
Low word of base address of string

Exit conditions

Substring contains characters copied from string. If the starting index is 0, the maximum length of the substring is 0, or the starting index is beyond the length of the string, the substring has a length of 0 and the Carry flag is set to 1. If the substring would extend beyond the end of the string or would exceed its specified maximum length, only the available characters from the string (up to the maximum length of the substring) are copied into the substring; the Carry flag is set in this case also. If no problems occur in forming the substring, the Carry flag is cleared.

Examples

1. Data: String = 10'LET Y1 = R7 + X4' ($10_{16} = 16_{10}$ is the length of the string)
   Maximum length of substring = 2
   Number of bytes to copy = 2
   Starting index = 5

   Result: Substring = 02'Y1' (2 is the length of the substring).
   We have copied 2 bytes from the string starting at character #5 (that is, characters 5 and 6).
   Carry = 0, since no problems occur in forming the substring

2. Data: String = 0E'8657 POWELL ST' ($0E_{16} = 14_{10}$ is the length of the string)
   Maximum length of substring = $10_{16} = 16_{10}$
   Number of bytes to copy = $0D_{16} = 13_{10}$
   Starting index = 06

   Result: Substring = 09'POWELL ST' (09 is the length of the substring)
   Carry = 1, since there were not enough characters available in the string to provide the specified number of bytes to copy.

3. Data: String = 16'9414 HEGENBERGER DRIVE' ($16_{16} = 22_{10}$ is the length of the string)
   Maximum length of substring = $10_{16} = 16_{10}$

Number of bytes to copy = $11_{16} = 17_{10}$
Starting index = 06

Result: Substring = 10'HEGENBERGER DRIV' ($10_{16} = 16_{10}$ is the length of the substring)
Carry = 1, since the number of bytes to copy exceeded the maximum length of the substring

---

Registers used A0, A1, CCR, D0, D1, D2

Execution time Approximately

23 × NUMBER OF BYTES COPIED plus 268 cycles overhead

NUMBER OF BYTES COPIED is the number specified if no problems occur, or the number available or the maximum length of the substring if copying would extend beyond either the string or the substring. If, for example, NUMBER OF BYTES COPIED = 12_{10} ($0C_{16}$), the execution time is

$$23 \times 12 + 268 = 276 + 268 = 544 \text{ cycles}$$

Program size: 94 bytes

Data memory required 6 stack bytes

Special cases

1. If the number of bytes to copy is 0, the program assigns the substring a length of 0 and clears the Carry flag, indicating no error.

2. If the maximum length of the substring is 0, the program assigns the substring a length of 0 and sets the Carry flag to 1, indicating an error.

3. If the starting index of the substring is 0, the program assigns the substring a length of 0 and sets the Carry flag to 1, indicating an error.

4. If the source string does not even reach the specified starting index, the program assigns the substring a length of 0 and sets the Carry flag to 1, indicating an error.

5. If the substring would extend beyond the end of the source string, the program places all the available characters in the substring and sets the Carry flag to 1, indicating an error. The available characters are the ones from the starting index to the end of the string.

6. If the substring would exceed its specified maximum length, the program places only the specified maximum number of characters in the substring. It sets the Carry flag to 1, indicating an error.

```
*       Title           Copy a Substring from a String
*       Name:           COPY
*
*       Purpose:        Copy a substring from a string given a starting
*                       index and the number of bytes.
*
*       Entry:          TOP OF STACK
*                         High word of return address
*                         Low word of return address
*                         Number of bytes to copy (less than 256)
*                         Starting index to copy from (less than 256)
*                         Maximum length of destination string
*                         High word of destination string address
*                         Low word of destination string address
*                         High word of source string address
*                         Low word of source string address
*
*                         Each string consists of a length byte
*                         followed by a maximum of 255 characters.
*
*       Exit:           Destination string := The substring from the
*                         string.
*                       If no errors then
*                         Carry := 0
*                       else
*                         begin
*                           the following conditions cause an
*                           error and the Carry flag = 1.
*                           if (index = 0) or (maxlen = 0) or
*                              (index > length(source) then
*                             the destination string will have a zero
*                             length.
*                           if (index + count - 1) > length(source))
*                           then
*                             the destination string becomes everything
*                             from index to the end of source string.
*                         end
*
*       Registers Used: A0,A1,CCR,D0,D1,D2
*
*       Time:           Approximately (23 X count) cycles plus
*                       268 cycles overhead
```

```
*
*       Size:           Program 94 bytes
*                       Data    6 stack bytes
*

COPY
        *
        *OBTAIN PARAMETERS FROM STACK
        *
        MOVEM.W   4(SP),D0-D2     GET NUMBER OF BYTES TO COPY, STARTING
                                  * INDEX, MAXIMUM LENGTH OF SUBSTRING
        MOVEM.L   10(SP),A0-A1    GET BASE ADDRESSES OF SUBSTRING (A0),
                                  * SOURCE STRING (A1)
        *
        *EXIT IF ZERO BYTES TO COPY, ZERO MAXIMUM SUBSTRING
        * LENGTH, OR ZERO STARTING INDEX
        *LENGTH OF SUBSTRING IS ZERO IN ALL CASES
        *
        CLR.B     (A0)            LENGTH OF SUBSTRING = 0
        TST.W     D0              CHECK NUMBER OF BYTES TO COPY
        BEQ.S     OKEXIT          BRANCH IF ZERO BYTES TO COPY, NO
                                  * ERROR.  SUBSTRING WILL JUST HAVE
                                  * ZERO LENGTH.  NOTE TST CLEARS
                                  * CARRY
        TST.W     D2              CHECK MAXIMUM LENGTH OF SUBSTRING
        BEQ.S     EREXIT          TAKE ERROR EXIT IF SUBSTRING HAS ZERO
                                  * MAXIMUM LENGTH
        TST.W     D1              CHECK STARTING INDEX
        BEQ.S     EREXIT          *TAKE ERROR EXIT IF STARTING INDEX IS
                                  * ZERO (LENGTH BYTE)
        *
        *CHECK IF SOURCE STRING REACHES STARTING INDEX
        *TAKE ERROR EXIT IF IT DOESN'T
        *
        MOVEM.W   D3-D5,-(SP)     SAVE EXTRA DATA REGISTERS IN STACK
        MOVE.B    (A1),D3         GET LENGTH OF SOURCE STRING
        CMP.B     D1,D3           COMPARE STARTING INDEX TO LENGTH
                                  * OF SOURCE STRING
        BCS.S     EREXIT          TAKE ERROR EXIT IF STARTING INDEX
                                  * BEYOND END OF SOURCE STRING
        *
        *CHECK IF THERE ARE ENOUGH CHARACTERS IN SOURCE STRING
        * TO SATISFY THE NEED
        *THERE ARE IF STARTING INDEX + NUMBER OF BYTES TO COPY - 1
        * IS LESS THAN OR EQUAL TO THE LENGTH OF THE SOURCE
        * STRING
        *
        CLR.B     D4              INDICATE NO TRUNCATION NEEDED
                                  * FLAG IN D4
        MOVE.B    D0,D5           COUNT = NUMBER OF BYTES TO COPY
        ADD.B     D1,D5           ADD COUNT TO STARTING INDEX
        BCS.S     REDLEN          BRANCH IF SUM IS GREATER THAN 255
        SUBQ.B    #1,D5           CALCULATE INDEX OF LAST BYTE IN AREA
                                  * SPECIFIED FOR COPYING
        CMP.B     D3,D5           COMPARE TO LENGTH OF SOURCE STRING
```

```
        BCS.S     CHKMAX          BRANCH IF SOURCE STRING IS LONGER
        *
        *CALLER ASKED FOR TOO MANY CHARACTERS
        *JUST RETURN EVERYTHING BETWEEN STARTING INDEX AND THE END OF
        *  THE SOURCE STRING
        *COUNT := LENGTH(SSTRG) - STARTING INDEX + 1
        *INDICATE TRUNCATION OF COUNT
        *
REDLEN
        MOVE.B    D3,D0           GET LENGTH OF SOURCE STRING
        SUBQ.W    D1,D0           COUNT = LENGTH - STARTING INDEX + 1
        ADDQ.W    #1,D0
        NOT.B     D4              INDICATE TRUNCATION OF COUNT BY
                                  * SETTING MARKER TO FF
        *
        *DETERMINE IF THERE IS ENOUGH ROOM IN THE SUBSTRING
        *CHECK IF COUNT IS LESS THAN OR EQUAL TO MAXIMUM LENGTH
        *  OF DESTINATION STRING.  IF NOT, SET COUNT TO
        *  MAXIMUM LENGTH
        *IF COUNT > MAXLEN THEN COUNT := MAXLEN
        *
CHKMAX
        CMP.W     D2,D0           COMPARE COUNT TO MAXIMUM SUBSTRING LENGTH
        BLS.S     MOVSTR          BRANCH (NO PROBLEM) IF COUNT IS LESS
                                  * THAN OR EQUAL TO MAXIMUM
        MOVE.W    D2,D0           OTHERWISE, REPLACE COUNT WITH MAXIMUM
        MOVE.B    #$FF,D4         INDICATE TRUNCATION OF COUNT
        *
        *SET LENGTH OF DESTINATION STRING
        *SOURCE POINTER = BASE ADDRESS OF SOURCE STRING + STARTING
        *  INDEX
        *DESTINATION POINTER = BASE ADDRESS OF SUBSTRING + 1 (TO
        *  ACCOUNT FOR LENGTH BYTE
        *
MOVSTR
        MOVE.B    D0,(A0)+        LENGTH OF DESTINATION STRING = COUNT
        ADDA.W    D1,A1           POINT TO FIRST CHARACTER IN AREA TO
                                  * BE COPIED FROM SOURCE STRING
        SUBQ.W    #1,D0           ADJUST COUNT FOR LOOP EXIT ON -1
        *
        *MOVE SUBSTRING FROM COPY AREA TO DESTINATION STRING
        *
MOVBYT
        MOVE.B    (A1)+,(A0)+     MOVE BYTE FROM SOURCE STRING TO
                                  * DESTINATION STRING
        DBRA      D0,MOVBYT       COUNT BYTES
        LSR.B     #1,D4           MAKE CARRY INDICATE WHETHER REQUEST WAS
                                  * FULLY SATISFIED (1 IF SO, 0 IF NOT)
        MOVEM.W   (SP)+,D3-D5     RESTORE EXTRA REGISTERS FROM STACK
OKEXIT
        RTS                       EXIT TO RETURN ADDRESS
        *
        *ERROR EXIT - SET CARRY TO 1
        *
EREXIT
        MOVE      #1,CCR          SET CARRY TO 1, INDICATING ERROR
```

```
        RTS

*
*       SAMPLE EXECUTION:
*

SC5D
        PEA       SSTG              PUSH ADDRESS OF SOURCE STRING INTO
                                    * STACK
        PEA       DSTG              PUSH ADDRESS OF DESTINATION STRING
                                    * INTO STACK
        MOVE.W    (CNT),D0          GET NUMBER OF CHARACTERS TO COPY
        MOVE.W    (IDX),D1          GET STARTING INDEX FOR COPYING
        MOVE.W    (MXLEN),D2        GET MAXIMUM LENGTH OF SUBSTRING
        MOVEM.W   D0-D2,-(SP)       PUSH PARAMETERS ONTO STACK
        JSR       COPY          COPY SUBSTRING
                                *COPYING 3 CHARACTERS STARTING AT INDEX 4
                                * FROM '12.345E+10' GIVES '345'
                                *NOTE THAT VALID INDEXES START AT 1,
                                * NOT 0
        BRA.S     SC5D          LOOP THROUGH TEST

*
*DATA SECTION
*
IDX     DC.W      4             STARTING INDEX FOR COPYING
CNT     DC.W      3             NUMBER OF CHARACTERS TO COPY
MXLEN   DC.W      $20           MAXIMUM LENGTH OF DESTINATION STRING
SSTG    DC.B      $0A           LENGTH OF STRING
        DC.B      '12.345E+10                     ' 32 BYTE MAX
DSTG    DC.B      0             LENGTH OF SUBSTRING
        DC.B      '                               ' 32 BYTE MAX

        END
```

5E Delete a substring from a string (DELETE)

Deletes a substring from a string, given a starting index and a length. The string consists of at most 256 bytes, including an initial byte containing the length. The Carry flag is cleared if the deletion can be performed as specified. The Carry flag is set if the starting index is 0 or beyond the length of the string; the string is left unchanged in either case. If the deletion extends beyond the end of the string, the Carry flag is set to 1 and only the characters from the starting index to the end of the string are deleted. The string is Pascal-style with a length byte, rather than C language-style with a terminating character.

Procedure The program exits immediately if either the starting index or the number of bytes to delete is 0. It also exits if the starting index is beyond the length of the string. If none of these conditions holds, the program checks whether the string extends beyond the area to be deleted. If it does not, the program simply truncates the string by setting the new length to the starting index minus 1. If it does, the program compacts the string by moving the bytes above the deleted area down. The program then determines the new string's length and exits with the Carry cleared if the specified number of bytes were deleted, and with the Carry set to 1 if any errors occurred.

Entry conditions

Order in stack (starting from the top)

High word of return address
Low word of return address

Number of bytes to delete (less than 256)

Starting index to delete from (less than 256)

High word of base address of string
Low word of base address of string

Exit conditions

Substring deleted from string. If no errors occur, the Carry flag is cleared. If the starting index is 0 or beyond the length of the string, the

Carry flag is set and the string is unchanged. If the number of bytes to delete would go beyond the end of the string, the Carry flag is set and the characters from the starting index to the end of the string are deleted.

Examples

1. Data: String = 26'SALES FOR MARCH AND APRIL OF THIS YEAR' ($26_{16} = 38_{10}$ is the length of the string)
Number of bytes to delete = $0A_{16} = 10_{10}$
Starting index to delete from = $10_{16} = 16_{10}$
Result: String = 1C'SALES FOR MARCH OF THIS YEAR' ($1C_{16} = 28_{10}$ is the length of the string with 10 bytes deleted starting with the 16th character—the deleted material is 'AND APRIL ').
Carry = 0, since no problems occurred in the deletion.

2. Data: String = 28'THE PRICE IS \$3.00 (\$2.00 BEFORE JUNE 1)' ($28_{16} = 40_{10}$ is the length of the string).
Number of bytes to delete = $30_{16} = 48_{10}$
Starting index to delete from = $13_{16} = 19_{10}$
Result: String = 12'THE PRICE IS \$3.00' ($12_{16} = 18_{10}$ is the length of the string with all remaining bytes deleted).
Carry = 1, since there were not as many bytes left in the string as were supposed to be deleted.

Registers used A0, A1, CCR, D0, D1, D2

Execution time Approximately 23 × NUMBER OF BYTES MOVED DOWN + 238 cycles overhead if the string must be compacted. This is necessary if the deletion creates a 'hole' in the string that must be filled. NUMBER OF BYTES MOVED DOWN is equal to STRING LENGTH – STARTING INDEX – NUMBER OF BYTES TO DELETE.

228 cycles if the string can simply be truncated (i.e. the deletion continues all the way to the end).

Examples

1. STRING LENGTH = 20_{16} (32_{10})
   STARTING INDEX = 19_{16} (25_{10})
   NUMBER OF BYTES TO DELETE = 08

Since there are exactly 8 bytes left in the string starting at index 19_{16}, all the routine must do is truncate it (i.e. reduce its length). This takes 228 cycles.

2. STRING LENGTH = 40_{16} (64_{10})
   STARTING INDEX = 19_{16} (25_{10})
   NUMBER OF BYTES TO DELETE = 08

Since there are 20_{16} (32_{10}) bytes above the truncated area, the routine must move them down eight positions to fill the 'hole'. Thus NUMBER OF BYTES MOVED DOWN = 32_{10} and the execution time is

$$23 \times 32 + 238 = 736 + 238 = 974 \text{ cycles}$$

Program size 92 bytes

Data memory required 6 stack bytes

Special cases

1. If the number of bytes to delete is 0, the program exits with the Carry flag cleared (no errors) and the string unchanged.

2. If the string does not even extend to the specified starting index, the program exits with the Carry flag set to 1 (indicating an error) and the string unchanged.

3. If the number of bytes to delete exceeds the number available, the program deletes all bytes from the starting index to the end of the string and exits with the Carry flag set to 1 (indicating an error).

```
*       Title                Delete a Substring from a String
*       Name:                DELETE
*
*       Purpose:             Delete a substring from a string given a
*                            starting index and a length.
*
*       Entry:               TOP OF STACK
```

```
*                       High word of return address
*                       Low word byte of return address
*                       Number of bytes to delete (count)
*                       Starting index to delete from (index)
*                       High word of string address
*                       Low word of string address
*
*                       The string consists of a length byte
*                       followed by a maximum of 255 characters.
*
*       Exit:           Substring deleted.
*                       If no errors then
*                         Carry := 0
*                       else
*                         begin
*                           the following conditions cause an
*                           error with Carry = 1.
*                           if (index = 0) or (index > length(string))
*                             then do not change string
*                           if count is too large then
*                             delete only the characters from
*                             index to end of string
*                         end
*
*       Registers Used: A0,A1,CCR,D0,D1,D2
*
*       Time:           Approximately 23 X (LENGTH(STRG)-INDEX-COUNT+1)
*                       plus 238 cycles overhead
*
*       Size:           Program 92 bytes
*                       Data     6 stack bytes
*

DELETE
        *
        *OBTAIN PARAMETERS FROM STACK
        *
        MOVEM.W   4(SP),D0-D1     GET NUMBER OF BYTES TO DELETE,
                                  * STARTING INDEX TO DELETE FROM
        MOVEA.L   8(SP),A0        GET BASE ADDRESS OF STRING
        *
        *EXIT IF COUNT IS ZERO, STARTING INDEX IS ZERO, OR
        *  STARTING INDEX IS BEYOND THE END OF THE STRING
        *
        TST.W     D0              TEST NUMBER OF BYTES TO DELETE
        BEQ.S     OKEXIT          BRANCH (GOOD EXIT) IF NOTHING TO
                                  * DELETE
        TST.W     D1              TEST STARTING INDEX
        BEQ.S     EREXIT          BRANCH (ERROR EXIT) IF STARTING INDEX
                                  * IS ZERO - THAT IS, IN LENGTH BYTE
        CLR.W     D2              CLEAR UPPER BYTE OF STRING LENGTH
        MOVE.B    (A0),D2         GET STRING LENGTH
        CMP.B     D1,D2           CHECK IF STARTING INDEX IS WITHIN
                                  * STRING
        BCS.S     EREXIT          BRANCH (ERROR EXIT) IF STARTING INDEX
                                  * IS BEYOND END OF STRING
```

```
        *
        *CHECK WHETHER NUMBER OF CHARACTERS REQUESTED TO BE
        *  DELETED ARE PRESENT
        *THEY ARE IF STARTING INDEX + NUMBER OF BYTES TO DELETE - 1
        *  IS LESS THAN OR EQUAL TO STRING LENGTH
        *IF NOT, THEN DELETE ONLY TO END OF STRING
        *
        MOVEM.W   D3-D5,-(SP)     SAVE EXTRA DATA REGISTERS IN STACK
        CLR.B     D3              INDICATE NO TRUNCATION NECESSARY
        MOVE.W    D1,D4           COMPUTE STARTING INDEX + COUNT
        ADD.B     D0,D4
        BCS.S     TRUNC           TRUNCATE IF INDEX + COUNT > 255
        SUBQ.W    #1,D4           END OF DELETED AREA IS AT INDEX GIVEN
                                  * BY STARTING INDEX + COUNT - 1
        CMP.W     D2,D4           COMPARE END OF DELETED AREA TO
                                  * STRING LENGTH
        BCS.S     CNTOK           BRANCH IF MORE THAN ENOUGH CHARACTERS
        BEQ.S     TRUNC           TRUNCATE BUT NO ERROR (EXACTLY ENOUGH
                                  * CHARACTERS
        NOT.B     D3              INDICATE ERROR - NOT ENOUGH
                                  * CHARACTERS TO DELETE
        *
        *TRUNCATE THE STRING - NO COMPACTING NECESSARY
        *SIMPLY REDUCE ITS LENGTH TO STARTING INDEX - 1
        *
TRUNC
        SUBQ.W    #1,D1           STRING LENGTH = STARTING INDEX - 1
        MOVE.B    D1,(A0)         SET LENGTH BYTE
        BRA.S     SETERR          EXIT, SETTING CARRY FROM ERROR MARK
        *
        *SET LENGTH OF STRING AFTER DELETION
        *THIS IS ORIGINAL LENGTH MINUS NUMBER OF BYTES TO DELETE
        *
CNTOK
        MOVE.W    D2,D5           GET ORIGINAL STRING LENGTH
        SUB.W     D0,D5           SUBTRACT NUMBER OF BYTES TO DELETE
        MOVE.B    D5,(A0)         SET LENGTH BYTE
        *
        *SET PARAMETERS FOR COMPACTING THE STRING
        *SOURCE POINTER = FIRST BYTE ABOVE DELETED AREA.  THIS IS
        * BASE ADDRESS OF STRING + STARTING INDEX
        * + NUMBER OF BYTES TO DELETE + 1
        *DESTINATION POINTER = FIRST BYTE IN DELETED AREA.  THIS IS
        * BASE ADDRESS OF STRING + STARTING INDEX
        *NUMBER OF BYTES TO MOVE = STRING LENGTH - INDEX OF LAST
        * BYTE IN DELETED AREA
        *
        MOVEA.L   A0,A1           CALCULATE BASE ADDRESS PLUS STARTING
        ADDA.W    D1,A1             INDEX
        ADDA.W    D4,A0           CALCULATE ADDRESS AT END OF DELETED
        ADDQ.W    #1,A0           * AREA
        SUB.W     D4,D2           NUMBER OF CHARACTERS TO MOVE = STRING
                                  * LENGTH - INDEX AT END OF AREA
        SUBQ.W    #1,D2           ADJUST COUNT FOR LOOP EXIT ON -1
        *
        *COMPACT STRING BY MOVING ALL CHARACTERS ABOVE THE
```

```
        *  DELETED AREA DOWN
        *
MOVCHR
        MOVE.B    (A0)+,(A1)+       MOVE CHARACTER DOWN IN STRING
        DBRA      D2,MOVCHR         CONTINUE THROUGH ALL CHARACTERS
        *
        *SET CARRY FROM ERROR INDICATOR
        *REMOVE EXTRA STORAGE FROM STACK
        *
SETERR
        LSR.B     #1,D3             SET CARRY FROM ERROR INDICATOR
        MOVEM.W   (SP)+,D3-D5       RESTORE EXTRA DATA REGISTERS
OKEXIT
        RTS
        *
        *SET CARRY, INDICATING AN ERROR
        *
EREXIT
        MOVE      #1,CCR            SET CARRY, INDICATING ERROR
        RTS

*
*       SAMPLE EXECUTION:
*

SC5E
        PEA       SSTG              PUSH BASE ADDRESS OF STRING
                                    * ONTO STACK
        MOVE.W    (CNT),D0          GET NUMBER OF CHARACTERS TO DELETE
        MOVE.W    (IDX),D1          GET STARTING INDEX FOR DELETION
        MOVEM.W   D0-D1,-(SP)       PUSH PARAMETERS ONTO STACK
        JSR       DELETE            DELETE CHARACTERS
                           *DELETING 4 CHARACTERS STARTING AT INDEX 1
                           * FROM "JOE HANDOVER" LEAVES "HANDOVER"
        BRA.S     SC5E              LOOP THROUGH TEST

*
*DATA SECTION
*
IDX     DC.W      1         STARTING INDEX FOR DELETION
CNT     DC.W      4         NUMBER OF CHARACTERS TO DELETE
SSTG    DC.B      12        LENGTH OF STRING IN BYTES
        DC.B      'JOE HANDOVER' STRING
        END
```

5F Insert a substring into a string (INSERT)

Inserts a substring into a string, given a starting index. The string and substring each consist of at most 256 bytes, including an initial byte containing the length. The Carry flag is cleared if the insertion can be accomplished with no problems. The Carry flag is set if the starting index is 0 or beyond the length of the string. In the second case, the substring is concatenated to the end of the string. The Carry flag is also set if the insertion would make the string exceed a specified maximum length; in that case, the program inserts only enough of the substring to reach the maximum length. These are Pascal-style strings with a length byte, rather than C language-style strings with a terminating character.

Procedure The program exits immediately if the starting index or the length of the substring is 0. If neither is 0, the program checks whether the insertion would make the string longer than the specified maximum. If it would, the program truncates the substring. The program then checks whether the starting index is within the string. If not, the program simply concatenates the substring at the end of the string. If the starting index is within the string, the program must make room for the insertion by moving the remaining characters up in memory. This move must start at the highest address to avoid writing over any data. Finally, the program can move the substring into the open area. The program then determines the new string length. It exits with the Carry flag set to 0 if no problems occurred and to 1 if the starting index was 0, the substring had to be truncated, or the starting index was beyond the length of the string.

Entry conditions

Order in stack (starting from the top)

High word of return address
Low word of return address

Maximum length of string (less than 256)

Starting index at which to insert the substring (less than 256)

High word of base address of substring
Low word of base address of substring

High word of base address of string
Low word of base address of string

Exit conditions

Substring inserted into string. If no errors occur, the Carry flag is cleared. If the starting index or the length of the substring is 0, the Carry flag is set and the string is not changed. If the starting index is beyond the length of the string, the Carry flag is set and the substring is concatenated to the end of the string. If the insertion would make the string exceed its specified maximum length, the Carry flag is set and only enough of the substring is inserted to reach maximum length.

Examples

1. Data: String = 0A'JOHN SMITH' ($0A_{16} = 10_{10}$ is the length of the string)
   Substring = 08'WILLIAM ' (08 is the length of the substring)
   Maximum length of string = $14_{16} = 20_{10}$
   Starting index = 06

   Result: String = 12'JOHN WILLIAM SMITH' ($12_{16} = 18_{10}$ is the length of the string with the substring inserted)
   Carry = 0, since no problems occurred in the insertion

2. Data: String = 0A'JOHN SMITH' ($0A_{16} = 10_{10}$ is the length of the string)
   Substring = 0C'ROCKEFELLER' ($0C_{16} = 12_{10}$ is the length of the substring)
   Maximum length of string = $14_{16} = 20_{10}$
   Starting index = 06

   Result: String = 14'JOHN ROCKEFELLESMITH' ($14_{16} = 20_{10}$ is the length of the string with as much of the substring inserted as the maximum length would allow)
   Carry = 1, since some of the substring could not be inserted without exceeding the maximum length of the string

---

Registers used A0, A1, CCR, D0, D1, D2

Execution time Approximately

$$20 \times \text{NUMBER OF BYTES MOVED} + 20 \times \text{NUMBER OF BYTES INSERTED} + 226 \text{ cycles}$$

NUMBER OF BYTES MOVED is the number of bytes that must be moved to make room for the insertion. If the starting index is beyond the end of the string, this is 0 since the substring is simply placed at the end. Otherwise, this is STRING LENGTH − STARTING INDEX + 1, since the bytes at or above the starting index must be moved.

NUMBER OF BYTES INSERTED is the length of the substring if no truncation occurs. It is the maximum length of the string minus its current length if inserting the substring would produce a string longer than the maximum.

Examples

1. STRING LENGTH = 20_{16} (32_{10})
   STARTING INDEX = 19_{16} (25_{10})
   MAXIMUM LENGTH = 30_{16} (48_{10})
   SUBSTRING LENGTH = 06

That is, we want to insert a substring 6 bytes long, starting at the 25th character. Since 8 bytes must be moved up (NUMBER OF BYTES MOVED = 32 − 25 + 1) and 6 bytes must be inserted, the execution time is approximately

$$20 \times 8 + 20 \times 6 + 226 = 160 + 120 + 226 = 506 \text{ cycles}$$

2. STRING LENGTH = 20_{16} (32_{10})
   STARTING INDEX = 19_{16} (25_{10})
   MAXIMUM LENGTH = 24_{16} (36_{10})
   SUBSTRING LENGTH = 06

As opposed to Example 1, here we can insert only 4 bytes of the substring without exceeding the string's maximum length. Thus NUMBER OF BYTES MOVED = 8 and NUMBER OF BYTES INSERTED = 4. The execution time is approximately

$$20 \times 8 + 20 \times 4 + 226 = 160 + 80 + 226 = 466 \text{ cycles}$$

Program size 118 bytes

Data memory required None

Special cases

1. If the length of the substring (the insertion) is 0, the program exits with the Carry flag cleared (no errors) and the string unchanged.

2. If the starting index for the insertion is 0 (i.e. the insertion would start in the length byte), the program exits with the Carry flag set to 1 (indicating an error) and the string unchanged.

3. If the insertion makes the string exceed the specified maximum length, the program inserts only enough characters to reach the maximum length. The Carry flag is set to 1 to indicate that the insertion has been truncated.

4. If the starting index of the insertion is beyond the end of the string, the program concatenates the insertion at the end of the string and indicates an error by setting the Carry flag to 1.

5. If the original length of the string exceeds its specified maximum length, the program exits with the Carry flag set to 1 (indicating an error) and the string unchanged.

```
*       Title           Insert a Substring into a String
*       Name:           INSERT
*

*       Purpose:        Insert a substring into a string given a
*                       starting index.
*
*       Entry:          TOP OF STACK
*                         High word of return address
*                         Low word of return address
*                         Maximum length of (source) string
*                         Starting index to insert the substring
*                         High word of substring address
*                         Low word of substring address
*                         High word of (source) string address
*                         Low word of (source) string address
*
*                         Each string consists of a length byte
*                         followed by a maximum of 255 characters.
*
*       Exit:           Substring inserted into string.
*                       If no errors then
*                         Carry = 0
*                       else
*                         begin
*                           the following conditions cause the
*                           Carry flag to be set.
```

```
*                               if index = 0 then
*                                 do not insert the substring
*                               if length(string) > maximum length then
*                                 do not insert the substring
*                               if index > length(string) then
*                                 concatenate substring onto the end of the
*                                 source string
*                               if length(string)+length(substring) > maxlen
*                                 then insert only enough of the substring
*                                 to reach maximum length
*                             end
*
*       Registers Used: A0,A1,CCR,D0,D1,D2
*
*       Time:           Approximately
*                       20 X (LENGTH(STRING) - INDEX + 1) +
*                       20 X (LENGTH(SUBSTRING)) +
*                       226 cycles overhead
*
*       Size:           Program 118 bytes

INSERT
        *
        *OBTAIN PARAMETERS FROM STACK
        *
        MOVEM.W  4(SP),D0-D1      GET MAXIMUM LENGTH OF SOURCE STRING,
                                  * STARTING INDEX OF INSERTION
        MOVEM.L  8(SP),A0-A1      GET BASE ADDRESS OF SUBSTRING (A0),
                                  * STRING (A1)
        *
        *EXIT IF SUBSTRING LENGTH IS ZERO OR STARTING INDEX IS
        * ZERO
        *
        TST.W    D1,D1            TEST STARTING INDEX
        ORI      #1,CCR           INDICATE POSSIBLE ERROR BY SETTING
                                  * CARRY FLAG
        BEQ.S    EXITIN           EXIT, INDICATING ERROR, IF STARTING
                                  * INDEX IS ZERO (LENGTH BYTE)
        CLR.W    D2               CLEAR UPPER BYTE OF SUBSTRING LENGTH
        MOVE.B   (A0)+,D2         GET LENGTH OF SUBSTRING
        BEQ.S    EXITIN           EXIT IF NOTHING TO INSERT (NO ERROR)
        *
        *CHECK WHETHER THE STRING WITH THE INSERTION FITS IN THE
        * SOURCE STRING (I.E., IF ITS LENGTH IS LESS THAN OR EQUAL
        * TO THE MAXIMUM.
        *IF NOT, TRUNCATE THE SUBSTRING AND SET THE TRUNCATION FLAG
        *
        MOVEM.W  D3-D5,-(SP)      SAVE EXTRA DATA REGISTERS
        CLR.B    D3               CLEAR ERROR FLAG, ASSUMING NO ERRORS
                                  * IN INSERTION PROCESS
        MOVE.W   D2,D4            GET SUBSTRING LENGTH
        CLR.W    D5               CLEAR UPPER BYTE OF STRING LENGTH
        MOVE.B   (A1),D5          GET STRING LENGTH
        ADD.B    D5,D4            SUBSTRING LENGTH + STRING LENGTH
        BCS.S    TRUNC            TRUNCATE SUBSTRING IF SUM > 255
```

```
        CMP.B    D4,D0          COMPARE TO MAXIMUM STRING LENGTH
        BCC.S    SETLEN         BRANCH IF NEW LENGTH <= MAX LENGTH
*
*SUBSTRING DOES NOT FIT, SO TRUNCATE IT
*THAT IS, ONLY INSERT ENOUGH OF IT TO GIVE THE SOURCE
*  STRING ITS MAXIMUM LENGTH
*
TRUNC
        NOT.B    D3             SET ERROR FLAG TO INDICATE SUBSTRING
                                * WAS TRUNCATED
        MOVE.W   D0,D4          NUMBER OF CHARACTERS TO INSERT =
                                * MAXIMUM LENGTH - STRING LENGTH
        SUB.W    D5,D4
        BLS.S    EREXIT         EXIT, INDICATING ERROR FROM
                                * TRUNCATION IF STRING LENGTH >=
                                * MAXIMUM LENGTH
        MOVE.W   D4,D2          REPLACE SUBSTRING LENGTH WITH NUMBER
                                * OF CHARACTERS TO INSERT
        MOVE.W   D0,D4          NEW LENGTH = MAXIMUM LENGTH
*
*SET LENGTH AFTER INSERTION
*THIS IS OLD LENGTH PLUS NUMBER OF CHARACTERS TO INSERT
*THE VALUE IS EITHER SUBSTRING LENGTH PLUS STRING
*  LENGTH OR MAXIMUM LENGTH.
*
SETLEN  MOVE.B   D4,(A1)        SET NEW STRING LENGTH
*
*SET POINTERS FOR INSERTION
*SOURCE POINTER POINTS TO FIRST CHARACTER IN SUBSTRING
*DESTINATION POINTER POINTS TO CHARACTER AT STARTING
*  INDEX
*
        ADDA.W   D1,A1          POINT TO POSITION AT WHICH FIRST
                                * CHARACTER WILL BE INSERTED
*
*CHECK WHETHER STARTING INDEX IS WITHIN THE STRING.  IF NOT,
*  CONCATENATE SUBSTRING ONTO THE END OF THE STRING
*
        CMP.B    D5,D1          COMPARE STARTING INDEX, STRING LENGTH
        BLS.S    LENOK          BRANCH IF STARTING INDEX IS WITHIN
                                * STRING
        MOVE.W   D5,D1          ELSE SET STARTING INDEX TO END OF
        ADDQ.W   #1,D5            STRING (LENGTH + 1)
        MOVE.B   #$FF,D3        INDICATE ERROR IN INSERT
        BRA.S    MVESUB         JUST PERFORM MOVE, NOTHING TO OPEN UP
*
*OPEN UP A SPACE IN SOURCE STRING FOR THE SUBSTRING BY MOVING
*  THE CHARACTERS FROM THE END OF THE SOURCE STRING DOWN TO
*  INDEX, UP BY NUMBER OF CHARACTERS TO INSERT
*
LENOK
*
*CALCULATE NUMBER OF CHARACTERS TO MOVE
*  COUNT := STRING LENGTH - STARTING INDEX + 1
*
        MOVE.W   D5,D4          GET STRING LENGTH
```

```
        SUB.W     D1,D4              SUBTRACT STARTING INDEX
                                     * +1 BALANCED BY -1 FOR DBRA
        *
        *SET SOURCE AND DESTINATION POINTERS
        *SOURCE POINTER POINTS TO LAST CHARACTER IN STRING
        *DESTINATION POINTER POINTS FURTHER ON BY NUMBER OF
        *  CHARACTERS TO INSERT
        *
        MOVEM.L   A2-A3,-(SP)        SAVE EXTRA ADDRESS REGISTERS
        MOVEA.L   A1,A2
        ADDA.W    D5,A2              CALCULATE ADDRESS AT END OF STRING
        MOVEA.L   A2,A3
        ADDA.W    D4,A3              CALCULATE ADDRESS AT END OF STRING
                                     * WITH INSERTION
        *
        *MOVE CHARACTERS UP IN MEMORY TO MAKE ROOM FOR SUBSTRING
        *
MVUP    MOVE.B    (A2)+,(A3)+        MOVE CHARACTER UP IN MEMORY
        DBRA      D4,MVUP            COUNT CHARACTERS
        MOVEM.L   (SP)+,A2-A3        RESTORE EXTRA ADDRESS REGISTERS
        *
        *MOVE SUBSTRING INTO THE OPEN AREA
        *
MVESUB
        SUBQ.W    #1,D2              COUNT = SUBSTRING LENGTH - 1 TO
                                     * EXIT ON -1
MVCHAR
        MOVE.B    (A0)+,(A1)+        MOVE SUBSTRING INTO OPEN AREA
        DBRA      D2,MVCHAR
        *
        *SET CARRY AS ERROR INDICATOR FROM ERROR FLAG
        *
EREXIT
        LSR.B     #1,D3              SET CARRY FROM ERROR FLAG
        MOVEM.W   (SP)+,D3-D5        RESTORE EXTRA DATA REGISTERS
EXITIN  RTS                          EXIT

*
*       SAMPLE EXECUTION:
*

SC5F
        PEA       STG                PUSH STRING ADDRESS INTO STACK
        PEA       SSTG               PUSH SUBSTRING ADDRESS INTO STACK
        MOVE.W    (MXLEN),D0         GET MAXIMUM LENGTH OF STRING
        MOVE.W    (IDX),D1           GET STARTING INDEX
        MOVEM.W   D0-D1,-(SP)        PUSH PARAMETERS ONTO STACK
        JSR       INSERT             INSERT SUBSTRING
                          *RESULT OF INSERTING '-' INTO '123456' AT
                          * INDEX 1 IS '-123456'
        BRA.S     SC5F               LOOP THROUGH TEST

*
*DATA SECTION
IDX     DC.W      1           STARTING INDEX FOR INSERTION
```

```
MXLEN    DC.W     $20       MAXIMUM LENGTH OF DESTINATION
STG      DC.B     6         LENGTH OF STRING
         DC.B     '123456                           ' 32 BYTE MAX
SSTG     DC.B     1         LENGTH OF SUBSTRING
         DC.B     '-                                ' 32 BYTE MAX

         END
```

5G Remove spaces from a string (SPACES)

Removes excess spaces from a string, including leading spaces, trailing spaces, and extra spaces within the string itself. The string consists of at most 256 bytes, including an initial byte containing the length. This is a Pascal-style string with a length byte, rather than a C language-style string with a terminating character.

Procedure The program exits immediately if the length of the string is 0. Otherwise, it first removes all leading spaces. It then sets a flag whenever it finds a space and deletes all subsequent spaces. If it reaches the end of the string with that flag set, it deletes the final trailing space as well. Finally, it adjusts the string's length.

Entry conditions

Base address of string in register A0

Exit conditions

Excess spaces removed from string. The string is left with no leading or trailing spaces and no groups of consecutive spaces inside it.

Examples

1. Data: String = 0F' JOHN SMITH ' ($0F_{16} = 15_{10}$ is the length of the string)
   Result: String = 0A'JOHN SMITH' ($0A_{16} = 10_{10}$ is the length of the string with the extra spaces removed)

2. Data: String = 1B' PORTLAND, OREGON '($1B_{16} = 27_{10}$ is the length of the string)
   Result: String = 10'PORTLAND, OREGON' ($10_{16} = 16_{10}$ is the length of the string with the extra spaces removed)

Registers used A0, A1, CCR, D0, D1, D2

Execution time Approximately

$$50 \times \text{LENGTH OF STRING IN BYTES} + 140$$

If, for example, the string is 1C hex (28 decimal) bytes long, this is

$$50 \times 28 + 140 = 1400 + 140 = 1540 \text{ cycles}$$

Program size 74 bytes

Data memory required 6 stack bytes

```
*
*       Title               Remove Extra Spaces from a String
*       Name:               SPACES
*

*       Purpose:            Remove leading, trailing, and extra
*                           internal spaces from a string
*
*       Entry:              Register A0 = Base address of string
*
*                             The string consists of a length byte
*                             followed by a maximum of 255 characters.
*
*       Exit:               Leading, trailing, and excess internal
*                           spaces removed
*
*       Registers Used: A0,A1,CCR,D0,D1,D2
*
*       Time:               Approximately
*                            50 X (LENGTH(STRG)) + 140 cycles overhead
*
*       Size:               Program 74 bytes
*                           Data     6 stack bytes
*

SPACES
         *
         *SAVE BASE ADDRESS OF STRING
         *START COMPACTED STRING'S LENGTH AT ZERO
         *INDICATE INITIALLY LAST CHARACTER WAS NOT A SPACE
         *
         MOVE.L    A0,-(SP)   SAVE BASE ADDRESS OF STRING IN STACK
         MOVE.W    D3,-(SP)   SAVE EXTRA DATA REGISTER
         CLR.W     D0         CLEAR UPPER BYTE OF STRING LENGTH
         CLR.W     D1         COMPACTED STRING'S LENGTH = 0
         CLR.B     D2         INDICATE LAST CHARACTER WAS NOT A SPACE
                              *  (D2 = 0)
         *
         *EXIT IF STRING LENGTH IS ZERO
```

```
        *
        MOVE.B    (A0)+,D0  GET STRING LENGTH
        BEQ.S     SETLEN    BRANCH (EXIT) IF STRING LENGTH IS ZERO
        *
        *REMOVE ALL LEADING SPACES
        *
        SUBQ.W    #1,D0     ADJUST COUNT FOR LOOP EXIT ON -1
        MOVEA.L   A0,A1     START POINTERS TO BOTH ORIGINAL, COMPACTED
                            *  STRINGS AT FIRST CHARACTER IN STRING
        MOVE.B    #SPACE,D3 GET SPACE FOR COMPARISON
LEADSP
        CMP.B     (A0)+,D3  EXAMINE NEXT CHARACTER
        BNE.S     TXTCHR    BRANCH IF NEXT CHARACTER NOT A SPACE
        DBRA      D0,LEADSP CONTINUE THROUGH ALL LEADING SPACES
        BRA.S     SETLEN    BRANCH IF ALL CHARACTERS EXAMINED - THIS
                            *  MEANS ALL CHARACTERS WERE SPACES SO
                            *  COMPACTED STRING IS EMPTY
        *
        *WORK THROUGH MAIN PART OF STRING, OMITTING SPACES
        * THAT OCCUR IMMEDIATELY AFTER OTHER SPACES
        *
        *CHECK IF CURRENT CHARACTER IS A SPACE
        *IF SO, CHECK IF PREVIOUS CHARACTER WAS A SPACE
        *IF SO, OMIT CHARACTER FROM COMPACTED STRING
        *IF NOT, MARK CHARACTER AS A SPACE
        *
TXTCHR
        SUBQ.L    #1,A0     GO BACK TO FIRST NON-BLANK CHARACTER
MVCHAR
        MOVE.B    (A0)+,D3  GET NEXT CHARACTER
        CMPI.B    #SPACE,D3 IS IT A SPACE?
        BNE.S     MARKCH    BRANCH IF CHARACTER IS NOT A SPACE
        TST.B     D2        CHECK IF LAST CHARACTER WAS A SPACE
        BNE.S     CNTCHR    BRANCH IF IT WAS, THUS DROPPING A SPACE
                            * THAT OCCURS AFTER ANOTHER SPACE
        NOT.B     D2        INDICATE CURRENT CHARACTER IS A SPACE
        BRA.S     SVCHR     GO SAVE FIRST SPACE
        *
        *INDICATE CURRENT CHARACTER IS NOT A SPACE
        *
MARKCH
        CLR.B     D2        INDICATE CURRENT CHARACTER NOT A SPACE
        *
        *SAVE CURRENT CHARACTER IN COMPACTED STRING
        *
SVCHR
        MOVE.B    D3,(A1)+  SAVE CHARACTER IN COMPACTED STRING
        ADDQ.W    #1,D1     ADD 1 TO LENGTH OF COMPACTED STRING
        *
        *COUNT CHARACTERS
        *
CNTCHR  DBRA      D0,MVCHAR   BRANCH IF ANY CHARACTERS LEFT
        *
        *OMIT LAST CHARACTER IF IT WAS A SPACE
        *
        TST.B     D2        CHECK IF FINAL CHARACTER WAS A SPACE
```

```
        BEQ.S     SETLEN    BRANCH IF IT WAS NOT
        SUBQ.W    #1,D1     OMIT FINAL CHARACTER IF IT WAS A SPACE BY
                            *  REDUCING LENGTH OF COMPACTED STRING
                            *  BY 1
        *
        *SET LENGTH OF COMPACTED STRING
        *
SETLEN
        MOVE.W    (SP)+,D3  RESTORE EXTRA DATA REGISTER
        MOVEA.L   (SP)+,A0  RESTORE BASE ADDRESS OF STRING
        MOVE.B    D1,(A0)   SAVE LENGTH OF COMPACTED STRING
        *
        *EXIT
        *
EXITRE  RTS

*
*CHARACTER DEFINITION
*
SPACE   EQU       $20       ASCII SPACE CHARACTER


*
*       SAMPLE EXECUTION:
*


SC5G
        LEA       STG,A0    GET BASE ADDRESS OF STRING
        JSR       SPACES    REMOVE SPACES
                            *RESULT OF REMOVING EXTRA SPACES FROM
                            * ' JOHN  SMITH  ' IS 'JOHN SMITH'
        BRA.S     SC5G      REPEAT TEST

*
*DATA SECTION
*
STG     DC.B      $0E       LENGTH OF STRING IN BYTES
        DC.B      ' JOHN  SMITH  '   STRING

        END
```

6 Array operations

6A 8-bit array summation (ASUM8)

Adds the 8-bit elements of an array, producing a 16-bit sum.

Procedure The program starts the sum at zero and clears the high byte of a 16-bit register. It then moves elements one at a time to the low byte of the register and adds the register to the sum. This is equivalent to extending each 8-bit element to 16 bits.

Entry conditions

Base address of array in register A0
Size of array in bytes in low word of register D0

Exit conditions

Sum in low word of register D0

Example

Data: Size of array in bytes = (D0) = 0008

Array elements
$F7_{16} = 247_{10}$
$23_{16} = 35_{10}$
$31_{16} = 49_{10}$
$70_{16} = 112_{10}$
$5A_{16} = 90_{10}$
$16_{16} = 22_{10}$
$CB_{16} = 203_{10}$
$E1_{16} = 225_{10}$
Result: Sum = (D0) = $03D7_{16} = 983_{10}$

Registers used A0, CCR, D0, D1, D2

Execution time Approximately 22 cycles per byte-length element plus 48 cycles overhead. If, for example, the array consists of $1C_{16}$ (28_{10}) elements, the execution time is approximately

$$22 \times 28 + 48 = 616 + 48 = 664 \text{ cycles}$$

Program size 22 bytes

Data memory required None

Special case An array size of 0 causes an immediate exit with a sum of 0.

```
*
*
*       Title             8-Bit Array Summation
*       Name:             ASUM8
*
*
*       Purpose:          Sum an array of 8-bit elements,
*                         yielding a 16-bit result.
*
*       Entry:            Register A0 = Base address of array
*                         Register D0 = Size of array in bytes
*
*       Exit:             Register D0 = Sum
*
*       Registers Used:  A0,CCR,D0,D1,D2
*
```

```
*       Time:              Approximately 22 cycles per element plus
*                          48 cycles overhead
*
*       Size:              Program 22 bytes
*
        *
        *TEST ARRAY LENGTH
        *EXIT WITH SUM = 0 IF ARRAY HAS NO ELEMENTS
        *
ASUM8
        CLR.W     D1              START SUM AT ZERO
        CLR.W     D2              CLEAR HIGH BYTE OF ELEMENTS
        TST.W     D0              TEST ARRAY LENGTH
        BEQ.S     EXITAS          BRANCH (EXIT) IF ARRAY LENGTH IS
                                  * ZERO - SUM IS ZERO IN THIS CASE
        *
        *EXTEND 8-BIT ELEMENTS TO 16 BITS WITH HIGH BYTE ALWAYS ZERO
        *ADD EXTENDED ELEMENTS TO 16-BIT SUM
        *
        SUBQ.W    #1,D0           COUNT = ARRAY LENGTH-1 TO EXIT ON -1
SUMLP
        MOVE.B    (A0)+,D2        GET NEXT ELEMENT (HIGH BYTE IS
                                  * ALWAYS ZERO)
        ADD.W     D2,D1           ADD EXTENDED ELEMENT TO SUM
        DBRA      D0,SUMLP        CONTINUE THROUGH ALL ELEMENTS
EXITAS
        MOVE.W    D1,D0           RETURN SUM IN LOW WORD OF D0
        RTS


*
*       SAMPLE EXECUTION
*
*
SC6A
        MOVEA.L   #BUF,A0         GET BASE ADDRESS OF BUFFER
        MOVE.W    (BUFSZ),D0      GET BUFFER SIZE IN BYTES
        JSR       ASUM8           SUM ELEMENTS IN BUFFER
                                  *SUM OF TEST DATA IS 07F8 HEX,
                                  * REGISTER D0 = $07F8
        BRA.S     SC6A            LOOP FOR ANOTHER TEST

*TEST DATA, CHANGE FOR OTHER VALUES
BSIZE   EQU       $10             SIZE OF BUFFER IN BYTES
BUFSZ   DC.W      BSIZE           SIZE OF BUFFER IN BYTES

BUF     DC.B      0               BUFFER
        DC.B      $11             DECIMAL ELEMENTS ARE 0,17,34,51,68
        DC.B      $22             85,102,119,135,153,170,187,204
        DC.B      $33             221,238,255
        DC.B      $44
        DC.B      $55
        DC.B      $66
        DC.B      $77
        DC.B      $88
        DC.B      $99
```

```
DC.B    $AA
DC.B    $BB
DC.B    $CC
DC.B    $DD
DC.B    $EE
DC.B    $FF            SUM = 07F8 (2040 DECIMAL)

END
```

6B 16-Bit array summation (ASUM16)

Adds the 16-bit elements of an array, producing a 32-bit sum. The elements are arranged in the usual 68000 format (more significant byte first).

Procedure The program starts the sum at zero and clears the high word of a 32-bit register. It then moves elements one at a time to the low word of the register and adds the register to the sum. This is equivalent to extending each 16-bit element to 32 bits.

Entry conditions

Base address of array in A0
Size of array in 16-bit words in low word of register D0

Exit conditions

32-bit sum in D0

Example

Data: Size of array (in 16-bit words) = (D0) = 0008
Array elements
$F7A1_{16} = 63\,393_{10}$
$239B_{16} = 9115_{10}$
$31D5_{16} = 12\,757_{10}$
$70F2_{16} = 28\,914_{10}$
$5A36_{16} = 23\,094_{10}$
$166C_{16} = 5740_{10}$
$CBF5_{16} = 52\,213_{10}$
$E107_{16} = 57\,607_{10}$
Result: Sum = $03DBA1_{16} = 252\,833_{10}$

Registers used A0, CCR, D0, D1, D2

Execution time 26 cycles per 16-bit element plus 52 cycles overhead. If, for example, the array consists of 12_{16} (18_{10}) elements, the execution time is

$$26 \times 18 + 52 = 468 + 52 = 520 \text{ cycles}$$

Program size 22 bytes

Data memory required None

Special case An array size of 0 causes an immediate exit with a sum of 0.

```
*
*
*       Title           16-Bit Array Summation
*       Name:           ASUM16
*

*       Purpose:        Sum an array of word-length (16-bit)
*                       elements, yielding a 32-bit result.
*
*       Entry:          Register A0 = Base address of array
*                       Register D0 = Size of array (in 16-bit words)
*
*       Exit:           Register D0 = 32-bit sum
*
*       Registers Used: A0,CCR,D0,D1,D2
*
*       Time:           Approximately 26 cycles per element plus
*                       52 cycles overhead
*
*       Size:           Program 22 bytes
*
*

ASUM16
         *
         *TEST ARRAY LENGTH
         *EXIT WITH SUM = 0 IF ARRAY HAS NO ELEMENTS
         *
         CLR.L     D1              START 32-BIT SUM AT ZERO
         CLR.L     D2              CLEAR HIGH WORD OF ELEMENTS
         TST.W     D0              TEST ARRAY LENGTH
         BEQ.S     EXITS1          BRANCH (EXIT) IF ARRAY LENGTH IS
                                   * ZERO - SUM IS ZERO IN THIS CASE
         *
         *EXTEND 16-BIT ELEMENTS TO 32 BITS WITH HIGH WORD ALWAYS ZERO
```

```
        *ADD EXTENDED ELEMENTS TO 32-BIT SUM
        *
        SUBQ.W    #1,D0          COUNT = ARRAY LENGTH-1 TO EXIT ON -1
SUMLP   MOVE.W    (A0)+,D2       GET NEXT ELEMENT (UPPER WORD IS
                                 * ALWAYS ZERO)
        ADD.L     D2,D1          ADD EXTENDED ELEMENT TO SUM
        DBRA      D0,SUMLP       CONTINUE THROUGH ALL ELEMENTS
        *
        *EXIT
        *
EXITS1
        MOVE.L    D1,D0          RETURN 32-BIT SUM IN D0
        RTS

*
*       SAMPLE EXECUTION
*

*
SC6B
        MOVEA.L   #BUF,A0        GET BASE ADDRESS OF BUFFER
        MOVE.W    (BUFSZ),D0     GET SIZE OF BUFFER IN WORDS
        JSR       ASUM16         SUM WORD-LENGTH ELEMENTS IN BUFFER
                                 * SUM OF TEST DATA IS 31FF8 HEX,
                                 * REGISTER D0 = $00031FF8
        BRA.S     SC6B           LOOP FOR ANOTHER TEST

*TEST DATA, CHANGE FOR OTHER VALUES
BSIZE   EQU       $10                    SIZE OF BUFFER IN WORDS
BUFSZ   DC.W      BSIZE          SIZE OF BUFFER IN WORDS

BUF     DC.W      0              BUFFER
        DC.W      $111           DECIMAL ELEMENTS ARE 0,273,546,819,1092
        DC.W      $222           1365,1638,1911,2184,2457,2730,3003,3276
        DC.W      $333           56797,61166,65535
        DC.W      $444
        DC.W      $555
        DC.W      $666
        DC.W      $777
        DC.W      $888
        DC.W      $999
        DC.W      $AAA
        DC.W      $BBB
        DC.W      $CCC
        DC.W      $DDDD
        DC.W      $EEEE
        DC.W      $FFFF          SUM = $31FF8 (204792 DECIMAL)

        END
```

6C Find maximum byte-length element (MAXELM)

Finds the maximum value in an array of unsigned 8-bit elements.

Procedure The program exits immediately (setting Carry to 1) if the array has no elements. Otherwise, the program assumes that the element at the base address is the maximum. It then works through the array, comparing the supposed maximum with each element and retaining the larger value and its address. Finally, the program clears Carry to indicate a valid result.

Entry conditions

Base address of array in register A0
Size of array in bytes in low word of register D0

Exit conditions

Largest unsigned element in low byte of register D0
Address of largest unsigned element in register A0

Carry = 0 if result is valid, 1 if size of array is 0 and result is meaningless.

Example

Data: Size of array (in bytes) = (D0) = 0008
Array elements
$35_{16} = 53_{10}$ $44_{16} = 68_{10}$
$A6_{16} = 166_{10}$ $59_{16} = 89_{10}$
$D2_{16} = 210_{10}$ $7A_{16} = 122_{10}$
$1B_{16} = 27_{10}$ $CF_{16} = 207_{10}$
Result: The largest unsigned element is element 2 ($D2_{16} = 210_{10}$)
(D0) = largest element ($D2_{16}$)
(A0) = BASE + 2 (lowest address containing $D2_{16}$)
Carry = 0, indicating that array size is non-zero and the result is valid.

Registers used A0, A1, CCR, D0, D1, D2

Execution time Approximately 30–54 cycles per element plus 52 cycles overhead. The larger number is necessary when the program replaces the presumed maximum value with the current element. If, on average, this occurs in half of the iterations, the execution time is approximately

$$(30 + 54) \times \text{ARRAY SIZE}/2 + 52 \text{ cycles}$$

If, for example, ARRAY SIZE = $18_{16} = 24_{10}$ bytes, the approximate execution time is

$$84 \times 12 + 52 = 1008 + 52 = 1060 \text{ cycles}$$

Program size 32 bytes

Data memory required None

Special cases

1. An array size of 0 causes an immediate exit with Carry set to 1 to indicate an invalid result.

2. If the largest unsigned value occurs more than once, the program returns with the lowest possible address. That is, it returns with the address closest to the base address that contains the maximum value.

```
*
*
*       Title           Find Maximum Byte-Length Element
*       Name:           MAXELM
*
*
*       Purpose:        Given the base address and size of an array,
*                       find the largest element.
*
*       Entry:          Register A0 = Base address of array
*                       Register D0 = Size of array in bytes
*
*       Exit:           If size of array not zero then
*                         Carry = 0
*                         Register D0 = Largest element
*                         Register A0 = Address of that element
```

```
*                           If there are duplicate values of the largest
*                           element, register A0 contains the address
*                           nearest to the base address.
*                        else
*                          Carry = 1
*
*       Registers Used: A0,A1,CCR,D0,D1
*
*       Time:            Approximately 30 to 54 cycles per byte
*                        plus 52 cycles overhead
*
*       Size:            Program 32 bytes
*
*

MAXELM
        *
        *EXIT WITH CARRY SET IF NO ELEMENTS IN ARRAY
        *
        TST.W   D0          TEST NUMBER OF ELEMENTS IN ARRAY
        ORI     #1,CCR      SET CARRY IN CASE NO ELEMENTS IN
                            * ARRAY
        BEQ.S   EXITMX      BRANCH (EXIT) WITH CARRY SET IF NO
                            * ELEMENTS - INDICATES INVALID RESULT
        *
        *EXAMINE ELEMENTS ONE AT A TIME, COMPARING EACH ONE'S VALUE
        * WITH CURRENT MAXIMUM AND ALWAYS KEEPING LARGER VALUE AND
        * ITS ADDRESS.  IN THE FIRST ITERATION, TAKE THE FIRST
        * ELEMENT AS THE CURRENT MAXIMUM.
        *
        ADDQ.L  #1,A0       SET POINTER AS IF PROGRAM HAD JUST
                            * EXAMINED THE FIRST ELEMENT AND FOUND
                            * IT TO BE LARGER THAN PREVIOUS MAXIMUM
MAXLP
        LEA     -1(A0),A1 SAVE ADDRESS OF ELEMENT JUST EXAMINED
                            * AS ADDRESS OF MAXIMUM
        MOVE.B  (A1),D1     SAVE ELEMENT JUST EXAMINED AS MAXIMUM
        *
        *COMPARE CURRENT ELEMENT TO MAXIMUM
        *KEEP LOOKING UNLESS CURRENT ELEMENT IS LARGER
        *
MAXLP1
        SUBQ.W  #1,D0       COUNT ELEMENTS
        BEQ.S   EXITLP      BRANCH (EXIT) IF ALL ELEMENTS EXAMINED
        CMP.B   (A0)+,D1    COMPARE CURRENT ELEMENT TO MAXIMUM
                            * ALSO MOVE POINTER TO NEXT ELEMENT
        BCC.S   MAXLP1      CONTINUE UNLESS CURRENT ELEMENT LARGER
        BCS.S   MAXLP       ELSE CHANGE MAXIMUM
                            *TO RETURN LAST OCCURRENCE RATHER THAN
                            * FIRST OCCURRENCE, CHANGE THE CONDITIONAL
                            * BRANCHES TO BHI AND BLS. NOTE: BCS HERE
                            * IS EQUIVALENT TO BRA, SINCE BCC PRECEDES
                            * IT.
        *
        *MOVE RESULTS FOR PROPER RETURN.  THESE MOVES ALSO
        * CLEAR CARRY TO INDICATE VALID RESULT - MAXIMUM FOUND
```

```
        *
EXITLP
        MOVE.B    D1,D0       RETURN MAXIMUM IN D0
        MOVEA.L   A1,A0       RETURN ADDRESS OF MAXIMUM IN A0
EXITMX  RTS

*
*       SAMPLE EXECUTION:
*

SC6C
        MOVEA.L   #ARY,A0     GET BASE ADDRESS OF ARRAY
        MOVE.W    #SZARY,D0   GET SIZE OF ARRAY IN BYTES
        JSR       MAXELM      FIND LARGEST UNSIGNED ELEMENT
                              *RESULT FOR TEST DATA IS
                              * D0 = FF HEX (MAXIMUM), A0 = ADDRESS OF
                              * FF IN ARY.
        BRA.S     SC6C        LOOP FOR MORE TESTING

SZARY   EQU       $10         SIZE OF ARRAY IN BYTES
ARY     DC.B      8
        DC.B      7
        DC.B      6
        DC.B      5
        DC.B      4
        DC.B      3
        DC.B      2
        DC.B      1
        DC.B      $FF
        DC.B      $FE
        DC.B      $FD
        DC.B      $FC
        DC.B      $FB
        DC.B      $FA
        DC.B      $F9
        DC.B      $F8

        END
```

6D Find minimum byte-length element (MINELM)

Finds the minimum value in an array of unsigned 8-bit elements.

Procedure The program exits immediately (setting Carry to 1) if the array has no elements. Otherwise, the program assumes that the element at the base address is the minimum. It then works through the array, comparing the current minimum to each element and retaining the smaller value and its address. Finally, the program clears Carry to indicate a valid result.

Entry conditions

Base address of array in register A0
Size of array in bytes in low word of register D0

Exit conditions

Smallest unsigned element in low byte of register D0
Address of smallest unsigned element in register A0
Carry = 0 if result is valid, 1 if size of array is 0 and result is meaningless.

Example

Data: Size of array (in bytes) = (D0) = 0008

Array elements

$35_{16} = 53_{10}$ $44_{16} = 68_{10}$
$A6_{16} = 166_{10}$ $59_{16} = 89_{10}$
$D2_{16} = 210_{10}$ $7A_{16} = 122_{10}$
$1B_{16} = 27_{10}$ $CF_{16} = 207_{10}$

Result: The smallest unsigned element is element 3 ($1B_{16} = 27_{10}$)
(D0) = smallest element ($1B_{16}$)
(A0) = BASE + 3 (lowest address containing $1B_{16}$)
Carry= 0, indicating that array size is non-zero and the result is valid.

Registers used A0, A1, CCR, D0, D1

Execution time Approximately 30 to 54 cycles per element plus 52 cycles overhead. The larger number applies when the program replaces the presumed minimum value with the current element. If, on the average, this occurs in half of the iterations, the execution time is approximately

$$(30 + 54) \times \text{ARRAY SIZE}/2 + 52 \text{ cycles}$$

If, for example, ARRAY SIZE = $14_{16} = 20_{10}$, the approximate execution time is

$$84 \times 10 + 52 = 840 + 52 = 892 \text{ cycles}$$

Program size 32 bytes

Data memory required None

Special cases

1. An array size of 0 causes an immediate exit with Carry set to 1 to indicate an invalid result.

2. If the smallest unsigned value occurs more than once, the program returns with the lowest possible address. That is, it returns with the address closest to the base address that contains the minimum value.

```
*
*
*       Title               Find Minimum Byte-Length Element
*       Name:               MINELM
*
*
*       Purpose:            Given the base address and size of an array,
*                           find the smallest element
*
*       Entry:              Register A0 = Base address of array
*                           Register D0 = Size of array in bytes
*
*       Exit:               If size of array not zero then
*                             Carry = 0
*                             Register D0 = Smallest element
*                             Register A0 = Address of that element
*                              If there are duplicate values of the smallest
*                              element, register A0 contains the address
*                              nearest to the base address.
*                           else
```

```
*                       Carry = 1
*
*       Registers Used: A0,A1,CCR,D0,D1
*
*       Time:           Approximately 30 to 54 cycles per byte
*                       plus 52 cycles overhead
*
*       Size:           Program 32 bytes
*
MINELM
        *
        *EXIT WITH CARRY SET IF ARRAY CONTAINS NO ELEMENTS
        *
        TST.W     D0         TEST NUMBER OF ELEMENTS IN ARRAY
        ORI       #1,CCR     SET CARRY IN CASE NO ELEMENTS IN ARRAY
        BEQ.S     EXITMN     BRANCH (EXIT) WITH CARRY SET IF NO
                             * ELEMENTS - INDICATES INVALID RESULT
        *
        *EXAMINE ELEMENTS ONE AT A TIME, COMPARING EACH VALUE WITH
        * THE CURRENT MINIMUM AND ALWAYS KEEPING THE SMALLER VALUE
        * AND ITS ADDRESS.  IN THE FIRST ITERATION, TAKE THE FIRST
        * ELEMENT AS THE CURRENT MINIMUM.
        *
        ADDQ.L    #1,A0      SET POINTER AS IF PROGRAM HAD JUST
                             * EXAMINED THE FIRST ELEMENT AND FOUND
                             * IT TO BE SMALLER THAN PREVIOUS MINIMUM
MINLP
        LEA       -1(A0),A1  SAVE ADDRESS OF ELEMENT JUST EXAMINED
                             * AS ADDRESS OF MINIMUM
        MOVE.B    (A1),D1    SAVE ELEMENT JUST EXAMINED AS MINIMUM
        *
        *COMPARE CURRENT ELEMENT TO SMALLEST
        *KEEP LOOKING UNLESS CURRENT ELEMENT IS SMALLER
        *
MINLP1
        SUBQ.W    #1,D0      COUNT ELEMENTS
        BEQ.S     EXITLP     BRANCH (EXIT) IF ALL ELEMENTS EXAMINED
        CMP.B     (A0)+,D1   COMPARE CURRENT ELEMENT TO MINIMUM
                             * ALSO MOVE POINTER TO NEXT ELEMENT
        BLS.S     MINLP1     CONTINUE UNLESS CURRENT ELEMENT SMALLER
        BHI.S     MINLP      ELSE CHANGE MINIMUM
                             *TO RETURN LAST OCCURRENCE RATHER THAN
                             * FIRST OCCURRENCE, CHANGE THE CONDITIONAL
                             * BRANCHES TO BCS AND BCC. NOTE: BHI IS
                             * EQUIVALENT TO BRA HERE, SINCE BLS
                             * PRECEDES IT
        *
        *MOVE RESULTS FOR PROPER RETURN.  THESE MOVES ALSO
        * CLEAR CARRY TO INDICATE VALID RESULT - MINIMUM FOUND
        *
EXITLP
        MOVE.B    D1,D0      RETURN MINIMUM IN D0
        MOVEA.L   A1,A0      RETURN ADDRESS OF MINIMUM IN A0
EXITMN
        RTS
```

```
*
*         SAMPLE EXECUTION:
*

SC6D
          MOVEA.L   #ARY,A0    GET BASE ADDRESS OF ARRAY
          MOVE.W    #SZARY,D0  GET SIZE OF ARRAY IN BYTES
          JSR       MINELM     FIND MINIMUM VALUE IN ARRAY
                               *RESULT FOR TEST DATA IS
                               * D0 = 1 HEX (MINIMUM), A0 = ADDRESS OF
                               * 1 IN ARY.
          BRA.S     SC6D       LOOP FOR ANOTHER TEST

SZARY     EQU       $10        SIZE OF ARRAY IN BYTES
ARY       DC.B      8
          DC.B      7
          DC.B      6
          DC.B      5
          DC.B      4
          DC.B      3
          DC.B      2
          DC.B      1
          DC.B      $FF
          DC.B      $FE
          DC.B      $FD
          DC.B      $FC
          DC.B      $FB
          DC.B      $FA
          DC.B      $F9
          DC.B      $F8

          END
```

6E Binary search (BINSCH)

Searches an array of unsigned 8-bit elements for a value. The elements are assumed to be arranged in ascending order. Clears Carry if it finds the value and sets Carry to 1 if it does not. Returns the address of the value if found.

Procedure The program searches by repeatedly comparing the value with the middle remaining element. After each comparison, it discards the part of the array that cannot contain the value (because of the ordering). The program retains upper and lower bounds for the part still being searched. If the value is larger than the middle element, the program discards that element and everything below it. The new lower bound is the address of the middle element plus 1. If the value is smaller than the middle element, the program discards that element and everything above it. The new upper bound is the address of the middle element minus 1. The program exits if it finds a match or if there is nothing left to search.

For example, assume that the array is

$$01_{16}, 02_{16}, 05_{16}, 07_{16}, 09_{16}, 09_{16}, 0D_{16}, 10_{16}, 2E_{16}, 37_{16}, 5D_{16}, 7E_{16}, A1_{16}, B4_{16}, D7_{16}, E0_{16}$$

and the value being sought is $0D_{16}$. The procedure works as follows.

In the first iteration, the lower bound is the base address and the upper bound is the address of the last element. So we have

$$\begin{aligned}\text{LOWER BOUND} &= \text{BASE}\\ \text{UPPER BOUND} &= \text{BASE} + \text{LENGTH} - 1 = \text{BASE} + 0F_{16}\\ \text{GUESS} &= (\text{UPPER BOUND} + \text{LOWER BOUND})/2\\ &= \text{BASE} + 7 \text{ (the result is truncated)}\\ (\text{GUESS}) &= \text{ARRAY}(7) = 10_{16} = 16_{10}\end{aligned}$$

Since the value ($0D_{16}$) is less than ARRAY(7), we can discard the elements beyond #6. So we have

$$\begin{aligned}\text{LOWER BOUND} &= \text{BASE}\\ \text{UPPER BOUND} &= \text{GUESS} - 1 = \text{BASE} + 6\\ \text{GUESS} &= (\text{UPPER BOUND} + \text{LOWER BOUND})/2\\ &= \text{BASE} + 3\\ (\text{GUESS}) &= \text{ARRAY}(3) = 07\end{aligned}$$

Since the value ($0D_{16}$) is greater than ARRAY(3), we can discard the elements below #4. So we have

LOWER BOUND = GUESS + 1 = BASE + 4
UPPER BOUND = BASE + 6
GUESS = (UPPER BOUND + LOWER BOUND)/2
= BASE + 5
(GUESS) = ARRAY(5) = 09

Since the value ($0D_{16}$) is greater than ARRAY(5), we can discard the elements below #6. So we have

LOWER BOUND = GUESS + 1 = BASE + 6
UPPER BOUND = BASE + 6
GUESS = (UPPER BOUND + LOWER BOUND)/2
= BASE + 6
(GUESS) = ARRAY(6) = $0D_{16}$

Since the value ($0D_{16}$) is equal to ARRAY(6), we have found the element. If, on the other hand, the value were $0E_{16}$, the new lower bound would be BASE + 7 and there would be nothing left to search.

Entry conditions

Order in stack (starting from the top)

High word of return address
Low word of return address

Value to find (less than 256)
Size of array in bytes

High word of base address of array (address of smallest unsigned element)
Low word of base address of array (address of smallest unsigned element)

Exit conditions

Carry = 0 if the value is found, 1 if it is not found.
If the value is found, (A0) = its address.

Examples

Length of array = $10_{16} = 16_{10}$
Elements of array are 01_{16}, 02_{16}, 05_{16}, 07_{16}, 09_{16}, 09_{16}, $0D_{16}$, 10_{16}, $2E_{16}$,

37_{16}, $5D_{16}$, $7E_{16}$, $A1_{16}$, $B4_{16}$, $D7_{16}$, $E0_{16}$

1. Data: Value to find = $0D_{16}$
   Result: Carry = 0, indicating value found
   (A0) = BASE + 6 (address containing $0D_{16}$)

2. Data: Value to find = $9B_{16}$
   Result: Carry = 1, indicating value not found

Registers used A0, A1, CCR, D0, D1, D2

Execution time Approximately 107 cycles per iteration plus 135 cycles overhead. A binary search takes on the order of $\log_2 N$ iterations, where N is the number of elements in the array.

If, for example, $N = 32$, the binary search takes about $\log_2 32 = 5$ iterations. The execution time is then approximately

$$107 \times 5 + 135 = 535 + 135 = 670 \text{ cycles}$$

Program size 74 bytes

Data memory required 4 stack bytes

Special case A size of 0 causes an immediate exit with Carry set to 1. That is, the array contains no elements and the value surely cannot be found.

```
*
*
*       Title           Binary Search
*       Name:           BINSCH
*
*
*       Purpose:        Search an ordered array of unsigned bytes,
*                       with a maximum size of 65,535 elements.
*
*
*       Entry:          TOP OF STACK
*                         High word of return address
*                         Low word of return address
*                         Value to find (less than 256)
*                         Length (size) of array in bytes
*                         High word of base address of array
```

```
*                     Low word of base address of array
*
*       Exit:         If the value is found then
*                       Carry = 0
*                       Register A0 = Address of value
*                     Else
*                       Carry = 1
*
*       Registers Used: A0,A1,CCR,D0,D1
*
*       Time:         Approximately 107 cycles per iteration of
*                     the search loop plus 135 cycles overhead
*
*                     A binary search takes on the order of log
*                     base 2 of N iterations, where N is the number of
*                     elements in the array.
*
*       Size:         Program 74 bytes
*                     Data     4 stack bytes
*

*
BINSCH
        *
        *OBTAIN PARAMETERS FROM STACK
        *
        MOVEM.W   4(SP),D0-D1      GET VALUE TO FIND (D0), SIZE OF
                                   * ARRAY IN BYTES (D1)
        MOVEA.L   8(SP),A1         GET BASE ADDRESS OF ARRAY
        *
        *EXIT INDICATING VALUE NOT FOUND IF ARRAY CONTAINS NO ELEMENTS
        *
        TST.W     D1               CHECK NUMBER OF ELEMENTS
        ORI       #1,CCR           SET CARRY IN CASE ARRAY HAS NO
                                   * ELEMENTS
        BEQ       EXITBI           BRANCH (EXIT) IF NO ELEMENTS
                                   * VALUE SURELY CANNOT BE FOUND
        *
        *INITIALIZE UPPER AND LOWER BOUNDS FOR SEARCH
        *LOWER BOUND = BASE ADDRESS
        *UPPER BOUND = ADDRESS OF LAST ELEMENT =
        * BASE ADDRESS + SIZE - 1
        *
        MOVE.L    A2,-(SP)         SAVE EXTRA ADDRESS REGISTER IN STACK
        LEA       -1(A1,D1.W),A2   GET ADDRESS OF LAST ELEMENT
        *
        *ITERATION OF BINARY SEARCH
        *1) COMPARE VALUE TO MIDDLE ELEMENT
        *2) IF THEY ARE NOT EQUAL, DISCARD HALF THAT
        *   CANNOT POSSIBLY CONTAIN VALUE (BECAUSE OF ORDERING)
        *3) CONTINUE IF THERE IS ANYTHING LEFT TO SEARCH
        *
SRLOOP
        MOVE.L    A1,D2            GET LOWER BOUND
                                   *MUST USE DATA REGISTER TO DIVIDE SUM
                                   * AND CARRY BY 2.  THIS CANNOT BE
```

```
                                  * DONE IN AN ADDRESS REGISTER
        ADD.L     A2,D2           ADD UPPER BOUND.  NOTE THIS COULD
                                  * PRODUCE A CARRY (IN EXTEND FLAG)
        ROXR.L    #1,D2           DIVIDE SUM (INCLUDING EXTEND FLAG) BY
                                  * 2 TO FIND ADDRESS OF MIDDLE ELEMENT
        BCC.S     CHKMID          BRANCH IF NO CARRY
        ADDQ.L    #1,D2           ELSE ROUND UPWARD BY ADDING CARRY TO
                                  * QUOTIENT
        *
        *IF ADDRESS OF MIDDLE ELEMENT IS GREATER THAN UPPER BOUND,
        * THEN ELEMENT IS NOT IN ARRAY
        *
CHKMID
        MOVEA.L   D2,A0           MOVE ADDRESS TO ADDRESS REGISTER
        CMPA.L    A2,A0           COMPARE ADDRESS OF MIDDLE ELEMENT TO
                                  * UPPER BOUND
        BHI.S     NOTFND          BRANCH (NOT FOUND) IF ADDRESS ABOVE
                                  * UPPER BOUND
        *
        *IF ADDRESS OF MIDDLE ELEMENT IS LESS THAN LOWER BOUND, THEN
        * ELEMENT IS NOT IN ARRAY
        *
        CMPA.L    A1,A0           COMPARE ADDRESS OF MIDDLE ELEMENT TO
                                  * LOWER BOUND
        BCS.S     NOTFND          BRANCH (NOT FOUND) IF ADDRESS BELOW
                                  * LOWER BOUND
        *
        *CHECK IF MIDDLE ELEMENT IS THE VALUE BEING SOUGHT
        *
        CMP.B     (A0),D0         COMPARE ELEMENT WITH VALUE SOUGHT
        BHI.S     RPLCLW          BRANCH IF VALUE LARGER THAN ELEMENT
        BEQ.S     FOUND           BRANCH IF VALUE FOUND
                                  *NOTE CARRY = 0 IN THIS CASE
                                  *CHECK FOR EXACT MATCH LAST SINCE
                                  * SUCCESS IS UNLIKELY
        *
        *VALUE IS SMALLER THAN ELEMENT AT MIDDLE ADDRESS
        *MAKE MIDDLE ADDRESS - 1 INTO NEW UPPER BOUND
        *
        SUBQ.L    #1,A0           SUBTRACT 1 SINCE VALUE MUST BE
                                  * FURTHER DOWN IN ARRAY
        MOVEA.L   A0,A2           SAVE MIDDLE ADDRESS - 1 AS UPPER
                                  * BOUND
        BRA.S     SRLOOP          CONTINUE SEARCHING
        *
        *VALUE IS LARGER THAN ELEMENT AT MIDDLE ADDRESS
        *MAKE MIDDLE ADDRESS + 1 INTO NEW LOWER BOUND
        *
RPLCLW
        ADDQ.L    #1,A0           ADD 1 SINCE VALUE MUST BE
                                  * FURTHER UP IN ARRAY
        MOVEA.L   A0,A1           SAVE MIDDLE ADDRESS + 1 AS LOWER
                                  * BOUND
        BRA.S     SRLOOP          CONTINUE SEARCHING
        *
        *EXIT WITH CARRY INDICATING SUCCESS OR FAILURE
```

```
        *
NOTFND
        ORI         #1,CCR          SET CARRY, INDICATING VALUE NOT FOUND
FOUND
        MOVEA.L     (SP)+,A2        RESTORE EXTRA ADDRESS REGISTER
EXITBI
        MOVEA.L     (SP)+,A1        GET RETURN ADDRESS
        ADDQ.L      #8,SP           REMOVE PARAMETERS FROM STACK
        JMP         (A1)            EXIT TO RETURN ADDRESS

*
*       SAMPLE EXECUTION
*

*
SC6E
        *SEARCH FOR A VALUE THAT IS IN THE ARRAY
        PEA         BUFFER          PUSH BASE ADDRESS OF ARRAY INTO STACK
        MOVE.W      (BUFSZ),D1      GET ARRAY SIZE IN BYTES
        MOVE.W      #7,D0           GET VALUE TO FIND
        MOVEM.W     D0-D1,-(SP)     PUSH PARAMETERS INTO STACK
        JSR         BINSCH          BINARY SEARCH
                                    * CARRY = 0 (VALUE FOUND)
                                    * A0 = ADDRESS OF 7 IN ARRAY
                                    * (BUFFER + 4)

        *SEARCH FOR A VALUE THAT IS NOT IN THE ARRAY
        PEA         BUFFER          PUSH BASE ADDRESS OF ARRAY INTO STACK
        MOVE.L      (BUFSZ),D1      GET ARRAY SIZE IN BYTES
        MOVE.W      #0,D0           GET VALUE TO FIND (ZERO)
        MOVEM.W     D0-D1,-(SP)     PUSH PARAMETERS INTO STACK
        JSR         BINSCH          BINARY SEARCH
                                    * CARRY = 1 (VALUE NOT FOUND)
        BRA.S       SC6E            LOOP FOR MORE TESTS
*
*DATA
*
BSIZE   EQU         $10       SIZE OF BUFFER IN BYTES
BUFSZ   DC.W        BSIZE     SIZE OF BUFFER IN BYTES
BUFFER  DC.B        1         BUFFER
        DC.B        2
        DC.B        4
        DC.B        5
        DC.B        7
        DC.B        9
        DC.B        10
        DC.B        11
        DC.B        23
        DC.B        50
        DC.B        81
        DC.B        123
        DC.B        191
        DC.B        199
        DC.B        250
        DC.B        255

        END
```

6F Shell sort (SSORT)

Arranges an array of unsigned word-length elements into ascending order using a Shell sort. Each iteration sorts a subset of the array consisting of elements separated by a gap or increment. A Shell sort is intermediate in efficiency between a crude insertion or bubble sort and a quicksort.

Procedure The program first deals with subsets of the array consisting of elements separated by a large gap. It then reduces the size of the gap between elements until it reaches 1. The idea here is that sorting subsets puts most elements in the proper order by the time the entire array has to be handled. Shell's method is efficient because later sorts (with smaller gaps) never undo the ordering of earlier sorts (with larger gaps). This has been proved mathematically.

The program follows Shell's original suggestion of starting with a gap one-half the size of the array and dividing it in half (with truncation) after each iteration. Knuth (see the references) describes other methods of generating gaps; since none has been proved to be superior in all cases, we have chosen the simplest approach.

Entry conditions

Base address of array in A0
Number of elements in low word of D0

Exit conditions

Array sorted into ascending order, considering the elements as unsigned words. Thus, the smallest unsigned word ends up stored starting at the base address.

Example

Data: Array size = $0C_{16} = 12_{10}$
Elements = $2B_{16}$, 57_{16}, $1D_{16}$, 26_{16},
22_{16}, $2E_{16}$, $0C_{16}$, 44_{16},
17_{16}, $4B_{16}$, 37_{16}, 27_{16}.

Result: In the first iteration, the step is size/2 = 6
Ordering elements separated by 6 gives:
$0C_{16}$, 44_{16}, 17_{16}, 26_{16},
22_{16}, 27_{16}, $2B_{16}$, 57_{16},
$1D_{16}$, $4B_{16}$, 37_{16}, $2E_{16}$
In the second iteration, the step is half the previous step (3)
Ordering elements separated by 3 gives:
$0C_{16}$, 22_{16}, 17_{16}, 26_{16},
37_{16}, $1D_{16}$, $2B_{16}$, 44_{16},
27_{16}, $4B_{16}$, 57_{16}, $2E_{16}$
In the third iteration, the step is half the previous step with truncation (1)
Finally, ordering elements separated by 1 gives:
$0C_{16}$, 17_{16}, $1D_{16}$, 22_{16},
26_{16}, 27_{16}, $2B_{16}$, $2E_{16}$,
37_{16}, 44_{16}, $4B_{16}$, 57_{16}

References

D. E. Knuth, *The Art of Computer Programming. Volume 3: Searching and Sorting*, Addison-Wesley, Reading, MA, 1973, pp. 84–95.

Y. Langsam *et al.*, *Data Structures for Personal Computers*, Prentice-Hall, Englewood Cliffs, NJ, 1985, pp. 459–462. The algorithms in this book are available as BASIC programs on disk for various computers. Other versions of the book are available for PL/I and Pascal.

Registers used A0, A1, CCR, D0, D1, D2

Execution time Approximately 72 cycles per comparison. The number of comparisons has been proved to be proportional to $N \times (\log_2 N)^2$ where N is the number of elements. In practice, the program took the following amounts of time on an Atari 520ST based on an 8 MHz 68000 chip:

2 s for 8K words
4 s for 16K words
6 s for 24K words

Program size 70 bytes

Data memory required 20 stack bytes

```
*       Title           Shell sort
*       Name:           SSORT
*
*       Purpose:        Arrange an array of unsigned words into
*                       ascending order using a Shell sort
*
*       Entry:          Base address of array in register A0
*                       Size of array in words in low word of
*                       register D0
*
*       Exit:           Array sorted into ascending order.
*
*       Registers Used: A0,A1,CCR,D0,D1,D2
*
*       Time:           Approximately 72 cycles per comparison.
*                       The number of comparisons is proportional to
*                       N X (log N)^2 where N is the size of the array.
*
*                       For example, sorting a 16,384-word array took
*                       about 4 s on an Atari 520ST with an 8 MHz 68000.
*
*       Size:           Program 70 bytes
*                       Data    20 stack bytes
*

*
*
SSORT
          *
          *EXIT IF NO SORTING NECESSARY (LESS THAN 2 ELEMENTS
          *  IN ARRAY)
          *
          CMPI.W    #2,D0          EXIT IF LENGTH LESS THAN 2
          BCS.S     SRTEND          (NO SORTING NECESSARY)
          *
          *SAVE EXTRA REGISTERS IN STACK
          *
          MOVEM.L   D3-D6/A2,-(A7) SAVE EXTRA REGISTERS IN STACK
          *
          *START GAP AT ARRAY LENGTH
          *NEXT GAP IS PREVIOUS GAP DIVIDED BY 2 WITH TRUNCATION
          *
          MOVE.W    D0,D1          INITIAL GAP = ARRAY LENGTH
NXTGAP    LSR.W     #1,D1          NEXT GAP IS PREVIOUS GAP DIVIDED
                                   * BY 2 WITH TRUNCATION
          BEQ.S     CLNSTK         DONE SORTING IF GAP IS ZERO
          *
          *SORT SUBSETS OF ELEMENTS SEPARATED BY CURRENT GAP
          *USE SIMPLE INSERTION SORT ON EACH SUBSET
```

```
        *SORT EACH SUBSET AS FAR AS TOP UPPER INDEX
        *CONTINUE UNTIL TOP UPPER INDEX BEYOND END OF ARRAY
        *
        MOVE.W   D1,D2          START TOP UPPER INDEX AT GAP-1
        SUBQ.W   #1,D2
        CLR.L    D3             COMPUTE DISTANCE BETWEEN ELEMENTS
                                * THIS IS TWICE THE GAP AND COULD BE
                                * MORE THAN 16 BITS, SO START BY
                                * CLEARING 32-BIT REGISTER
        MOVE.L   D1,D3          GET GAP
        ADD.L    D3,D3          DISTANCE = GAP X 2 (A 32-BIT NUMBER)
NXTSUB
        ADDQ.W   #1,D2          ADD 1 TO TOP UPPER INDEX FOR NEXT
                                * SUBSET
        CMP.W    D2,D0          CHECK IF TOP UPPER INDEX IN ARRAY
        BCS.S    NXTGAP         BRANCH IF TOP UPPER INDEX BEYOND
                                * END OF ARRAY
                                *ALL SUBSETS WITH CURRENT GAP ARE
                                * SORTED WHEN THIS HAPPENS
        *
        *SORT SUBSET WITH GIVEN GAP UP TO TOP UPPER INDEX
        *USE STANDARD INSERTION METHOD, EXCHANGING ELEMENTS
        *  WHEN NECESSARY
        *
        MOVE.W   D2,D4          START AT TOP UPPER INDEX
        CLR.L    D5             CLEAR 32-BIT INDEX FOR TOP ELEMENT
                                * IN ARRAY OF WORD-LENGTH ELEMENTS
        MOVE.W   D2,D5          GET TOP UPPER INDEX
        ADD.L    D5,D5          DOUBLE INDEX FOR WORD-LENGTH
                                * ELEMENTS
        LEA      (A0,D5.L),A1   POINT TO TOP ELEMENT IN SUBSET
        MOVE.W   (A1),D6        GET TOP ELEMENT
NXTPR
        SUB.W    D1,D4          CHECK IF THERE IS ANOTHER ELEMENT
                                * FURTHER DOWN IN SUBSET
        BCS.S    NXTSUB         JUMP IF NO MORE ELEMENTS, HENCE
                                * SUBSET IS SORTED
        MOVEA.L  A1,A2          COMPARE NEXT PAIR OF ELEMENTS
                                * SEPARATED BY GAP
        SUBA.L   D3,A1          STEP IS GAP X 2 SINCE ELEMENTS ARE
                                * WORD-LENGTH
        CMP.W    (A1),D6        COMPARE NEXT PAIR OF ELEMENTS
        BCC.S    NXTSUB         DONE IF PAIR IN ORDER SINCE LATER
                                * PAIRS HAVE ALREADY BEEN SORTED
        MOVE.W   (A1),(A2)      EXCHANGE PAIR IF OUT OF ORDER
        MOVE.W   D6,(A1)        TOP ELEMENT STAYS THE SAME FOR NEXT
                                * COMPARISON
        BRA.S    NXTPR          CONTINUE THROUGH PARTIAL SUBSET
        *
        *CLEAN STACK AND EXIT
        *
CLNSTK
        MOVEM.L  (A7)+,D3-D6/A2 RESTORE EXTRA REGISTERS FROM STACK
SRTEND
        RTS                     EXIT
```

```
*
*
*       SAMPLE EXECUTION
*
*
SC6F
        *
        *SORT AN ARRAY BETWEEN BEGBUF (FIRST ELEMENT)
        * AND ENDBUF (LAST ELEMENT)
        *
        MOVEA.L  #BEGBUF,A0    GET BASE ADDRESS OF ARRAY
        MOVE.W   (SZARY),D0    GET SIZE OF ARRAY IN WORDS
        JSR      SSORT         SORT USING SHELL SORT
                               *RESULT FOR TEST DATA IS
                               * 0,1,2,3, ... ,14,15
        BRA.S    SC6F          LOOP TO REPEAT TEST

*
*DATA SECTION
*
BEGBUF  DC.W     15
        DC.W     14
        DC.W     13
        DC.W     12
        DC.W     11
        DC.W     10
        DC.W     9
        DC.W     8
        DC.W     7
        DC.W     6
        DC.W     5
        DC.W     4
        DC.W     3
        DC.W     2
        DC.W     1
        DC.W     0
SZARY   DC.W     16            SIZE OF ARRAY IN WORDS
        END
```

6G Quicksort (QSORT)

Arranges an array of unsigned word-length elements into ascending order using a quicksort algorithm. Each iteration selects an element and divides the array into two parts, one containing all elements larger than the selected element and the other containing all elements smaller than the selected element. Elements equal to the selected element may end up in either part. The parts are then sorted recursively in the same way. The algorithm continues until all parts contain either no elements or only 1 element. An alternative is to stop recursion when a part contains few enough elements (say, less than 20) to make a bubble sort practical.

The parameters are the array's base address, the address of its last element, and the lowest available stack address. The array can thus occupy all available memory, as long as there is room for the stack. Since the procedures that obtain the selected element, compare elements, move forward and backward in the array, and swap elements are all subroutines, they could be changed readily to handle other types of elements.

Ideally, quicksort should divide the array in half during each iteration. How closely the procedure approaches this ideal depends on how well the selected element is chosen. Since this element serves as a midpoint or pivot, the best choice would be the central value (or median). Of course, the true median is unknown. A simple but reasonable approximation is to select the median of the first, middle, and last elements.

Procedure The program first deals with the entire array. It selects the median of the current first, middle, and last elements as a central element. It moves that element to the first position and divides the array into two parts or partitions. It then operates recursively on the parts, dividing them into parts and stopping when a part contains no elements or only one element. Since each recursion places 6 bytes on the stack, the program must guard against overflow by checking whether the stack has reached to within a small buffer of its lowest available position.

Note that the selected element always ends up in the correct position after an iteration. Therefore, it need not be included in either partition.

Our rule for choosing the middle element is as follows, assuming that the first element is #1:

1. If the array has an odd number of elements, take the center one. For example, if the array has 11 elements, take #6.

2. If the array has an even number of elements and its base address is even, take the element on the lower (base address) side of the centre. For example, if the array starts in 0300_{16} and has 12 elements, take #6.

3. If the array has an even number of elements and its base address is odd, take the element on the upper side of the centre. For example, if the array starts in 0301_{16} and has 12 elements, take #7.

Entry conditions

Order in stack (starting from the top)

High word of return address
Low word of return address

High word of base address of array
Low word of base address of array

High word of address of last word in array
Low word of address of last word in array

High word of lowest available stack address
Low word of lowest available stack address

Exit conditions

Array sorted into ascending order, considering the elements as unsigned words. Thus, the smallest unsigned word ends up stored starting at the base address. Carry = 0 if the stack did not overflow and the result is proper. Carry = 1 if the stack overflowed and the final array is not sorted.

Example

Data: Length (size) of array = $0C_{16} = 12_{10}$
Elements = $2B_{16}$, 57_{16}, $1D_{16}$, 26_{16}, 22_{16}, $2E_{16}$, $0C_{16}$, 44_{16}, 17_{16}, $4B_{16}$, 37_{16}, 27_{16}.

Result: In the first iteration, we have:

Selected element = median of the first (#1 = $2B_{16}$), middle (#6 = $2E_{16}$), and last (#12 = 27_{16}) elements. The selected element is therefore #1 ($2B_{16}$), and no swapping is necessary since it is already in the first position.

At the end of the iteration, the array is

27_{16}, 17_{16}, $1D_{16}$, 26_{16},
22_{16}, $0C_{16}$, $2B_{16}$, 44_{16},
$2E_{16}$, $4B_{16}$, 37_{16}, 57_{16}

The first partition, consisting of elements less than $2B_{16}$, is 27_{16}, 17_{16}, $1D_{16}$, 26_{16}, 22_{16}, and $0C_{16}$.

The second partition, consisting of elements greater than $2B_{16}$, is 44_{16}, $2E_{16}$, $4B_{16}$, 37_{16}, and 57_{16}.

Note that the selected element ($2B_{16}$) is now in the correct position and need not be included in either partition.

We may now sort the first partition recursively in the same way:

Selected element = median of the first (#1 = 27_{16}), middle (#3 = $1D_{16}$), and last (#6 = $0C_{16}$) elements. Here, #3 is the median and must be exchanged initially with #1.

The final order of the elements in the first partition is:

$0C_{16}$, 17_{16}, $1D_{16}$, 26_{16}, 22_{16}, 27_{16}.

The first partition of the first partition (consisting of elements less than $1D_{16}$) is $0C_{16}$, 17_{16}. We will call this the (1,1) partition for short.

The second partition of the first partition (consisting of elements greater than $1D_{16}$) is 26_{16}, 22_{16}, and 27_{16}.

As in the first iteration, the selected element ($1D_{16}$) is in the correct position and need not be considered further.

We may now sort the (1,1) partition recursively as follows:

Selected element = median of the first (#1 = $0C_{16}$), middle (#1 = $0C_{16}$), and last (#2 = 17_{16}) elements. Thus the selected element is the first element (#1 = $0C_{16}$), and no initial swap is necessary.

The final order is obviously the same as the initial order, and the two resulting partitions contain 0 and 1 element, respectively. Thus the next iteration concludes the recursion, and we then sort the other partitions by the same method. Obviously, quicksort's overhead becomes a major factor for arrays containing only a few elements. This is why one might use a bubble sort once quicksort has created small enough partitions.

Note that the example array does not contain any identical elements. During an iteration, elements that are the same as the selected element are never moved. Thus they may end up in either partition. Strictly speaking, then, the two partitions consist of elements 'less than or possibly equal to the selected element' and elements 'greater than or possibly equal to the selected element.'

References

N. Dale and S.C. Lilly, *Pascal Plus Data Structures*, D.C. Heath, Lexington, MA, 1985, pp. 300–307, 440–441.

D.E. Knuth, *The Art of Computer Programming. Volume 3: Searching and Sorting*, Addison-Wesley, Reading, MA, 1973, pp. 114–123.

Y. Langsam, *et al.*, *Data Structures for Personal Computers*, Prentice-Hall, Englewood Cliffs, NJ, 1985, pp. 430–437. The algorithms in this book are available as BASIC programs for various computers. Other versions of the book are available for Pascal and PL/I.

Registers used A0, A1, CCR, D0, D1, D2

Execution time Approximately $N \times \log_2 N$ loops through PARTLP plus $2 \times N + 1$ overhead calls to SORT. Each iteration of PARTLP takes approximately 65 or 150 cycles (depending on whether an exchange is necessary), and each overhead call to SORT takes approximately 340 cycles. Thus the total execution time is on the order of

$$65 \times \mathrm{N} \times \log_2 \mathrm{N} + 340 \times (2 \times \mathrm{N} + 1) \text{ cycles}$$

assuming relatively few exchanges. In practice, sorting a 24K word array using an Atari 520 ST with an 8 MHz 68000 chip takes about 1 s.

Program size 224 bytes

Data memory required 16 bytes anywhere in RAM for pointers to the first and last element of a partition (4 bytes starting at addresses FIRST and LAST, respectively), a pointer to the bottom of the stack (4 bytes starting at address STKBTM), and the original value of the stack pointer (4 bytes starting at address OLDSP). Each recursion level requires 12 bytes of stack space, and the routines themselves require another 16 bytes.

Special case If the stack overflows (i.e., comes too close to its boundary), the program exits with Carry set to 1.

```
*       Title           Quicksort
*       Name:           QSORT
*
*       Purpose:        Arrange an array of unsigned words into
*                       ascending order using a quicksort.
*
*       Entry:          TOP OF STACK
*                         High word of return address
*                         Low word of return address
*                         High word of address of first word in array
*                         Low word of address of first word in array
*                         High word of address of last word in array
*                         Low word of address of last word in array
*                         High word of lowest available stack address
*                         Low word of lowest available stack address
*
*       Exit:           If the stack did not overflow then
*                         The array is sorted into ascending order.
*                         Carry = 0
*                       Else
*                         Carry = 1
*
*       Registers Used: A0,A1,CCR,D0,D1,D2
*
*       Time:           The timing is highly data-dependent but the
*                       quicksort algorithm takes approximately
*                       N X log (N) loops through PARTLP. There will be
*                                2
*                       2 X N+1 calls to Sort. The number of recursions
*                       will probably be a fraction of N but if all
*                       data is the same, the recursion could be up to
*                       N. Therefore, the amount of stack space should
*                       be maximized. NOTE: Each recursion level takes
*                       12 bytes of stack space.
*
*                       In the above discussion, N is the number of
*                       array elements.
*
*                       In practice, sorting a 24K word array took
*                       about 1 second on an Atari 520ST with an
*                       8 MHz 68000 chip.
*
*       Size:           Program 224 bytes
*                       Data     16 bytes
*
*
QSORT
        *
        *WATCH FOR STACK OVERFLOW
        *CALCULATE A THRESHOLD TO WARN OF OVERFLOW
        * (30 HEX BYTES FROM THE END OF THE STACK)
```

```
        *SAVE THIS THRESHOLD FOR LATER COMPARISONS
        *ALSO SAVE THE POSITION OF THIS ROUTINE'S RETURN ADDRESS
        * IN THE EVENT WE MUST ABORT BECAUSE OF STACK OVERFLOW
        *
        MOVEM.L   (SP)+,D0-D1/A0-A1   GET RETURN ADDRESS (D0),
                                 * ADDRESS OF FIRST ELEMENT (D1),
                                 * ADDRESS OF LAST ELEMENT (A0),
                                 * LOWEST STACK ADDRESS (A1)
        MOVE.L    D0,-(SP)       PUT RETURN ADDRESS BACK IN STACK
        MOVEA.L   SP,OLDSP       SAVE CURRENT STACK POINTER IN CASE
                                 * WE MUST ABORT
        LEA       $30(A1),A1     ADD 30 HEX BYTE BUFFER TO STACK
                                 * END
        MOVE.L    A1,STKBTM      SAVE STACK THRESHOLD FOR LATER
                                 * COMPARISONS
        MOVEA.L   A0,A1          MOVE ADDRESS OF LAST ELEMENT TO A1
        MOVEA.L   D1,A0          MOVE ADDRESS OF FIRST ELEMENT TO A0
        *
        *WORK RECURSIVELY THROUGH THE QUICKSORT ALGORITHM AS
        * FOLLOWS:
        *  1. CHECK IF THE PARTITION CONTAINS 0 OR 1 ELEMENT.
        *     MOVE UP A RECURSION LEVEL IF IT DOES.
        *  2. USE MEDIAN TO OBTAIN A REASONABLE CENTRAL VALUE
        *     FOR DIVIDING THE CURRENT PARTITION INTO TWO
        *     PARTS.
        *  3. MOVE THROUGH THE ARRAY SWAPPING ELEMENTS THAT
        *     ARE OUT OF ORDER UNTIL ALL ELEMENTS BELOW THE
        *     CENTRAL VALUE ARE AHEAD OF ALL ELEMENTS ABOVE
        *     THE CENTRAL VALUE.  SUBROUTINE COMPARE
        *     COMPARES ELEMENTS, SWAP EXCHANGES ELEMENTS,
        *     PREV MOVES UPPER BOUNDARY DOWN ONE ELEMENT,
        *     AND NEXT MOVES LOWER BOUNDARY UP ONE ELEMENT.
        *  4. CHECK IF THE STACK IS ABOUT TO OVERFLOW.  IF IT
        *     IS, ABORT AND EXIT.
        *  5. ESTABLISH THE BOUNDARIES FOR THE FIRST PARTITION
        *     (CONSISTING OF ELEMENTS LESS THAN THE CENTRAL VALUE)
        *     AND SORT IT RECURSIVELY.
        *  6. ESTABLISH THE BOUNDARIES FOR THE SECOND PARTITION
        *     (CONSISTING OF ELEMENTS GREATER THAN THE CENTRAL
        *     VALUE) AND SORT IT RECURSIVELY.
        *
SORT
        *
        *SAVE BASE ADDRESS AND ADDRESS OF LAST ELEMENT
        * IN CURRENT PARTITION
        *
        MOVE.L    A0,FIRST       SAVE BASE ADDRESS
        MOVE.L    A1,LAST        SAVE ADDRESS OF LAST ELEMENT
        *
        *CHECK IF PARTITION CONTAINS 0 OR 1 ELEMENTS
        * IT DOES IF FIRST IS EITHER LARGER THAN (0)
        * OR EQUAL TO (1) LAST.
        *
        *STOP WHEN FIRST >= LAST
        *
        CMPA.L    A1,A0          COMPARE ADDRESSES OF FIRST AND
```

```
                                  * LAST ELEMENTS
        BCC.S   EXITPR            RETURN IF FIRST >= LAST
                                  *THIS PART IS SORTED
*
*START ANOTHER ITERATION ON THIS PARTITION
*USE MEDIAN TO FIND A REASONABLE CENTRAL ELEMENT
*MOVE CENTRAL ELEMENT TO FIRST POSITION
*
        JSR     MEDIAN            SELECT CENTRAL ELEMENT, MOVE IT
                                  * TO FIRST POSITION
        CLR.B   D1                BIT 0 OF REGISTER D1 = DIRECTION
                                  * IF IT IS 0 THEN DIRECTION IS UP
                                  * ELSE DIRECTION IS DOWN
*
*REORDER ARRAY BY COMPARING OTHER ELEMENTS WITH THE
* CENTRAL ELEMENT.  START BY COMPARING THAT ELEMENT WITH
* LAST ELEMENT.  EACH TIME WE FIND AN ELEMENT THAT
* BELONGS IN THE FIRST PART (THAT IS, IT IS LESS THAN
* THE CENTRAL ELEMENT), SWAP IT INTO THE FIRST PART IF IT
* IS NOT ALREADY THERE AND MOVE THE BOUNDARY OF THE
* FIRST PART DOWN ONE ELEMENT.  SIMILARLY, EACH TIME WE
* FIND  AN ELEMENT THAT BELONGS IN THE SECOND PART (THAT
* IS,  IT IS GREATER THAN THE CENTRAL ELEMENT),  SWAP IT
* INTO THE SECOND PART IF IT IS NOT ALREADY THERE AND MOVE
* THE BOUNDARY OF THE SECOND PART UP ONE ELEMENT.
*ULTIMATELY, THE BOUNDARIES COME TOGETHER
* AND THE DIVISION OF THE ARRAY IS THEN COMPLETE
*NOTE THAT ELEMENTS EQUAL TO THE CENTRAL ELEMENT ARE NEVER
* SWAPPED AND SO MAY END UP IN EITHER PART
*
PARTLP
*
*LOOP SORTING UNEXAMINED PART OF PARTITION
* UNTIL THERE IS NOTHING LEFT IN IT
*
        CMPA.L  A1,A0             COMPARE LOWER, UPPER BOUNDARIES
                                  * OF PARTITION
        BCC.S   DONE              EXIT WHEN UPPER BOUNDARY AT OR BELOW
                                  * LOWER BOUNDARY - THIS MEANS
                                  * EVERYTHING HAS BEEN EXAMINED
*
*COMPARE NEXT 2 ELEMENTS.  IF OUT OF ORDER,  SWAP THEM
*AND CHANGE DIRECTION OF SEARCH
* IF FIRST > LAST THEN SWAP
*
        MOVE.W  (A0),D0           GET FIRST ELEMENT
        CMP.W   (A1),D0           COMPARE FIRST TO LAST ELEMENT
        BCS.S   REDPRT            JUMP IF IN ORDER
*
*ELEMENTS OUT OF ORDER, SWAP THEM AND CHANGE DIRECTION
*
        NOT.B   D1                CHANGE DIRECTION
        JSR     SWAP              SWAP ELEMENTS
*
*REDUCE SIZE OF UNEXAMINED AREA
*IF NEW ELEMENT LESS THAN CENTRAL ELEMENT, MOVE
```

```
        * UPPER BOUNDARY DOWN
        *IF NEW ELEMENT GREATER THAN CENTRAL ELEMENT, MOVE
        * LOWER BOUNDARY UP
        *IF ELEMENTS EQUAL, CONTINUE IN CURRENT DIRECTION
        *
REDPRT
        TST.B     D1             CHECK DIRECTION
        BEQ.S     UP             JUMP IF MOVING UP
        JSR       NEXT           MOVE UPPER BOUNDARY DOWN ONE ELEMENT
        BRA.S     PARTLP         JUMP TO CHECK NEXT ELEMENT
UP
        JSR       PREV           MOVE LOWER BOUNDARY UP ONE ELEMENT
        BRA.S     PARTLP
        *
        *THIS PARTITION HAS NOW BEEN SUBDIVIDED INTO TWO
        * PARTITIONS. ONE STARTS AT THE UPPER BOUNDARY AND ENDS JUST
        * ABOVE THE CENTRAL ELEMENT. THE OTHER STARTS JUST BELOW
        * THE CENTRAL ELEMENT AND CONTINUES TO THE LOWER BOUNDARY.
        * THE CENTRAL ELEMENT IS NOW IN ITS PROPER SORTED POSITION
        * AND NEED NOT BE INCLUDED IN EITHER PARTITION
        *
DONE
        *
        *FIRST CHECK WHETHER STACK MIGHT OVERFLOW
        *IF IT IS GETTING TOO CLOSE TO THE BOTTOM, ABORT
        * THE PROGRAM AND EXIT
        *
        CMPA.L    STKBTM,SP      COMPARE STACK POINTER TO THRESHOLD
        BCS.S     ABORT          ABORT IF STACK IS TOO LARGE
        *
        *ESTABLISH BOUNDARIES FOR FIRST (LOWER) PARTITION
        *LOWER BOUNDARY IS SAME AS BEFORE
        *UPPER BOUNDARY IS ELEMENT JUST BELOW CENTRAL ELEMENT
        *THEN RECURSIVELY QUICKSORT FIRST PARTITION
        *
        MOVEA.L   LAST,A1        GET UPPER BOUNDARY
        MOVEM.L   A0-A1,-(SP)    SAVE CENTRAL ADDRESS, UPPER BOUNDARY
        MOVEA.L   A0,A1          SET UPPER BOUNDARY TO CENTRAL ADDRESS
        MOVEA.L   FIRST,A0       GET LOWER BOUNDARY
        CMPA.L    A1,A0          CHECK WHETHER CENTRAL ELEMENT IS AT
                                 * LOWER BOUNDARY
        BEQ.S     SKPDEC         DO NOT MOVE POINTER DOWN IF ALREADY
                                 * AT LOWER BOUNDARY
        JSR       PREV           OTHERWISE, UPPER BOUNDARY IS AT
                                 * ELEMENT JUST BELOW CENTRAL ELEMENT
SKPDEC
        JSR       SORT           QUICKSORT FIRST PART
        *
        *ESTABLISH BOUNDARIES FOR SECOND (UPPER) PARTITION
        *UPPER BOUNDARY IS SAME AS BEFORE
        *LOWER BOUNDARY IS ELEMENT JUST ABOVE CENTRAL ELEMENT
        *THEN RECURSIVELY QUICKSORT SECOND PARTITION
        *
        MOVEM.L   (SP)+,A0-A1    RESTORE CENTRAL ADDRESS, UPPER
                                 * BOUNDARY
        JSR       NEXT           LOWER BOUNDARY = ELEMENT JUST ABOVE
```

```
                                   *  CENTRAL ELEMENT
        JSR        SORT            QUICKSORT SECOND PART
        MOVE.W     #0,CCR          CLEAR CARRY, INDICATING NO ERRORS
EXITPR
        RTS                        GOOD EXIT
        *
        *ERROR EXIT, SET CARRY TO 1
        *
ABORT
        MOVEA.L    OLDSP,SP        GET ORIGINAL STACK POINTER
        MOVE.W     #1,CCR          INDICATE ERROR BY SETTING CARRY
        RTS                        RETURN WITH ERROR INDICATOR TO
                                   * ORIGINAL CALLER

*************************************************
*ROUTINE: MEDIAN
*PURPOSE: DETERMINE WHICH ELEMENT IN A PARTITION
*     SHOULD BE USED AS THE CENTRAL ELEMENT OR PIVOT
*ENTRY: ADDRESS OF FIRST ELEMENT IN REGISTER A0
*       ADDRESS OF LAST ELEMENT IN REGISTER A1
*EXIT:  CENTRAL ELEMENT IN FIRST POSITION
*       A0,A1 UNCHANGED
*REGISTERS USED: CCR,D0,D1,D2
*************************************************

MEDIAN
        *
        *DETERMINE ADDRESS OF MIDDLE ELEMENT
        * MIDDLE := ALIGNED(FIRST + LAST) DIV 2
        *
        MOVEM.L    A1-A2,-(SP)     SAVE ADDRESS REGISTERS
        MOVE.L     A1,D0           ADD FIRST AND LAST IN A DATA REGISTER
                                   * SO WE CAN DIVIDE BY 2 AND ALIGN
        ADD.L      A0,D0           NOTE THIS COULD PRODUCE A CARRY
        ROXR.L     #1,D0           DIVIDE SUM (INCLUDING CARRY) BY 2
        ANDI.L     #$FFFFFE,D0     CLEAR LOWEST BIT TO ALIGN CENTRAL
        MOVE.L     D0,A2           SAVE CENTRAL ADDRESS
        MOVE.L     A0,D0           GET ADDRESS OF FIRST ELEMENT
        ANDI.L     #1,D0           CLEAR ALL BUT LOWEST BIT
        ADDA.L     D0,A2           ADD TO CENTRAL TO ALIGN ADDRESSES
        *
        *DETERMINE MEDIAN OF FIRST, MIDDLE, LAST ELEMENTS
        *COMPARE FIRST AND MIDDLE
        *
        MOVE.W     (A0),D0         GET FIRST ELEMENT
        MOVE.W     (A1),D1         GET LAST ELEMENT
        MOVE.W     (A2),D2         GET MIDDLE ELEMENT
        CMP.W      D2,D0           COMPARE FIRST AND MIDDLE
        BCC.S      MIDD1           JUMP IF FIRST IS >= MIDDLE
        *
        *WE KNOW (MIDDLE > FIRST)
        * SO COMPARE MIDDLE AND LAST
        *
        CMP.W      D2,D1           COMPARE LAST TO MIDDLE
        BCC.S      SWAPMF          JUMP IF LAST IS >= MIDDLE
        *
```

```
        *
        *WE KNOW (MIDDLE > FIRST) AND (MIDDLE > LAST)
        * SO COMPARE FIRST AND LAST (MEDIAN IS LARGER ONE)
        *
        CMP.W     D0,D1            COMPARE LAST TO FIRST
        BCS.S     SWAPLF           JUMP IF LAST > FIRST
        BRA.S     MEXIT            EXIT IF FIRST IS >= LAST
                                   *FIRST IS MEDIAN
        *
        *WE KNOW FIRST >= MIDDLE
        *SO COMPARE FIRST AND LAST
        *
MIDD1
        CMP.W     D0,D1            EXIT IF LAST >= FIRST
        BCC.S     MEXIT            FIRST IS MEDIAN
        *
        *WE KNOW (FIRST >= MIDDLE) AND (FIRST > LAST)
        * SO COMPARE MIDDLE AND LAST (MEDIAN IS LARGER ONE)
        *
        CMP.W     D2,D1            COMPARE LAST TO MIDDLE
        BHI.S     SWAPLF           JUMP IF LAST > MIDDLE
                                   * LAST IS MEDIAN
        *
        *MIDDLE IS MEDIAN, MOVE ITS POINTER TO LAST
        *
SWAPMF
        MOVEA.L   A2,A1            MOVE MIDDLE'S POINTER TO LAST
        *
        *LAST IS MEDIAN, SWAP IT WITH FIRST
        *
SWAPLF
        JSR       SWAP             SWAP LAST, FIRST
        *
        *RESTORE LAST AND EXIT
        *
MEXIT
        MOVEM.L   (SP)+,A1-A2      RESTORE ADDRESS REGISTERS
        RTS

*******************************************
*ROUTINE: SWAP
*PURPOSE: SWAP ELEMENTS POINTED TO BY A0,A1
*ENTRY:   A0 = ADDRESS OF ELEMENT 1
*      A1 = ADDRESS OF ELEMENT 2
*EXIT:  ELEMENTS SWAPPED
*REGISTERS USED: CCR,D0
*******************************************

SWAP
        MOVE.W    (A0),D0          GET FIRST ELEMENT
        MOVE.W    (A1),(A0)        MOVE SECOND ELEMENT TO FIRST POSITION
        MOVE.W    D0,(A1)          MOVE FIRST ELEMENT TO SECOND POSITION
        RTS

*******************************************
*ROUTINE: NEXT
```

```
*PURPOSE: MAKE A0 POINT TO NEXT ELEMENT
*ENTRY: A0 = ADDRESS OF CURRENT ELEMENT
*EXIT:  A0 = ADDRESS OF NEXT ELEMENT
*REGISTERS USED: A0,CCR
******************************************

NEXT
        ADDQ.L  #2,A0           MOVE POINTER TO NEXT ELEMENT
        RTS

******************************************
*ROUTINE: PREV
*PURPOSE: MAKE A1 POINT TO PREVIOUS ELEMENT
*ENTRY: A1 = ADDRESS OF CURRENT ELEMENT
*EXIT:  A1 = ADDRESS OF PREVIOUS ELEMENT
*REGISTERS USED: A1,CCR
******************************************

PREV
        SUBQ.L  #2,A1           MOVE POINTER TO PREVIOUS ELEMENT
        RTS

*
*DATA SECTION
*
FIRST   DS.L    1               POINTER TO FIRST ELEMENT IN PARTITION
LAST    DS.L    1               POINTER TO LAST ELEMENT IN PARTITION
OLDSP   DS.L    1               POINTER TO ORIGINAL RETURN ADDRESS
                                * (INITIAL STACK POINTER)
STKBTM  DS.L    1               THRESHOLD FOR STACK OVERFLOW

*
*       SAMPLE EXECUTION
*

*
*PROGRAM SECTION
SC6G
        *
        *SORT AN ARRAY BETWEEN BEGBUF (FIRST ELEMENT)
        * AND ENDBUF (LAST ELEMENT)
        *LET STACK EXPAND 1000 HEX BYTES
        *
        MOVEA.L SP,A2           GET CURRENT STACK ADDRESS
        SUBA.L  #$1000,A2       SUBTRACT 1000 HEX TO SPECIFY END OF
                                *  STACK ADDRESS
        MOVEA.L #BEGBUF,A0      GET ADDRESS OF FIRST ELEMENT
        MOVEA.L #ENDBUF,A1      GET ADDRESS OF LAST ELEMENT
        MOVEM.L A0-A2,-(SP)     PUSH PARAMETERS INTO STACK
        JSR     QSORT           SORT USING QUICKSORT
                                *RESULT FOR TEST DATA IS
                                * 0,1,2,3, ... ,14,15
        BRA.S   SC6G            LOOP TO REPEAT TEST

*
*DATA SECTION
```

```
*
BEGBUF  DC.W    15
        DC.W    14
        DC.W    13
        DC.W    12
        DC.W    11
        DC.W    10
        DC.W    9
        DC.W    8
        DC.W    7
        DC.W    6
        DC.W    5
        DC.W    4
        DC.W    3
        DC.W    2
        DC.W    1
ENDBUF  DC.W    0
        END
```

6H Merge sort (MSORT)

Merges two lists of unsigned 16-bit elements into ascending order. Both original lists are assumed to be already arranged in ascending order. The merged list replaces list 1, the list with the base address higher in the stack.

Procedure The program starts at the end of the expanded list (i.e. the extension of list 1 to include the elements of list 2). It repeatedly compares the next remaining elements of the two lists, moves the larger element into the merged list, and updates the counters and pointers. If there are elements left from the second list when the first list is done, they are moved to the front of the expanded list.

Entry conditions

Order in stack (starting from the top)

High word of return address
Low word of return address

High word of base address of list 1
Low word of base address of list 1

Size of list 1 in words

High word of base address of list 2
Low word of base address of list 2

Size of list 2 in words

Exit conditions

List 1 replaced by list 1 merged with list 2. List 1 is sorted into ascending order, considering the elements as unsigned words. Thus, the smallest unsigned word ends up stored starting at the base address of list 1.

Example

Data: Length (size) of list 1 = $0C_{16} = 12_{10}$

Elements = $0D_{16}$, 17_{16}, $1D_{16}$, 22_{16},
26_{16}, 27_{16}, $2B_{16}$, $2E_{16}$,
37_{16}, 44_{16}, $4B_{16}$, 57_{16}.
Length (size) of list 2 = 08
Elements = $0B_{16}$, 12_{16}, 13_{16}, 17_{16},
25_{16}, $2D_{16}$, 41_{16}, 62_{16}

Result: Length (size) of list 1 = $14_{16} = 20_{10}$
Elements = $0B_{16}$, $0D_{16}$, 12_{16}, 13_{16},
17_{16}, 17_{16}, $1D_{16}$, 22_{16},
25_{16}, 26_{16}, 27_{16}, $2B_{16}$,
$2D_{16}$, $2E_{16}$, 37_{16}, 41_{16},
44_{16}, $4B_{16}$, 57_{16}, 62_{16}

References

D.E. Knuth, *The Art of Computer Programming. Volume 3: Searching and Sorting*, Addison-Wesley, Reading, MA, 1973, pp. 159–170, 198–209.

Y. Langsam *et al., Data Structures for Personal Computers*, Prentice-Hall, Englewood Cliffs, NJ, 1985, pp. 467–470, 474–476. The algorithms in this book are available as BASIC programs for various computers. Other versions of the book have algorithms in Pascal and PL/I.

Registers used A0, A1, CCR, D0, D1, D2

Execution time Approximately 60 cycles per element plus 250 cycles overhead. If, for example, the two lists have 1000 and 500 elements, respectively, the execution time is approximately

$$60 \times (1000 + 500) + 250 = 90{,}250 \text{ cycles}$$

Program size 98 bytes

Data memory required 8 stack bytes

Special cases

1. If list 1 has zero length, the program simply moves list 2 to list 1.
2. If list 2 has zero length, the program returns list 1 unchanged.

```
*       Title           Merge sort
*       Name:           MSORT
*
*       Purpose:        Merges two lists of 16-bit elements into one.
*                       Both original lists and the merged list are
*                       arranged in ascending order.
*
*       Entry:          TOP OF STACK
*                         High word of return address
*                         Low word of return address
*                         High word of base address of list 1
*                         Low word of base address of list 1
*                         Size of list 1 in words
*                         High word of base address of list 2
*                         Low word of base address of list 2
*                         Size of list 2 in words
*
*       Exit:           List 1 has its original contents combined
*                         list 2. Combined list is sorted into ascending
*                         order.
*
*       Registers Used: A0,A1,CCR,D0,D1,D2
*
*       Time:           Approximately 60 cycles per element plus
*                       250 cycles overhead
*
*       Size:           Program 98 bytes
*                       Data     8 stack bytes
*
*
MSORT
        *
        *OBTAIN PARAMETERS FROM STACK
        *EXIT (DONE) IF LIST 2 HAS NO ELEMENTS
        *
        MOVEM.L   D3/A2,-(SP)     SAVE EXTRA REGISTERS IN STACK
        CLR.L     D2              CLEAR UPPER WORDS OF SIZES TO ALLOW
        CLR.L     D3               32-BIT OVERALL LENGTHS IN BYTES
        MOVEA.L   12(SP),A0       GET BASE ADDRESS OF LIST 1
        MOVE.W    16(SP),D0       GET SIZE OF LIST 1 IN WORDS
        MOVEA.L   18(SP),A1       GET BASE ADDRESS OF LIST 2
        MOVE.W    22(SP),D1       GET SIZE OF LIST 2 IN WORDS
        BEQ.S     EXITMS          NO MERGE NECESSARY IF LIST 2 HAS
                                  * NO ELEMENTS
        *
        *SET POINTERS JUST BEYOND LAST ELEMENTS IN LISTS
        *POINTER = BASE ADDRESS OF LIST + 2 X (SIZE OF LIST) SINCE
        * SIZE IS IN WORDS
```

```
        *
        MOVE.W    D1,D2           GET SIZE OF LIST 2
        ADD.L     D2,D2           DOUBLE SIZE OF LIST 2 (ALLOW 32-BIT
                                  * RESULT)
        LEA       (A1,D2.L),A1    POINTER 2 = BASE L2 + 2 X SIZE L2
        MOVE.W    D0,D3           GET SIZE OF LIST 1
        ADD.L     D3,D3           DOUBLE SIZE OF LIST 1 (ALLOW 32-BIT
                                  * RESULT)
        ADD.L     D3,D2           2 X SIZE L2 + 2 X SIZE L1
        LEA       (A0,D2.L),A2    POINTER TO COMBINED LIST = BASE L1
                                  * + 2 X (SIZE L1 + SIZE L2)
        SUBQ.W    #1,D1           REDUCE LIST 2 SIZE BY 1 TO EXIT
                                  * ON -1
        TST.W     D0              TEST LENGTH OF LIST 1
        BEQ.S     MVREM           SIMPLY MOVE LIST 2 TO LIST 1 IF LIST
                                  * 1 HAS NO ELEMENTS
        LEA       (A0,D3.L),A0    POINTER 1 = BASE L1 + 2 X SIZE L1
        *
        *MERGE LISTS BY COMPARING NEXT ELEMENTS AND MOVING LARGER
        *  ELEMENT TO COMBINED LIST
        *
        SUBQ.W    #1,D0           REDUCE LIST 1 SIZE BY 1 TO EXIT ON -1
CMPNXT
        MOVE.W    -2(A0),D2       GET NEXT ELEMENT FROM LIST 1
        CMP.W     -2(A1),D2       COMPARE TO ELEMENT FROM LIST 2
        BHI.S     MVLST1          JUMP IF LIST 1 ELEMENT IS LARGER
        *
        *LIST 2 ELEMENT IS LARGER
        *MOVE IT TO COMBINED LIST AND PROCEED TO NEXT ELEMENT
        *  IN LIST 2
        *
        MOVE.W    -(A1),-(A2)     MOVE LIST 2 ELEMENT INTO MERGED LIST
        DBRA      D1,CMPNXT       COUNTDOWN ON LIST 2
        BRA.S     EXITMS          DONE IF ALL LIST 2 ELEMENTS MERGED
                                  * SINCE REMAINING LIST 1 ELEMENTS
                                  * ARE ALREADY WHERE THEY BELONG
        *
        *LIST 1 ELEMENT IS LARGER
        *MOVE IT TO COMBINED LIST AND PROCEED TO NEXT ELEMENT
        *  IN LIST 1
        *
MVLST1
        MOVE.W    -(A0),-(A2)     MOVE LIST 1 ELEMENT INTO MERGED LIST
        DBRA      D0,CMPNXT       COUNTDOWN ON LIST 1
        *
        *LIST 1 IS MERGED COMPLETELY INTO COMBINED LIST
        *MOVE REMAINING ELEMENTS FROM LIST 2 TO FRONT OF COMBINED
        *  LIST
        *
MVREM
        MOVE.W    -(A1),-(A2)     MOVE LIST 2 ELEMENT INTO MERGED LIST
        DBRA      D1,MVREM        COUNTDOWN ON LIST 2
EXITMS
        MOVEM.L   (SP)+,D3/A2     RESTORE EXTRA REGISTERS FROM STACK
        MOVEA.L   (SP)+,A0        GET RETURN ADDRESS
        LEA       12(SP),SP       REMOVE PARAMETERS FROM STACK
```

```
        JMP      (A0)            EXIT TO RETURN ADDRESS

*

*
*       SAMPLE EXECUTION
*

*
SC6H
        *
        *MERGE AN ARRAY BETWEEN BEGBF1 (FIRST ELEMENT)
        * AND ENDBF1 (LAST ELEMENT) WITH AN ARRAY BETWEEN
        * BEGBF2 (FIRST ELEMENT) AND ENDBF2 (LAST ELEMENT)
        *
        MOVE.W   SIZE2,D0        GET SIZE OF LIST 2
        MOVE.W   D0,-(SP)        PUSH SIZE OF LIST 2
        PEA      BEGBF2          PUSH BASE ADDRESS OF LIST 2
        MOVE.W   SIZE1,D0        GET SIZE OF LIST 1
        MOVE.W   D0,-(SP)        PUSH SIZE OF LIST 1
        PEA      BEGBF1          PUSH BASE ADDRESS OF LIST 1
        JSR      MSORT           MERGE LISTS
                                 *RESULT FOR TEST DATA IS
                                 * 0,1,2,3, ... ,14,15
        BRA.S    SC6H            LOOP TO REPEAT TEST

*
*DATA SECTION
*
SIZE1   DC.W     8               SIZE OF LIST 1
BEGBF1  DC.W     1               LIST 1
        DC.W     3
        DC.W     5
        DC.W     7
        DC.W     9
        DC.W     11
        DC.W     13
        DC.W     15
        DS.W     8               EXTRA SPACE REQUIRED TO MERGE
                                 * ELEMENTS FROM LIST 2
SIZE2   DC.W     8               SIZE OF LIST 2
BEGBF2  DC.W     0               LIST 2
        DC.W     2
        DC.W     4
        DC.W     6
        DC.W     8
        DC.W     10
        DC.W     12
        DC.W     14

        END
```

6I RAM test (RAMTST)

Tests a RAM area specified by a 32-bit base address and a 32-bit length in bytes. Writes the values 0, FF_{16}, 10101010_2 (AA_{16}), and 01010101_2 (55_{16}) into each byte and checks whether they can be read back correctly. Puts 1 in each bit position of each byte and checks whether it can be read back correctly with all other bits cleared. Clears Carry if all tests run correctly; if it finds an error, it exits immediately, setting Carry, and returning the test value and the address at which the error occurred.

Procedure The program performs the single value tests (with 0, FF_{16}, AA_{16}, and 55_{16}) by first filling the memory area and then comparing each byte with the specified value. Filling the entire area first should provide enough delay between writing and reading to detect a failure to retain data (perhaps caused by improperly designed refresh circuitry). The program then performs the walking bit test, starting with bit 7; here it writes the data into memory and reads it back immediately for a comparison.

Entry conditions

Area size in bytes in register D0
Base address of test area in register A0

Exit conditions

1. If a memory error is found:
   Carry = 1
   Address containing error in register A0
   Test value in low byte of register D0
2. If no error is found:
   Carry = 0
   All bytes in test area contain 0

Example

Data: Base address = 010380_{16}
Length (size) of area = 030000_{16}

Result: Area tested is the 30000_{16} bytes starting at address 010380_{16}, i.e. addresses 010380_{16} through $04037F_{16}$. The order of the tests is:

1. Write and read 0
2. Write and read FF_{16}
3. Write and read AA_{16} (10101010_2)
4. Write and read 55_{16} (01010101_2)
5. Walking bit test, starting with 1 in bit 7. That is, start with 10000000_2 (80_{16}) and move the 1 one position right for each subsequent test of a byte.

Registers used A0, A1, CCR, D0, D1, D2

Execution time Approximately 630 cycles per byte tested. Thus, for example, to test an area of size $20\,400_{16} = 132\,096_{10}$ would take

$$630 \times 132\,096 = \text{about } 83\,000\,000 \text{ cycles}$$

This is about 8.3 s at a typical 68000 clock rate of 10 MHz.

Program size 110 bytes

Data memory required None

Special cases

1. An area size of zero causes an immediate exit with no memory tested. Carry is cleared to indicate no errors.

2. Since the routine changes all bytes in the tested area, using it to test an area that includes itself will yield unpredictable results.

Note that Case 1 means you cannot ask this routine to test the entire memory, but such a request would be meaningless anyway since it would require the routine to test itself.

3. Testing a ROM causes a return with an error indication after the first occasion on which the test value differs from the memory's contents.

```
*
*
*       Title               RAM Test
*       Name:               RAMTST
*
*       Purpose:            Test a RAM (read/write memory) area as follows:
*                             1) Write all 0 and test
*                             2) Write all 11111111 binary and test
*                             3) Write all 10101010 binary and test
*                             4) Write all 01010101 binary and test
*                             5) Shift a single 1 through each bit,
*                                while clearing all other bits
*
*                             If the program finds an error, it exits
*                             immediately with the Carry flag set and
*                             indicates the test value and where the
*                             error occurred.
*
*       Entry:              Area size in bytes in D0
*                           Base address of area in A0
*
*       Exit:               If there are no errors then
*                             Carry = 0
*                             test area contains 0 in all bytes
*                           else
*                             Carry = 1
*                             Register A0 = Address of error
*                             Low byte of register D0 = test value
*
*       Registers Used: A0,A1,CCR,D0,D1,D2
*
*       Time:               Approximately 630 cycles per byte tested
*
*       Size:               Program 110 bytes

*
RAMTST
        *
        *EXIT INDICATING NO ERROR IF AREA SIZE IS ZERO
        *
        TST.L     D0          TEST AREA SIZE
        BEQ.S     EXITRT      EXIT WITH CARRY = 0 IF AREA SIZE IS 0
                              * CARRY = 0 (NO ERROR) IN THIS CASE
                              * BECAUSE OF TST
        *
        *FILL MEMORY WITH 0 AND TEST
        *
        CLR.B     D1          GET ZERO VALUE
        JSR       FILCMP      FILL AND TEST MEMORY
        BCS.S     EXITRT      BRANCH (EXIT) IF ERROR FOUND
        *
        *FILL MEMORY WITH FF HEX (ALL 1'S) AND TEST
        *
        MOVE.B    #$FF,D1     GET ALL 1'S VALUE
        JSR       FILCMP      FILL AND TEST MEMORY
```

```
         BCS.S     EXITRT    BRANCH (EXIT) IF ERROR FOUND
         *
         *FILL MEMORY WITH ALTERNATING 1'S AND 0'S AND TEST
         *
         MOVE.B    #$AA,D1   GET ALTERNATING 1'S AND 0'S PATTERN
         JSR       FILCMP    FILL AND TEST MEMORY
         BCS.S     EXITRT    BRANCH (EXIT) IF ERROR FOUND
         *
         *FILL MEMORY WITH ALTERNATING 0'S AND 1'S AND TEST
         *
         MOVE.B    #$55,D1   GET ALTERNATING 0'S AND 1'S PATTERN
         JSR       FILCMP    FILL AND TEST MEMORY
         BCS.S     EXITRT    BRANCH (EXIT) IF ERROR FOUND
         *
         *PERFORM WALKING BIT TEST. PLACE A 1 IN BIT 7 AND
         * SEE IF IT CAN BE READ BACK.  THEN MOVE THE 1 TO
         * BITS 6, 5, 4, 3, 2, 1, AND 0 AND SEE IF IT CAN
         * BE READ BACK
         *
         MOVEA.L   A0,A1     GET BASE ADDRESS OF TEST AREA
         MOVE.L    D0,D2     GET BYTE COUNT
WLKLP
         MOVE.B    #$80,D1   MAKE BIT 7 1, ALL OTHER BITS 0
WLKLP1
         MOVE.B    D1,(A1)   STORE TEST PATTERN IN MEMORY
         CMP.B     (A1),D1   TRY TO READ IT BACK
         BNE.S     EXITCS    BRANCH (EXIT) IF ERROR FOUND
         LSR.B     #1,D1     SHIFT PATTERN TO MOVE 1 BIT RIGHT
                             *COULD ALSO START WITH BIT 0 AND USE
                             * ADD.B D1,D1 TO MOVE THE 1 BIT LEFT
         BNE.S     WLKLP1    CONTINUE UNTIL PATTERN BECOMES ZERO
                             * THAT IS, UNTIL 1 BIT MOVES ALL THE
                             * WAY ACROSS THE BYTE
         MOVE.B    D1,(A1)+  CLEAR BYTE JUST CHECKED
                             * NOTE D1 MUST CONTAIN 0 OR BNE
                             * WOULD HAVE BRANCHED
         SUBQ.L    #1,D2     COUNT BYTES
         BNE.S     WLKLP
         MOVE      #0,CCR    ALL BYTES TESTED WITH NO ERRORS SO
                             * CLEAR CARRY TO INDICATE SUCCESS
EXITRT   RTS
         *
         *FOUND AN ERROR - SET CARRY TO INDICATE IT
         *
EXITCS
         MOVEA.L   A1,A0     GET ADDRESS IN WHICH ERROR OCCURRED
         ORI       #1,CCR    SET CARRY TO INDICATE ERROR
         RTS

*******************************************
*ROUTINE: FILCMP
*PURPOSE: FILL MEMORY WITH A VALUE AND TEST
*         THAT IT CAN BE READ BACK
*ENTRY:   LOW BYTE OF D1 = TEST VALUE
*         LOW WORD OF D0 = BYTE COUNT
*         A0 = BASE ADDRESS OF TEST AREA
```

```
*EXIT:    IF NO ERRORS THEN
*           CARRY = 0
*         ELSE
*           CARRY = 1
*           A0 = ADDRESS OF ERROR
*           LOW BYTE OF D1 = TEST VALUE
*REGISTERS USED: A0,A1,CCR,D0,D1,D2
*******************************************

FILCMP
          *
          *FILL MEMORY WITH TEST VALUE
          *
          MOVEA.L    A0,A1            GET BASE ADDRESS OF AREA
          MOVE.L     D0,D2            GET BYTE COUNT
FILWRD
          MOVE.B     D1,(A1)+         FILL MEMORY WITH TEST VALUE
          SUBQ.L     #1,D2            COUNT BYTES
          BNE.S      FILWRD
          *
          *COMPARE MEMORY AND TEST VALUE
          *
          MOVEA.L    A0,A1            GET BASE ADDRESS OF AREA
          MOVE.L     D0,D2            GET WORD COUNT
CMPWRD
          CMP.B      (A1)+,D1         COMPARE MEMORY WITH TEST VALUE
          BNE.S      EREXIT           BRANCH (ERROR EXIT) IF NOT EQUAL
          SUBQ.L     #1,D2            COUNT BYTES
          BNE.S      CMPWRD
          *
          *NO ERRORS FOUND, CLEAR CARRY AND EXIT
          *
          MOVE       #0,CCR           INDICATE NO ERRORS BY CLEARING CARRY
          RTS
          *
          *ERROR FOUND, SET CARRY, POINT TO ERROR, AND EXIT
          *
EREXIT
          LEA        -1(A1),A0        GET ADDRESS OF ERROR (-1 BECAUSE
                                      * OF AUTOPOSTINCREMENT)
          MOVE       #1,CCR           INDICATE AN ERROR BY SETTING CARRY
          RTS

*
*         SAMPLE EXECUTION
*

*
SC6I
          *
          *TEST RAM FROM 02000 HEX THROUGH 3300F HEX
          *  SIZE OF AREA = 31010 HEX BYTES
          *
          MOVE.L     #$31010,D0       GET AREA SIZE IN BYTES
          MOVEA.L    #$2000,A0        GET BASE ADDRESS OF AREA
          JSR        RAMTST           TEST MEMORY
```

```
                                  *CARRY WILL BE 0 IF NO MEMORY ERRORS
                                  * ARE FOUND IN THIS AREA

        END
```

6J Jump table (JTAB)

Transfers control to a 32-bit address selected from a table according to an index. The addresses are stored in the usual 68000 format with the most significant byte first, starting at address JMPTBL. The size of the table (number of addresses) is a constant LENSUB. If the index is greater than or equal to LENSUB, the program returns control immediately with Carry set to 1.

Procedure The program first checks whether the index is greater than or equal to the size of the table (LENSUB). If it is, the program returns control with the Carry flag set. If it is not, the program obtains the starting address of the appropriate subroutine from the table and jumps to it. The result is like an indexed JSR instruction with range checking and automatic accounting for the 32-bit length of complete memory addresses.

Entry conditions

Index in D0

Exit conditions

If (D0) is greater than LENSUB, an immediate return with Carry = 1. Otherwise, control is transferred to appropriate subroutine as if an indexed call had been performed. The return address remains at the top of the stack.

Example

Data: LENSUB (size of subroutine table) = 03
Table consists of addresses SUB0, SUB1, and SUB2
Index = (D0) = 2
Result: Control transferred to address SUB2

Registers used A0, CCR, D0

Execution time 52 cycles besides the time required to execute the actual subroutine

Program size 22 bytes plus 4 × LENSUB bytes for the table of starting addresses, where LENSUB is the number of subroutines

Data memory required None

Special case Entry with an index greater than or equal to LENSUB causes an immediate exit with Carry set to 1.

```
*       Title               Jump Table
*       Name:               JTAB
*
*       Purpose:            Given an index, jump to the subroutine with
*                           that index in a table
*
*       Entry:              Subroutine number (0 to LENSUB-1, the number of
*                             subroutines) in AX. LENSUB must be less than
*                             or equal to 16,383.
*
*       Exit:               If the routine number is valid then
*                             execute the routine
*                           else
*                             Carry = 1
*
*       Registers Used: A0,CCR,D0
*
*       Time:               52 cycles plus execution time of subroutine
*
*       Size:               Program 22 bytes plus size of table (4 X LENSUB)
*

*
*         EXIT WITH CARRY SET IF ROUTINE NUMBER IS INVALID
*         THAT IS, IF IT IS TOO LARGE FOR TABLE (>LENSUB - 1)
*
JTAB
          CMP.W     #LENSUB,D0        COMPARE ROUTINE NUMBER, TABLE LENGTH
          BCS.S     EREXIT            BRANCH (EXIT) IF ROUTINE NUMBER TOO
                                      * LARGE (CARRY = 1 IF JUMP OCCURS)
*
*         INDEX INTO TABLE OF DOUBLE-WORD-LENGTH ADDRESSES
*         OBTAIN ROUTINE ADDRESS FROM TABLE AND TRANSFER CONTROL
*           TO IT
*
          ASL.W     #2,D0             MULTIPLY INDEX BY 4 TO ACCOUNT FOR
                                      * LONG WORD-LENGTH ENTRIES
```

```
        MOVEA.L   #JMPTBL,A0       GET BASE ADDRESS OF JUMP TABLE
        JMP       (A0,D0.W)        JUMP TO INDEXED ADDRESS
*
*       ERROR EXIT - EXIT WITH CARRY SET
*
EREXIT
        RTS                        NOTE CARRY MUST BE SET AT THIS POINT
                                   * OR BCS WOULD NOT HAVE BRANCHED

LENSUB  EQU       3                NUMBER OF SUBROUTINES IN TABLE

*
*JUMP TABLE
*
JMPTBL
        DC.L      SUB0             STARTING ADDRESS FOR ROUTINE 0
        DC.L      SUB1             STARTING ADDRESS FOR ROUTINE 1
        DC.L      SUB2             STARTING ADDRESS FOR ROUTINE 2


*
*THREE TEST SUBROUTINES FOR JUMP TABLE
*
SUB0
        MOVEQ     #1,D0            TEST ROUTINE 0 SETS (D0) = 1
        RTS

SUB1
        MOVEQ     #2,D0            TEST ROUTINE 1 SETS (D0) = 2
        RTS

SUB2
        MOVEQ     #3,D0            TEST ROUTINE 2 SETS (D0) = 3
        RTS

*
*       SAMPLE EXECUTION
*

*
*PROGRAM SECTION
SC6J
        CLR.W     D0               EXECUTE ROUTINE 0
        JSR       JTAB             AFTER EXECUTION, (D0) = 1
        MOVEQ     #1,D0            EXECUTE ROUTINE 1
        JSR       JTAB             AFTER EXECUTION, (D0) = 2
        MOVEQ     #2,D0            EXECUTE ROUTINE 2
        JSR       JTAB             AFTER EXECUTION, (D0) = 3
        MOVEQ     #3,D0            EXECUTE ROUTINE 3
        JSR       JTAB             AFTER EXECUTION, CARRY = 1
                                   * INDICATING BAD ROUTINE NUMBER
        BRA.S     SC6J             LOOP FOR MORE TESTS

        END
```

6K Matrix multiplication (MATMUL)

Multiplies two square matrixes and saves the result in a third matrix. The matrixes consist of unsigned 8-bit elements.

Procedure The program starts by clearing the entire result area. It then multiplies each row of matrix 1 by each column of matrix 2 to obtain the elements of the result matrix. Matrix 1 is the matrix with the base address higher in the stack.

Entry conditions

Order in stack (starting from the top)

High word of return address
Low word of return address

High word of base address of result matrix
Low word of base address of result matrix

High word of base address of matrix 1
Low word of base address of matrix 1

High word of base address of matrix 2
Low word of base address of matrix 2

Size of matrixes in bytes

Exit conditions

Result matrix = matrix 1 × matrix 2

Example

Data: Size of matrixes = 3 by 3

$$\text{Matrix 1} = \begin{matrix} 1 & 2 & 3 \\ 4 & 3 & 2 \\ 3 & 1 & 2 \end{matrix}$$

$$\text{Matrix 2} = \begin{matrix} 1 & 2 & 3 \\ 2 & 3 & 1 \\ 4 & 1 & 2 \end{matrix}$$

Result:

		11	0B	0B
Result matrix	=	12	13	13
		0D	0B	0E

The elements are hexadecimal numbers

Registers used A0, A1, CCR, D0, D1, D2

Execution time Approximately 130 × $SIZE^3$ + 65 × $SIZE^2$ + 30 × SIZE + 430 cycles, where SIZE is the number of rows or columns in the square matrixes. If, for example, the matrixes are 4 by 4, the execution time is

$$130 \times 4^3 + 65 \times 4^2 + 30 \times 4 + 430 = 8320 + 1040 + 120 + 430 = 9910 \text{ cycles}$$

Program size 112 bytes

Data memory required 36 stack bytes

Special case If the size of the matrixes is 0, the program returns immediately with no memory locations changed. Carry is set to 1 to indicate an error.

```
*       Title           Matrix Multiplication
*       Name:           MATMUL
*
*       Purpose:        Multiplies two square matrixes of
*                       byte-length elements
*       Entry:          TOP OF STACK
*                         High word of return address
*                         Low word of return address
*                         High word of base address of result matrix
*                         Low word of base address of result matrix
*                         High word of base address of matrix 1
*                         Low word of base address of matrix 1
*                         High word of base address of matrix 2
*                         Low word of base address of matrix 2
```

```
*                    Size of matrixes in bytes
*
*       Exit:        Result matrix = matrix 1 X matrix 2
*
*       Registers Used: A0,A1,CCR,D0,D1,D2
*
*       Time:        Approximately 130 X size^3 + 65 X size^2 +
*                      30 X size + 430 cycles where size is the
*                      number or rows or columns in the square
*                      matrixes
*
*       Size:        Program 112 bytes
*                    Data     36 stack bytes
*
MATMUL
        LINK       A6,#0              USE A6 AS FRAME POINTER
                                      * NOTE: A6 CONTAINS STACK POINTER
                                      * VALUE AFTER OLD A6 SAVED ON STACK
        MOVEM.L    A2-A5/D3-D6,-(SP)    SAVE EXTRA REGISTERS IN STACK
        MOVEM.L    8(A6),A0-A2        GET MATRIX ADDRESSES FROM STACK
                                      * (MR IN A0, M1 IN A1, M2 IN A2)

        MOVE.W     20(A6),D0          GET SIZE OF MATRIXES
        ORI.W      #1,CCR             INDICATE POSSIBLE ERROR
        BEQ.S      MEXIT              EXIT WITH ERROR INDICATOR IF
                                      * SIZE = 0
        *
        *CLEAR ENTIRE RESULT AREA
        *
        MOVE.W     D0,D1              NUMBER OF ELEMENTS = SIZE SQUARED
        MULU       D1,D1
        SUBQ.W     #1,D1              SUBTRACT 1 TO EXIT ON -1
        MOVEA.L    A0,A3              GET BASE ADDRESS OF RESULT AREA
CLRELM
        CLR.B      (A3)+              CLEAR NEXT ELEMENT
        DBRA       D1,CLRELM          COUNT ELEMENTS
        *
        *MULTIPLY MATRIXES AS FOLLOWS:
        *FOR I = 0 TO SIZE - 1
        *FOR J = 0 TO SIZE - 1
        *FOR K = 0 TO SIZE - 1
        *  DO MR (I,J) = M1(I,K) X M2(K,J) + MR(I,J)
        *
        *THAT IS, EACH ELEMENT OF RESULT MATRIX CONSISTS OF A ROW
        *  OF MATRIX 1 TIMES A COLUMN OF MATRIX 2
        *
        MOVE.W     D0,D1              GET SIZE - 1
        SUBQ.W     #1,D1
        MOVE.W     D1,D2              ROW COUNTER = SIZE - 1
        MOVEA.L    A1,A3              SAVE POINTER TO FIRST ELEMENT IN ROW
                                      * OF MATRIX 1 CURRENTLY BEING USED
                                      * IN MULTIPLY - M1(I,0)
        MOVEA.L    A2,A4              SAVE POINTER TO BASE ADDRESS OF
                                      * MATRIX 2.  THIS IS FIRST ELEMENT
                                      * IN COLUMN OF MATRIX 2 USED IN
```

```
                                  * MULTIPLY WHEN STARTING A NEW ROW
                                  * IN PRODUCT MATRIX
         MOVEA.L   A2,A5          SAVE POINTER TO FIRST ELEMENT IN
                                  * COLUMN OF MATRIX 2 CURRENTLY
                                  * BEING USED IN MULTIPLY - M2(0,J)
NXTROW   MOVEA.L   A4,A5          MOVE COLUMN POINTER BACK TO COLUMN 0
                                  * TO START A NEW ROW IN PRODUCT
                                  * MATRIX - M2(0,0)
         MOVE.W    D1,D3          COLUMN COUNTER = SIZE - 1
NXTCOL   MOVEA.L   A3,A1          MAKE ROW POINTER POINT TO FIRST
                                  * ELEMENT IN CURRENT ROW (I)
         MOVEA.L   A5,A2          MAKE COLUMN POINTER POINT TO FIRST
                                  * ELEMENT IN CURRENT COLUMN (J)
         MOVE.W    D1,D4          ELEMENT COUNTER = SIZE - 1
         *
         *COMPUTE NEXT ELEMENT (I,J) OF PRODUCT AS A ROW (I) OF MATRIX
         *  1 TIMES A COLUMN (J) OF MATRIX 2
         *
COMPEL
         *
         *MULTIPLY M1(I,K) TIMES M2(K,J)
         *
         CLR.W     D5             EXTEND M1(I,K) TO 16 BITS
         MOVE.B    (A1),D5        GET M1(I,K)
         CLR.W     D6             EXTEND M2(K,J) TO 16 BITS
         MOVE.B    (A2),D6        GET M2(K,J)
         MULU      D6,D5          MULTIPLY M1(I,K) X M2(K,J)
         *
         *ADD PRODUCT OF M1(I,K) AND M2(K,J) TO MR(I,J)
         *
         ADD.B     D5,(A0)        UPDATE BYTE-LENGTH ELEMENT IN PRODUCT
                                  * MATRIX
         *
         *CONTINUE COMPUTING ROW OF MATRIX 1 X COLUMN OF MATRIX 2
         *
         ADDQ.L    #1,A1          POINT TO NEXT ELEMENT IN CURRENT
                                  * ROW OF M1
         ADDA.L    D0,A2          POINT TO NEXT ELEMENT IN CURRENT
                                  * COLUMN OF M2
         DBRA      D4,COMPEL      CONTINUE THROUGH ROW X COLUMN
         *
         *PROCEED TO NEXT ELEMENT IN RESULT MATRIX
         *
         ADDQ.L    #1,A0          POINT TO NEXT ELEMENT IN RESULT MATRIX
         ADDQ.L    #1,A5          MOVE COLUMN STARTING POINT TO NEXT
                                  * ELEMENT - THAT IS, M2(0,J)
         DBRA      D3,NXTCOL      COUNT COLUMNS
         *
         *PROCEED TO NEXT ROW IN RESULT MATRIX
         *
         ADDA.L    D0,A3          MOVE ROW STARTING POINT TO NEXT
                                  * ROW - THAT IS, M2(I,0)
         DBRA      D2,NXTROW      COUNT ROWS
         MOVE      #0,CCR         CLEAR CARRY, GOOD EXIT
         *
         *REMOVE PARAMETERS FROM STACK AND EXIT
```

```
        *
MEXIT
        MOVEM.L   (SP)+,A2-A5/D3-D6   RESTORE EXTRA REGISTERS FROM
                                      * STACK
        UNLK      A6                  RESTORE FRAME POINTER
        MOVEA.L   (SP)+,A0            GET RETURN ADDRESS
        LEA       14(SP),SP           REMOVE PARAMETERS FROM STACK
        JMP       (A0)                EXIT TO RETURN ADDRESS

*
*PROGRAM SECTION
SC6K
        MOVE.W    #MSIZE,-(SP)        PUSH MATRIX SIZE INTO STACK
        PEA       MAT2                PUSH BASE ADDRESS OF MATRIX 2
        PEA       MAT1                PUSH BASE ADDRESS OF MATRIX 1
        PEA       MATR                PUSH BASE ADDRESS OF RESULT MATRIX
        JSR       MATMUL              DO MATRIX MULTIPLICATION
                                      *RESULT IN MATR =
                                      *  $33, $2F, $2B, $27
                                      *  $27, $2B, $2F, $33
                                      *  $7B, $77, $73, $6F
                                      *  $6F, $73, $77, $7B
        BRA.S     SC6K                LOOP FOR MORE TESTS
*
*DATA SECTION
*
MSIZE     EQU     4                   SIZE OF MATRIXES
MAT1      DC.B    1,2,3,4             MATRIX 1
          DC.B    4,3,2,1
          DC.B    5,6,7,8
          DC.B    8,7,6,5
MAT2      DC.B    1,2,3,4             MATRIX 2
          DC.B    5,6,7,8
          DC.B    8,7,6,5
          DC.B    4,3,2,1
MATR      DS.B    MSIZE*MSIZE         RESULT MATRIX
          END
```

7 Data structure manipulation

7A Queue manager (INITQ, INSRTQ, REMOVQ)

Manages a queue of 16-bit words on a first-in, first-out basis. The queue may contain up to 65 535 word-length elements plus a 14-byte header and an overflow word (used to distinguish a full queue from an empty queue). The manager consists of the following routines:

1. INITQ starts the queue's head and tail pointers at the base address of its data area, sets the queue's length to zero, and sets its end pointer to just beyond the end of its data area.
2. INSRTQ inserts an element at the queue's tail if there is room for it.
3. REMOVQ removes an element from the queue's head if one is available.

These routines assume a data area of fixed length. The actual queue may occupy any part of it. If either the head or the tail reaches the end pointer, the routine simply sets it back to the base address, thus providing wraparound.

The queue header contains the following:

1. Head pointer (address of oldest element in queue).
2. Tail pointer (address at which next entry will be placed).
3. End pointer (address just beyond the end of the data area).

4. Queue length (number of word-length elements). The queue length is a 16-bit number.

Note that the queue never occupies the entire data area. It is full when its tail pointer is one element behind its head pointer. This leaves one word (an overflow word) unoccupied. The queue is empty when its tail pointer and head pointer are equal. An alternative approach is to keep the size of the data area in the header. This makes the header larger (and the routines somewhat longer) but eliminates the need for an overflow word.

Procedure

1. INITQ sets the head and tail pointers to the base address of the data area, sets the queue's length to zero, and sets the end pointer to the address just beyond the end of the data area.

2. INSRTQ stores the element at the tail and increases the tail pointer. If this moves the tail pointer beyond the end of the data area, INSRTQ sets it back to the base address. It then checks whether the queue was already full (i.e. whether increasing the tail pointer made it equal to the head pointer). If so, it discards the incremented tail pointer and sets Carry to indicate an overflow. If not, it saves the incremented tail pointer and clears Carry.

3. REMOVQ checks whether the queue is empty. If so, it sets Carry to indicate an underflow. If not, it removes the element from the head and increases the head pointer. If this moves the head pointer beyond the end of the data area, REMOVQ sets it back to the base address.

A sequence of INSRTQs and REMOVQs make the head 'chase' the tail across the data area. The occupied part of the area starts at the head and ends just before the tail. Note that INSRTQ puts an element in the overflow word if the queue is full, but this word is not actually part of the queue and the element cannot be retrieved.

Entry conditions

1. INITQ
Base address of queue in register A0
Capacity of queue in words in low word of register D0

2. INSRTQ

Base address of queue in register A0
Element to be inserted in low word of register D0

3. REMOVQ
Base address of queue in register A0

Exit conditions

1. INITQ
Head pointer and tail pointer both set to base address of data area, queue length set to zero, and end pointer set to address just beyond the end of the data area.

2. INSRTQ
Element inserted into queue, queue length increased by 1, and tail pointer adjusted if queue is not full; otherwise, Carry = 1.

3. REMOVQ
Element removed from queue in low word of register D0, queue length reduced by 1, and head pointer adjusted if queue is not empty; otherwise, Carry = 1.

Example

A typical sequence of queue operations proceeds as follows:

1. Initialize the queue. Call INITQ to set the head and tail pointers to the data area's base address, the queue length to zero, and the end pointer to the address just beyond the end of the data area.

2. Insert an element. Call INSRTQ to insert the element, increase the tail pointer by 2, and increase the queue length by 1.

3. Insert another element. Call INSRTQ again to insert the element, increase the tail pointer by 2, and increase the queue length by 1.

4. Remove an element. Call REMOVQ to remove an element, increase the head pointer by 2, and decrease the queue length by 1. Since the queue is organized on a first-in, first-out basis, the element removed is the first one inserted.

Reference

Y. Langsam *et al.*, *Data Structures for Personal Computers*, Prentice-Hall, Englewood Cliffs, NJ, 1985, pp. 154–164.

Registers used

1. INITQ: A0, A1, CCR, D0, D1
2. INSRTQ: A0, A1, CCR, D0
3. REMOVQ: A0, A1, CCR, D0

Execution time

1. INITQ: 113 cycles
2. INSRTQ: 166 cycles
3. REMOVQ: 165 cycles

Program size

1. INITQ: 24 bytes
2. INSRTQ: 40 bytes
3. REMOVQ: 40 bytes

Data memory required None

```
*       Title           Queue Manager
*       Name:           INITQ, INSRTQ, REMOVQ
*
*       Purpose:        This program consists of three
*                       subroutines that manage a queue.
*
*                       INITQ initializes an empty queue.
*                       INSRTQ inserts a 16-bit element into
*                         the queue.
*                       REMOVQ removes a 16-bit element from
*                         the queue.
*
*       Entry:          INITQ
*                         Base address of queue in A0
*                         Queue capacity in 16-bit elements in low word
```

```
*                       of D0
*
*                     INSRTQ
*                       Base address of queue in A0
*                       Element to be inserted in low word of D0
*
*                     REMOVQ
*                       Base address of queue in A0
*
*       Exit:         INITQ
*                       Head pointer = Base address of data area
*                       Tail pointer = Base address of data area
*                       End pointer = Base address of data area +
*                         2 X Queue capacity in 16-bit elements + 2
*                       Queue length = 0 (a 16-bit number)
*
*                     INSRTQ
*                       If queue is not full,
*                         Element added to queue
*                         Tail pointer = Tail pointer + 2
*                         Queue length = Queue length + 1
*                         Carry = 0
*                       else Carry = 1
*
*                     REMOVQ
*                       If queue is not empty,
*                         Element removed from queue in low word
*                           of D0
*                         Head pointer = Head pointer + 2
*                         Queue length = Queue length - 1
*                         Carry = 0
*                       else Carry = 1
*
*       Registers Used: INITQ
*                         A0,A1,CCR,D0,D1
*                       INSRTQ
*                         A0,A1,CCR,D0
*                       REMOVQ
*                         A0,A1,CCR,D0
*
*       Time:           INITQ
*                         113 cycles
*                       INSRTQ
*                         166 cycles
*                       REMOVQ
*                         165 cycles
*
*       Size:           Program 104 bytes
*

*
*       OFFSET DEFINITIONS FROM BASE ADDRESS OF QUEUE
*
HDPTR   EQU     0               HEAD POINTER
TLPTR   EQU     4               TAIL POINTER
ENDPTR  EQU     8               END POINTER
```

```
QLENG     EQU       10                QUEUE LENGTH
DAREA     EQU       14                DATA AREA
*
*INITIALIZE AN EMPTY QUEUE
*HEADER CONTAINS:
*     1) HEAD POINTER (ADDRESS OF OLDEST ELEMENT)
*     2) TAIL POINTER (NEXT AVAILABLE ADDRESS)
*     3) END POINTER (ADDRESS JUST BEYOND END OF DATA AREA)
*     4) QUEUE LENGTH IN WORDS
*
INITQ
          *
          *SET QUEUE LENGTH IN HEADER TO ZERO
          *
          CLR.W     (A0)+             QUEUE LENGTH = ZERO
          *
          *INITIALIZE HEAD AND TAIL POINTERS TO START OF DATA AREA
          *
          LEA       DAREA(A0),A1      POINT TO START OF DATA AREA
          MOVE.L    A1,(A0)+          HEAD POINTER = START OF DATA AREA
          MOVE.L    A1,(A0)+          TAIL POINTER = START OF DATA AREA
          *
          *INITIALIZE END POINTER TO ADDRESS JUST BEYOND DATA AREA
          *
          CLR.L     D1                CLEAR EXTENDED QUEUE SIZE
          MOVE.W    D0,D1             QUEUE SIZE = QUEUE CAPACITY TIMES
                                      * 2 SINCE CAPACITY IS IN WORDS
          ADD.L     D1,D1             THIS IS A 32-BIT QUANTITY SINCE
                                      * LENGTH COULD BE 65,535
          ADDQ.L    #2,D1             ADD 2 EXTRA BYTES (OVERFLOW WORD)
                                      * TO DISTINGUISH AN EMPTY QUEUE
                                      * FROM A FULL ONE
          ADDA.L    D1,A1             ADD QUEUE SIZE TO BASE ADDRESS
          MOVE.L    A1,(A0)           END POINTER = ADDRESS JUST BEYOND
                                      * DATA AREA
          RTS

*
*INSERT AN ELEMENT INTO A QUEUE
*
INSRTQ
          *
          *STORE ELEMENT AT TAIL, THEN CHECK IF QUEUE WAS FULL
          *
          MOVEA.L   TLPTR(A0),A1      GET TAIL POINTER
          MOVE.W    D0,(A1)+          INSERT ELEMENT AT TAIL AND INCREASE
                                      * TAIL POINTER BY 2
                                      *IF QUEUE WAS ALREADY FULL, THIS
                                      * STORES ELEMENT IN OVERFLOW WORD
                                      * WHICH IS NOT ACTUALLY PART OF THE
                                      * QUEUE
          *
          *IF TAIL POINTER HAS REACHED END OF DATA AREA, SET IT
          *  BACK TO BASE ADDRESS
          *
          CMPA.L    ENDPTR(A0),A1     COMPARE TAIL POINTER TO END POINTER
```

```
        BNE.S    STORTP          BRANCH IF TAIL NOT AT END OF DATA
                                 * AREA
        LEA      DAREA(A0),A1    OTHERWISE, MOVE TAIL POINTER BACK TO
                                 * BASE ADDRESS OF DATA AREA
        *
        *CHECK IF QUEUE WAS ALREADY FULL
        *IT WAS IF INCREMENTED TAIL POINTER IS EQUAL TO HEAD POINTER
        *IF SO, EXIT WITHOUT UPDATING TAIL POINTER
        *IT THEN RETAINS ITS OLD VALUE AND THE ELEMENT IS NOT
        *  ACTUALLY ENTERED INTO THE QUEUE
        *IF NOT, UPDATE TAIL POINTER AND ADD 1 TO QUEUE LENGTH
        *CARRY INDICATES WHETHER INSERT SUCCEEDED (0 IF IT DID, 1
        *  IF NOT)
        *
STORTP
        CMPA.L   HDPTR(A0),A1    COMPARE TAIL POINTER TO HEAD POINTER
        ORI      #1,CCR          INDICATE QUEUE FULL (OVERFLOW) BY
                                 * SETTING CARRY
        BEQ.S    EXITIS          BRANCH (EXIT) IF QUEUE WAS FULL
        MOVE.L   A1,TLPTR(A0)    SAVE UPDATED TAIL POINTER
        ADDQ.W   #1,QLENG(A0)    ADD 1 TO QUEUE LENGTH
        MOVE     #0,CCR          CLEAR CARRY TO INDICATE ELEMENT WAS
                                 * INSERTED INTO QUEUE SUCCESSFULLY
EXITIS
        RTS

*
*REMOVE AN ELEMENT FROM A QUEUE
*
REMOVQ
        *
        *CHECK IF QUEUE IS EMPTY BY COMPARING HEAD AND TAIL POINTERS
        *EQUAL POINTERS INDICATE AN EMPTY QUEUE
        *EXIT WITH CARRY SET IF QUEUE IS EMPTY
        *
        MOVEA.L  HDPTR(A0),A1    GET HEAD POINTER
        CMPA.L   TLPTR(A0),A1    COMPARE TO TAIL POINTER
        ORI      #1,CCR          INDICATE QUEUE EMPTY (UNDERFLOW) BY
                                 * SETTING CARRY
        BEQ.S    EXITRQ          BRANCH (EXIT) IF QUEUE IS EMPTY
        *
        *QUEUE NOT EMPTY, SO REMOVE ELEMENT FROM HEAD
        *SUBTRACT 1 FROM QUEUE LENGTH
        *
        MOVE.W   (A1)+,D0        GET ELEMENT FROM HEAD OF QUEUE AND
                                 * MOVE HEAD POINTER UP ONE ELEMENT
        SUBQ.W   #1,QLENG(A0)    SUBTRACT 1 FROM QUEUE LENGTH
        *
        *IF HEAD POINTER HAS REACHED END OF DATA AREA, SET IT BACK
        *  TO BASE ADDRESS OF DATA AREA
        *
        CMPA.L   ENDPTR(A0),A1   COMPARE HEAD POINTER TO END POINTER
        BEQ.S    STORHP          BRANCH IF NOT AT END OF DATA AREA
        MOVEA.L  DAREA(A0),A1    OTHERWISE, MOVE HEAD POINTER BACK
                                 * TO BASE ADDRESS OF DATA AREA
STORHP
```

```
        MOVE.L   A1,HDPTR(A0)   SAVE UPDATED HEAD POINTER
        MOVE     #0,CCR         INDICATE QUEUE NON-EMPTY,
                                * ELEMENT FOUND BY CLEARING CARRY
EXITRQ
        RTS                     EXIT, CARRY INDICATES WHETHER
                                * ELEMENT WAS FOUND (0 IF SO,
                                * 1 IF NOT)

*
*       SAMPLE EXECUTION
*
*
SC7A
        *
        *INITIALIZE EMPTY QUEUE
        *
        MOVE.W   #NELEM,D0      DATA AREA HAS ROOM FOR 12 WORD-LENGTH
                                * ELEMENTS
        MOVEA.L  #QUEUE,A0      GET BASE ADDRESS OF QUEUE BUFFER
        JSR      INITQ          INITIALIZE QUEUE
                                *NOT ACTUALLY NECESSARY IN THIS
                                * SEQUENCE TO EVER LOAD BASE ADDRESS
                                * AGAIN SINCE NONE OF THE QUEUE
                                * ROUTINES CHANGE IT
        *
        *INSERT ELEMENTS INTO QUEUE
        *
        MOVE.W   #$AAAA,D0      ELEMENT TO BE INSERTED IS AAAA
        MOVEA.L  #QUEUE,A0      GET BASE ADDRESS OF QUEUE
        JSR      INSRTQ         INSERT ELEMENT INTO QUEUE
        MOVE.W   #$BBBB,D0      ELEMENT TO BE INSERTED IS BBBB
        MOVEA.L  #QUEUE,A0      GET BASE ADDRESS OF QUEUE
        JSR      INSRTQ         INSERT ELEMENT INTO QUEUE
        *
        *REMOVE ELEMENT FROM QUEUE
        *
        MOVEA.L  #QUEUE,A0      GET BASE ADDRESS OF QUEUE
        JSR      REMOVQ         REMOVE ELEMENT FROM QUEUE
                                * (D0) = $AAAA (FIRST ELEMENT
                                * INSERTED)
        BRA.S    SC7A           REPEAT TEST

*
*DATA
*
HEADLN  EQU      7              HEADER LENGTH IN WORDS
NELEM   EQU      12             NUMBER OF ELEMENTS IN QUEUE
QUEUE   DS.W     HEADLN+NELEM+1 QUEUE BUFFER CONSISTS OF A 14 BYTE
                                * HEADER FOLLOWED BY 26 BYTES FOR
                                * DATA. THIS IS ENOUGH ROOM FOR 12
                                * WORD-LENGTH ELEMENTS PLUS AN
                                * OVERFLOW WORD.

        END
```

7B Stack manager (INITST, PUSHS, POPS, STKTOP)

Manages a stack of 16-bit words on a first-in, last-out basis. The stack can contain up to 65 535 elements. Consists of the following routines:

1. INITST initializes the stack header, consisting of the stack pointer and its upper and lower bounds.

2. PUSHS inserts an element into the stack if there is room for it.

3. POPS removes an element from the stack if one is available.

4. STKTOP returns the top element and its address.

Procedures

1. INITST sets the stack pointer and its lower bound to the base address of the stack's data area. It sets the upper bound to the address of the last word in the data area.

2. PUSHS checks whether the stack pointer exceeds its upper bound. If so, it sets the Carry flag to indicate overflow. If not, it inserts the element at the stack pointer, increases the stack pointer by 2, and clears the Carry flag.

3. POPS checks whether decreasing the stack pointer by 2 will make it less than its lower bound. If so, it sets the Carry flag to indicate underflow. If not, it decreases the stack pointer by 2, removes the element, and clears the Carry flag.

4. STKTOP checks whether decreasing the stack pointer by 2 will make it less than its lower bound. If so, it sets the Carry flag to indicate an empty stack. If not, it returns the top element and its address and clears the Carry flag. Note that the top element's address is not the stack pointer, but rather the location immediately below it.

The software stack differs from the 68000's hardware stack in the following regards:

1. It grows up in memory (i.e. toward higher addresses), whereas the hardware stack grows down (i.e. toward lower addresses).

2. Its pointer contains the next available memory address, whereas the hardware pointer contains the last occupied address.

Entry conditions

1. INITST
Base address of stack in register A0
Size of stack data area in words in low word of register D0

2. PUSHS
Base address of stack in register A0
Element in low word of register D0

3. POPS
Base address of stack in register A0

4. STKTOP
Base address of stack in register A0

Exit conditions

1. INITST
Stack header set up with:
  Stack pointer = Base address of stack's data area
  Lower bound = Base address of stack's data area
  Upper bound = Address of last word in stack's data area

2. PUSHS
Element inserted into stack and stack pointer increased if there is room in the data area; otherwise, Carry = 1, indicating an overflow.

3. POPS
Element removed from stack in low word of register D0 and stack pointer decreased if stack was not empty; otherwise, Carry = 1, indicating an underflow.

4. STKTOP
Top element in low word of register D0 and its address in register A1 if stack is not empty; otherwise, Carry = 1, indicating an empty stack.

Example

A typical sequence of stack operations proceeds as follows:

1. Initialize the empty stack with INITST. This sets the stack pointer and the lower bound to the base address of the stack's data area, and the upper bound to the address of the last word in the data area.

2. Insert an element. Call PUSHS to store an element at the top of the stack and increase the stack pointer by 2.

3. Insert another element. Call PUSHS to store a second element at the top of the stack and increase the stack pointer by 2.

4. Remove an element. Call POPS to decrease the stack pointer by 2 and remove an element from the top of the stack. Since the stack is organized on a last-in, first-out basis, the element removed is the latest one inserted.

You can use STKTOP at any time to obtain the top element and its address without popping the stack. This allows you to use the top of the stack as an extra register. You can examine its contents, replace them, or exchange them with a hardware register. You can also determine the stack's current position if you need to save it or index from it. The wide range of uses is why we include STKTOP, even though it is not an elementary operation (it is equivalent to POPS followed immediately by PUSHS).

Reference

Y. Langsam *et al.*, *Data Structures for Personal Computers*, Prentice-Hall, Englewood Cliffs, NJ, 1985, pp. 108–118.

Registers used

1. INITST: A0, A1, CCR, D0, D1
2. PUSHS: A0, A1, CCR, D0
3. POPS: A0, A1, CCR, D0
4. STKTOP: A0, A1, CCR, D0

Execution time

1. INITST: 108 cycles
2. PUSHS: 101 cycles
3. POPS: 92 cycles
4. STKTOP: 74 cycles

Program size

1. INITST: 28 bytes
2. PUSHS: 22 bytes
3. POPS: 20 bytes
4. STKTOP: 16 bytes

Data memory required None

```
*       Title           Stack Manager
*       Name:           INITST, PUSHS, POPS, STKTOP
*
*       Purpose:        This program consists of four
*                       subroutines that manage a stack.
*
*                       INITST initializes the stack pointer and
*                         the stack's upper and lower bounds
*                       PUSHS inserts a 16-bit element into
*                         the stack.
*                       POPS removes a 16-bit element from
*                         the stack.
*                       STKTOP returns the top element and its
*                         address without changing the stack
*
*       Entry:          INITST
*                         Base address of stack in A0
*                         Size of stack data area in words in low word
*                           of D0
*                       PUSHS
*                         Base address of stack in A0
*                         Element in low word of D0
*                       POPS
*                         Base address of stack in A0
*                       STKTOP
*                         Base address of stack in A0
*
*       Exit:           INITST
*                         Stack header set up with:
*                           Stack pointer = Base address of stack
*                             data area
*                           Lower bound = Base address of stack
*                             data area
*                           Upper bound = Address of last word
*                             in stack data area
*
*                       PUSHS
*                         If stack pointer is at or below upper
*                         bound,
*                            Element inserted into stack
*                            Stack pointer = Stack pointer + 2
```

```
*                             Carry = 0
*                           else Carry = 1
*
*                        POPS
*                          If stack pointer - 2 is at or above lower
*                          bound,
*                             Element removed from stack in low word
*                               of D0
*                             Stack pointer = Stack pointer - 2
*                             Carry = 0
*                          else Carry = 1
*
*                        STKTOP
*                          If stack pointer - 2 is at or above lower
*                          bound,
*                             Top element in low word of D0
*                             Top element's address (stack pointer - 2)
*                               in A1
*                             Carry = 0
*                           else Carry = 1
*
*       Registers Used: INITST
*                          A0,A1,CCR,D0,D1
*                        PUSHS
*                          A0,A1,CCR,D0
*                        POPS
*                          A0,A1,CCR,D0
*                        STKTOP
*                          A0,A1,CCR,D0
*
*       Time:            INITST
*                          108 cycles
*                        PUSHS
*                          101 cycles
*                        POPS
*                          92 cycles
*                        STKTOP
*                          74 cycles
*
*       Size:            Program 86 bytes
*
*                                                                   *


*
*         OFFSET DEFINITIONS FROM BASE ADDRESS OF STACK
*
STKPTR    EQU      0                 STACK POINTER
LWRBND    EQU      4                 LOWER BOUND
UPRBND    EQU      8                 UPPER BOUND
DAREA     EQU      12                DATA AREA

*
*INITIALIZE AN EMPTY STACK
*HEADER CONTAINS:
*    1) STACK POINTER (4 BYTES)
*    2) LOWER BOUND (4 BYTES)
*    3) UPPER BOUND (4 BYTES)
```

```
*
        *
        *STACK POINTER = BASE ADDRESS OF STACK DATA AREA
        *LOWER BOUND = BASE ADDRESS OF STACK DATA AREA
        *
INITST
        LEA       DAREA(A0),A1     COMPUTE BASE ADDRESS OF STACK DATA
                                   * AREA (BASE OF STACK + HEADER SIZE)
        MOVE.L    A1,STKPTR(A0)    STORE IT AS INITIAL STACK POINTER
        MOVE.L    A1,LWRBND(A0)    STORE IT AS LOWER BOUND ALSO
        *
        *UPPER BOUND = ADDRESS OF LAST WORD IN STACK DATA AREA
        *
        SUBQ.W    #1,D0            INDEX OF LAST WORD = STACK SIZE - 1
        CLR.L     D1               EXTEND STACK SIZE IN BYTES TO 32 BITS
        MOVE.W    D0,D1
        ADD.L     D1,D1            MULTIPLY INDEX TIMES 2 SINCE
                                   * ELEMENTS ARE WORD-LENGTH
                                   * THIS IS A 32-BIT QUANTITY
        ADDA.L    D1,A1            ADD DOUBLED INDEX TO BASE ADDRESS OF
                                   * STACK DATA AREA
        MOVE.L    A1,UPRBND(A0)    STORE SUM AS UPPER BOUND OF STACK
        RTS

*
*INSERT A 16-BIT ELEMENT INTO A STACK
*
PUSHS
        *
        *EXIT INDICATING OVERFLOW (CARRY SET) IF STACK IS FULL
        *
        MOVEA.L   UPRBND(A0),A1    GET UPPER BOUND
        CMPA.L    STKPTR(A0),A1    COMPARE TO STACK POINTER
        BCS.S     PSEXIT           BRANCH IF STACK POINTER IS
                                   * ABOVE UPPER BOUND
                                   * NOTE: THIS COMPARISON HANDLES
                                   * SITUATIONS IN WHICH THE STACK
                                   * POINTER HAS BECOME MISALIGNED OR
                                   * HAS GONE OUTSIDE ITS NORMAL RANGE.
                                   *CARRY = 1 IF A BRANCH OCCURS, 0 IF
                                   * NOT
        *
        *NO OVERFLOW - INSERT ELEMENT INTO STACK
        *UPDATE STACK POINTER
        *
        MOVEA.L   STKPTR(A0),A1    GET STACK POINTER
        MOVE.W    D0,(A1)+         INSERT ELEMENT INTO STACK AND
                                   * INCREASE STACK POINTER
        MOVE.L    A1,STKPTR(A0)    SAVE UPDATED STACK POINTER
                                   *CARRY IS CLEARED, INDICATING
                                   * SUCCESSFUL PUSH, BY MOVE
PSEXIT
        RTS                        EXIT, CARRY INDICATES WHETHER
                                   * PUSH WORKED (0) OR STACK WAS
                                   * FULL (1)
```

```
*
*REMOVE A 16-BIT ELEMENT FROM A STACK
*
POPS
        *
        *EXIT INDICATING UNDERFLOW (CARRY = 1) IF STACK IS EMPTY
        *
        MOVEA.L   STKPTR(A0),A1   GET STACK POINTER
        SUBQ.L    #2,A1           DECREASE STACK POINTER BY 2
        CMPA.L    LWRBND(A0),A1   COMPARE TO LOWER BOUND
        BCS.S     EXITPOP         BRANCH (EXIT) IF BELOW LOWER BOUND
                                  * NOTE: THIS COMPARISON HANDLES
                                  * SITUATIONS IN WHICH THE STACK
                                  * POINTER HAS BECOME MISALIGNED OR
                                  * GONE OUTSIDE ITS NORMAL RANGE.
                                  * CARRY IS SET IF A BRANCH OCCURS,
                                  * CLEARED IF NOT.
        *
        *NO UNDERFLOW - REMOVE ELEMENT AND DECREASE STACK POINTER
        *
        MOVE.W    (A1),D0         REMOVE ELEMENT FROM STACK
                                  * AND CLEAR CARRY, INDICATING SUCCESS
        MOVE.L    A1,STKPTR(A0)   SAVE UPDATED STACK POINTER
EXITPOP
        RTS                       EXIT - CARRY INDICATES WHETHER
                                  * POP WORKED (0) OR STACK WAS
                                  * EMPTY (1)
*
*RETURN TOP ELEMENT AND ITS ADDRESS
*
STKTOP
        *
        *EXIT INDICATING ERROR (CARRY = 1) IF STACK IS EMPTY
        *
        MOVEA.L   STKPTR(A0),A1   GET STACK POINTER
        SUBQ.L    #2,A1           DECREASE STACK POINTER BY 2
        CMPA.L    LWRBND(A0),A1   COMPARE TO LOWER BOUND
        BCS.S     EXITTOP         BRANCH (EXIT) IF BELOW LOWER BOUND
                                  * NOTE: THIS COMPARISON HANDLES
                                  * SITUATIONS IN WHICH THE STACK
                                  * POINTER HAS BECOME MISALIGNED OR
                                  * GONE OUTSIDE ITS NORMAL RANGE.
                                  * CARRY IS SET IF A BRANCH OCCURS,
                                  * CLEARED IF NOT.
        *
        *NO ERROR - RETURN TOP ELEMENT AND ITS ADDRESS
        *
        MOVE.W    (A1),D0         RETURN TOP ELEMENT IN D0
                                  * CLEAR CARRY TO INDICATE SUCCESS
                                  * NOTE STACK POINTER DOES NOT CHANGE
EXITTOP
        RTS                       EXIT - CARRY INDICATES WHETHER
                                  * ELEMENT VALID (0) OR STACK WAS
                                  * EMPTY (1)
```

```
*
*       SAMPLE EXECUTION
*
*
SC7B
          *
          *INITIALIZE EMPTY STACK
          *
          MOVEA.L   #STACK,A0       GET BASE ADDRESS OF STACK
          MOVE.W    #STKSZ,D0       GET SIZE OF STACK DATA AREA IN WORDS
          JSR       INITST          INITIALIZE STACK HEADER
          *
          *PUT ELEMENT 1 IN STACK
          *
          MOVE.W    ELEM1,D0        GET ELEMENT 1
                                    *NOTE THAT THE STACK ADDRESS STAYS
                                    * IN A0 SINCE NONE OF THE STACK
                                    * ROUTINES CHANGE THAT REGISTER
                                    * (STKTOP RETURNS THE ADDRESS OF
                                    * THE TOP ELEMENT IN A1)
          JSR       PUSHS           PUT ELEMENT 1 IN STACK
          *
          *PUT ELEMENT 2 IN STACK
          *
          MOVE.W    ELEM2,D0        GET ELEMENT 2
          MOVEA.L   #STACK,A0       GET BASE ADDRESS OF STACK AREA
          JSR       PUSHS           PUT ELEMENT 2 IN STACK
          *
          *REMOVE ELEMENT FROM STACK
          *
          MOVEA.L   #STACK,A0       GET BASE ADDRESS OF STACK AREA
          JSR       POPS            REMOVE ELEMENT FROM STACK TO D0
                                    * D0 NOW CONTAINS ELEMENT 2
                                    * SINCE STACK IS ORGANIZED ON A
                                    * LAST-IN, FIRST-OUT BASIS

          *
          *OBTAIN TOP ELEMENT AND ITS ADDRESS
          *
          MOVEA.L   #STACK,A0       GET BASE ADDRESS OF STACK AREA
          JSR       STKTOP          GET TOP ELEMENT AND ITS ADDRESS
                                    * D0 NOW CONTAINS ELEMENT 1
                                    * A1 CONTAINS ADDRESS STACK, THE
                                    * TOP OCCUPIED ADDRESS
                                    *NOTE THAT STKTOP DOES NOT CHANGE
                                    * THE STACK OR ITS POINTER
          BRA.S     SC7B            LOOP FOR MORE TESTS

*
*DATA
*
STACK     DS.B      22              STACK HAS ROOM FOR 12-BYTE HEADER
                                    * AND 10 BYTES OF DATA (5 WORD-
                                    * LENGTH ELEMENTS)
ELEM1     DC.W      $1111           WORD-LENGTH ELEMENT
ELEM2     DC.W      $2222           WORD-LENGTH ELEMENT
```

```
STKSZ   EQU     5                    SIZE OF STACK DATA AREA IN WORDS

        END
```

7C Singly linked list manager (INLST, RMLST, NFOLLO)

Manages a linked list of elements, each of which has the address of its successor (or 0 if it has no successor) in its first four bytes. Consists of the following routines:

1. INLST inserts an element into the list, given its predecessor.

2. RMLST removes an element from the list (if one exists), given its predecessor.

3. NFOLLO determines the number of successors to a given element.

Note that you can add or remove elements anywhere in the linked list. All you need is the address of the predecessor to provide the linkage.

Procedures

1. INLST obtains the link from the predecessor, changes that link to the new element, and sets the new element's link to the one from the predecessor.

2. RMLST first determines if a successor exists. If not, it sets the Carry flag. If so, it obtains that element's link and puts it in the current element. This unlinks the element and removes it from the list.

3. NFOLLO starts the element count at −1. It then repeatedly adds 1 to the element count and replaces the current element with its link until it finds a zero link (indicating no successor).

Entry conditions

1. INLST
Base address of predecessor in A0
Base address of new element in A1

2. RMLST
Base address of predecessor in A0

3. NFOLLO
Base address of given element in A0

Exit conditions

1. INLST
Element inserted into list with predecessor linked to it. It is linked to the element that had been linked to the predecessor.

2. RMLST
If a successor exists, it is removed from the list, its base address is placed in register A0, and Carry = 0.

Otherwise, Carry = 1.

3. NFOLLO
Number of elements after given element in low word of D0.

Example

A typical sequence of operations on a linked list is:

1. Initialize the empty list by setting the link in the header to zero.

2. Insert an element by using the base address of the header as the predecessor.

3. Insert another element by using the base address of the element just inserted as the predecessor.

4. Remove the first element by using the base address of the header as the predecessor. Note that we can remove either element from the list by supplying the appropriate predecessor.

These routines require the user to keep track of the list's length separately. An alternative approach is to put the length in the header and update it during each insertion or removal. While NFOLLO can determine the list's length at any time, it is slow for long lists since it must examine each element.

Note that the routines allow the link to be anywhere in an element. They do not take advantage of its actually being in the first four bytes.

Reference

Y. Langsam *et al.*, *Data Structures for Personal Computers*, Prentice-Hall, Englewood Cliffs, NJ, 1985, pp. 164–189.

Registers used

1. INLST: A0, A1, CCR, D0
2. RMLST: A0, A1, CCR, D0
3. NFOLLO: A0, CCR, D0, D1

Execution time

1. INLST: 68 cycles
2. RMLST: 102 cycles
3. NFOLLO: 32 cycles per element plus 22 cycles overhead.

Program size

1. INLST: 14 bytes
2. RMLST: 24 bytes
3. NFOLLO: 14 bytes

Data memory required None

```
*       Title           Singly Linked List Manager
*       Name:           INLST, RMLST, NFOLLO
*
*       Purpose:        This program consists of three subroutines
*                       that manage a singly linked list.
*
*                       INLST inserts an element into the linked
*                         list.
*                       RMLST removes an element from the linked
*                         list.
*                       NFOLLO determines the number of elements
*                         following a given element.
*
*       Entry:          INLST
*                          Predecessor's address in register A0
*                          Entry's address in register A1
*                       RMLST
*                          Predecessor's address in register A0
*                       NFOLLO
*                          Given element's address in register A0
*
*       Exit:           INLST
*                         Element added to list
*                       RMLST
```

```
*                     If successor exists,
*                       its address is in register A0
*                       Carry = 0
*                     else
*                       Carry = 1
*                   NFOLLO
*                     Number of elements in register D0
*
*       Registers Used: INLST
*                     A0,A1,CCR,D0
*                   RMLST
*                     A0,A1,CCR,D0
*                   NFOLLO
*                     A0,CCR,D0,D1
*
*       Time:       INLST
*                     68 cycles
*                   RMLST
*                     102 cycles
*                   NFOLLO
*                     32 cycles per element plus 22 cycles
*                       overhead
*
*       Size:       Program 52 bytes
*
*
*
*         OFFSET FROM BASE ADDRESS OF LIST ELEMENT
*
FLINK   EQU       0                ADDRESS OF NEXT ELEMENT

*
*         INSERT AN ELEMENT INTO A SINGLY LINKED LIST
*

INLST
        *
        *UPDATE LINKS TO INCLUDE NEW ELEMENT
        *LINK PREDECESSOR TO NEW ELEMENT
        *LINK NEW ELEMENT TO ELEMENT FORMERLY LINKED TO
        *  PREDECESSOR
        *
        MOVE.L    FLINK(A0),D0    GET LINK FROM PREDECESSOR
        MOVE.L    D0,FLINK(A1)    STORE LINK IN NEW ELEMENT
        MOVE.L    A1,FLINK(A0)    STORE NEW ELEMENT AS LINK IN
                                  * PREDECESSOR
        *
        *EXIT
        *
        RTS

*
*         REMOVE AN ELEMENT FROM A SINGLY LINKED LIST
*
RMLST
        *
```

```
        *EXIT INDICATING FAILURE (CARRY SET) IF NO SUCCESSOR
        *
        MOVE.L   FLINK(A0),D0    GET LINK TO POSSIBLE SUCCESSOR
        ORI      #1,CCR          INDICATE SUCCESSOR IS NULL BY
                                 * SETTING CARRY
        BEQ.S    RMEXIT          BRANCH IF SUCCESSOR IS NULL
        *
        *UNLINK REMOVED ELEMENT BY TRANSFERRING ITS LINK TO
        *  PREDECESSOR
        *
        MOVEA.L  D0,A1
        MOVE.L   FLINK(A1),D0    GET LINK FROM REMOVED ELEMENT
        MOVE.L   D0,FLINK(A0)    MOVE LINK TO PREDECESSOR
        MOVEA.L  A1,A0           EXIT WITH REMOVED ELEMENT IN A0
                                 * MOVES CLEAR CARRY
        *
        *EXIT
        *
RMEXIT
        RTS                      CARRY = 0 IF ELEMENT FOUND, 1
                                 * IF NOT
*
*       DETERMINE NUMBER OF SUCCESSORS TO A GIVEN ELEMENT
*
NFOLLO
        *
        *COUNT ELEMENTS UNTIL ENCOUNTERING ONE WITH A ZERO LINK
        *  (NO SUCCESSOR)
        *
        MOVEQ    #1,D0           START ELEMENT COUNT AT -1
CHKNXT  ADDQ.W   #1,D0           ADD 1 TO ELEMENT COUNT
        MOVEA.L  FLINK(A0),A0    REPLACE ELEMENT WITH SUCCESSOR
        MOVE.L   A0,D1           TEST IF SUCCESSOR EXISTS
        BNE.S    CHKNXT          BRANCH (CONTINUE) IF SUCCESSOR
                                 * EXISTS
        RTS                      EXIT

*                                                               *
*       SAMPLE EXECUTION                                        *
*                                                               *
*
SC7C
        *
        *INITIALIZE EMPTY LINKED LIST
        *
        CLR.L    FLINK(LLHDR)    CLEAR LINK FIELD IN LIST HEADER
                                 * 0 INDICATES NO SUCCESSOR
        *
        *INSERT AN ELEMENT INTO LINKED LIST
        *
        MOVEA.L  #LLHDR,A0       GET PREDECESSOR (HEADER)
        MOVEA.L  #ELEM1,A1       GET BASE ADDRESS OF ELEMENT 1
        JSR      INLST           INSERT ELEMENT INTO LIST
        *
        *INSERT ANOTHER ELEMENT INTO LINKED LIST
        *
```

```
        MOVEA.L   #ELEM1,A0       GET PREDECESSOR (ELEMENT 1)
        MOVEA.L   #ELEM2,A1       GET BASE ADDRESS OF ELEMENT 2
        JSR       INLST           INSERT ELEMENT INTO LIST
        *
        *DETERMINE LENGTH OF LIST
        *
        MOVEA.L   #LLHDR,A0       GET ADDRESS OF HEADER
        JSR       NFOLLO          DETERMINE NUMBER OF ELEMENTS
                                  * FOLLOWING HEADER.  RESULT
                                  * SHOULD BE (D0) = 2

        *
        *REMOVE FIRST ELEMENT FROM LINKED LIST
        *
        MOVEA.L   #LLHDR,A0       GET PREDECESSOR
        JSR       RMLST           REMOVE ELEMENT FROM LIST
                                  *END UP WITH HEADER LINKED TO
                                  * SECOND ELEMENT
                                  *A0 CONTAINS ADDRESS OF
                                  * FIRST ELEMENT
        BRA.S     SC7C            REPEAT TEST

*
*DATA
*
LLHDR   DS.L      1               LINKED LIST HEADER (LINK ONLY)
ELEM1   DS.L      1               ELEMENT 1 - HEADER (LINK) ONLY
ELEM2   DS.L      1               ELEMENT 2 - HEADER (LINK) ONLY
        END
```

7D Doubly linked list manager (INSRDL, INSLDL, DELDL)

Manages a doubly linked list of elements. Each element contains the address of its successor (or 0 if it has no successor) in its first four bytes. It contains the address of its predecessor (or 0 if it has no predecessor) in its next four bytes. The manager consists of the following routines:

1. INSRDL inserts an element into the list, given its predecessor. That is, it inserts to the right.

2. INSLDL inserts an element into the list, given its successor. That is, it inserts to the left.

3. DELDL deletes an element from the list by linking its successor (if it has one) directly to its predecessor (if it has one) and vice versa.

As with a singly linked list, you can add or remove elements anywhere. All you need is the address of the predecessor (for INSRDL) or successor (for INSLDL) to insert an element. No parameters are needed to delete an element, since each one contains links to both its successor and its predecessor.

Procedures

1. INSRDL first obtains the forward link from the predecessor. It then changes the links as follows:

(a) The new element becomes the forward link of the predecessor.
(b) The predecessor becomes the backward link of the new element.
(c) The old forward link from the predecessor becomes the forward link of the new element.
(d) The new element becomes the backward link of the predecessor's successor if the old forward link was non-null.

2. INSLDL works just like INSRDL except that it first obtains the backward link from the successor. Here, of course, the successor is known to exist, whereas the backward link might be null (i.e. the successor might not have a predecessor).

3. DELDL first obtains the element's forward and backward links. If a successor exists, it sets that element's backward link to the deleted element's backward link. If a predecessor exists, it sets that element's forward link to the deleted element's forward link. This unlinks the element, removing it from the list. An optional extension would be to clear the element's links so no trace remains of its previous state. This would help maintain security, but would also increase the difficulty of 'undoing' deletions.

Entry conditions

1. INSRDL
Address of predecessor in register A0
Address of new element in register A1

2. INSLDL
Address of successor in register A0
Address of new element in register A1

3. DELDL
Address of element to be deleted in register A0

Note that the programs all take a general approach to the positions of the links, rather than taking advantage of the fact that the forward link is at offset 0.

Exit conditions

1. INSRDL
Element added to list after its predecessor. The new links make it the successor of its predecessor and the predecessor of its predecessor's successor if such an element exists.

2. INSLDL
Element added to list before its successor. The new links make it the predecessor of its successor and the successor of its successor's predecessor if such an element exists.

3. DELDL
Element removed from the list. The new links make its successor the successor of its predecessor, and its predecessor the predecessor of its successor, assuming that these elements exist.

Example

A typical sequence of operations on a doubly linked list is:

1. Initialize the empty list by setting both links in the header to zero.

2. Insert an element with INSRDL, using the header's address as its predecessor.

3. Insert another element with INSRDL, by using the address of the element just added as the predecessor. An alternative is to insert the new element between the header and the previous element (with INSLDL).

4. Delete the first element with DELDL, leaving only the header and the second element.

Note that we can delete either element and we can insert elements on either side of existing elements.

Reference

Y. Langsam *et al.*, *Data Structures for Personal Computers*, Prentice-Hall, Englewood Cliffs, NJ, 1985, pp. 210–217.

Registers used

1. INSRDL: A0, A1, CCR, D0
2. INSLDL: A0, A1, CCR, D0
3. DELDL: A0, A1, CCR, D0

Execution time

1. INSRDL: 116 cycles
2. INSLDL: 116 cycles
3. DELDL: 108 cycles

Program size

1. INSRDL: 26 bytes
2. INSLDL: 26 bytes
3. DELDL: 26 bytes

Data memory required None

```
*       Title           Doubly Linked List Manager
*       Name:           INSRDL, INSLDL, DELDL
*
*       Purpose:        This program consists of three subroutines
*                       that manage a doubly linked list.
*
*                       INSRDL inserts an element into the doubly
*                         linked list as the successor of a given
*                         element.
*                       INSLDL inserts an element into the doubly
*                         linked list as the predecessor of a given
*                         element.
*                       DELDL removes an element from the
*                         doubly linked list.
*
*       Entry:          INSRDL
*                         Predecessor in register A0
*                         New element in register A1
*                       INSLDL
*                         Successor in register A0
*                         New element in register A1
*                       DELDL
*                         Element in register A0
*
*       Exit:           INSRDL
*                         Element inserted into list after predecessor
*                       INSLDL
*                         Element inserted into list before successor
*                       DELDL
*                         Element removed from list
*
*       Registers Used: INSRDL
*                         A0,A1,CCR,D0
*                       INSLDL
*                         A0,A1,CCR,D0
*                       DELDL
*                         A0,A1,CCR,D0
*
*       Time:           INSRDL
*                         116 cycles
*                       INSLDL
*                         116 cycles
*                       DELDL
*                         108 cycles
*
*       Size:           Program 78 bytes                        *
*                                                               *

*
*         OFFSETS FROM BASE ADDRESS OF LIST ELEMENTS
*
FDLINK  EQU     0               FORWARD LINK (ADDRESS OF NEXT
*                                 ELEMENT)
```

```
BKLINK   EQU      4                 BACKWARD LINK (ADDRESS OF PREVIOUS
*                                     ELEMENT)
*
*
*        INSERT AN ELEMENT INTO A DOUBLY LINKED LIST, GIVEN ITS
*          PREDECESSOR
*        THAT IS, INSERT AN ELEMENT TO THE RIGHT OF A GIVEN ELEMENT
*
INSRDL
         *
         *UPDATE LINKS TO INCLUDE NEW ELEMENT
         *MAKE NEW ELEMENT PREDECESSOR'S FORWARD LINK
         *MAKE PREDECESSOR NEW ELEMENT'S BACKWARD LINK
         *MOVE PREDECESSOR'S PREVIOUS FORWARD LINK TO NEW ELEMENT
         *
         MOVE.L   FDLINK(A0),D0     GET FORWARD LINK FROM PREDECESSOR
         MOVE.L   A1,FDLINK(A0)     MAKE NEW ELEMENT INTO PREDECESSOR'S
                                    * FORWARD LINK
         MOVE.L   A0,BKLINK(A1)     MAKE PREDECESSOR NEW ELEMENT'S
                                    * BACKWARD LINK
         MOVE.L   D0,FDLINK(A1)     MOVE PREDECESSOR'S PREVIOUS FORWARD
                                    * LINK TO NEW ELEMENT
                                    *THIS ALSO SETS FLAGS ACCORDING TO
                                    * FORWARD LINK
         *
         *IF PREDECESSOR HAS A SUCCESSOR, LINK IT TO NEW ELEMENT
         *THAT IS, MAKE NEW ELEMENT SUCCESSOR'S BACKWARD LINK
         *
         BEQ.S    INREXT            BRANCH IF SUCCESSOR IS NULL
         MOVEA.L  D0,A0             MAKE NEW ELEMENT SUCCESSOR'S
         MOVE.L   A1,BKLINK(A0)      BACKWARD LINK
         *
         *EXIT
         *
INREXT
         RTS                        EXIT

*
*        INSERT AN ELEMENT INTO A DOUBLY LINKED LIST, GIVEN ITS
*          SUCCESSOR
*        THAT IS, INSERT AN ELEMENT TO THE LEFT OF A GIVEN ELEMENT
*
INSLDL
         *
         *UPDATE LINKS TO INCLUDE NEW ELEMENT
         *MAKE NEW ELEMENT SUCCESSOR'S BACKWARD LINK
         *MAKE SUCCESSOR NEW ELEMENT'S FORWARD LINK
         *MOVE PREDECESSOR'S PREVIOUS BACKWARD LINK TO NEW ELEMENT
         *
         MOVE.L   BKLINK(A0),D0     GET BACKWARD LINK FROM SUCCESSOR
         MOVE.L   A1,BKLINK(A0)     MAKE NEW ELEMENT INTO SUCCESSOR'S
                                    * BACKWARD LINK
         MOVE.L   A0,FDLINK(A1)     MAKE SUCCESSOR NEW ELEMENT'S
                                    * FORWARD LINK
         MOVE.L   D0,BKLINK(A1)     MOVE SUCCESSOR'S PREVIOUS BACKWARD
                                    * LINK TO NEW ELEMENT
```

```
                                  *THIS ALSO SETS FLAGS ACCORDING TO
                                  * BACKWARD LINK
        *
        *IF SUCCESSOR HAS A PREDECESSOR, LINK IT TO NEW ELEMENT
        *THAT IS, MAKE NEW ELEMENT PREDECESSOR'S FORWARD LINK
        *
        BEQ.S     INLEXT          BRANCH IF PREDECESSOR IS NULL
        MOVEA.L   D0,A0           MAKE NEW ELEMENT PREDECESSOR'S
        MOVE.L    A1,FDLINK(A0)    FORWARD LINK
        *
        *EXIT
        *
INLEXT
        RTS                       EXIT

*
*       REMOVE AN ELEMENT FROM A DOUBLY LINKED LIST
*
DELDL
        *
        *GET ELEMENT'S FORWARD AND BACKWARD LINKS
        *
        MOVEA.L   FDLINK(A0),A1   GET ELEMENT'S FORWARD LINK
        MOVEA.L   BKLINK(A0),A0   GET ELEMENT'S BACKWARD LINK
                                  *NOTE THAT MOVEA DOES NOT AFFECT
                                  * FLAGS, SO A ZERO LINK WILL NOT
                                  * SET THE ZERO FLAG
        *
        *IF ELEMENT HAS A SUCCESSOR, MOVE ELEMENT'S BACKWARD
        *  LINK TO SUCCESSOR
        *
        MOVE.L    A1,D0           CHECK IF SUCCESSOR EXISTS
        BEQ.S     CHKPR           BRANCH IF SUCCESSOR IS NULL
        MOVE.L    A0,BKLINK(A1)   MOVE ELEMENT'S BACKWARD LINK
                                  * TO SUCCESSOR
        *
        *IF ELEMENT HAS A PREDECESSOR, MOVE ELEMENT'S FORWARD
        *  LINK TO PREDECESSOR
        *
CHKPR
        MOVE.L    A0,D0           CHECK IF PREDECESSOR EXISTS
        BEQ.S     DELEXT          BRANCH IF PREDECESSOR IS NULL
        MOVE.L    A1,FDLINK(A0)   MOVE ELEMENT'S FORWARD LINK
                                  * TO PREDECESSOR
DELEXT
        RTS                       EXIT

*
*       SAMPLE EXECUTION
*
*
SC7D
        *
        *INITIALIZE EMPTY DOUBLY LINKED LIST
        *
        MOVEA.L   #HEADER,A0      GET BASE ADDRESS OF HEADER
```

```
         CLR.L     FDLINK(A0)       CLEAR HEADER'S FORWARD LINK
         CLR.L     BKLINK(A0)       CLEAR HEADER'S BACKWARD LINK
                                    *0 INDICATES NO LINK IN THAT
                                    * DIRECTION
         *
         *INSERT ELEMENT INTO DOUBLY LINKED LIST
         *
         MOVEA.L   #HEADER,A0       GET BASE ADDRESS OF PREDECESSOR
                                    * (HEADER)
         MOVEA.L   #ELEM1,A1        GET ELEMENT 1
         JSR       INSRDL           INSERT ELEMENT 1 INTO LIST AFTER
                                    * HEADER
         *
         *INSERT ANOTHER ELEMENT INTO DOUBLY LINKED LIST
         *
         MOVEA.L   #ELEM1,A0        GET SUCCESSOR
         MOVEA.L   #ELEM2,A1        GET ELEMENT 2
         JSR       INSLDL           INSERT ELEMENT 2 INTO LIST BEFORE
                                    * ELEMENT 1
         *
         *REMOVE FIRST ELEMENT FROM DOUBLY LINKED LIST
         *
         MOVEA.L   #ELEM1,A0        GET ELEMENT
         JSR       DELDL            REMOVE ELEMENT 1 FROM LIST
                                    *END UP WITH HEADER LINKED TO
                                    * ELEMENT 2

         BRA.S     SC7D             REPEAT TEST
*
*DATA
*
HEADER   DS.L      2                HEADER WITH BACKWARD AND FORWARD
                                    * LINKS
ELEM1    DS.L      2                ELEMENT 1 - HEADER (LINKS) ONLY
ELEM2    DS.L      2                ELEMENT 2 - HEADER (LINKS) ONLY
         END
```

7E Dynamic memory allocation (INITFS, ALLOCM, DALLOC)

Allocates memory dynamically in blocks of arbitrary size. The free space is organized as a linked list; each element has a header containing its size and a link to the next element. Consists of the following routines:

1. INITFS initializes the free space as a single block with a null link.
2. ALLOCM obtains a block of given size from the list.
3. DALLOC releases a block of given size to the list.

These routines allow you to obtain and release memory blocks of any size.

Procedures

1. INITFS first determines if there is enough free memory for a header and some data. If not, it sets Carry. If so, it clears the link to the next element, sets the size of the free area to the given size minus the header's size (six bytes), and clears Carry.

2. ALLOCM searches the list for elements large enough to satisfy the request. It accepts either the element closest in size to the request or the first element within a threshold of the request size. If it finds such an element, it reduces its size by the request and returns a pointer to the allocated memory. The pointer is set to the furthest available part of the block to maintain the header. The Carry is cleared if the request can be satisfied and set otherwise.

3. DALLOC first determines if enough memory has been released to hold a header and some data. If not, it sets Carry. If so, it links the released area to the initial element, forms its header, and clears Carry. This links the released area to the element to which the initial element had been linked; its size is the amount of memory released minus the size of the header.

Entry conditions

1. INITFS
Base address of free area in A0
Size of free area in bytes in low word of D0

2. ALLOCM
Base address of free area in A0
Size of request in bytes in low word of D0

3. DALLOC
Base address of free area in A0
Base address of released area in A1
Size of released area in low word of D0

Exit conditions

1. INITFS
Free area established as a single block with a header containing a null link. Its size is the number of bytes allocated minus the header's size. Carry = 0 if enough space was allocated for the header and some data, and 1 if not.

2. ALLOCM If a large enough block exists, the base address of the selected block is returned in A0 and Carry = 0. The selected block is either the one closest in size to the request or the first one that has a size within a threshold of the request. Otherwise, Carry = 1.

3. DALLOC
If enough memory was released to hold a header and some data, it is linked to the list and Carry = 0. Otherwise, Carry = 1.

Example

A typical sequence of memory allocations and releases is:

1. Make the free space into a single list element by calling INITFS.

2. Obtain memory for an overall program's temporary storage by calling ALLOCM.

3. Obtain memory for a subprogram's temporary storage by calling ALLOCM.

4. Free the memory used by the subprogram by calling DALLOC when it finishes running.

5. Obtain memory for a second subprogram's temporary storage by calling ALLOCM.

6. Obtain memory for a subsubprogram's temporary storage by calling ALLOCM.

7. Free the memory used by the subsubprogram by calling DALLOC when it finishes running.

8. Free the memory used by the second subprogram by calling DALLOC when it finishes running.

9. Free the memory used by the overall program by calling DALLOC when it finishes running.

Note that, even if the sequence allocates and releases equal amounts of memory, the system will not return to its initial state. Released blocks will become additional elements with their own headers rather than being combined into a single element. Obviously, this fragments free memory and creates many headers. Eventually, the system cannot grant any sizeable request for memory. In actual applications, this usually forces the running of a compaction or *garbage collection* routine that combines small blocks or returns the system to its initial state as a single large block of free memory.

There are many methods for efficient allocation and deallocation of memory (see the references). The one we have implemented here is to search for the block that is closest in size to the request or has a size within a threshold of the request. This approach avoids breaking up large blocks to satisfy small requests. The threshold prevents the allocation routine from wasting time searching for a closer fit that is only a marginal improvement.

References

M. Augenstein and A. Tenenbaum, *Data Structures and PL/I Programming*, Prentice-Hall, Englewood Cliffs, NJ, 1979, Chapter 10. There is also a Pascal version of this book from the same publisher.

D. E. Knuth, *The Art of Computer Programming. Volume 1: Fundamental Algorithms*, 2nd edn, Addison-Wesley, Reading, MA, 1973, pp. 435–455.

Registers used

1. INITFS: A0, CCR, D0

2. ALLOCM: A0, A1, CCR, D0, D1, D2
3. DALLOC: A0, A1, CCR, D0

Execution time

1. INITFS: 71 cycles
2. ALLOCM: 56–88 cycles per block that must be examined plus 63 cycles overhead
3. DALLOC: 97 cycles

Program size

1. INITFS: 20 bytes
2. ALLOCM: 66 bytes
3. DALLOC: 28 bytes

Data memory required None

Special case

An attempt to initialize or release an amount of memory that is less than or equal to the size of the header will result in an immediate return with the Carry set to 1.

```
*       Title           Dynamic Memory Allocation
*       Name:           INITFS, ALLOCM, DALLOC
*
*       Purpose:        This program consists of three subroutines
*                       that allocate memory dynamically, that is, on
*                       a demand basis in units of variable size.
*
*                       INITFS initializes the free memory area as
*                         a linked list with a single element.
*                       ALLOCM allocates a block of memory of specified
*                         size. It searches the list for an element
*                         whose size most closely matches the request.
*                       DALLOC releases a block of memory of specified
*                         size
*
*       Entry:          INITFS
*                         Base address of free area in A0
```

```
*                         Size of free area in bytes in low word of D0
*                       ALLOCM
*                         Base address of free area in A0
*                         Size of request in bytes in low word of D0
*                       DALLOC
*                         Base address of free memory in A0
*                         Base address of released area in A1
*                         Size of released area in low word of D0
*
*       Exit:           INITFS
*                         Free area set up as a linked list consisting
*                           of a single element
*                       ALLOCM
*                         If a block of sufficient size exists,
*                           base address of selected block is in
*                             register A0
*                           Carry = 0
*                         else
*                           Carry = 1
*                         If more than one such block exists, the
*                           one closest in size to the request or the
*                           first one encountered within a threshold of
*                           the size of the request is allocated.
*                       DALLOC
*                         If the released block is large enough, it is
*                           placed in the linked list
*                           Carry = 0
*                         else
*                           Carry = 1
*
*       Registers Used: INITFS
*                         A0,CCR,D0
*                       ALLOCM
*                         A0,A1,CCR,D0,D1,D2
*                       DALLOC
*                         A0,A1,CCR,D0
*
*       Time:           INITFS
*                         71 cycles
*                       ALLOCM
*                         56-88 cycles per block that must be examined
*                         plus 63 cycles overhead
*                       DALLOC
*                         97 cycles
*
*       Size:           Program 114 bytes                                 *
*                                                                         *

*
*DECLARATIONS
*
HEADLN    EQU     6                 LENGTH OF HEADER IN BYTES
DIFLMT    EQU     $20               BLOCK SIZE DIFFERENCE LIMIT
                                    *SIZE DIFFERENCES LESS THAN THIS
                                    * LIMIT ARE CONSIDERED SMALL ENOUGH
                                    * TO HALT THE BLOCK SEARCH.  THIS
```

```
                                        * LIMIT HELPS AVOID WASTING TIME
                                        * WHEN ONLY A MINOR IMPROVEMENT IS
                                        * POSSIBLE. IF THE LIMIT IS 0, THE
                                        * BLOCK WITH THE SMALLEST SIZE
                                        * DIFFERENCE IS CHOSEN.
*
*       OFFSET DEFINITIONS FROM BASE ADDRESS OF BLOCKS
*
FLINK   EQU     0               ADDRESS OF NEXT BLOCK
BSIZE   EQU     4               SIZE OF BLOCK IN BYTES (INCLUDING
                                * THE HEADER)

*
*       INITIALIZE FREE SPACE AS A LINKED LIST WITH A SINGLE ELEMENT
*
INITFS
        *
        *CHECK IF ENOUGH SPACE AVAILABLE FOR HEADER
        *IF NOT (OR JUST ENOUGH), EXIT WITH CARRY SET
        *
        SUB.W   #HEADLN,D0      IS THERE ENOUGH ROOM FOR HEADER?
        BLS.S   INITERR         BRANCH TO ERROR EXIT IF NOT
        *
        *SET UP HEADER FOR SINGLE BLOCK OF FREE MEMORY:
        *  LINK TO NEXT ELEMENT = NULL (0) IN FIRST TWO BYTES
        *  SIZE OF AREA = ALLOCATED AREA MINUS HEADER SIZE IN
        *    NEXT TWO BYTES
        *
        MOVE.W  D0,BSIZE(A0)    SET BLOCK SIZE IN HEADER
        CLR.L   FLINK(A0)       CLEAR LINK (MAKE IT NULL)
                                *THIS ALSO CLEARS CARRY, INDICATING
                                * NO ERRORS
        RTS
        *
        *ERROR EXIT WITH CARRY SET
        *
INITERR
        ORI     #1,CCR          ERROR - BLOCK TOO SMALL (SET CARRY)
        RTS
*
*       ALLOCATE A BLOCK OF MEMORY
*
ALLOCM
        *
        *INITIALIZE VARIABLES FOR BLOCK SIZE SEARCH
        *
        CLR.L   D1              INITIALIZE BLOCK ADDRESS TO NULL
        MOVEA.L D1,A1
        MOVE.W  #$FFFF,D1       INITIALIZE SMALLEST DIFFERENCE
                                * REGISTER TO MAXIMUM DIFFERENCE
        *
        *CHECK NEXT ELEMENT TO SEE IF IT CAN SATISFY REQUEST
        *
GETBSZ
        MOVE.W  BSIZE(A0),D2    GET BLOCK SIZE
        CMP.W   D0,D2           IS NEXT ELEMENT LARGE ENOUGH?
```

```
        BCS.S      CHKNXT           BRANCH IF IT IS TOO SMALL
        SUB.W      D0,D2            CALCULATE SIZE DIFFERENCE
        CMP.W      #DIFLMT,D2       COMPARE DIFFERENCE TO THRESHOLD
        BHI.S      CMPSML           CONTINUE IF DIFFERENCE ABOVE LIMIT
        MOVE.W     D2,D1            DIFFERENCE AT OR BELOW LIMIT, SO
                                    * SAVE DIFFERENCE OF SELECTED BLOCK
        MOVEA.L    A0,A1            SAVE BASE ADDRESS OF SELECTED BLOCK
        BRA.S      GETSP            ALLOCATE MEMORY FROM SELECTED BLOCK
CMPSML
        CMP.W      D1,D2            COMPARE CURRENT DIFFERENCE TO
                                    * SMALLEST DIFFERENCE FOUND SO FAR
        BCC.S      CHKNXT           BRANCH IF CURRENT DIFFERENCE NOT
                                    * SMALLER, SO NOT WORTH KEEPING
        MOVE.W     D2,D1            SAVE NEW DIFFERENCE AS SMALLEST
        MOVEA.L    A0,A1            SAVE BASE ADDRESS OF BLOCK WITH
                                    * SMALLEST SIZE DIFFERENCE
        *
        *CHECK IF THERE ARE MORE BLOCKS IN LIST
        *
CHKNXT
        MOVEA.L    FLINK(A0),A0     GET LINK TO NEXT ELEMENT
        MOVE.L     A0,D2            IS THERE A NEXT ELEMENT?
        BNE.S      GETBSZ           BRANCH IF THERE IS (LINK NONZERO)
        *
        *NO MORE ELEMENTS - CHECK IF A BLOCK WAS FOUND
        *
        MOVE.L     A1,D2            CHECK IF BLOCK FOUND
        BEQ.S      ALLERR           JUMP IF NO BLOCK FOUND
        *
        *BLOCK WITH SMALLEST SIZE DIFFERENCE FOUND
        *ALLOCATE THAT BLOCK'S LAST BYTES
        *REDUCE BLOCK'S SIZE BY THE NUMBER OF BYTES ALLOCATED
        *
GETSP
        SUB.W      D0,BSIZE(A1)     NEW SIZE IS OLD SIZE MINUS SIZE
                                    * OF REQUEST
                                    * THIS ALSO CLEARS CARRY
        LEA        HEADLN(A1,D1.W),A0 BASE ADDRESS OF ALLOCATED AREA =
                                    * BASE ADDRESS OF ELEMENT +
                                    * DIFFERENCE + HEADER LENGTH
                                    *THIS ALLOCATES THE END OF THE DATA
                                    * AREA, LEAVING THE FIRST PART
                                    * (INCLUDING THE HEADER) AVAILABLE
                                    * FOR LATER REQUESTS
        *
        *EXIT
        *
        RTS
        *
        *SET CARRY TO INDICATE FAILURE AND EXIT
        *
ALLERR
        ORI        #1,CCR           NO BLOCK FOUND, SO SET CARRY
        RTS
```

```
*
*DEALLOCATE A BLOCK OF MEMORY
*
DALLOC
        *
        *ERROR EXIT IF RELEASED BLOCK TOO SMALL TO HOLD HEADER
        *  OR JUST LARGE ENOUGH FOR IT
        *
        SUB.W     #HEADLN,D0       IS BLOCK LARGE ENOUGH FOR HEADER?
        BLS.S     DALERR           BRANCH IF NOT LARGE ENOUGH
        *
        *PUT RELEASED BLOCK IN LINKED LIST - LINK IT TO BLOCK AT
        *  BOTTOM OF FREE AREA AND ESTABLISH ITS SIZE
        *
        MOVE.W    D0,BSIZE(A1)     BLOCK SIZE = RELEASED AREA - SIZE
                                   * OF HEADER
                                   * THIS ALSO CLEARS CARRY
        MOVE.L    FLINK(A0),D0     GET LINK FROM BLOCK AT BOTTOM OF
                                   * FREE AREA
        MOVE. L   A1,FLINK(A0)     LINK RELEASED BLOCK TO BLOCK AT
                                   * BOTTOM
        MOVE.L    D0,FLINK(A1)     LINK RELEASED BLOCK TO BLOCK THAT
                                   * WAS LINKED TO BOTTOM
        *
        *EXIT
        *
        RTS
        *
        *ERROR EXIT - SET CARRY - BLOCK TOO SMALL
DALERR
        ORI       #1,CCR           ERROR - BLOCK TOO SMALL
        RTS

*                                                                  *
*       SAMPLE EXECUTION
*
*
SC7E
        *
        *INITIALIZE FREE MEMORY AREA
        *
        MOVEA.L   #FREEM,A0        GET BASE ADDRESS OF FREE AREA
        MOVE.W    #FSIZE,D0        GET SIZE OF FREE AREA (100 HEX BYTES)
        JSR       INITFS           INITIALIZE FREE AREA AS LINKED LIST
        *
        *REQUEST MEMORY
        *
        MOVEA.L   #FREEM,A0        GET BASE ADDRESS OF FREE AREA
        MOVE.W    #$20,D0          REQUEST 20 HEX BYTES
        JSR       ALLOCM           THIS WILL ALLOCATE BYTES E0-FF HEX
                                   * ADDRESS FREEM+$E0 RETURNED IN A0
        MOVEA.L   #FREEM,A0        GET BASE ADDRESS OF FREE AREA
        MOVE.W    #$30,D0          REQUEST 30 HEX BYTES
        JSR       ALLOCM           THIS WILL ALLOCATE BYTES B0-DF HEX
                                   * ADDRESS FREEM+$B0 RETURNED IN A0
        *
```

```
        *RELEASE MEMORY
        *
        MOVEA.L   #FREEM,A0       GET BASE ADDRESS OF FREE AREA
        MOVEA.L   #FREEM+$E0,A1   RELEASED AREA STARTS AT FREEM+$E0
        MOVE.W    #$20,D0         RELEASE 20 HEX BYTES
        JSR       DALLOC          THE RESULT HERE WILL BE AN
                                  * AREA OF B0 HEX BYTES STARTING
                                  * AT ADDRESS FREEM. ONLY AA OF
                                  * THESE BYTES WILL BE AVAILABLE
                                  * SINCE THE FIRST 6 ARE USED AS
                                  * A HEADER.  THIS AREA WILL BE
                                  * LINKED TO AN AREA OF 20 HEX
                                  * BYTES (1A AVAILABLE) STARTING
                                  * AT ADDRESS FREEM+$E0
        *
        *REQUEST MEMORY
        *
        MOVEA.L   #FREEM,A0       GET BASE ADDRESS OF FREE AREA
        MOVE.W    #$10,D0         REQUEST 10 HEX BYTES
        JSR       ALLOCM          THIS WILL ALLOCATE BYTES $F0-$FF
                                  *ADDRESS FREEM+$F0 RETURNED IN A0
        BRA.S     SC7E            REPEAT TEST

*
*DATA
*
FSIZE   EQU       $100            SIZE OF FREE AREA IN BYTES
FREEM   DS.B      $100            FREE AREA
        END
```

8 Input/output

8A Read a line from a terminal (RDLINE)

Reads a line of ASCII characters ending with a carriage return and saves it in a buffer. Defines the control characters Control H (08 hex), which deletes the latest character, and Control X (18 hex), which deletes the entire line. Sends a bell character (07 hex) to the terminal if the buffer overflows. Echoes each character placed in the buffer. Echoes non-printable characters as an up-arrow or caret (^) followed by the printable equivalent (see Table 8-1). Sends a new line sequence (typically consisting of carriage return and line feed characters) to the terminal before exiting.

Table 8-1 ASCII control characters and printable equivalents

Name	Hex value	Printable equivalent
NUL	00	Control @
SOH	01	Control A
STX	02	Control B
ETX	03	Control C
EOT	04	Control D
ENQ	05	Control E
ACK	06	Control F
BEL	07	Control G
BS	08	Control H

HT	09	Control I
LF	0A	Control J
VT	0B	Control K
FF	0C	Control L
CR	0D	Control M
SO	0E	Control N
SI	0F	Control O
DLE	10	Control P
DC1	11	Control Q
DC2	12	Control R
DC3	13	Control S
DC4	14	Control T
NAK	15	Control U
SYN	16	Control V
ETB	17	Control W
CAN	18	Control X
EM	19	Control Y
SUB	1A	Control Z
ESC	1B	Control [
FS	1C	Control \
GS	1D	Control]
RS	1E	Control ^
VS	1F	Control _

RDLINE assumes the following system-dependent subroutines:

1. RDCHAR reads a character from the terminal and puts it in the low byte of register D0.

2. WRCHAR sends the character in the low byte of register D0 to the terminal.

3. WRNEWL sends a new line sequence to the terminal.

These subroutines are assumed to preserve all user registers except A0, A1, CCR, D0, D1, and D2 (in accordance with the Macintosh assembly language interface as described in Apple Computer, Inc., *Inside Macintosh*, Addison-Wesley, Reading, MA, 1985, pp. I-94–I-95).

RDLINE is an example of a terminal input handler. The control characters and I/O subroutines in an actual system will, of course, be computer-dependent. A specific example in the listing is for an Atari 520ST running GEMDOS.

Procedure The program starts the loop by reading a character. If it is a carriage return, the program sends a new line sequence to the terminal and exits. Otherwise, it checks for the special characters Control H and Control X. If the buffer is not empty, Control H makes the program reduce both the buffer pointer and the character count by 1 and send a backspace string (cursor left, space, cursor left) to the terminal. Control X makes the program delete characters until it empties the buffer.

If the character is not special, the program determines whether the buffer is full. If so, the program sends a bell character to the console. If not, the program stores the character in the buffer, echoes it to the display, and increments both the character count and the buffer pointer.

Before echoing a character or deleting one from the display, the program must determine whether it is printable. If not (i.e. it is a non-printable ASCII control character), the program must display or delete two characters, the control indicator (up-arrow or caret) and the printable equivalent (see Table 8-1). Note, however, that the character is stored in its non-printable form.

Entry conditions

Base address of buffer in register A0
Length (size) of buffer in bytes in low word of register D0

Exit conditions

Number of characters in the buffer in low word of register D0

Examples

1. Data: Line from keyboard is 'ENTERcr'
   Result: Character count = 5 (line length)
   Buffer contains 'ENTER'
   'ENTER' echoed to terminal, followed by the new line sequence (carriage return, line feed)
   Note that the 'cr' (carriage return) character does not appear in the buffer

2. Data: Line from keyboard is 'DMcontrolHNcontrolXENTET-controlHRcr'
   Result: Character count = 5 (length of final line after deletions)

Buffer contains 'ENTER'
'DMBackspaceStringNBackspaceStringBackspaceS-tringENTET BackspaceStringR' sent to screen, followed by a new line sequence. The backspace string deletes a character from the screen and moves the cursor left one column.
The sequence of operations is as follows:

Character typed	Initial buffer	Final buffer	Sent to terminal
D	empty	'D'	D
M	'D'	'DM'	M
control H	'DM'	'D'	backspace string
N	'D'	'DN'	N
control X	'DN'	empty	2 backspace strings
E	empty	'E'	E
N	'E'	'EN'	N
T	'EN'	'ENT'	T
E	'ENT'	'ENTE'	E
T	'ENTE'	'ENTET'	T
control H	'ENTET'	'ENTE'	backspace string
R	'ENTE'	'ENTER'	R
cr	'ENTER'	'ENTER'	New line string

What happened is the following:

(a) The operator types 'D', 'M'
(b) The operator sees that 'M' is wrong (it should be 'N'), presses control H to delete it, and types 'N'.
(c) The operator then sees that the initial 'D' is also wrong (it should be 'E'). Since the error is not the latest character, the operator presses control X to delete the entire line, and then types 'ENTET'.
(d) The operator notes that the second 'T' is wrong (it should be 'R'), presses control H to delete it, and types 'R'.
(e) The operator types a carriage return to end the line.

Registers used A0, A1, CCR, D0, D1, D2

Execution time Approximately 151 cycles to put an ordinary character in the buffer, not considering the execution time of either RDCHAR or WRCHAR.

Program size 108 bytes

Data memory required None

Special cases

1. If the buffer is empty, typing Control H (delete one character) or Control X (delete the entire line) has no effect.

2. If the program receives an ordinary character when the buffer is full, it discards the character and sends a Bell character to the terminal (ringing the bell).

```
*       Title           Read Line
*       Name:           RDLINE
*
*       Purpose:        Read characters from an input device until
*                       a carriage return is found. Defines the
*                       control characters
*                         Control H -- Delete latest character.
*                         Control X -- Delete all characters.
*                       Any other control character is placed in
*                       the buffer and displayed as the equivalent
*                       printable ASCII character preceded by an
*                       up-arrow or caret.
*
*       Entry:          Base address of buffer in register A0
*                       Length of buffer in bytes in low word of
*                         register D0
*
*       Exit:           Number of characters in buffer in low word of
*                         register D0
*
*       Registers Used: A0,A1,CCR,D0,D1,D2
*
*       Time:           Not applicable.
*
*       Size:           Program 108 bytes
*

*EQUATES
BELL    EQU     $07     BELL CHARACTER
BSKEY   EQU     $08     BACKSPACE KEYBOARD CHARACTER (CONTROL-H)
```

```
CR      EQU     $0D      CARRIAGE RETURN FOR CONSOLE
CRKEY   EQU     $0D      CARRIAGE RETURN KEYBOARD CHARACTER
CSRLFT  EQU     $08      MOVE CURSOR LEFT FOR CONSOLE
CTLOFF  EQU     $40      OFFSET FROM CONTROL CHARACTER TO PRINTED
                         * FORM (E.G., CONTROL-X TO X)
DELKEY  EQU     $18      DELETE LINE KEYBOARD CHARACTER (CONTROL-X)
LF      EQU     $0A      LINE FEED FOR CONSOLE
SPACE   EQU     $20      SPACE CHARACTER (ALSO MARKS END OF CONTROL
                         * CHARACTERS IN ASCII SEQUENCE)
STERM   EQU     $00      STRING TERMINATOR FOR GEMDOS (ASCII NUL)
UPARRW  EQU     $5E      UP-ARROW OR CARET USED AS CONTROL INDICATOR

RDLINE
        *
        *INITIALIZE CHARACTER COUNT TO ZERO, SAVE BUFFER LENGTH
        *  AND BUFFER POINTER
        *
        CLR.W   D1             CHARACTER COUNT = ZERO
        MOVE.W  D0,D2          SAVE BUFFER LENGTH
        *
        *READ LOOP
        *READ CHARACTERS UNTIL A CARRIAGE RETURN IS TYPED
        *
RDLOOP
        JSR     RDCHAR         READ CHARACTER FROM KEYBOARD
                               *DOES NOT ECHO CHARACTER
        *
        *CHECK FOR CARRIAGE RETURN, EXIT IF FOUND
        *
        CMPI.B  #CR,D0         CHECK FOR CARRIAGE RETURN
        BEQ.S   EXITRD         END OF LINE IF CARRIAGE RETURN
        *
        *CHECK FOR BACKSPACE AND DELETE CHARACTER IF FOUND
        *
        CMPI.B  #BSKEY,D0      CHECK FOR BACKSPACE KEY
        BNE.S   RDLP1          BRANCH IF NOT BACKSPACE
        JSR     BACKSP         IF BACKSPACE, DELETE ONE CHARACTER
        BRA.S   RDLOOP         THEN START READ LOOP AGAIN
        *
        *CHECK FOR DELETE LINE CHARACTER AND EMPTY BUFFER IF FOUND
        *
RDLP1
        CMPI.B  #DELKEY,D0     CHECK FOR DELETE LINE KEY
        BNE.S   RDLP2          BRANCH IF NOT DELETE LINE
DEL1
        JSR     BACKSP         DELETE A CHARACTER
        BNE.S   DEL1           CONTINUE UNTIL BUFFER EMPTY
                               *THIS ACTUALLY BACKS UP OVER EACH
                               * CHARACTER RATHER THAN JUST MOVING
                               * UP A LINE
        BRA.S   RDLOOP
        *
        *KEYBOARD ENTRY IS NOT A SPECIAL CHARACTER
        *CHECK IF BUFFER IS FULL
        *IF FULL, RING BELL AND CONTINUE
        *IF NOT FULL, STORE CHARACTER AND ECHO
```

```
        *
RDLP2
        CMP.W    D1,D2           COMPARE COUNT AND BUFFER LENGTH
        BHI.S    STRCH           JUMP IF BUFFER NOT FULL
        MOVE.B   #BELL,D0        BUFFER FULL, RING BELL
        JSR      WRCHAR
        BRA.S    RDLOOP          THEN CONTINUE THE READ LOOP
        *
        *BUFFER NOT FULL, STORE CHARACTER
        *
STRCH
        MOVE.B   D0,(A0)+        STORE CHARACTER IN BUFFER
                                 * AND INCREASE BUFFER POINTER
        ADDQ.W   #1,D1           ADD 1 TO CHARACTER COUNT
        *
        *IF CHARACTER IS CONTROL, THEN OUTPUT
        * UP-ARROW FOLLOWED BY PRINTABLE EQUIVALENT
        *
        CMPI.B   #SPACE,D0       CONTROL CHARACTER IF CODE IS
                                 * BELOW SPACE (20 HEX) IN ASCII
                                 * SEQUENCE
        BCC.S    PRCH            JUMP IF A PRINTABLE CHARACTER
        MOVE.W   D0,-(SP)        SAVE NONPRINTABLE CHARACTER
        MOVE.B   #UPARRW,D0      WRITE UP-ARROW OR CARET
        JSR      WRCHAR
        MOVE.W   (SP)+,D0        RECOVER NONPRINTABLE CHARACTER
        ADDI.B   #CTLOFF,D0      CHANGE TO PRINTABLE FORM
PRCH
        JSR      WRCHAR          ECHO CHARACTER TO TERMINAL
        BRA.S    RDLOOP          THEN CONTINUE READ LOOP
        *
        *EXIT
        *SEND NEW LINE SEQUENCE (USUALLY CR,LF) TO TERMINAL
        *LINE LENGTH = CHARACTER COUNT
        *
EXITRD
        JSR      WRNEWL          ECHO NEW LINE SEQUENCE
        MOVE.W   D1,D0           LINE LENGTH = CHARACTER COUNT
        RTS

*************************************************************
*
* THE FOLLOWING SUBROUTINES ARE TYPICAL EXAMPLES FOR AN
*  ATARI 520ST RUNNING GEMDOS
*
*************************************************************

*************************************************************
*ROUTINE: RDCHAR
*PURPOSE: READ A CHARACTER FROM STANDARD INPUT BUT DO NOT
*         ECHO TO STANDARD OUTPUT
*ENTRY: NONE
*EXIT: LOW BYTE OF REGISTER D0 = CHARACTER
*REGISTERS USED: CCR,D0
```

```
*****************************************************************

RDCHAR:
        *
        *WAIT FOR CHARACTER FROM KEYBOARD
        *RETURN WITH IT IN LOW BYTE OF REGISTER DO
        *
        MOVE.L    A0,-(SP)     PRESERVE REGISTER A0
        MOVE.W    #7,-(SP)     GEMDOS FUNCTION 7, STANDARD
                               * CHARACTER INPUT
        TRAP      #1
        ADDQ.L    #2,SP        REMOVE GEMDOS PARAMETER FROM STACK
        MOVEA.L   (SP)+,A0     RESTORE REGISTER A0
        RTS                    RETURN WITH CHARACTER IN LOW BYTE
                               * OF REGISTER D0

*****************************************************************
*ROUTINE: WRCHAR
*PURPOSE: WRITE CHARACTER TO STANDARD OUTPUT DEVICE
*ENTRY: LOW BYTE OF REGISTER D0 = CHARACTER
*EXIT:  NONE
*REGISTERS USED: CCR,D0
*****************************************************************

WRCHAR
        *
        *WRITE A CHARACTER TO STANDARD OUTPUT DEVICE
        *
        MOVE.L    A0,-(SP)     PRESERVE REGISTER A0
        MOVE.W    D0,-(SP)     PUSH CHARACTER ONTO STACK
        MOVE.W    #2,-(SP)     GEMDOS FUNCTION 2, STANDARD CHARACTER
                               * OUTPUT
        TRAP      #1
        ADDQ.L    #4,SP        REMOVE GEMDOS PARAMETERS FROM STACK
        MOVE.L    (SP)+,A0     RESTORE REGISTER A0
        RTS

*****************************************************************
*ROUTINE: WRNEWL
*PURPOSE: ISSUE NEW LINE SEQUENCE TO VIDEO DISPLAY (STANDARD OUTPUT)
*         NORMALLY, THIS SEQUENCE IS A CARRIAGE RETURN AND
*          LINE FEED, BUT SOME OUTPUT DEVICES REQUIRE ONLY
*         A CARRIAGE RETURN.
*ENTRY: NONE
*EXIT:  NONE
*REGISTERS USED: A1,CCR,D0
*****************************************************************

WRNEWL
        *
        *SEND NEW LINE STRING TO STANDARD OUTPUT
        *
        MOVEA.L   #NLSTRG,A1   POINT TO NEW LINE STRING
        JSR       WRSTRG       SEND STRING TO STANDARD OUTPUT
        RTS
NLSTRG  DC.B      CR,LF,STERM NEW LINE STRING
```

```
*********************************************************
*ROUTINE: BACKSP
*PURPOSE: PERFORM A DESTRUCTIVE BACKSPACE
*ENTRY: D1 = NUMBER OF CHARACTERS IN BUFFER
*       A0 = NEXT AVAILABLE BUFFER ADDRESS
*EXIT:  IF NO CHARACTERS IN BUFFER
*          Z = 1
*       ELSE
*          Z = 0
*          CHARACTER REMOVED FROM BUFFER
*REGISTERS USED: A0,A1,CCR,D0,D1
*********************************************************

BACKSP
        *
        *CHECK FOR EMPTY BUFFER
        *
        TST.W     D1             TEST NUMBER OF CHARACTERS
        BEQ.S     EXITBS         BRANCH (EXIT) IF BUFFER EMPTY
        *
        *OUTPUT BACKSPACE STRING
        * TO REMOVE CHARACTER FROM DISPLAY
        *
        MOVE.B    -(A0),D0       GET CHARACTER
        CMPI.B    #SPACE,D0      IS IT A CONTROL CHARACTER?
        BCC.S     BS1            NO, BRANCH, DELETE ONLY ONE CHARACTER
        MOVEA.L   #BSSTRG,A1     YES, DELETE 2 CHARACTERS
                                 * (UP-ARROW AND PRINTABLE EQUIVALENT)
        JSR       WRSTRG         WRITE BACKSPACE STRING
BS1     MOVEA.L   #BSSTRG,A1
        JSR       WRSTRG         WRITE BACKSPACE STRING
        *
        *SUBTRACT 1 FROM CHARACTER COUNT
        *
        SUBQ.W    #1,D1          ONE LESS CHARACTER IN BUFFER
EXITBS
        RTS
*
*DESTRUCTIVE BACKSPACE STRING FOR VIDEO DISPLAY
*MOVES CURSOR LEFT, PRINTS SPACE OVER CHARACTER, MOVES
*  CURSOR LEFT
*
BSSTRG  DC.B      CSRLFT,SPACE,CSRLFT,STERM

*********************************************************
*ROUTINE: WRSTRG
*PURPOSE: OUTPUT STRING TO VIDEO DISPLAY (STANDARD OUTPUT)
*ENTRY: A1 = BASE ADDRESS OF STRING
*EXIT:  NONE
*REGISTERS USED: A1,CCR,D0,D1
*********************************************************

WRSTRG
        MOVE.L    A0,-(SP)       PRESERVE REGISTER A0
        MOVE.L    A1,-(SP)       PUSH STRING BASE ADDRESS ONTO STACK
        MOVE.W    #9,-(SP)       GEMDOS FUNCTION 9 - PRINT STRING
```

```
        TRAP      #1
        ADDQ.L    #6,SP         REMOVE GEMDOS PARAMETERS FROM STACK
        MOVEA.L   (SP)+,A0      RESTORE REGISTER A0
        RTS
*
*       SAMPLE EXECUTION:
*
*EQUATES
PROMPT  EQU       '?'           OPERATOR PROMPT = QUESTION MARK

SC8A
        *
        *READ LINE FROM STANDARD INPUT DEVICE
        *
        MOVE.B    #PROMPT,D0    WRITE PROMPT (?)
        JSR       WRCHAR
        LEA       INBUFF,A0     GET INPUT BUFFER ADDRESS
        MOVE.W    LENBUF,D0     GET LENGTH OF BUFFER
        JSR       RDLINE        READ LINE
        TST.W     D0            CHECK LINE LENGTH
        BEQ.S     SC8A          READ NEXT LINE IF LENGTH IS 0
        *
        *ECHO LINE TO CONSOLE
        *
        MOVE.W    D0,D1         SAVE NUMBER OF CHARACTERS IN BUFFER
        SUBQ.W    #1,D1         ADJUST COUNT TO EXIT ON -1
        LEA       INBUFF,A0     POINT TO START OF BUFFER
WRBUFF
        MOVE.B    (A0)+,D0      WRITE NEXT CHARACTER
        JSR       WRCHAR
        DBRA      D1,WRBUFF     CONTINUE UNTIL ALL CHARACTERS SENT
        JSR       WRNEWL        THEN END WITH CR,LF
        BRA.S     SC8A          READ NEXT LINE


*DATA SECTION
LENBUF  EQU       16            LENGTH OF INPUT BUFFER
INBUFF  DS.W      LENBUF        INPUT BUFFER

        END
```

8B Write a line to an output device (WRLINE)

Writes characters until it empties a buffer with given length and base address. Assumes the system-dependent subroutine WRCHAR, which sends the character in the low byte of register D0 to an output device.

WRLINE is an example of an output driver. The actual I/O subroutines will, of course, be computer-dependent. A specific example in the listing is for an Atari 520ST running GEMDOS.

Procedure The program exits immediately if the buffer is empty. Otherwise, it sends characters to the output device one at a time until it empties the buffer. The program saves its temporary data in memory rather than in registers to avoid dependence on WRCHAR.

Entry conditions

Base address of buffer in register A0
Number of characters in the buffer in low word of register D0

Exit conditions

None

Example

Data: Number of characters = 5
Buffer contains 'ENTER'
Result: 'ENTER' sent to the output device.

Registers used A0, CCR, D0

Execution time 69 cycles overhead plus 57 cycles per byte. This does not, of course, include the execution time of WRCHAR.

Program size 30 bytes

Data memory required None

Special case An empty buffer results in an immediate exit with nothing sent to the output device.

```
*       Title             Write a Line to an Output Device
*       Name:             WRLINE
*
*       Purpose:          Write characters to standard
*                           output device
*
*       Entry:            Base address of buffer in register A0
*                         Number of characters in buffer in low word of
*                           register D0
*
*       Exit:             None
*
*       Registers Used: A0,CCR,D0
*
*       Time:             Indeterminate, depends on the speed of the
*                         WRCHAR routine.
*
*       Size:             Program 30 bytes
*

WRLINE
        *
        *EXIT IMMEDIATELY IF BUFFER IS EMPTY
        *
        LINK    A6,#-2          ALLOCATE MEMORY FOR COUNTER
        TST.W   D0              TEST NUMBER OF CHARACTERS IN BUFFER
        BEQ.S   EXITWL          BRANCH (EXIT) IF BUFFER EMPTY
                                * A0 = BASE ADDRESS OF BUFFER
        *
        *LOOP SENDING CHARACTERS TO OUTPUT DEVICE
        *
        MOVE.W  D0,-2(A6)       SAVE CHARACTER COUNT IN LOCAL MEMORY
                                * TO AVOID DEPENDENCE ON WRCHAR
WRLLP
        MOVE.B  (A0)+,D0        GET NEXT CHARACTER
        JSR     WRCHAR          SEND CHARACTER
        SUBQ.W  #1,-2(A6)       CONTINUE UNTIL ALL CHARACTERS SENT
        BNE.S   WRLLP
EXITWL
        UNLK    A6              DEALLOCATE LOCAL MEMORY
        RTS                     EXIT

************************************************************
*
* THE FOLLOWING SUBROUTINES ARE TYPICAL EXAMPLES FOR AN
* ATARI 520ST RUNNING GEMDOS
```

```
*
**********************************************************

****************************************
*ROUTINE: WRCHAR
*PURPOSE: WRITE CHARACTER TO OUTPUT DEVICE
*ENTRY: LOW BYTE OF REGISTER D0 = CHARACTER
*EXIT:  NONE
*REGISTERS USED: A0,CCR,D0
****************************************

WRCHAR
*
*       SEND CHARACTER TO STANDARD OUTPUT DEVICE FROM LOW BYTE OF
*         REGISTER D0
*
        MOVE.L  A0,-(SP)          PRESERVE REGISTER A0
        MOVE.W  D0,-(SP)          PUSH CHARACTER ONTO STACK
        MOVE.W  #2,-(SP)          GEMDOS FUNCTION 2, STANDARD CHARACTER
                                  * OUTPUT
        TRAP    #1
        ADDQ.L  #4,SP             REMOVE GEMDOS PARAMETERS FROM STACK
        MOVEA.L (SP)+,A0          RESTORE REGISTER A0
        RTS

*
*       SAMPLE EXECUTION:
*

*CHARACTER EQUATES
CR      EQU     $0D               CARRIAGE RETURN FOR KEYBOARD
LF      EQU     $0A               LINE FEED FOR VIDEO DISPLAY
PROMPT  EQU     '?'               OPERATOR PROMPT = QUESTION MARK

SC8B
        *
        *READ LINE FROM KEYBOARD
        *
        MOVE.B  #PROMPT,D0        OUTPUT PROMPT (?)
        JSR     WRCHAR
        LEA     INBUFF,A0         POINT TO INPUT BUFFER
        MOVE.W  #LENBUF,D0        GET BUFFER SIZE
        JSR     RDLINE            READ LINE
        MOVE.W  D0,INBUFF         SAVE NUMBER OF CHARACTERS READ
        MOVE.B  #CR,D0            OUTPUT CARRIAGE RETURN
        JSR     WRCHAR
        MOVE.B  #LF,D0            OUTPUT LINE FEED
        JSR     WRCHAR
        *
        *WRITE LINE ON VIDEO DISPLAY
        *
        LEA     INBUFF,A0         POINT TO NUMBER OF CHARACTERS IN
                                  * BUFFER
        MOVE.W  (A0)+,D0          GET LINE LENGTH
```

```
        JSR     WRLINE          WRITE LINE
        LEA     CRLF,A0         OUTPUT CARRIAGE RETURN, LINE FEED
        MOVEQ   #2,D0           LENGTH OF CRLF STRING
        JSR     WRLINE          WRITE CRLF STRING
        BRA.S   SC8B            REPEAT CLEAR, READ, WRITE SEQUENCE

*DATA SECTION
CRLF    DC.B    CR,LF           CARRIAGE RETURN, LINE FEED
LENBUF  EQU     $10             LENGTH OF INPUT BUFFER
INBUFF  DC.W    LENBUF          LENGTH OF INPUT BUFFER
        DS.B    LENBUF          DATA BUFFER

        END
```

8C Parity checking and generation (CKPRTY, GEPRTY)

Generates and checks parity. GEPRTY generates odd parity for a 7-bit character and puts it in bit 7. This gives the byte even parity, as it makes the total number of 1 bits even. CKPRTY sets the Carry flag to 0 if a data byte has even parity and to 1 otherwise. A byte's parity is even if it has an even number of 1 bits and odd otherwise.

Procedures The basic approach here is to exclusive-OR all the bits together. The algorithm is a three-stage approach as suggested by J. R. Thompson ('Software Provides Rapid Parity Check', *EDN*, 18 September 1986, p. 316). The first stage exclusive-ORs bits 0–3 with the bit positions four higher. The second stage exclusive-ORs the pairs of bits, leaving the combined even-numbered bits in bit 1 and the combined odd-numbered bits in bit 0. The final stage exclusive-ORs the two combinations, producing even parity in bit 0. This emulates the three logic levels in a typical parity generator chip such as the 74180.

1. GEPRTY clears data bit 7 before starting the algorithm. Afterward, it shifts odd parity into bit 7.

2. CKPRTY concludes by shifting odd parity into the Carry and Extend flags.

Entry conditions

1. GEPRTY
Data in low byte of register D0

2. CKPRTY
Data in low byte of register D0

Exit conditions

1. GEPRTY
Data with odd parity in bit 7 in low byte of register D0

2. CKPRTY
Carry = 0 if the data has even parity, 1 if it had odd parity

Examples

1. GEPRTY

(a) Data: (D0) = 42_{16} = 01000010_2 (ASCII B)

Result: (D0) = 42_{16} = 01000010_2 (ASCII B with bit 7 cleared)
Odd parity is 0, as 01000010_2 has an even number (2) of 1 bits

(b) Data: (D0) = 43_{16} = 01000011_2 (ASCII C)

Result: (D0) = $C3_{16}$ = 11000011_2 (ASCII C with bit 7 set)
Odd parity is 1, as 01000011_2 has an odd number (3) of 1 bits.

2. CKPRTY

(a) Data: (D0) = 42_{16} = 01000010_2 (ASCII B)

Result: Carry = 0, since 01000010_2 has an even number (2) of 1 bits.

(b) Data: (D0) = 43_{16} = 01000011_2 (ASCII C)

Result: Carry = 1, since 01000011_2 has an odd number (3) of 1 bits.

Registers used

1. GEPRTY: CCR, D0, D1, D2
2. CKPRTY: CCR, D0, D1

Execution time

1. GEPRTY: 136 cycles. 100 cycles if CKPRTY's code is repeated instead of being called.
2. CKPRTY: 80 cycles

Program size

1. GEPRTY: 12 bytes (30 bytes as a stand-alone program)
2. CKPRTY: 22 bytes

Data memory required None

```
*       Title              Generate and Check Parity
*       Name:              GEPRTY, CKPRTY
*
*
*       Purpose:           GEPRTY generates odd parity in bit 7
*                          for a 7-bit character.  The overall
*                          parity of the byte is even.
*
*                          CKPRTY checks the parity of a byte
*
*       Entry:             GEPRTY - Data in low byte of register D0
*                          CKPRTY - Data in low byte of register D0
*
*       Exit:              GEPRTY - Data with odd parity in bit 7
*                            in low byte of register D0
*                          CKPRTY - Carry = 0 if parity is even,
*                            Carry = 1 if parity is odd
*
*       Registers Used: GEPRTY - CCR,D0,D1,D2
*                          CKPRTY - CCR,D0,D1
*
*       Time:              GEPRTY - 136 cycles
*                          CKPRTY - 80 cycles
*
*       Size:              Program  34 bytes
*
*


*
*       GENERATE ODD PARITY IN BIT 7.  THIS GIVES OVERALL
*         DATA BYTE EVEN PARITY.
*
GEPRTY
        ADD.B   D0,D0      DROP DATA BIT 7 BY CLEARING IT
        MOVE.B  D0,D2      SAVE SHIFTED DATA
        *
        *COMPUTE ODD PARITY WITH 3 STAGES OF EXCLUSIVE-ORS
        *
        BSR     CKPRTY     COMPUTE ODD PARITY (IN CARRY AND
                           * EXTEND FLAGS
        *
        *MOVE ODD PARITY TO BIT 7 OF DATA
        *
        MOVE.B  D2,D0      RESTORE SHIFTED DATA
        ROXR.B  #1,D0      ROTATE TO FORM BYTE WITH ODD PARITY IN BIT 7
                           * RESULT HAS EVEN PARITY
        RTS
*
*       CHECK PARITY
*
CKPRTY
        MOVE.B  D0,D1      FIRST STAGE EXCLUSIVE-ORS BIT PAIRS IN
                           * BIT POSITIONS 0-3
        LSR.B   #4,D1
        EOR.B   D1,D0
        MOVE.B  D0,D1      SECOND STAGE EXCLUSIVE-ORS EVEN,ODD BITS
```

```
                         * IN BIT POSITIONS 0 AND 1
        LSR.B   #2,D1
        EOR.B   D1,D0
        MOVE.B  D0,D1    THIRD STAGE EXCLUSIVE-ORS ALL BITS IN
                         * BIT POSITION 0
        LSR.B   #1,D1
        EOR.B   D1,D0    ODD PARITY IS NOW IN BIT 0
        LSR.B   #1,D0    MOVE ODD PARITY TO CARRY, EXTEND FLAGS
        RTS
*
*       SAMPLE EXECUTION:
*

        *
        *GENERATE PARITY FOR VALUES FROM 0..127 AND STORE THEM
        * IN BUFFER 1
        *
SC8C
        LEA     BUFR1,A0       GET BASE ADDRESS OF BUFFER
        CLR.B   D0             START DATA AT ZERO
GPARTS
        MOVE.W  D0,-(SP)       SAVE DATA IN STACK
        JSR     GEPRTY         GIVE DATA BYTE EVEN PARITY
        MOVE.B  D0,(A0)+       SAVE DATA BYTE WITH EVEN PARITY
        MOVE.W  (SP)+,D0       RESTORE DATA FROM STACK
        ADDQ.B  #1,D0          ADD 1 TO DATA VALUE
        CMP.B   #128,D0        HAVE WE REACHED HIGHEST VALUE?
        BNE.S   GPARTS         BRANCH IF NOT DONE
        *
        *CHECK PARITY FOR ALL BYTES IN BUFFER 1
        *CARRY = 1 IF ROUTINE FINDS A PARITY ERROR, REGISTER
        *  A0 POINTS TO THE BYTE WITH THE ERROR
        *CARRY = 0 IF ROUTINE FINDS NO PARITY ERRORS
        *
        LEA     BUFR1,A0       GET BASE ADDRESS OF BUFFER
        MOVE.B  #129,D3        CHECK 128 BYTES
CPARTS
        SUBQ.B  #1,D3          COUNT BYTES
        BEQ.S   CPEXIT
        MOVE.B  (A0)+,D0       GET NEXT DATA BYTE
        JSR     CKPRTY         CHECK PARITY
        BCC.S   CPARTS         IF NO ERROR, CONTINUE THROUGH VALUES
        SUBQ.L  #1,A0          PARITY ERROR - MAKE A0 POINT TO IT
CPEXIT
        BRA.S   SC8C           BRANCH FOR ANOTHER TEST
*
*DATA SECTION
*
BUFR1   DS.B    128            BUFFER FOR DATA VALUES WITH ODD PARITY
                               * IN BIT 7. BYTES HAVE EVEN PARITY.

        END
```

8D CRC16 checking and generation (ICRC16, CRC16, GCRC16)

Generates a 16-bit cyclic redundancy check (CRC) based on the IBM Binary Synchronous Communications protocol (BSC or Bisync). Uses the polynomial $X^{16} + X^{15} + X^2 + 1$. Entry point ICRC16 initializes the CRC to 0 and the polynomial to its bit pattern. Entry point CRC16 combines the previous CRC with the one generated from the current data byte. Entry point GCRC16 returns the CRC.

Procedure Subroutine ICRC16 initializes the CRC to 0 and the polynomial to a 1 in each bit position corresponding to a power of X present in the formula. Subroutine CRC16 updates the CRC for a data byte. It shifts both the data and the CRC left eight times; after each shift, it exclusive-ORs the CRC with the polynomial if the exclusive-OR of the data bit and the CRC's most significant bit is 1. Subroutine CRC16 leaves the CRC in memory locations CRC (more significant byte) and CRC+1 (less significant byte). Subroutine GCRC16 loads the CRC into the low word of register D0.

Entry conditions

1. For ICRC16: none

2. For CRC16: data byte in low byte of register D0, previous CRC in memory locations CRC (more significant byte) and CRC+1 (less significant byte), CRC polynomial in memory locations PLY (more significant byte) and PLY+1 (less significant byte).

3. For GCRC16: CRC in memory locations CRC (more significant byte) and CRC+1 (less significant byte).

Exit conditions

1. For ICRC16:
0 (initial CRC value) in memory locations CRC (more significant byte) and CRC+1 (less significant byte)
CRC polynomial in memory locations PLY (more significant byte) and PLY+1 (less significant byte)

2. For CRC16: CRC with current data byte included in memory locations CRC (more significant byte) and CRC+1 (less significant byte)

3. For GCRC16: CRC in low word of register D0

Examples

1. Generating a CRC.
Call ICRC16 to initialize the polynomial and start the CRC at 0.
Call CRC16 repeatedly to update the CRC for each data byte.
Call GCRC16 to obtain the final CRC.

2. Checking a CRC.
Call ICRC16 to initialize the polynomial and start the CRC at 0.
Call CRC16 repeatedly to update the CRC for each data byte (including the stored CRC) for checking.
Call GCRC16 to obtain the final CRC; it will be 0 if there were no errors.

Note that only ICRC16 depends on the particular CRC polynomial used. To change the polynomial, simply change the data ICRC16 loads into memory locations PLY (more significant byte) and PLY+1 (less significant byte).

Reference

J. E. McNamara, *Technical Aspects of Data Communications*, 3rd edn, Digital Press, Digital Equipment Corp., Billerica, MA, 1989. This book contains explanations of CRC and communications protocols.

Registers used

1. By ICRC16: CCR

2. By CRC16: CCR

3. By GCRC16: CCR, D0

Execution time

1. For ICRC16: 58 cycles

2. For CRC16: 180 cycles overhead plus an average of 67 cycles per data byte, assuming that the previous CRC and the polynomial must be EXCLUSIVE-ORed in half of the iterations.

3. For GCRC16: 32 cycles

Program size

1. For ICRC16: 16 bytes
2. For CRC16: 54 bytes
3. For GCRC16: 8 bytes

Data memory required Four bytes anywhere in RAM for the CRC (two bytes starting at address CRC) and the polynomial (two bytes starting at address PLY). CRC16 also requires 20 stack bytes.

```
*       Title              Generate CRC-16
*       Name:              ICRC16, CRC16, GCRC16
*
*       Purpose:           Generate a 16 bit CRC based on IBM's Binary
*                          Synchronous Communications protocol. The CRC is
*                          based on the following polynomial:
*                            (^ indicates "to the power")
*                                X^16 + X^15 + X^2 + 1
*
*                          To generate a CRC:
*                                1)  Call ICRC16 to initialize the CRC
*                                    polynomial and clear the CRC.
*                                2)  Call CRC16 for each data byte.
*                                3)  Call GCRC16 to obtain the CRC.
*                                    It should then be appended to the data,
*                                    high byte first.
*
*                          To check a CRC:
*                                1)  Call ICRC16 to initialize the CRC.
*                                2)  Call CRC16 for each data byte and
*                                    the 2 bytes of CRC previously generated.
*                                3)  Call GCRC16 to obtain the CRC. It will
*                                    be zero if no errors occurred.
*
*       Entry:             ICRC16 - None
*                          CRC16  - Data byte in low byte of Register D0
*                          GCRC16 - None
*
*       Exit:              ICRC16 - CRC, PLY initialized
*                          CRC16  - CRC updated
*                          GCRC16 - CRC in low word of register D0
*
*       Registers Used:    ICRC16 - CCR
*                          CRC16  - CCR
*                          GCRC16 - CCR,D0
*
*       Time:              ICRC16 - 58 cycles
*                          CRC16 - 180 cycles overhead plus an average of
*                          67 cycles per data byte.  The loop timing
*                          assumes that half the iterations require
```

```
*                       EXCLUSIVE-ORing the CRC and the polynomial.
*                       GCRC16 - 32 cycles
*
*       Size:           Program 78 bytes
*                       Data     4 bytes plus 20 stack bytes (CRC16)
*
*

CRC16
        *
        *SAVE ALL REGISTERS
        *
        MOVEM.L D0-D4,-(SP)     SAVE ALL REGISTERS
        *
        *LOOP THROUGH EACH DATA BIT, GENERATING THE CRC
        *
        MOVEQ   #7,D3           8 BITS PER BYTE (MINUS 1 FOR DBRA)
        MOVE.W  PLY,D2          GET POLYNOMIAL
        MOVE.W  CRC,D1          GET CURRENT CRC VALUE
        MOVE.B  D0,D4           SAVE DATA
CRCLP
        ANDI.B  #%10000000,D0   GET BIT 7 OF DATA
        ASL.W   #8,D0
        EOR.W   D0,D1           EXCLUSIVE-OR BIT 7 WITH BIT 15 OF CRC
        ADD.W   D1,D1           SHIFT 16-BIT CRC LEFT
        BCC.S   CRCLP1          BRANCH IF BIT 7 OF EXCLUSIVE-OR IS 0
        *
        *BIT 7 IS 1, SO EXCLUSIVE-OR CRC WITH POLYNOMIAL
        *
        EOR.W   D2,D1           EXCLUSIVE-OR CRC WITH POLYNOMIAL
        *
        *SHIFT DATA LEFT AND COUNT BITS
        *
CRCLP1
        ADD.B   D4,D4           SHIFT DATA LEFT
        MOVE.B  D4,D0           SAVE SHIFTED DATA
        DBRA    D3,CRCLP        JUMP IF NOT THROUGH 8 BITS
        MOVE.W  D1,CRC          SAVE UPDATED CRC
        *
        *RESTORE REGISTERS AND EXIT
        *
        MOVEM.W (SP)+,D0-D4     RESTORE ALL REGISTERS
        RTS

****************************************
*ROUTINE: ICRC16
*PURPOSE: INITIALIZE CRC AND PLY
*ENTRY: NONE
*EXIT: CRC AND POLYNOMIAL INITIALIZED
*REGISTERS USED: CCR
****************************************

ICRC16
        CLR.W   CRC             INITIALIZE CRC TO 0
        MOVE.W  #$8005,PLY      PLY = 8005 HEX
                                *8005 HEX REPRESENTS X^16+X^15+X^2+1
```

```
                                        *  THERE IS A 1 IS IN EACH BIT
                                        *  POSITION FOR WHICH A POWER APPEARS
                                        *  IN THE FORMULA (BITS 0, 2, AND 15)
        RTS

*****************************************
*ROUTINE: GCRC16
*PURPOSE: GET CRC VALUE
*ENTRY: NONE
*EXIT: LOW WORD OF REGISTER D0 = CRC VALUE
*REGISTERS USED: CCR,D0
*****************************************

GCRC16
        MOVE.W  CRC,D0              D0 = CRC
        RTS

*DATA
CRC     DS.W    1                   CRC VALUE
PLY     DS.W    1                   POLYNOMIAL VALUE


*
*       SAMPLE EXECUTION:
*

        *
        *GENERATE CRC FOR THE NUMBER 1 AND CHECK IT
        *
SC8D
        JSR     ICRC16              INITIALIZE CRC, POLYNOMIAL
        MOVE.B  #1,D0               GENERATE CRC FOR 1
        JSR     CRC16
        JSR     GCRC16
        MOVE.W  D0,D2               SAVE CRC IN REGISTER D2
        JSR     ICRC16              INITIALIZE AGAIN
        MOVE.B  #1,D0
        JSR     CRC16               CHECK CRC BY GENERATING IT FOR DATA
        MOVE.W  D2,D0               AND STORED CRC ALSO - HIGH BYTE FIRST
        LSR.W   #8,D0
        JSR     CRC16
        MOVE.B  D2,D0               THEN LOW BYTE
        JSR     CRC16
        JSR     GCRC16              CRC SHOULD BE ZERO IN D0

        *
        *GENERATE CRC FOR THE SEQUENCE 0,1,2,...,255 AND CHECK IT
        *
        JSR     ICRC16              INITIALIZE CRC, POLYNOMIAL
        CLR.B   D0                  START DATA BYTES AT 0
GENLP
        JSR     CRC16               UPDATE CRC
        ADDQ.B  #1,D0               ADD 1 TO PRODUCE NEXT DATA BYTE
        BNE.S   GENLP               BRANCH IF NOT DONE
        JSR     GCRC16              GET RESULTING CRC
```

```
        MOVE.W  D0,D1           AND SAVE IT IN D1
        *
        *CHECK CRC BY GENERATING IT AGAIN
        *
        JSR     ICRC16          INITIALIZE CRC, POLYNOMIAL
        CLR.B   D0              START DATA BYTES AT 0
CHKLP
        JSR     CRC16           UPDATE CRC
        ADDQ.B  #1,D0           ADD 1 TO PRODUCE NEXT DATA BYTE
        BNE.S   CHKLP           BRANCH IF NOT DONE
        *
        *INCLUDE STORED CRC IN CHECK
        *
        MOVE.W  D1,D0           INCLUDE HIGH BYTE OF CRC
        LSR.W   #8,D0
        JSR     CRC16
        MOVE.B  D1,D0           INCLUDE LOW BYTE OF CRC
        JSR     CRC16

        JSR     GCRC16          GET RESULTING CRC
                                *IT SHOULD BE 0
        BRA.S   SC8D            REPEAT TEST

        END
```

8E I/O device table handler (IOHDLR)

Performs input and output in a device-independent manner using I/O control blocks and an I/O device table. The I/O device table is a linked list; each entry contains a link to the next entry, the device number, and starting addresses for routines that initialize the device, determine its input status, read data from it, determine its output status, and write data to it. An I/O control block is an array containing device number, operation number, device status, and the base address and length of the device's buffer. The user must provide IOHDLR with the base address of an I/O control block and the data if only one byte is to be written. IOHDLR returns the status byte and the data (if only one byte is read).

This subroutine is an example of handling input and output in a device-independent manner. The I/O device table must be constructed using subroutines INITDL, which creates an empty device list, and INSDL, which inserts a device into the list.

An applications program will perform input or output by obtaining or constructing an I/O control block and then calling IOHDLR. IOHDLR uses the I/O device table to determine how to transfer control to the I/O driver.

Procedure The program first initializes the status byte to 0, indicating no errors. It then searches the device table, trying to match the device number in the I/O control block. If it does not find a match, it exits with an error number in the status byte. If it finds a match, it checks for a valid operation and transfers control to the appropriate routine from the device table entry. That routine must then transfer control back to the original caller. If the operation is invalid (the operation number is too large or the starting address for the routine is 0), the program returns with an error number in the status byte.

Subroutine INITDL initializes the device list, setting the initial link to 0.

Subroutine INSDL inserts an entry into the device list, making its address the head of the list and setting its link field to the previous head of the list.

Entry conditions

1. For IOHDLR:
Base address of input/output control block in register A0

Data byte (if the operation is to write 1 byte) in low byte of register D0

2. For INITL: None

3. For INSDL: Base address of a device table entry in register A0

Exit conditions

1. For IOHDLR:
I/O control block status byte in low byte of register D0 if an error is found; otherwise, the routine exits to the appropriate I/O driver.
Data byte in low byte of register D0 if the operation is to read one byte.

2. For INITL:
Device list header (addresses DVLST through DVLST+3) cleared to indicate empty list.

3. For INSDL:
Device table entry added to list.

Example

The example in the listing uses the following structure:

INPUT/OUTPUT OPERATIONS

Operation Number	Operation
0	Initialize device
1	Determine input status
2	Read 1 byte from input device
3	Read *N* bytes (usually 1 line) from input device
4	Determine output status
5	Write 1 byte to output device
6	Write *N* bytes (usually 1 line) to output device

INPUT/OUTPUT CONTROL BLOCK

Index	Contents
0	Device number
1	Operation number
2	Status
3	Unused
4–7	Base address of buffer

8–9	Buffer length

DEVICE TABLE ENTRY

Index	**Contents**
0–3	Link field (base address of next element)
4	Device number
5–7	Unused
8–B	Starting address of device initialization routine
C–F	Starting address of input status determination routine
10–13	Starting address of input driver (read 1 byte only)
14–17	Starting address of input driver (read *N* bytes or 1 line)
18–1B	Starting address of output status determination routine
1C–1F	Starting address of output driver (write 1 byte only)
20–23	Starting address of output driver (write *N* bytes or 1 line)

If an operation is irrelevant or undefined (such as output status determination for a keyboard or input driver for a printer), the corresponding starting address in the device table is 0.

STATUS VALUES

Value	**Description**
0	No errors
1	Bad device number (no such device)
2	Bad operation number (no such operation or invalid operation)
3	Input data available or output device ready
254	Buffer too small for GEMDOS function 10 (Read Edited String)

Registers used

1. By IOHDLR: A0, A1, CCR, D0, D1, D2

2. By INITDL: CCR

3. By INSDL: A0, A1, CCR

Execution time

1. For IOHDLR: 197 cycles overhead plus 54 cycles for each unsuccessful match of a device number

2. For INITDL: 46 cycles

3. For INSDL: 72 cycles

Program size

1. For IOHDLR: 92 bytes
2. For INITL: 8 bytes
3. For INSDL: 16 bytes

Data memory required 5 bytes anywhere in RAM for the device list header (4 bytes starting at address DVLST) and temporary storage for data to be written without a buffer (1 byte at address BDATA). Another byte must generally be wasted to provide word alignment.

```
*       Title           I/O Device Table Handler
*       Name:           IOHDLR
*
*       Purpose:        Perform I/O in a device independent manner.
*                       This can be done by accessing all devices
*                       in the same way using an I/O Control Block
*                       (IOCB) and a device table. The routines here
*                       allow the following operations:
*
*                       Operation number  Description
*                           0               Initialize Device
*                           1               Determine input status
*                           2               Read 1 byte
*                           3               Read N bytes
*                           4               Determine output status
*                           5               Write 1 byte
*                           6               Write N bytes
*
*                       Adding operations such as Open, Close, Delete,
*                       Rename,  and Append would allow for more complex
*                       devices such as floppy or hard disks.
*
*                       A IOCB is an array consisting of elements
*                       with the following form:
*
*                       IOCB + 0 = Device Number
*                       IOCB + 1 = Operation Number
*                       IOCB + 2 = Status
*                       IOCB + 3 = Unused
*                       IOCB + 4-7 = Buffer address
*                       IOCB + 8-9 = Buffer length
*
*                       The device table is implemented as a linked
*                       list. Two routines maintain the list: INITDL,
*                       which initializes it to empty, and INSDL,
*                       which inserts a device into it.
*                       A device table entry has the following form:
*
*                       DVTBL + 0-3 = Link field
```

```
*                           DVTBL + 4 = Device Number
*                           DVTBL + 5-7 = Unused
*                           DVTBL + 8-B = Device initialization routine
*                           DVTBL + C-F = Input status routine
*                           DVTBL + 10-13 = Input 1 byte routine
*                           DVTBL + 14-17 = Input N bytes routine
*                           DVTBL + 18-1B = Output status routine
*                           DVTBL + 1C-1F = Output 1 byte routine
*                           DVTBL + 20-23 = Output N bytes routine
*
*       Entry:              Base address of IOCB in register A0
*                           For write 1 byte, data in low byte of
*                             register D0 (no buffer is used).
*
*       Exit:               Copy of the IOCB status byte in low byte
*                             of register D0, except contains the data for
*                             read 1 byte (no buffer is used).
*                           Status byte of IOCB is 0 if the operation was
*                             completed successfully; otherwise, it contains
*                             the error number.
*
*                           Status value    Description
*                               0           No errors
*                               1           Bad device number
*                               2           Bad operation number
*                               3           Input data available or output
*                                           device ready
*                             254           Buffer too small for GEMDOS
*                                           function 10 (Read Edited String)
*
*
*       Registers Used: A0,A1,CCR,D0,D1,D2
*
*       Time:               197 cycles overhead plus 54 cycles for each
*                           device in the list which is not the one
*                           requested
*
*       Size:               Program    116 bytes
*                           Data    5 bytes
*
*IOCB AND DEVICE TABLE EQUATES
IOCBDN  EQU     0           IOCB DEVICE NUMBER
IOCBOP  EQU     1           IOCB OPERATION NUMBER
IOCBST  EQU     2           IOCB STATUS
IOCBBA  EQU     4           IOCB BUFFER BASE ADDRESS
IOCBBL  EQU     8           IOCB BUFFER LENGTH
DTLNK   EQU     0           DEVICE TABLE LINK FIELD
DTDN    EQU     4           DEVICE TABLE DEVICE NUMBER
DTSR    EQU     8           BEGINNING OF DEVICE TABLE SUBROUTINES
*OPERATION NUMBERS
NUMOP   EQU     7           NUMBER OF OPERATIONS
INIT    EQU     0           INITIALIZATION
ISTAT   EQU     1           INPUT STATUS
R1BYTE  EQU     2           READ 1 BYTE
RNBYTE  EQU     3           READ N BYTES
```

```
OSTAT    EQU    4       OUTPUT STATUS
W1BYTE   EQU    5       WRITE 1 BYTE
WNBYTE   EQU    6       WRITE N BYTES
*STATUS VALUES
NOERR    EQU    0       NO ERRORS
DEVERR   EQU    1       BAD DEVICE NUMBER
OPERR    EQU    2       BAD OPERATION NUMBER
DEVRDY   EQU    3       INPUT DATA AVAILABLE OR OUTPUT DEVICE READY
BUFERR   EQU    254     BUFFER TOO SMALL FOR GEMDOS READ CONSOLE BUFFER

IOHDLR
        *
        *SAVE IOCB ADDRESS AND DATA (IF ANY)
        *
        MOVEA.L A0,A1           SAVE IOCB ADDRESS
        MOVE.B  D0,BDATA        SAVE DATA BYTE FOR WRITE 1 BYTE
        *
        *INITIALIZE STATUS BYTE TO INDICATE NO ERRORS
        *
        MOVE.B  #NOERR,IOCBST(A0)  SAVE NO ERRORS STATUS IN IOCB
        *
        *CHECK FOR VALID OPERATION NUMBER (WITHIN LIMIT)
        *
        MOVE.B  IOCBOP(A0),D1   GET OPERATION NUMBER FROM IOCB
        CMPI.B  #NUMOP,D1       IS OPERATION NUMBER WITHIN LIMIT?
        BCC.S   BADOP           JUMP IF OPERATION NUMBER TOO LARGE
        *
        *SEARCH DEVICE LIST FOR THIS DEVICE
        *
        MOVE.B  IOCBDN(A0),D0   GET IOCB DEVICE NUMBER
        MOVEA.L DVLST,A0        GET FIRST ENTRY IN DEVICE LIST
        *
        *A0 = POINTER TO DEVICE LIST
        *D0 = REQUESTED DEVICE NUMBER
        *D1 = OPERATION NUMBER
        *
SRCHLP
        *CHECK IF AT END OF DEVICE LIST (LINK FIELD = 0)
        MOVE.L  A0,D2           TEST LINK FIELD (NOTE THAT TST CANNOT
                                * BE APPLIED TO AN ADDRESS REGISTER)
        BEQ.S   BADDN           BRANCH IF NO MORE DEVICE ENTRIES
        *
        *CHECK IF CURRENT ENTRY IS DEVICE IN IOCB
        *
        CMP.B   DTDN(A0),D0     COMPARE DEVICE NUMBER, REQUESTED DEVICE
        BEQ.S   FOUND           BRANCH IF DEVICE FOUND
        *
        *DEVICE NOT FOUND, SO ADVANCE TO NEXT DEVICE
        * TABLE ENTRY THROUGH LINK FIELD
        * MAKE CURRENT DEVICE = LINK
        *
        MOVEA.L (A0),A0         CURRENT ENTRY = LINK
        BRA.S   SRCHLP          CHECK NEXT ENTRY IN DEVICE TABLE
        *
        *FOUND DEVICE,  SO VECTOR TO APPROPRIATE ROUTINE IF ANY
        *D1 = OPERATION NUMBER IN IOCB
```

```
        *
FOUND
        *GET ROUTINE ADDRESS (ZERO INDICATES INVALID OPERATION)
        MOVEQ    #0,D2              EXTEND OPERATION NUMBER TO 16 BITS
        MOVE.B   D1,D2
        ASL.W    #2,D2              MULTIPLY OPERATION NUMBER TIMES 4 TO
                                    * INDEX INTO TABLE OF 32-BIT ADDRESSES
        MOVEA.L DTSR(A0,D2.W),A0 GET SUBROUTINE ADDRESS
        MOVE.L   A0,D2              TEST SUBROUTINE ADDRESS
        BEQ.S    BADOP              JUMP IF OPERATION INVALID (ADDRESS = 0)
        MOVE.L   A0,-(SP)           SAVE SUBROUTINE ADDRESS ON STACK
        MOVE.B   BDATA,D0           D0 = DATA BYTE FOR WRITE 1 BYTE
        MOVEA.L A1,A0               GET BASE ADDRESS OF IOCB
        RTS                         GOTO SUBROUTINE
BADDN
        MOVE.B   #DEVERR,D0         ERROR CODE -- NO SUCH DEVICE
        BRA.S    EREXIT
BADOP
        MOVE.B   #OPERR,D0          ERROR CODE -- NO SUCH OPERATION

EREXIT
        MOVEA.L A1,A0               POINT TO IOCB
        MOVE.B   D0,IOCBST(A0)      SET STATUS BYTE IN IOCB
        RTS
****************************************
*ROUTINE: INITDL
*PURPOSE: INITIALIZE DEVICE LIST TO EMPTY
*ENTRY: NONE
*EXIT: DEVICE LIST SET TO NO ITEMS
*REGISTERS USED: CCR
****************************************

INITDL
        *INITIALIZE DEVICE LIST HEADER TO 0 TO INDICATE NO DEVICES
        CLR.L    DVLST              HEADER = 0 (EMPTY LIST)
        RTS


****************************************
*ROUTINE: INSDL
*PURPOSE: INSERT DEVICE INTO DEVICE LIST
*ENTRY: REGISTER A0 = ADDRESS OF DEVICE TABLE ENTRY
*EXIT: DEVICE INSERTED INTO DEVICE LIST
*REGISTERS USED: A1,CCR
****************************************

INSDL
        MOVEA.L DVLST,A1            GET CURRENT HEAD OF DEVICE LIST
        MOVE.L   A1,(A0)            STORE CURRENT HEAD OF DEVICE LIST
        MOVE.L   A0,DVLST           MAKE DVLST POINT TO NEW DEVICE
        RTS

*
*DATA SECTION
```

```
DVLST   DS.L    1                   DEVICE LIST HEADER
BDATA   DS.B    1                   DATA BYTE FOR WRITE 1 BYTE
        DS.B    1                   WASTE A BYTE TO ALIGN TO WORD BOUNDARY

*
*       SAMPLE EXECUTION:
*
*
*CHARACTER EQUATES
CR      EQU     $0D                 CARRIAGE RETURN CHARACTER
LF      EQU     $0A                 LINE FEED CHARACTER

SC8E
        *INITIALIZE DEVICE LIST
        JSR     INITDL              CREATE EMPTY DEVICE LIST

        *SET UP CONSOLE AS DEVICE 1 AND INITIALIZE IT
        LEA     CONDV,A0            POINT TO CONSOLE DEVICE ENTRY
        JSR     INSDL               ADD CONSOLE TO DEVICE LIST
        LEA     IOCB,A0             POINT TO I/O CONTROL BLOCK
        MOVE.B  #INIT,IOCBOP(A0)    INITIALIZE OPERATION
        MOVE.B  #1,IOCBDN(A0)       DEVICE NUMBER = 1
        JSR     IOHDLR              INITIALIZE CONSOLE

        *SET UP PRINTER AS DEVICE 2 AND INITIALIZE IT
        LEA     PRTDV,A0            POINT TO PRINTER DEVICE ENTRY
        JSR     INSDL               ADD PRINTER TO DEVICE LIST
        LEA     IOCB,A0             POINT TO I/O CONTROL BLOCK
        MOVE.B  #INIT,IOCBOP(A0)    INITIALIZE OPERATION
        MOVE.B  #2,IOCBDN(A0)       DEVICE NUMBER = 2
        JSR     IOHDLR              INITIALIZE PRINTER

        *
        *LOOP READING LINES FROM CONSOLE, AND ECHOING THEM TO
        * THE CONSOLE AND PRINTER UNTIL A BLANK LINE IS ENTERED
        *
TSTLP
        LEA     IOCB,A0             POINT TO I/O CONTROL BLOCK
        LEA     BUFFER,IOCBBA(A0)   SAVE BUFFER ADDRESS IN IOCB
        MOVE.B  #1,IOCBDN(A0)       DEVICE NUMBER = 1 (CONSOLE)
        MOVE.B  #RNBYTE,IOCBOP(A0)  OPERATION IS READ N BYTES
        MOVE.B  #LENBUF,IOCBBL(A0)  SET BUFFER LENGTH TO LENBUF
        JSR     IOHDLR              READ LINE FROM CONSOLE
        *
        *SEND LINE FEED TO CONSOLE
        *
        LEA     IOCB,A0             POINT TO I/O CONTROL BLOCK
        MOVE.B  #W1BYTE,IOCBOP(A0)  OPERATION IS WRITE 1 BYTE
        MOVE.B  #LF,D0              CHARACTER IS LINE FEED
        JSR     IOHDLR              WRITE 1 BYTE (LINE FEED)
        *
        *ECHO LINE TO DEVICES 1 AND 2
        *
        MOVE.B  #1,D0               ECHO LINE TO DEVICE 1
        JSR     ECHO
        MOVE.B  #2,D0               ECHO LINE TO DEVICE 2
```

```
        JSR     ECHO
        *
        *STOP IF LINE LENGTH IS 0
        *
        MOVE.W  IOCB+IOCBBL,D0  GET LINE LENGTH
        BEQ.S   TSTLP           JUMP IF LENGTH NOT ZERO

        BRA.S   SC8E            AGAIN

ECHO
        *
        *OUTPUT LINE
        *
        LEA     IOCB,A0         GET BASE ADDRESS OF IOCB
        MOVE.B  D0,IOCBDN(A0)   SET DEVICE NUMBER IN IOCB
                                *NOTE THAT ECHO WILL SEND A LINE
                                * TO ANY DEVICE. THE DEVICE NUMBER
                                * IS IN THE LOW BYTE OF REGISTER D0
        MOVE.B  #WNBYTE,IOCBOP(A0)  SET OPERATION TO WRITE N BYTES
        JSR     IOHDLR          WRITE N BYTES
        *
        *OUTPUT CARRIAGE RETURN/LINE FEED
        *
        LEA     IOCB,A0         GET BASE ADDRESS OF IOCB
        MOVE.B  #W1BYTE,IOCBOP(A0) SET OPERATION TO WRITE 1 BYTE
        MOVE.B  #CR,D0          CHARACTER IS CARRIAGE RETURN
        JSR     IOHDLR          WRITE 1 BYTE
        LEA     IOCB,A0         GET BASE ADDRESS OF IOCB
        MOVE.B  #LF,D0          CHARACTER IS LINE FEED
        JSR     IOHDLR          *WRITE 1 BYTE
        RTS

*
*       DATA SECTION
*
LENBUF  EQU     127             I/O BUFFER LENGTH
BUFFER  DS.B    LENBUF          I/O BUFFER
        DS.B    1               WASTE BYTE TO ALIGN TO WORD BOUNDARY

*IOCB FOR PERFORMING IO
IOCB    DS.B    1               DEVICE NUMBER
        DS.B    1               OPERATION NUMBER
        DS.B    1               STATUS
        DS.B    1               UNUSED
        DS.L    1               BUFFER ADDRESS
        DS.W    1               BUFFER LENGTH

*DEVICE TABLE ENTRIES
CONDV   DS.L    1               LINK FIELD
        DC.B    1               DEVICE 1
        DS.B    3               UNUSED
        DC.L    CINIT           CONSOLE INITIALIZE
        DC.L    CISTAT          CONSOLE INPUT STATUS
        DC.L    CIN             CONSOLE INPUT 1 BYTE
        DC.L    CINN            CONSOLE INPUT N BYTES
```

```
        DC.L    COSTAT              CONSOLE OUTPUT STATUS
        DC.L    COUT                CONSOLE OUTPUT 1 BYTE
        DC.L    COUTN               CONSOLE OUTPUT N BYTES

PRTDV   DS.L    1                   LINK FIELD
        DC.B    2                   DEVICE 2
        DS.B    3                   UNUSED
        DC.L    PINIT               PRINTER INITIALIZE
        DC.L    0                   NO PRINTER INPUT STATUS
        DC.L    0                   NO PRINTER INPUT 1 BYTE
        DC.L    0                   NO PRINTER INPUT N BYTES
        DC.L    POSTAT              PRINTER OUTPUT STATUS
        DC.L    POUT                PRINTER OUTPUT 1 BYTE
        DC.L    POUTN               PRINTER OUTPUT N BYTES


************************************
*CONSOLE I/O ROUTINES
************************************

*CONSOLE INITIALIZE
CINIT
        CLR.B   D0                  STATUS = NO ERRORS
        RTS                         NO INITIALIZATION NECESSARY

*CONSOLE INPUT STATUS
CISTAT
        MOVE.L  A0,-(SP)            SAVE REGISTER A0
        MOVE.W  #11,-(SP)           CALL GEMDOS STATUS CHECK FUNCTION
        TRAP    #1
        ADDQ.L  #2,SP               REMOVE GEMDOS PARAMETER FROM STACK
        MOVE.L  (SP)+,A0            RESTORE REGISTER A0
        MOVE.B  D0,IOCBST(A0)       STORE STATUS IN IOCB
        RTS

*CONSOLE READ 1 BYTE
CIN
        MOVE.L  A0,-(SP)            SAVE REGISTER A0
        MOVE.W  #1,-(SP)            CALL GEMDOS CONSOLE INPUT FUNCTION
        TRAP    #1
        ADDQ.L  #2,SP               REMOVE GEMDOS PARAMETER FROM STACK
        MOVE.L  (SP)+,A0            RESTORE REGISTER A0
        RTS                         EXIT WITH CHARACTER IN LOW BYTE OF
                                    * REGISTER D0

*CONSOLE READ N BYTES
CINN
        MOVE.W  IOCBBL(A0),D0       GET BUFFER LENGTH
        CMP.W   #3,D0               BUFFER MUST BE AT LEAST 3 CHARACTERS
                                    * TO ALLOW FOR MAX LENGTH AND COUNT
        BCC.S   CINN1               JUMP IF BUFFER LONG ENOUGH
        MOVE.B  #BUFERR,IOCBST(A0) SET ERROR STATUS - BUFFER
                                    * TOO SMALL - NO ROOM FOR DATA
CINN1   ADDQ.B  #1,D0               ADD ONE BACK TO FIND AMOUNT OF ROOM
                                    * IN BUFFER FOR DATA (2 BYTES OVERHEAD)
        MOVEA.L IOCBBA(A0),A1       GET BUFFER ADDRESS FROM IOCB
```

```
        MOVE.B  D0,(A1)          SET MAXIMUM LENGTH IN BUFFER
        MOVE.L  A0,-(SP)         SAVE REGISTER A0
        MOVE.L  A1,-(SP)         PUSH BUFFER ADDRESS ONTO STACK
        MOVE.W  #10,-(SP)        CALL GEMDOS READ CONSOLE BUFFER FUNCTION
        TRAP    #1
        ADDQ.L  #6,SP            REMOVE GEMDOS PARAMETERS FROM STACK
        MOVE.L  (SP)+,A0         RESTORE REGISTER A0
        *
        *RETURN NUMBER OF CHARACTERS READ IN IOCB
        *
        MOVEQ   #0,D0
        MOVE.B  1(A1),D0         GET NUMBER OF CHARACTERS READ
        MOVE.W  D0,IOCBBL(A0)    SET BUFFER LENGTH IN IOCB
        *
        *MOVE DATA TO FIRST BYTE OF BUFFER
        *
        BEQ.S   CINEND           EXIT IF NO CHARACTERS
        SUBQ.W  #1,D0            REDUCE COUNT BY 1 FOR DBRA LOOP
        MOVE.L  A0,-(SP)         SAVE REGISTER A0
        MOVEA.L A1,A0            COPY BUFFER POINTER
CINMOV  MOVE.B  2(A0),(A0)+      MOVE A BYTE
        DBRA    D0,CINMOV        CONTINUE UNTIL ALL BYTES MOVED
        MOVE.L  (SP)+,A0         RESTORE REGISTER A0
CINEND  RTS

*CONSOLE OUTPUT STATUS
COSTAT
        MOVE.B  #DEVRDY,D0       STATUS - ALWAYS READY TO OUTPUT
        RTS

*CONSOLE WRITE 1 BYTE
COUT
        MOVE.L  A0,-(SP)         SAVE REGISTER A0
        MOVE.W  D0,-(SP)         PUSH CHARACTER TO WRITE ONTO STACK
        MOVE.W  #2,-(SP)         CALL GEMDOS CONSOLE WRITE FUNCTION
        TRAP    #1
        ADDQ.L  #4,SP            REMOVE GEMDOS PARAMETERS FROM STACK
        MOVE.L  (SP)+,A0         RESTORE REGISTER A0
        CLR.B   D0               STATUS = NO ERRORS
        RTS

*CONSOLE WRITE N BYTES
COUTN
        LEA     COUT,A0          A0=ADDRESS OF OUTPUT CHARACTER ROUTINE
        JSR     OUTN             CALL OUTPUT N CHARACTERS
        CLR.B   D0               STATUS = NO ERRORS
        RTS

***************************************
*PRINTER ROUTINES
***************************************

*PRINTER INITIALIZE
PINIT
        CLR.B   D0               NOTHING TO DO, RETURN NO ERRORS
```

```
        RTS

*PRINTER OUTPUT STATUS
POSTAT
        MOVE.B  #DEVRDY,D0         STATUS = ALWAYS READY
        RTS

*PRINTER OUTPUT 1 BYTE
POUT
        MOVE.L  A0,-(SP)           SAVE REGISTER A0
        MOVE.W  D0,-(SP)           PUSH CHARACTER TO PRINT ONTO STACK
        MOVE.W  #5,-(SP)           CALL GEMDOS PRINTER OUTPUT FUNCTION
        TRAP    #1
        ADDQ.L  #4,SP              REMOVE GEMDOS PARAMETERS FROM STACK
        MOVE.L  (SP)+,A0           RESTORE REGISTER A0
        CLR.B   D0                 STATUS = NO ERRORS
        RTS

*PRINTER OUTPUT N BYTES
POUTN
        MOVEA.L #POUT,A0           A0 = ADDRESS OF OUTPUT ROUTINE
        JSR     OUTN               OUTPUT N CHARACTERS
        CLR.B   D0                 STATUS = NO ERRORS
        RTS

************************************************************
*ROUTINE: OUTN
*PURPOSE: OUTPUT N CHARACTERS
*ENTRY: REGISTER A0 = CHARACTER OUTPUT SUBROUTINE ADDRESS
*       REGISTER A1 = BASE ADDRESS OF AN IOCB
*EXIT: DATA OUTPUT
*REGISTERS USED: A0,A1,CCR
************************************************************
OUTN
        MOVE.L  A2,-(SP)           SAVE REGISTER A2
        MOVEA.L A0,A2              SET A2 = OUTPUT ROUTINE ADDRESS
        *
        *GET NUMBER OF BYTES, EXIT IF LENGTH IS 0
        * D1 = NUMBER OF BYTES
        *GET OUTPUT BUFFER ADDRESS FROM IOCB
        * A0 = BUFFER ADDRESS
        *
        MOVE.W  IOCBBL(A1),D1      GET BUFFER LENGTH FROM IOCB
        BEQ.S   EXOUTN             EXIT IF BUFFER EMPTY
        MOVEA.L IOCBBA(A1),A0      GET BUFFER ADDRESS FROM IOCB
        SUBQ.W  #1,D1              REDUCE COUNT BY 1 FOR DBRA LOOP
        *
        *SEND DATA FROM BUFFER TO OUTPUT DEVICE
        *
OUTLP
        MOVE.B  D0,(A0)+           GET DATA FROM BUFFER
        MOVE.W  D1,-(SP)           SAVE COUNT IN STACK
        JSR     DOSUB              OUTPUT CHARACTER
        MOVE.W  (SP)+,D1           RESTORE COUNT
        DBRA    D1,OUTLP           CONTINUE UNTIL ALL BYTES SENT
EXOUTN  MOVE.L  (SP)+,A2           RESTORE REGISTER A2
```

```
        RTS

DOSUB   JMP     (A2)            GOTO ROUTINE

        END
```

8F Initialize I/O ports (IPORTS)

Initializes a set of I/O ports from an array of port device addresses and data values. Examples are given of initializing the common 68000 programmable I/O devices: 6821 Peripheral Interface Adapter, 6840 Programmable Timer, 6850 Asynchronous Communications Interface Adapter, 68230 Parallel Interface/Timer, and 68901 Multifunction Peripheral (contains an 8-bit parallel port, a USART, four 8-bit timers, and a 16-level interrupt controller).

This subroutine provides a generalized method for initializing I/O sections. The initialization may involve data ports, data direction registers that specify whether bits are inputs or outputs, control or command registers that determine the operating modes of programmable devices, counters (in timers), priority registers, vector registers, address registers (in DMA controllers or memory management units), and other external registers or storage locations.

The user may perform the following tasks with this routine:

1. Assign bidirectional I/O lines as inputs or outputs.

2. Put initial values in output ports.

3. Enable or disable interrupts from peripheral chips.

4. Determine operating modes, such as whether inputs are latched, whether strobes are produced, how priorities are assigned, which inputs and outputs are sensed or enabled, how interrupts are terminated, whether timers operate continuously or only on demand, and whether I/O is asynchronous, synchronous, or uses a block-oriented protocol.

5. Load starting values into timers and counters.

6. Select bit rates for communications.

7. Clear or reset devices that are not tied to the overall system reset line.

8. Initialize priority registers or assign initial priorities to interrupts or other operations.

9. Set vectors used in servicing interrupts, DMA requests, and other inputs.

10. Choose active logic levels or transitions.

Procedure The program loops through the port entries, obtaining each port's memory address and initial value from the array and storing the value in the address. This approach does not depend on the number or type of devices in the I/O section. The user may add or delete devices or change the initialization by changing the array rather than the program. The approach is thus well suited to expandable systems with a wide range of accessories or models. It also allows easy replacement or updating of I/O devices.

Each array entry consists of the following:

1. Port address (4 bytes)
2. Initial value to be sent to the port
3. An unused byte for word boundary alignment

Entry conditions

Base address of array of port addresses and initial values in register A0
Number of entries in array (number of ports to initialize) in low word of register D0

Exit conditions

All data values sent to port addresses.

Example

Data: Number of ports to initialize = 3
Array elements are:
Port 1's memory address
Initial value for port 1
Unused byte
Port 2's memory address
Initial value for port 2
Unused byte
Port 3's memory address
Initial value for port 3
Unused byte

Note that each element consists of 6 bytes organized as follows:
Port's memory address (4 bytes)

Initial value for port (1 byte)
Unused byte for word boundary alignment

Registers used A0, A1, CCR, D0

Execution time 36 cycles overhead plus 43 cycles per port entry. If, for example, there are 10 ports, the execution time is

$$36 + 10 \times 43 = 466 \text{ cycles}$$

Program size 18 bytes plus the size of the table (6 bytes per port).

Data memory required None

```
*       Title           Initialize I/O Ports
*       Name:           IPORTS
*
*       Purpose:        Initialize I/O ports from an array of port
*                       addresses and values.
*
*       Entry:          Register A0 = Base address of array
*                       Register D0 = Number of ports
*
*                       The array consists of elements organized
*                       as follows:  port address, initial value,
*                       and 1 unused byte for word-length alignment.
*                          array+0-3 = Port 1 address
*                          array+4 = Value to store in port 1 address
*                          array+5 = Unused for alignment
*                          array+6-9 = Port 2 address
*                          array+A = Value to store in port 2 address
*                          array+B = Unused for alignment
*                                .
*                                .
*                                .
*
*       Exit:           None
*
*       Registers Used: A0,A1,CCR,D0
*
*       Time:           36 cycles overhead plus 43 cycles per port
*
*       Size:           Program 18 bytes
*
```

```
IPORTS
        *
        *EXIT IMMEDIATELY IF NUMBER OF PORTS IS ZERO
        *
        TST.W   D0              TEST NUMBER OF PORTS
        BEQ.S   EXIPOR          EXIT IF NO PORTS TO INITIALIZE
        *
        *LOOP, INITIALIZING PORTS
        *
        SUBQ.W  #1,D0           REDUCE COUNT BY 1 FOR DBRA EXIT ON -1
INITPT
        MOVEA.L (A0)+,A1        GET NEXT PORT ADDRESS
        MOVE.B  (A0)+,(A1)      GET VALUE AND SEND IT TO PORT
        ADDQ.L  #1,D0           MOVE ON TO NEXT PORT ADDRESS
                                * ALL ELEMENTS ARE WORD-ALIGNED
        DBRA    D0,INITPT       CONTINUE UNTIL ALL PORTS INITIALIZED
EXIPOR  RTS

*
*       SAMPLE EXECUTION:
*


*
*INITIALIZE
*  6821 PERIPHERAL INTERFACE ADAPTER (PIA) - PARALLEL INTERFACE
*  6840 PROGRAMMABLE TIMER MODULE (PTM)
*  6850 ASYNCHRONOUS COMMUNICATIONS INTERFACE ADAPTER (ACIA) - UART
*  68230 PARALLEL INTEFACE/TIMER (PI/T)
*  68901 MULTIFUNCTION PERIPHERAL (MFP) - PARALLEL, SERIAL, TIMERS,
*     INTERRUPT CONTROLLER
*
*ARBITRARY PORT ADDRESSES
*
*  NOTE: PI/T AND MFP GENERALLY HAVE ODD ADDRESSES SO THAT THEIR
*     INTERRUPT VECTORS (EXCEPTION VECTOR NUMBERS) WILL APPEAR ON THE
*     LOWER HALF OF THE DATA BUS (REMEMBER THAT 68000-BASED SYSTEMS
*     HAVE THE LOW BYTE OF A WORD AT THE HIGHER OR ODD ADDRESS).
*  6800-FAMILY DEVICES SUCH AS THE 6821 PIA, 6840 PTM, AND 6850
*     ACIA CAN HAVE EITHER EVEN OR ODD ADDRESSES, AS THEY DO NOT
*     PRODUCE INTERRUPT VECTORS ANYWAY.
*
*  6820/6821 PIA ADDRESSES
*

PIA     EQU     $FFFFA400       6821 PIA BASE ADDRESS
PIADRA  EQU     PIA             6821 PIA DATA REGISTER A
PIADDRA EQU     PIA             6821 PIA DATA DIRECTION REGISTER A
PIACRA  EQU     PIA+2           6821 PIA CONTROL REGISTER A
PIADRB  EQU     PIA+4           6821 PIA DATA REGISTER B
PIADDRA EQU     PIA+4           6821 PIA DATA DIRECTION REGISTER A
PIACRB  EQU     PIA+6           6821 PIA CONTROL REGISTER B
*
*  6840 PTM ADDRESSES
*
PTM     EQU     $FFFFA200       6840 PTM BASE ADDRESS
PTMC13  EQU     PTM             6840 PTM CONTROL REGISTERS 1,3
```

```
PTMCR2  EQU     PTM+2           6840 PTM CONTROL REGISTER 2
PTM1MS  EQU     PTM+4           6840 PTM TIMER 1 MSB
PTM1LS  EQU     PTM+6           6840 PTM TIMER 1 LSB
PTM2MS  EQU     PTM+8           6840 PTM TIMER 2 MSB
PTM2LS  EQU     PTM+10          6840 PTM TIMER 2 LSB
PTM3MS  EQU     PTM+12          6840 PTM TIMER 3 MSB
PTM3LS  EQU     PTM+14          6840 PTM TIMER 3 LSB
*
*  6850 ACIA ADDRESSES
*
ACIA    EQU     $FFFFFC04       6850 ACIA BASE ADDRESS
ACIACR  EQU     ACIA            6850 ACIA CONTROL REGISTER
ACIASR  EQU     ACIA            6850 ACIA STATUS REGISTER
ACIADR  EQU     ACIA+2          6850 ACIA DATA REGISTER
*
*  68230 PARALLEL INTERFACE/TIMER ADDRESSES
*
PIT     EQU     $FFFFA101       68230 PI/T BASE ADDRESS
PITGCR  EQU     PIT             68230 GENERAL CONTROL REGISTER
PITSRR  EQU     PIT+2           68230 SERVICE REQUEST REGISTER
PITDDRA EQU     PIT+4           68230 DATA DIRECTION REGISTER A
PITDDRB EQU     PIT+6           68230 DATA DIRECTION REGISTER B
PITDDRC EQU     PIT+8           68230 DATA DIRECTION REGISTER C
PITIVR  EQU     PIT+$0A         68230 INTERRUPT VECTOR REGISTER
PITCRA  EQU     PIT+$0C         68230 CONTROL REGISTER A
PITCRB  EQU     PIT+$0E         68230 CONTROL REGISTER B
PITDRA  EQU     PIT+$10         68230 DATA REGISTER A
PITDRB  EQU     PIT+$12         68230 DATA REGISTER B
PITARA  EQU     PIT+$14         68230 ALTERNATE REGISTER A
PITARB  EQU     PIT+$16         68230 ALTERNATE REGISTER B
PITDRC  EQU     PIT+$18         68230 DATA REGISTER C
PITSR   EQU     PIT+$1A         68230 STATUS REGISTER
PITTCR  EQU     PIT+$20         68230 TIMER CONTROL REGISTER
PITTIVR EQU     PIT+$22         68230 TIMER INTERRUPT VECTOR REGISTER
PITCPRH EQU     PIT+$26         68230 COUNTER PRELOAD REGISTER HIGH
PITCPRM EQU     PIT+$28         68230 COUNTER PRELOAD REGISTER MID
PITCPRL EQU     PIT+$2A         68230 COUNTER PRELOAD REGISTER LOW
PITCRH  EQU     PIT+$2E         68230 COUNT REGISTER HIGH
PITCRM  EQU     PIT+$30         68230 COUNT REGISTER MID
PITCRL  EQU     PIT+$32         68230 COUNT REGISTER LOW
PITTSR  EQU     PIT+$34         68230 TIMER STATUS REGISTER
*
*  68901 MULTIFUNCTION PERIPHERAL ADDRESSES
*
MFP     EQU     $FFFFFA00       68901 MFP BASE ADDRESS
MFPGPIR EQU     MFP             68901 GENERAL-PURPOSE I/O REGISTER
MFPAER  EQU     MFP+2           68901 ACTIVE EDGE REGISTER
MFPDDR  EQU     MFP+4           68901 DATA DIRECTION REGISTER
MFPIERA EQU     MFP+6           68901 INTERRUPT ENABLE REGISTER A
MFPIERB EQU     MFP+8           68901 INTERRUPT ENABLE REGISTER B
MFPIPRA EQU     MFP+$0A         68901 INTERRUPT PENDING REGISTER A
MFPIPRB EQU     MFP+$0C         68901 INTERRUPT PENDING REGISTER B
MFPISRA EQU     MFP+$0E         68901 INTERRUPT IN-SERVICE REGISTER A
MFPISRB EQU     MFP+$10         68901 INTERRUPT IN-SERVICE REGISTER B
MFPIMRA EQU     MFP+$12         68901 INTERRUPT MASK REGISTER A
MFPIMRB EQU     MFP+$14         68901 INTERRUPT MASK REGISTER B
```

```
MFPVR    EQU      MFP+$16              68901 VECTOR REGISTER
MFPTACR EQU       MFP+$18              68901 TIMER A CONTROL REGISTER
MFPTBCR EQU       MFP+$1A              68901 TIMER B CONTROL REGISTER
MFPTCDCR EQU      MFP+$1C              68901 TIMERS C,D CONTROL REGISTER
MFPTADR EQU       MFP+$1E              68901 TIMER A DATA REGISTER
MFPTBDR EQU       MFP+$20              68901 TIMER B DATA REGISTER
MFPTCDR EQU       MFP+$22              68901 TIMER C DATA REGISTER
MFPTDDR EQU       MFP+$24              68901 TIMER D DATA REGISTER
MFPSCR   EQU      MFP+$26              68901 SYNCHRONOUS CHARACTER REGISTER
MFPUCR   EQU      MFP+$28              68901 USART CONTROL REGISTER
MFPRSR   EQU      MFP+$2A              68901 RECEIVER STATUS REGISTER
MFPTSR   EQU      MFP+$2C              68901 TRANSMITTER STATUS REGISTGER
MFPUDR   EQU      MFP+$2E              68901 USART DATA REGISTER
         SC8F
         LEA      PINIT,A0             POINT TO INITIALIZATION ARRAY
         MOVE.W   #NPORTS,D0           GET NUMBER OF PORT ENTRIES
         JSR      IPORTS               INITIALIZE PORTS
         BRA.S    SC8F                 REPEAT TEST

PINIT
*
*INITIALIZE 6820 OR 6821 PERIPHERAL INTERFACE ADAPTER (PIA)
*
*
         *
         *  PORT A = INPUT
         *  CA1 = DATA AVAILABLE, SET ON LOW TO HIGH TRANSITION,
         *    NO INTERRUPTS
         *  CA2 = DATA ACKNOWLEDGE HANDSHAKE, CLEARED BY READING DATA
         *     REGISTER B, SET TO 1 BY LOW TO HIGH TRANSITION ON CA1
         *
         DC.L     PIACRA               PIA CONTROL REGISTER A ADDRESS
         DC.B     %00000000            INDICATE NEXT ACCESS TO DATA
                                       * DIRECTION REGISTER (SAME ADDRESS
                                       * AS DATA REGISTER)
         DS.B     1                    UNUSED BYTE FOR ALIGNMENT
         DC.L     PIADDRA              PIA DATA DIRECTION REGISTER A ADDRESS
         DC.B     %00000000            ALL BITS INPUT
         DS.B     1                    UNUSED BYTE FOR ALIGNMENT
         DC.L     PIACRA               PIA CONTROL REGISTER A ADDRESS
         DC.B     %00100110            * BITS 7, 6 NOT USED
                                       * BIT 5 = 1 TO MAKE CA2 OUTPUT
                                       * BIT 4 = 0 TO MAKE CA2 A PULSE
                                       * BIT 3 = 0 TO MAKE CA2 INDICATE
                                       *    DATA REGISTER FULL
                                       * BIT 2 = 1 TO ADDRESS DATA REGISTER
                                       * BIT 1 = 1 TO MAKE CA1 ACTIVE
                                       *    LOW-TO-HIGH
                                       * BIT 0 = 0 TO DISABLE CA1 INTERRUPTS
         DS.B     1                    UNUSED BYTE FOR ALIGNMENT

         *
         *  PORT B = OUTPUT
         *  CB1 = DATA ACKNOWLEDGE, SET ON HIGH TO LOW TRANSITION,
         *    NO INTERRUPTS
```

```
        *  CB2 = DATA AVAILABLE, CLEARED BY WRITING TO DATA
        *    REGISTER B, SET TO 1 BY HIGH TO LOW TRANSITION ON CB1
        *
        DC.L    PIACRB              PIA CONTROL REGISTER B ADDRESS
        DC.B    %00000000           INDICATE NEXT ACCESS TO DATA
                                    * DIRECTION REGISTER (SAME ADDRESS
                                    * AS DATA REGISTER)
        DS.B    1                   UNUSED BYTE FOR ALIGNMENT
        DC.L    PIADRB              PIA DATA DIRECTION REGISTER B ADDRESS
        DC.B    %11111111           ALL BITS OUTPUT
        DS.B    1                   UNUSED BYTE FOR ALIGNMENT
        DC.L    PIACRB              PIA CONTROL REGISTER B ADDRESS
        DC.B    %00100100           * BITS 7, 6 NOT USED
                                    * BIT 5 = 1 TO MAKE CB2 OUTPUT
                                    * BIT 4 = 0 TO MAKE CB2 A PULSE
                                    * BIT 3 = 0 TO MAKE CB2 INDICATE
                                    *   DATA REGISTER FULL
                                    * BIT 2 = 1 TO ADDRESS DATA REGISTER
                                    * BIT 1 = 0 TO MAKE CB1 ACTIVE
                                    *   HIGH-TO-LOW
                                    * BIT 0 = 0 TO DISABLE CB1 INTERRUPTS
        DS.B    1                   UNUSED BYTE FOR ALIGNMENT

*
*INITIALIZE 6840 PROGRAMMABLE TIMER MODULE (PTM)
*
*
        *
        *  CLEAR ALL TIMER COUNTERS
        *  RESET TIMERS
        *  OPERATE TIMER 2 IN CONTINUOUS MODE, DECREMENTING COUNTER
        *    AFTER EACH CLOCK CYCLE
        *  SET TIME CONSTANT TO 12 CLOCK CYCLES
        *  THIS GENERATES A SQUARE WAVE WITH PERIOD 2 X (12 + 1)
        *    = 26 CYCLES
        *
        *  THIS INITIALIZATION PRODUCES A 2400 HZ CLOCK FOR USE
        *    IN DIVIDE BY 16 DATA TRANSMISSION
        *  IT ASSUMES A 1 MHZ INPUT CLOCK, SO A PERIOD OF
        *    (1,000,000)/(16 X 2400) = 26 CYCLES WILL GENERATE
        *    A 38,400 (16 X 2400) HZ SQUARE WAVE
        *  NOTE THAT THE 6840 PTM CANNOT OPERATE DIRECTLY FROM
        *    THE 68000 SYSTEM CLOCK BECAUSE OF ITS HIGH FREQUENCY
        *
        DC.L    PTM1MS              PTM TIMER 1 MS BYTE
        DC.B    0                   CLEAR TIMER 1 MS BYTE
        DS.B    1                   UNUSED BYTE FOR ALIGNMENT
        DC.L    PTM1LS              PTM TIMER 1 LS BYTE
        DC.B    0                   CLEAR TIMER 1 LS BYTE
        DS.B    1                   UNUSED BYTE FOR ALIGNMENT
        DC.L    PTM2MS              PTM TIMER 2 MS BYTE
        DC.B    0                   CLEAR TIMER 2 MS BYTE
        DS.B    1                   UNUSED BYTE FOR ALIGNMENT
        DC.L    PTM2LS              PTM TIMER 2 LS BYTE
        DC.B    0                   CLEAR TIMER 1 MS BYTE
```

```
        DS.B    1               UNUSED BYTE FOR ALIGNMENT
        DC.L    PTM3MS          PTM TIMER 3 MS BYTE
        DC.B    0               CLEAR TIMER 3 MS BYTE
        DS.B    1               UNUSED BYTE FOR ALIGNMENT
        DC.L    PTM3MS          PTM TIMER 3 LS BYTE
        DC.B    0               CLEAR TIMER 1 MS BYTE
        DS.B    1               UNUSED BYTE FOR ALIGNMENT
        DC.L    PTMCR2          PTM TIMER 2 CONTROL REGISTER
        DC.B    %00000001       ADDRESS TIMER 1 CONTROL REGISTER
        DS.B    1               UNUSED BYTE FOR ALIGNMENT
        DC.L    PTMC13          PTM TIMER 1,3 CONTROL REGISTER
        DC.B    %00000001       RESET TIMERS
        DS.B    1               UNUSED BYTE FOR ALIGNMENT
        DC.L    PTMC13          PTM TIMER 1,3 CONTROL REGISTER
        DC.B    0               REMOVE RESET
        DS.B    1               UNUSED BYTE FOR ALIGNMENT
        DC.L    PTMCR2          PTM TIMER 2 CONTROL REGISTER
        DC.B    %10000010       * BIT 7 = 1 TO PUT SQUARE WAVE
                                *    OUTPUT ON O2
                                * BIT 6 = 0 TO DISABLE INTERRUPT
                                * BIT 5 = 0 FOR PULSE MODE
                                * BIT 4 = 0 TO INITIALIZE COUNTER
                                *    ON WRITE TO LATCHES
                                * BIT 3 = 0 FOR CONTINUOUS OPERATION
                                * BIT 2 = 0 FOR 16-BIT OPERATION
                                * BIT 1 = 0 TO USE CPU CLOCK
                                * BIT 0 = 0 TO ADDRESS CONTROL
                                *    REGISTER 3
        DS.B    1               UNUSED BYTE FOR ALIGNMENT
        DC.L    PTM2MS          PTM TIMER 2 MS BYTE
        DC.B    0               MS BYTE OF COUNT
        DS.B    1               UNUSED BYTE FOR ALIGNMENT
        DC.L    PTM2LS          PTM TIMER 2 LS BYTE
        DC.B    12              LS BYTE OF COUNT
        DS.B    1               UNUSED BYTE FOR ALIGNMENT
*
*
*INITIALIZE 6850 ASYNCHRONOUS COMMUNICATIONS INTERFACE ADAPTER
*    (ACIA OR UART)
*
        *
        *  8 BIT DATA, NO PARITY
        *  1 STOP BIT
        *  DIVIDE MASTER CLOCK BY 16
        *  NO INTERRUPTS
        *
        *
        DC.L    ACIACR          ACIA CONTROL REGISTER ADDRESS
        DC.B    %00000011       PERFORM MASTER RESET - NOTE:
                                * 6850 HAS NO RESET INPUT
        DS.B    1               UNUSED BYTE FOR ALIGNMENT
        DC.L    ACIACR          ACIA CONTROL REGISTER ADDRESS
        DC.B    %00010101       * BIT 7 = 0 TO DISABLE RECEIVE
                                *    INTERRUPTS
                                * BIT 6 = 0 TO MAKE RTS LOW
                                * BIT 5 = 1 TO DISABLE TRANSMIT
```

```
                                   *   INTERRUPTS
                                   * BIT 4 = 1 TO SELECT 8-BIT DATA
                                   * BIT 3 = 0 FOR NO PARITY
                                   * BIT 2 = 1 FOR 1 STOP BIT
                                   * BIT 1 = 0, BIT 0 = 1 TO
                                   *   DIVIDE MASTER CLOCK BY 16
        DS.B   1                   UNUSED BYTE FOR ALIGNMENT
*
*
*INITIALIZE 68230 PARALLEL INTERFACE/TIMER (PIT)
*
        *
        *  SET PORT MODE 0, DISABLE HANDSHAKE LINES DURING MODE-SETTING,
        *    USE NEGATIVE LOGIC (ACTIVE-LOW) ON ALL HANDSHAKE LINES
        *  PORT A DOUBLE-BUFFERED OUTPUT WITH OUTPUT DEVICE
        *    READY ON H1, H2 MANUAL OUTPUT
        *  PORT B NON-LATCHED INPUT WITH NO STATUS CONTROL,
        *    H4 MANUAL OUTPUT
        *  HANDSHAKE INTERRUPT VECTOR BASE SET TO $50
        *  ENABLE HANDSHAKE LINES 1 AND 2
        *  TIMER INTERRUPT VECTOR BASE SET TO $54
        *  TIMER GENERATES 1000 HZ SQUARE WAVE ON TOUT PIN,
        *    ASSUMING A 4 MHZ CLOCK INPUT (63 X 32 = 2016 CYCLES
        *    PER TOGGLE) USING THE 5-BIT (DIVIDE-BY-32) PRESCALER
        *
        DC.L   PITGCR              PIT GENERAL CONTROL REGISTER
        DC.B   %00000000           *BITS 7, 6 = 00 FOR MODE 0,
                                   * UNIDIRECTIONAL 8-BIT MODE
                                   *BITS 5, 4 = 00 TO DISABLE
                                   * H34, H12 DURING MODE-SETTING
                                   *BITS 3-0 = 0 TO MAKE ALL
                                   * HANDSHAKE LINES ACTIVE-LOW
        DS.B   1                   UNUSED BYTE FOR ALIGNMENT
        DC.L   PITCRA              PIT CONTROL REGISTER A
        DC.B   %01100000           *BITS 7, 6 = 01 FOR SUBMODE
                                   * 01 - DOUBLE-BUFFERED OUTPUT
                                   *BITS 5, 4 = 10 TO MAKE H2
                                   * AN OUTPUT WITH VALUE GIVEN
                                   * BY BIT 3
                                   *BIT 3 = 0 TO MAKE H2 INIITALLY 0
                                   *BIT 2 = 0 TO DISABLE H2 INTERRUPTS
                                   *BIT 1 = 0 TO DISABLE H1 INTERRUPTS
                                   *BIT 0 = 0 TO HAVE H1S SET WHEN
                                   * FINAL OUTPUT LATCH IS EMPTY
        DS.B   1                   UNUSED BYTE FOR ALIGNMENT
        DC.L   PITCRB              PIT CONTROL REGISTER B
        DC.B   %10100000           BITS 7, 6 = 10 FOR SUBMODE
                                   * 1X - BIT I/O
                                   *BITS 5, 4 = 10 TO MAKE H4
                                   * AN OUTPUT WITH VALUE GIVEN
                                   * BY BIT 3
                                   *BIT 3 = 0 TO MAKE H4 INITIALLY 0
                                   *BIT 2 = 0 TO DISABLE H4 INTERRUPTS
                                   *BIT 1 = 0 TO DISABLE H3 INTERRUPTS
                                   *BIT 0 - DON'T CARE
        DS.B   1                   UNUSED BYTE FOR ALIGNMENT
```

```
        DC.L    PITDDRA                 PIT DATA DIRECTION REGISTER A
        DC.B    %11111111               ALL BITS OUTPUTS
        DS.B    1                       UNUSED BYTE FOR ALIGNMENT
        DC.L    PITDDRB                 PIT DATA DIRECTION REGISTER B
        DC.B    %00000000               ALL BITS INPUTS
        DS.B    1                       UNUSED BYTE FOR ALIGNMENT
        DC.L    PITIVR                  PIT INTERRUPT VECTOR REGISTER
        DC.B    $50                     SET INTERRUPT VECTOR BASE TO $50
        DS.B    1                       UNUSED BYTE FOR ALIGNMENT
                                        *NOW ENABLE H1 FOR HANDSHAKE OUTPUT
                                        * ON PORT A
        DC.L    PITGCR                  PIT GENERAL CONTROL REGISTER
        DC.B    %00010000               *BIT 4 = 1 TO ENABLE H1, H2
                                        * HANDSHAKE SIGNALS
        DS.B    1                       UNUSED BYTE FOR ALIGNMENT
        DC.L    PITTIVR                 PIT TIMER INTERRUPT VECTOR REGISTER
        DC.B    $54                     TIMER INTERRUPT VECTOR BASE = $54
        DS.B    1                       UNUSED BYTE FOR ALIGNMENT
        DC.L    PITCPRH                 PIT COUNTER PRELOAD REGISTER HIGH
        DC.B    0                       HIGH BYTE OF INITIAL COUNT = 0
        DS.B    1                       UNUSED BYTE FOR ALIGNMENT
        DC.L    PITCPRM                 PIT COUNTER PRELOAD REGISTER MID
        DC.B    0                       MIDDLE BYTE OF INITIAL COUNT = 0
        DS.B    1                       UNUSED BYTE FOR ALIGNMENT
        DC.L    PITCPRL                 PIT COUNTER PRELOAD REGISTER LOW
        DC.B    63                      SET INTERVAL TO 63 X 32 CLOCK CYCLES
                                        * PER TOGGLE
        DS.B    1                       UNUSED BYTE FOR ALIGNMENT
        DC.L    PITTCR                  PIT TIMER CONTROL REGISTER
        DC.B    %01000001               *BITS 7,6,5 = 010 TO TOGGLE TOUT
                                        *BITS 4,3 UNUSED IN SQUARE WAVE MODE
                                        *BITS 2,1 = 00 TO USE CLK INPUT,
                                        * PRESCALER
                                        *BIT 0 = 1 TO ENABLE TIMER
        DS.B    1                       UNUSED BYTE FOR ALIGNMENT
*
*
*INITIALIZE 68901 MULTIFUNCTION PERIPHERAL
*   HAS 8-BIT PARALLEL PORT, USART, 4 TIMERS, 16-LEVEL INTERRUPT
*     CONTROLLER
*
        *
        *  CLEAR I/O REGISTERS TO ENSURE PROPER STARTUP
        *  SET INTERRUPT VECTOR BASE TO $100, SOFTWARE END-OF-INTERRUPT
        *  MAKE INTERRUPT 2 TRIGGER ON 0 TO 1 TRANSITION, OTHERS
        *     TRIGGER ON 1 TO 0 TRANSITIONS
        *  TIMER C TO OPERATE IN DELAY MODE, INPUT CLOCK DIVIDED BY
        *     64, 192 X 64 INPUT CLOCK CYCLES PER DELAY INTERVAL
        *  TIMER D TO OPERATE IN DELAY MODE, INPUT CLOCK DIVIDED BY
        *     4, 16 X 4 INPUT CLOCK CYCLES PER DELAY INTERVAL
        *  USART OPERATES IN ASYNCHRONOUS MODE, INPUT CLOCK DIVIDED
        *     BY 16, 8 DATA BITS, 2 STOP BITS, NO PARITY
        *
        *
        DC.L    MFPGPIR                 CLEAR GENERAL-PURPOSE I/O REGISTER
        DC.B    %00000000
```

```
DS.B    1                       UNUSED BYTE FOR ALIGNMENT
DC.L    MFPAER                  CLEAR ACTIVE EDGE REGISTER
DC.B    %00000000
DS.B    1                       UNUSED BYTE FOR ALIGNMENT
DC.L    MFPDDR                  CLEAR DATA DIRECTION REGISTER
DC.B    %00000000
DS.B    1                       UNUSED BYTE FOR ALIGNMENT
DC.L    MFPIERA                 CLEAR INTERRUPT ENABLE REGISTER A
DC.B    %00000000
DS.B    1                       UNUSED BYTE FOR ALIGNMENT
DC.L    MFPIERB                 CLEAR INTERRUPT ENABLE REGISTER B
DC.B    %00000000
DS.B    1                       UNUSED BYTE FOR ALIGNMENT
DC.L    MFPIPRA                 CLEAR INTERRUPT PENDING REGISTER A
DC.B    %00000000
DS.B    1                       UNUSED BYTE FOR ALIGNMENT
DC.L    MFPIPRB                 CLEAR INTERRUPT PENDING REGISTER B
DC.B    %00000000
DS.B    1                       UNUSED BYTE FOR ALIGNMENT
DC.L    MFPISRA                 CLEAR INTERRUPT IN-SERVICE REGISTER A
DC.B    %00000000
DS.B    1                       UNUSED BYTE FOR ALIGNMENT
DC.L    MFPISRB                 CLEAR INTERRUPT IN-SERVICE REGISTER B
DC.B    %00000000
DS.B    1                       UNUSED BYTE FOR ALIGNMENT
DC.L    MFPIMRA                 CLEAR INTERRUPT MASK REGISTER A
DC.B    %00000000
DS.B    1                       UNUSED BYTE FOR ALIGNMENT
DC.L    MFPIMRB                 CLEAR INTERRUPT MASK REGISTER B
DC.B    %00000000
DS.B    1                       UNUSED BYTE FOR ALIGNMENT
DC.L    MFPVR                   CLEAR VECTOR REGISTER
DC.B    %00000000
DS.B    1                       UNUSED BYTE FOR ALIGNMENT
DC.L    MFPVR                   MFP VECTOR REGISTER
DC.B    %01001000               *BITS 7-4 = INTERRUPT VECTOR ($40)
                                *BIT 3 = 1 FOR SOFTWARE END-OF-
                                *  INTERRUPT
                                *BITS 2-0 UNUSED
DS.B    1                       UNUSED BYTE FOR ALIGNMENT
DC.L    MFPAER                  MFP ACTIVE EDGE REGISTER
DC.B    %00000100               INTERRUPT 2 TRIGGERS ON RISING EDGE,
                                * ALL OTHERS TRIGGER ON FALLING EDGES
DS.B    1                       UNUSED BYTE FOR ALIGNMENT
DC.L    MFPTCDCR                MFP TIMERS C AND D CONTROL REGISTER
DC.B    %01010001               *BIT 7 UNUSED
                                *BITS 6-4 = 101 TO PUT TIMER C
                                *  IN DELAY MODE, DIVIDE BY 64
                                *BIT 3 UNUSED
                                *BITS 2-0 = 001 TO PUT TIMER D
                                *  IN DELAY MODE, DIVIDE BY 4
DS.B    1                       UNUSED BYTE FOR ALIGNMENT
DC.L    MFPTCDR                 MFP TIMER C DATA REGISTER
DC.B    192                     STARTING COUNT IN TIMER C = 192
DS.B    1                       UNUSED BYTE FOR ALIGNMENT
DC.L    MFPTDDR                 MFP TIMER D DATA REGISTER
```

```
        DC.B    16              STARTING COUNT IN TIMER D = 16
        DS.B    1               UNUSED BYTE FOR ALIGNMENT
        DC.L    MFPSCR          CLEAR SYNCHRONOUS CHARACTER REGISTER
        DC.B    %00000000
        DS.B    1               UNUSED BYTE FOR ALIGNMENT
        DC.L    MFPUCR          MFP USART CONTROL REGISTER
        DC.B    %10011000       * BIT 7 = 1 TO DIVIDE INPUT CLOCK
                                *   BY 16
                                * BITS 6,5 = 00 FOR 8-BIT DATA
                                * BITS 4,3 = 11 FOR ASYNCHRONOUS
                                *   MODE WITH 2 STOP BITS
                                * BIT 2 = 0 FOR NO PARITY
                                * BITS 1,0 NOT USED
        DS.B    1               UNUSED BYTE
        DC.L    MFPRSR          MFP RECEIVER STATUS REGISTER
        DC.B    %00000001       ENABLE RECEIVER
        DS.B    1               UNUSED BYTE
        DC.L    MFPTSR          MFP TRANSMITTER STATUS REGISTER
        DC.B    %00000001       ENABLE TRANSMITTER
        DS.B    1               UNUSED BYTE
ENDPIN  DS.B    0               MARK END OF PORT ARRAY
NPORTS  EQU     (ENDPIN-PINIT)/6 NUMBER OF PORTS TO INITIALIZE

        END
```

8G Delay milliseconds (DELAY)

Provides a delay of between 1 and 65 536 ms, depending on the parameter supplied. A parameter value of 0 is interpreted as 65 536. The user must calculate the value CPMS (cycles per millisecond) to fit a particular computer. Typical values are 8000 for an 8 MHz clock and 10 000 for a 10 MHz clock.

In practice, you must reduce these values to compute the effective clock frequencies for instruction execution. Most computers use some clock periods for refresh and DMA transfers. If, for example, a computer uses 8.5% of its cycles for refresh, only 91.5% are left for instruction execution. The effective clock frequency as far as instruction execution is concerned is the system clock frequency divided by 1.093 (1/0.915).

Procedure The program simply counts down register D0 for the appropriate amount of time as determined by the user-supplied constant. Extra instructions account for the JSR instruction, RTS instruction, and routine overhead without changing anything.

Entry conditions

Number of milliseconds to delay (1–65 536) in low word of register D0.

Exit conditions

Returns after the specified number of milliseconds with (low word of D0) = 0

Example

Data: (low word of D0) = number of milliseconds = $002A_{16} = 42_{10}$
Result: Software delay of $2A_{16}$ (42_{10}) milliseconds, assuming that user supplies the proper value of CPMS.

Registers used CCR, D0

Execution time 1 ms × (low word of D0). If (low word of D0) = 0, the routine takes 65 536 ms

Program size 36 bytes

Data memory required None

Special case (low word of D0) = 0 causes a delay of 65 536 ms

```
*       Title           Delay Milliseconds
*       Name:           DELAY
*
*       Purpose:        Delay from 1 to 256 milliseconds
*
*       Entry:          Low word of Register D0 = number of milliseconds
*                         to delay. A 0 equals 65,536 milliseconds
*
*       Exit:           Returns to calling routine after the
*                       specified delay.
*
*       Registers Used: CCR,D0
*
*       Time:           1 millisecond X (low word of D0)
*
*       Size:           Program 36 bytes

*
*EQUATES
*CYCLES PER MILLISECOND - USER-SUPPLIED
*
CPMS    EQU     8000    8000 = 8 MHZ CLOCK (ATARI ST)
                        *4000 = 4 MHZ CLOCK (MOTOROLA MC68000ECB)
                        *7800 = 7.8 MHZ CLOCK (APPLE MACINTOSH)
                        *10000 = 10 MHZ
*
*EXECUTION TIMES AND OVERHEAD FACTORS
*
DBRAEX  EQU     10      EXECUTION TIME FOR DBRA WITH A BRANCH
                        * AS USED IN DELAY LOOPS
OVRHD1  EQU     72      EXECUTION TIME FOR CALLING DELAY AND
                        * DLY, LOADING D0 FOR THE LAST MS,
                        * AND RETURNING
                        * CONSISTS OF:
                        *   2 LONG JSR'S            - 44
                        *   MOVE.W                  - 8
                        *   EXCESS FOR EXITING DBRA - 4
                        *   RTS                     - 16
OVRHD2  EQU     55      EXECUTION TIME FOR MOVING THROUGH DLY
```

```
                             * ROUTINE THE LAST TIME
                             * CONSISTS OF:
                             *   MOVE.L D1,-(SP) - 13
                             *   SUBQ.W          - 4
                             *   BEQ WITH BRANCH - 10
                             *   MOVE.L (SP)+,D1 - 12
                             *   RTS             - 16
OVRHD3  EQU     34           OVERHEAD ASSOCIATED WITH INNER DLY LOOP
                             * CONSISTS OF:
                             *   SUBQ.W                  - 4
                             *   BEQ WITH NO BRANCH      - 8
                             *   MOVE.W #                - 8
                             *   EXCESS FOR EXITING DBRA - 4
                             *   BRA                     - 10
*
* LOOP CONSTANTS
*
INNERC  EQU     (CPMS-OVRHD3)/DBRAEX    NUMBER OF INNER LOOPS
                                        * REQUIRED FOR 1 MS
OUTERC  EQU     (CPMS-OVRHD1-OVRHD2)/DBRAEX  NUMBER OF OUTER LOOPS
                                             * REQUIRED FOR 1 MS

*
*METHOD:
* THE ROUTINE IS DIVIDED INTO 2 PARTS. THE CALL TO
* THE "DLY" ROUTINE DELAYS EXACTLY 1 LESS THAN THE
* NUMBER OF REQUIRED MILLISECONDS. THE LAST ITERATION
* TAKES INTO ACCOUNT THE OVERHEAD TO CALL "DELAY" AND
* "DLY".
*
DELAY
        *DO ALL BUT THE LAST MILLISECOND
        *
        JSR     DLY             DO ALL BUT LAST MILLISECOND
        *
        *DO LAST MILLISECOND, ACCOUNTING FOR
        * CALLS AND RETURNS
        *
        MOVE.W  #OUTERC,DO      DELAY LAST MILLISECOND
DELYMS  DBRA    DO,DELYMS
        RTS

*****************************************************
*ROUTINE: DLY
*PURPOSE: DELAY ROUTINE
*ENTRY: LOW WORD OF REGISTER DO = MILLISECOND COUNT
*EXIT: LOW WORD OF REGISTER DO = 0
*REGISTERS USED: CCR,DO
*****************************************************

DLY     MOVE.W  D1,-(SP)        PRESERVE REGISTER D1
DLYAGN  SUBQ.W  #1,DO           DECREMENT MILLISECOND COUNT
        BEQ.S   DLYDONE         BRANCH IF ALL MILLISECONDS DONE
*
*       COMPLETE MILLISECOND DELAY
*
        MOVE.W  #INNERC,D1      WAIT REST OF MILLISECOND
```

```
DLYMS    DBRA     D1,DLYMS
         BRA.S    DLYAGN
*
*        EXIT
*
DLYDONE MOVE.L   (SP)+,D1        RESTORE REGISTER D1
         RTS

*
*        SAMPLE EXECUTION:
*


SC8G
         *
         *DELAY 10 MINUTES
         * CALL DELAY 10 TIMES AT 60,000 MS (1 MINUTE) EACH
         *
         MOVE.W   #9,D1            10 TIMES (0A HEX) - REMEMBER THAT
                                   * DBRA EXITS ON -1
MINUTE
         MOVE.W   #60000,D0        60,000 MS (EA60 HEX)
         JSR      DELAY            WAIT 1 MINUTE
         DBRA     D1,MINUTE        CONTINUE UNTIL DONE

         BRA.S    SC8G             REPEAT OPERATION

         END
```

9 Interrupts

9A Unbuffered interrupt-driven input/output using a 6850 ACIA (SINTIO)

Performs interrupt-driven input and output using a 6850 ACIA (Asynchronous Communications Interface Adapter or UART) and single-character input and output buffers. Consists of the following subroutines:

1. INCH reads a character from the input buffer.
2. INST reports whether the input buffer is empty.
3. OUTCH writes a character into the output buffer.
4. OUTST reports whether the output buffer is full.
5. INIT initializes the 6850 ACIA, the interrupt vectors, and the software flags. The flags show whether data is available for transfer between the main program and the interrupt service routines.
6. IOSRVC determines which interrupt occurred and services it. In response to an input interrupt, it reads a character from the ACIA into the input buffer. In response to an output interrupt, it writes a character from the output buffer into the ACIA.

Procedures

1. INCH waits for a character to become available, clears the Data

Ready flag (RECDF), and loads the character into the low byte of register D0.

2. INST sets the Carry flag from the Data Ready flag (RECDF).

3. OUTCH waits for the output buffer to empty, stores the character in the buffer, and sets the Character Available flag (TRNDF). If no output interrupt is expected (i.e. it has been disabled because it occurred when no data was available), OUTCH sends the data to the ACIA immediately.

4. OUTST sets the Carry flag from the Character Available flag (TRNDF).

5. INIT clears the software flags, sets up the interrupt vectors, resets the ACIA (a master reset, since the device has no reset input), and determines the ACIA's operating mode by loading its control register. INIT starts the ACIA with input interrupts enabled and output interrupts disabled. See Subroutine 8F for more details on initializing a 6850 ACIA.

6. IOSRVC examines the ACIA's status register to identify an input interrupt (bit 0 = 1), an output interrupt (bit 1 = 1), or an interrupt from some other device. If an input interrupt occurred, the program reads the data, saves it in memory, and sets the Data Ready flag (RECDF). Lack of buffering results in the loss of unread data at this point.

If an output interrupt occurred, the program determines whether data is available. If not, it simply disables the output interrupt. If data is available, the program sends it to the ACIA, clears the Character Available flag (TRNDF), and enables both input and output interrupts.

Most 68000-based interrupt systems have a controller that responds to interrupt acknowledgements from the CPU and contains prioritization, vectoring, masking, and other management logic. For example, the popular 68901 Multifunction Peripheral (MFP) contains a 16-level interrupt controller. It can thus handle eight external interrupts (typically from 6800 family devices that lack vector-generating circuitry) and eight internal levels derived from the MFP's timers and USART. The 68901 MFP latches interrupt requests from peripheral chips, prioritizes them, and generates source identification to vector the 68000. The system must also have circuitry that converts interrupt request signals into interrupt inputs with the proper overall priority levels.

The special problem with the output interrupt is that it may occur when no data is available. We cannot ignore it or it will assert itself indefinitely, creating an endless loop. Nor can we clear an ACIA output interrupt without sending data to the device, as we can with other serial devices such as the Z80 SIO.

The solution is to disable output interrupts. But this creates a new problem when data is ready to be sent. That is, if output interrupts are disabled, they cannot inform the system that the ACIA is ready to transmit. The solution is to create a non-interrupt-driven entry to the ACIA output routine. This entry must check whether the ACIA's output register is empty before sending it a character.

The special sequence of operations is the following:

1. Output interrupt occurs before new data is available (that is, the ACIA becomes ready for data). The response is to disable the output interrupt, as there is no data to be sent. Note that this sequence will not occur initially, because INIT disables the output interrupt. Otherwise, the output interrupt would occur immediately, since the ACIA surely starts out empty and therefore ready to transmit data.

2. Output data becomes available. That is, the system now has data to transmit. But there is no use waiting for the output interrupt, since it has been disabled.

3. The main program calls the routine (OUTDAT) that sends data to the ACIA. Checking the ACIA's status shows that it is, in fact, ready to transmit a character (as it indicated by causing the output interrupt). The routine then sends the character and reenables interrupts.

Unserviceable interrupts occur only with output devices, since input devices always have data when they request service. Thus output devices cause more startup and sequencing problems in interrupt-driven systems than do input devices.

The solution shown here may, however, have a strange result. Assume that the system has output data but the ACIA is not ready for it. The system must then wait with interrupts disabled for the ACIA to become ready. That is, an interrupt-driven system must disable its interrupts and wait idly, polling the output device. We could solve this problem with an extra software flag (output interrupt expected). The service routine would change this flag if the output interrupt occurred when no data was available. The system could then check the flag and determine whether the output interrupt had already occurred (see Subroutines 9B and 9C).

Entry conditions

1. INCH: none
2. INST: none
3. OUTCH: character to transmit in low byte of register D0.
4. OUTST: none
5. INIT: none

Exit conditions

1. INCH: character in low byte of register D0.
2. INST: Carry = 0 if input buffer is empty, 1 if it is full.
3. OUTCH: none
4. OUTST: Carry = 0 if output buffer is empty, 1 if it is full.
5. INIT: none

Registers used

1. INCH: CCR, D0
2. INST: CCR, D0
3. OUTCH: CCR, D0
4. OUTST: CCR, D0
5. INIT: CCR, D0

Execution time

1. INCH: 123 cycles if a character is available
2. INST: 40 cycles
3. OUTCH: 280 cycles if the output buffer is empty and the ACIA is ready to transmit
4. OUTST: 40 cycles
5. INIT: 203 cycles

6. IOSRVC: 175 cycles to service an input interrupt, 246 cycles to service an output interrupt, 155 cycles to determine that the interrupt is from another device. These times include the processor's interrupt response time (44 cycles).

Program size 246 bytes

Data memory required 8 bytes anywhere in RAM for the received data (address RECDAT), receive data flag (address RECDF), transmit data (address TRNDAT), transmit data flag (address TRNDF), and the starting address of the next service routine (4 bytes at address NEXTSR).

```
*       Title           Simple interrupt input and output using a 6850
*                       ACIA and single character buffers.
*       Name:           SINTIO
*
*       Purpose:        This program consists of 5 subroutines that
*                       perform interrupt driven input and output using
*                       a 6850 ACIA.
*
*                       INCH
*                         Read a character.
*                       INST
*                         Report input status (whether input buffer
*                         is empty).
*                       OUTCH
*                         Write a character.
*                       OUTST
*                         Report output status (whether output buffer
*                         is full).
*                       INIT
*                         Initialize.
*
*       Entry:          INCH
*                         No parameters.
*                       INST
*                         No parameters.
*                       OUTCH
*                         Character to transmit in low byte of
*                           register D0.
*                       OUTST
*                         No parameters.
*                       INIT
*                         No parameters.
*
*       Exit:           INCH
```

```
*                         Received character in low byte of register D0.
*                       INST
*                         Carry = 0 if input buffer is empty,
*                         1 if character is available.
*                       OUTCH
*                         No parameters
*                       OUTST
*                         Carry = 0 if output buffer is empty,
*                         1 if it is full.
*                       INIT
*                         No parameters.
*
*       Registers Used: INCH
*                         CCR,D0
*                       INST
*                         CCR,D0
*                       OUTCH
*                         CCR,D0
*                       OUTST
*                         CCR,D0
*                       INIT
*                         CCR,D0
*
*       Time:           INCH
*                         123 cycles if a character is available
*                       INST
*                         40 cycles
*                       OUTCH
*                         280 cycles if output buffer is empty and
*                         the ACIA is ready to transmit
*                       OUTST
*                         40 cycles
*                       INIT
*                         203 cycles
*                       IOSRVC
*                         155 cycles minimum if the interrupt is not
*                           ours
*                         175 cycles to service an input interrupt
*                         246 cycles to service an output interrupt
*                         These include the processor's interrupt
*                         response time (44 cycles).
*
*       Size:           Program 246 bytes
*                       Data      8 bytes
*


*
*ARBITRARY 6850 ACIA MEMORY ADDRESSES (ATARI ST MIDI PORT)
*
ACIA     EQU     $FFFFFC04          6850 ACIA BASE ADDRESS
ACIACR   EQU     ACIA               6850 ACIA CONTROL REGISTER
ACIASR   EQU     ACIA               6850 ACIA STATUS REGISTER
ACIADR   EQU     ACIA+2             6850 ACIA DATA REGISTER
*
*ATARI 520ST INTERRUPT VECTOR
*
```

```
INTVEC  EQU     $0118              VECTOR TO INTERRUPT SERVICE ROUTINE
                                   * (USER INTERRUPT VECTOR 6)
*
*INTERRUPT ENABLE/DISABLE EQUATES
*
INTDIS  EQU     $2700              STATUS REGISTER VALUE TO DISABLE
                                   * ALL INTERRUPTS IN SUPERVISOR MODE
INTENB  EQU     $2000              STATUS REGISTER VALUE TO ENABLE
                                   * ALL INTERRUPTS IN SUPERVISOR MODE

*
*     READ A CHARACTER FROM INPUT BUFFER
*
INCH
        JSR     INST               GET INPUT STATUS
        BCC.S   INCH               WAIT IF NO CHARACTER AVAILABLE
        CLR.B   RECDF              INDICATE INPUT BUFFER EMPTY
        MOVE.B  RECDAT,D0          GET CHARACTER FROM INPUT BUFFER
        RTS
*
*     DETERMINE INPUT STATUS (CARRY = 1 IF DATA AVAILABLE, 0 IF NOT)
*
INST
        MOVE.B  RECDF,D0           GET DATA READY FLAG
        LSR.B   #1,D0              SET CARRY FROM DATA READY FLAG
                                   * CARRY = 1 IF CHARACTER AVAILABLE,
                                   * 0 IF NOT
        RTS

*
*    WRITE A CHARACTER INTO OUTPUT BUFFER AND THEN ON TO ACIA
*
OUTCH
        MOVE.W  D1,-(SP)           SAVE REGISTER D1
        MOVE.B  D0,D1              SAVE CHARACTER TO WRITE
*
*    WAIT FOR OUTPUT BUFFER TO EMPTY, STORE NEXT CHARACTER
*
WAITOC
        JSR     OUTST              GET OUTPUT STATUS
        BCS.S   WAITOC             WAIT IF OUTPUT BUFFER FULL
        MOVE.B  D1,TRNDAT          STORE CHARACTER IN BUFFER
        MOVE.B  #$FF,TRNDF         INDICATE BUFFER FULL
        JSR     OUTDAT             SEND CHARACTER TO OUTPUT PORT
        MOVE.W  (SP)+,D1           RESTORE REGISTER D1
        RTS

*
*    DETERMINE OUTPUT STATUS (CARRY = 1 IF OUTPUT BUFFER FULL)
*
OUTST
        MOVE.B  TRNDF,D0           GET TRANSMIT FLAG
        LSR.B   #1,D0              SET CARRY FROM TRANSMIT FLAG
        RTS                        CARRY = 1 IF BUFFER FULL, 0 IF NOT

*
```

```
*INITIALIZE INTERRUPT SYSTEM AND 6850 ACIA
*
INIT
        *
        *DISABLE INTERRUPTS DURING INITIALIZATION BUT SAVE
        *  PREVIOUS STATE OF INTERRUPT MASK
        *
        MOVE.W  SR,-(SP)        SAVE CURRENT STATUS (PARTICULARLY
                                * INTERRUPT MASK).  THIS IS A PRIVILEGED
                                * INSTRUCTION ON 68010 AND LATER
                                * PROCESSORS.
        MOVE.W  #INTDIS,SR      DISABLE INTERRUPTS DURING INITIALIZATION
                                * (ASSUME SUPERVISOR MODE)
        *
        *INITIALIZE ATARI 520ST INTERRUPT VECTOR
        *
        MOVE.L  INTVEC,NEXTSR   GET CURRENT INTERRUPT VECTOR
                                * AND SAVE IT AS ADDRESS OF NEXT SERVICE
                                * ROUTINE
        MOVE.L  #IOSRVC,INTVEC  GET ADDRESS OF OUR SERVICE ROUTINE
                                * AND SAVE IT AS INTERRUPT VECTOR
        *
        *INITIALIZE SOFTWARE FLAGS
        *
        CLR.B   RECDF           NO INPUT DATA AVAILABLE
        CLR.B   TRNDF           OUTPUT BUFFER EMPTY
        *
        *INITIALIZE 6850 ACIA (UART)
        *
        MOVE.B  #%00000011,ACIACR MASTER RESET ACIA (IT HAS NO RESET
                                * INPUT)
        MOVE.B  #%10010001,ACIACR SELECT ACIA OPERATING MODE
                              *BIT 7 = 1 TO ENABLE INPUT INTERRUPTS
                              *BITS 6,5 = 0 TO DISABLE OUTPUT INTERRUPTS
                              *BITS 4,3,2 = 100 FOR 8 DATA BITS, 2 STOP
                              *  BITS, NO PARITY
                              *BITS 1,0 = 01 FOR DIVIDE BY 16 CLOCK
        RTE                   RESTORE FLAGS AND EXIT (THIS RESTORES THE
                              * STATE OF THE INTERRUPT MASKS WHEN INIT
                              * WAS CALLED)


*
*GENERAL INTERRUPT HANDLER
*
IOSRVC
        *
        *GET ACIA STATUS: BIT 0 = 1 IF AN INPUT INTERRUPT,
        *  BIT 1 = 1 IF AN OUTPUT INTERRUPT
        *
        MOVE.W D0,-(SP)       SAVE REGISTER D0
        MOVE.B ACIASR,D0      GET ACIA STATUS
        LSR.B  #1,D0          EXAMINE RECEIVE DATA REGISTER FULL BIT
        BCS.S  RDHDLR         BRANCH IF AN INPUT INTERRUPT
        LSR.B  #1,D0          EXAMINE TRANSMIT DATA REGISTER EMPTY BIT
        BCS.S  WRHDLR         BRANCH IF AN OUTPUT INTERRUPT
```

```
        MOVE.W (SP)+,D0         RESTORE REGISTER D0
        MOVE.L NEXTSR,-(SP)     NOT THIS ACIA, EXAMINE NEXT INTERRUPT
        RTS
*
*INPUT (READ) INTERRUPT HANDLER
*
RDHDLR
        MOVE.B  ACIADR,RECDAT   READ DATA FROM 6850 ACIA
                                * AND SAVE IT IN INPUT BUFFER
        MOVE.B  #$FF,RECDF      INDICATE INPUT DATA AVAILABLE
        BRA.S   IOSREXIT        RESTORE REGISTER D0

*
*OUTPUT (WRITE) INTERRUPT HANDLER
*
WRHDLR
        MOVE.B  TRNDF,D0        TEST DATA AVAILABLE FLAG
        BEQ.S   NODATA          JUMP IF NO DATA TO TRANSMIT
        JSR     OUTDT1          ELSE SEND DATA TO 6850 ACIA
        BRA.S   IOSREXIT          (NO NEED TO TEST STATUS)
*
*IF AN OUTPUT INTERRUPT OCCURS WHEN NO DATA IS AVAILABLE,
* WE MUST DISABLE IT (IN THE 6850) TO AVOID AN ENDLESS LOOP.  LATER,
* WHEN A CHARACTER BECOMES AVAILABLE, WE CALL THE OUTPUT ROUTINE
* OUTDAT WHICH MUST TEST ACIA STATUS BEFORE SENDING THE DATA.
* THE OUTPUT ROUTINE MUST ALSO REENABLE THE OUTPUT INTERRUPT AFTER
* SENDING THE DATA.  THIS PROCEDURE OVERCOMES THE PROBLEM OF AN
* UNSERVICED OUTPUT INTERRUPT ASSERTING ITSELF REPEATEDLY, WHILE
* STILL ENSURING THAT OUTPUT INTERRUPTS ARE RECOGNIZED AND THAT
* DATA IS NEVER SENT TO AN ACIA THAT IS NOT READY FOR IT.
*THE PROBLEM IS THAT AN OUTPUT DEVICE MAY REQUEST SERVICE BEFORE
* THE COMPUTER HAS ANYTHING TO SEND (UNLIKE AN INPUT DEVICE THAT
* HAS DATA WHEN IT REQUESTS SERVICE).
*
NODATA
        MOVE.B  #%10010001,ACIACR ESTABLISH ACIA OPERATING MODE
                                  * WITH OUTPUT INTERRUPTS DISABLED
IOSREXIT
        MOVE.W  (SP)+,D0        RESTORE REGISTER D0
        RTE

****************************************
*ROUTINE: OUTDAT, OUTDT1 (OUTDAT IS NON-INTERRUPT DRIVEN ENTRY POINT)
*PURPOSE: SEND A CHARACTER TO THE ACIA
*ENTRY: TRNDAT = CHARACTER TO SEND
*EXIT: NONE
*REGISTERS USED: CCR,D0
****************************************

OUTDAT
        MOVE.B  ACIASR,D0       CAME HERE WITH INTERRUPTS DISABLED
        ANDI.B  #%00000010,D0   TEST WHETHER ACIA OUTPUT REGISTER EMPTY
        BEQ.S   OUTDAT          BRANCH (WAIT) IF IT IS NOT EMPTY
OUTDT1
        MOVE.B  TRNDAT,ACIADR   GET THE CHARACTER AND SEND IT TO ACIA
        CLR.B   TRNDF           INDICATE OUTPUT BUFFER EMPTY
```

```
        MOVE.B  #%10110001,ACIACR  ESTABLISH ACIA OPERATING MODE WITH
                                   * OUTPUT INTERRUPTS ENABLED
        RTS

*
*DATA SECTION
*
RECDAT  DS.B    1                  RECEIVE DATA
RECDF   DS.B    1                  RECEIVE DATA FLAG
                                   *  (0 = NO DATA, FF = DATA AVAILABLE)
TRNDAT  DS.B    1                  TRANSMIT DATA
TRNDF   DS.B    1                  TRANSMIT DATA FLAG
                                   *  (0 = BUFFER EMPTY, FF = BUFFER FULL)
NEXTSR  DS.L    1                  ADDRESS OF NEXT INTERRUPT SERVICE
                                   *  ROUTINE

*
*       SAMPLE EXECUTION:
*
*CHARACTER EQUATES
ESCAPE  EQU     $1B                ASCII ESCAPE CHARACTER
TESTCH  EQU     'A'                TEST CHARACTER = A

SC9A
        MOVE.L  #0,-(SP)           PUT 68000 IN SUPERVISOR MODE
        MOVE.W  #$20,-(SP)
        TRAP    #1
        MOVE.L  2(SP),USERSP       SAVE ORIGINAL STACK POINTER
        ADDQ.L  #6,SP              REMOVE GEMDOS PARAMETERS FROM STACK
        JSR     INIT               INITIALIZE 6850 ACIA, INTERRUPT SYSTEM
        MOVE.W  #INTENB,SR         ENABLE INTERRUPTS
        *
        *SIMPLE EXAMPLE - READ AND ECHO CHARACTERS
        * UNTIL AN ESC IS RECEIVED
        *
LOOP
        JSR     INCH               READ CHARACTER
        MOVE.W  D0,D1              SAVE CHARACTER
        JSR     OUTCH              ECHO CHARACTER
        CMPI.B  #ESCAPE,D1         IS CHARACTER AN ESCAPE?
        BNE.S   LOOP               STAY IN LOOP IF NOT
        *
        *AN ASYNCHRONOUS EXAMPLE
        * OUTPUT "A" TO CONSOLE CONTINUOUSLY BUT ALSO LOOK AT
        * INPUT SIDE, READING AND ECHOING ANY INPUT CHARACTERS.
        *
ASYNLP
        *
        *OUTPUT AN "A" IF OUTPUT IS NOT BUSY
        *
        JSR     OUTST              IS OUTPUT BUSY?
        BCS.S   ASYNLP             JUMP IF IT IS
        MOVE.B  #TESTCH,D0
        JSR     OUTCH              OUTPUT TEST CHARACTER
        *
        *CHECK INPUT PORT
```

```
        *ECHO CHARACTER IF ONE IS AVAILABLE
        *EXIT ON ESCAPE CHARACTER
        *
        JSR      INST               IS INPUT DATA AVAILABLE?
        BCC.S    ASYNLP             JUMP IF NOT (SEND ANOTHER "A")
        JSR      INCH               GET CHARACTER
        CMPI.B   #ESCAPE,D0         IS IT AN ESCAPE?
        BEQ.S    DONE               BRANCH IF IT IS
        JSR      OUTCH              ELSE ECHO CHARACTER
        BRA.S    ASYNLP             AND CONTINUE

DONE
        MOVE.L   USERSP,-(SP)       RESTORE 68000 TO USER MODE
        MOVE.W   #$20,-(SP)
        TRAP     #1
        ADDQ.L   #6,SP              REMOVE GEMDOS PARAMETERS FROM STACK
        BRA.S    SC9A               REPEAT TEST

USERSP  DS.L     1                  STORAGE FOR USER'S STACK POINTER

        END
```

9B Unbuffered interrupt-driven input/output using a 6821 PIA (PINTIO)

Performs interrupt-driven input and output using a 6821 PIA and single-character input and output buffers. Consists of the following subroutines:

1. INCH reads a character from the input buffer.

2. INST reports whether the input buffer is empty.

3. OUTCH writes a character into the output buffer.

4. OUTST reports whether the output buffer is full.

5. INIT initializes the 6821 PIA and the software flags. The flags show whether data is available for transfer between the main program and the interrupt service routines.

6. IOSRVC determines which interrupt occurred and services it. That is, it reads a character from the PIA into the input buffer in response to an input interrupt, and it writes a character from the output buffer into the PIA in response to an output interrupt.

Procedure

1. INCH waits for a character to become available, clears the Data Ready flag (RECDF), and loads the character into the low byte of register D0.

2. INST sets the Carry flag from the Data Ready flag (RECDF).

3. OUTCH waits for the output buffer to empty, puts the character from the low byte of register D0 into the buffer, and sets the character available flag (TRNDF). If an unserviced output interrupt has occurred (i.e. the output device has requested service when no data was available), OUTCH actually sends the data to the 6821 PIA immediately.

4. OUTST sets Carry from the Character Available flag (TRNDF).

5. INIT clears the software flags and initializes the 6821 PIA by loading its control and data direction registers. It makes port A an input port, port B an output port, control lines CA1 and CB1 active low-to-high, control line CA2 a brief output pulse indicating input acknowledge (active-low briefly after the CPU reads the data), and control line CB2 a write strobe (active-low after the CPU writes the data and lasting until the peripheral becomes ready again). INIT also enables the input interrupt on CA1 and the output interrupt on CB1. See Appendix B and Subroutine 8F for more details about initializing 6821 PIAs.

6. IOSRVC determines whether the interrupt was an input interrupt (bit 7 of PIA control register A = 1), an output interrupt (bit 7 of PIA control register B = 1), or the product of some other device. If an input interrupt occurred, the program reads the data, saves it in the input buffer, and sets the Data Ready flag (RECDF). Lack of buffering results in the loss of any unread data at this point.

If an output interrupt occurred, the program determines whether any data is available. If not, it simply clears the interrupt and clears the flag (OIE) that indicates the output device is actually ready (i.e. an output interrupt has occurred when no data was available). If data is available, the program sends it from the output buffer to the PIA, clears the Character Available flag (TRNDF), sets the Output Interrupt flag (OIE), and enables both input and output interrupts.

Most 68000-based interrupt systems have a controller that responds to interrupt acknowledgements from the CPU and contains prioritization, vectoring, masking, and other management logic. For example, the popular 68901 Multifunction Peripheral (MFP) contains a 16-level interrupt controller. It can thus handle eight external interrupts (typically from 6800 family devices that lack vector-generating circuitry) and eight internal levels derived from the MFP's timers and USART. The 68901 MFP latches interrupt requests from peripheral chips, prioritizes them, and generates source identification to vector the 68000. The system must also have circuitry that converts interrupt request signals into interrupt inputs with the proper overall priority levels.

The special problem with the output interrupt is that it may occur when no data is available to send. We cannot ignore it or it will assert itself indefinitely, causing an endless loop. The solution is simply to clear the 6821 interrupt by reading the data register in port B.

But now we have a new problem when output data becomes available. That is, since the interrupt has been cleared, it obviously cannot inform the system that the output device is ready. The solution is a flag that indicates (with a 0 value) that the output interrupt has occurred without being serviced. We call this flag OIE (Output Interrupt Expected).

The initialization routine clears OIE (since the output device surely starts out ready for data). The output service routine clears it when an output interrupt occurs that cannot be serviced (no data is available) and sets it after sending data to the 6821 PIA (in case it might have been cleared). Now the output routine OUTCH can check OIE to determine whether an output interrupt is expected. If not, OUTCH simply sends the data immediately.

Note that we can clear a PIA interrupt without actually sending any data (by simply reading the data port). We cannot do this with a 6850 ACIA (see Subroutines 9A and 9C), so the procedures for using it are different.

Unserviceable interrupts occur only with output devices, since input devices always have data when they request service. Thus output devices cause more startup and sequencing problems in interrupt-driven systems than do input devices.

Entry conditions

1. INCH : none
2. INST: none
3. OUTCH: character to transmit in low byte of register D0
4. OUTST: none
5. INIT: none

Exit conditions

1. INCH: character in low byte of register D0
2. INST: Carry = 0 if input buffer is empty, 1 if it is full.
3. OUTCH: none
4. OUTST: Carry = 0 if output buffer is empty, 1 if it is full.
5. INIT: none

Registers used

1. INCH: CCR, D0
2. INST: CCR, D0
3. OUTCH: CCR, D0

4. OUTST: CCR, D0

5. INIT: CCR, D0

Execution time

1. INCH: 123 cycles if a character is available

2. INST: 40 cycles

3. OUTCH: 171 cycles if the output buffer is not full; 107 additional cycles to send the data to the 6821 PIA if no output interrupt is expected

4. OUTST: 40 cycles

5. INIT: 308 cycles

6. IOSRVC: 150 cycles to service an input interrupt, 257 cycles to service an output interrupt; 138 cycles to determine that an interrupt is from another device. These times all include the CPU's interrupt response time (44 cycles).

Program size 268 bytes

Data memory required 9 bytes anywhere in RAM for the received data (address RECDAT), receive data flag (address RECDF), transmit data (address TRNDAT), transmit data flag (address TRNDF), output interrupt expected flag (address OIE), and the address of the next interrupt service routine (4 bytes starting at address NEXTSR).

```
*       Title           Simple interrupt input and output using a 6821
*                       Peripheral Interface Adapter and single
*                       character buffers.
*       Name:           PINTIO
*

*       Purpose:        This program consists of 5 subroutines that
*                       perform interrupt driven input and output using
*                       a 6821 PIA.
*
*                       INCH
*                         Read a character.
*                       INST
*                         Report input status (whether input buffer
*                         is empty).
*                       OUTCH
*                         Write a character.
```

```
*                       OUTST
*                         Report output status (whether output buffer
*                         is full).
*                       INIT
*                         Initialize 6821 PIA and interrupt system.
*
*       Entry:          INCH
*                         No parameters.
*                       INST
*                         No parameters.
*                       OUTCH
*                         Character to transmit in low byte of
*                           register D0.
*                       OUTST
*                         No parameters.
*                       INIT
*                         No parameters.
*
*       Exit:           INCH
*                         Character in low byte of register D0.
*                       INST
*                         Carry = 0 if input buffer is empty,
*                         1 if character is available.
*                       OUTCH
*                         No parameters
*                       OUTST
*                         Carry = 0 if output buffer is
*                         empty, 1 if it is full.
*                       INIT
*                         No parameters.
*
*       Registers Used: INCH
*                         CCR,D0
*                       INST
*                         CCR,D0
*                       OUTCH
*                         CCR,D0
*                       OUTST
*                         CCR,D0
*                       INIT
*                         CCR,D0
*
*       Time:           INCH
*                         123 cycles if a character is available
*                       INST
*                         40 cycles
*                       OUTCH
*                         171 cycles if output buffer is not full and
*                         output interrupt is expected
*                       OUTST
*                         40 cycles
*                       INIT
*                         308 cycles
*                       IOSRVC
*                         138 cycles minimum if the interrupt is not
*                           ours
```

```
*                           150 cycles to service an input interrupt
*                           257 cycles to service an output interrupt
*                           These include the processor's interrupt
*                           response time (44 cycles).
*
*       Size:               Program 268 bytes
*                           Data      9 bytes
*

*
*6821 PIA EQUATES
*ARBITRARY 6821 PIA MEMORY ADDRESSES
*
PIA     EQU     $FFFFA400       6821 PIA BASE ADDRESS
PIADRA  EQU     PIA             6821 PIA DATA REGISTER A
PIADDRA EQU     PIA             6821 PIA DATA DIRECTION REGISTER A
PIACRA  EQU     PIA+2           6821 PIA CONTROL REGISTER A
PIADRB  EQU     PIA+4           6821 PIA DATA REGISTER B
PIADDRB EQU     PIA+4           6821 PIA DATA DIRECTION REGISTER B
PIACRB  EQU     PIA+6           6821 PIA CONTROL REGISTER B
*
*ATARI 520ST INTERRUPT VECTOR
*
INTVEC  EQU     $006C           VECTOR TO INTERRUPT SERVICE ROUTINE
*                                  (AUTOVECTOR 3 - CHOSEN ARBITRARILY)
*
*INTERRUPT ENABLE/DISABLE EQUATES
*
INTDIS  EQU     $2700           STATUS REGISTER VALUE TO DISABLE
                                * ALL INTERRUPTS IN SUPERVISOR MODE
INTENB  EQU     $2000           STATUS REGISTER VALUE TO ENABLE
                                * ALL INTERRUPTS IN SUPERVISOR MODE

*
*READ A CHARACTER FROM INPUT BUFFER
*
INCH
        JSR     INST            GET INPUT STATUS
        BCC.S   INCH            WAIT IF NO CHARACTER AVAILABLE
        CLR.B   RECDF           INDICATE INPUT BUFFER EMPTY
        MOVE.B  RECDAT,D0       GET CHARACTER FROM INPUT BUFFER
        RTS

*
*DETERMINE INPUT STATUS (CARRY = 1 IF DATA AVAILABLE, 0 IF NOT)
*
INST
        MOVE.B  RECDF,D0        GET DATA READY FLAG
        LSR.B   #1,D0           SET CARRY FROM DATA READY FLAG
                                * CARRY = 1 IF CHARACTER AVAILABLE,
                                * 0 IF NOT
        RTS

*
*WRITE A CHARACTER INTO OUTPUT BUFFER
*
```

```
OUTCH
        MOVE.W  D1,-(SP)        SAVE REGISTER D1
        MOVE.B  D0,D1           SAVE CHARACTER TO WRITE
*
*WAIT FOR OUTPUT BUFFER TO EMPTY, STORE NEXT CHARACTER
*
WAITOC
        JSR     OUTST           GET OUTPUT STATUS
        BCS.S   WAITOC          WAIT IF OUTPUT BUFFER FULL
        MOVE.B  D1,TRNDAT       STORE CHARACTER IN OUTPUT BUFFER
        MOVE.B  #$FF,TRNDF      INDICATE OUTPUT BUFFER FULL
        TST.B   OIE             TEST OUTPUT INTERRUPT EXPECTED FLAG
        BNE.S   EXITOT          EXIT IF OUTPUT INTERRUPT EXPECTED
        JSR     OUTDAT          SEND CHARACTER IMMEDIATELY IF
                                * NO OUTPUT INTERRUPT EXPECTED
EXITOT
        RTS

*
*DETERMINE OUTPUT STATUS (CARRY = 1 IF OUTPUT BUFFER FULL)
*
OUTST
        MOVE.B  TRNDF,D0        GET TRANSMIT FLAG
        LSR.B   #1,D0           SET CARRY FROM TRANSMIT FLAG
        RTS                       CARRY = 1 IF BUFFER FULL, 0 IF NOT

*
*INITIALIZE INTERRUPT SYSTEM AND 6821 PIA
*
INIT
        *
        *DISABLE INTERRUPTS DURING INITIALIZATION BUT SAVE
        *  PREVIOUS STATE OF INTERRUPT MASK
        *
        MOVE.W  SR,-(SP)        SAVE CURRENT STATUS (PARTICULARLY
                                * INTERRUPT MASK)
        MOVE.W  #INTDIS,SR      DISABLE INTERRUPTS DURING INITIALIZATION
                                * (ASSUME SUPERVISOR MODE)
        *
        *INITIALIZE ATARI 520ST INTERRUPT VECTOR
        *
        MOVE.L  INTVEC,NEXTSR   GET CURRENT INTERRUPT VECTOR
                                * AND SAVE IT AS ADDRESS OF NEXT SERVICE
                                * ROUTINE
        MOVE.L  #IOSRVC,INTVEC  GET ADDRESS OF OUR SERVICE ROUTINE AND
                                * SAVE IT AS INTERRUPT VECTOR
        *
        *INITIALIZE SOFTWARE FLAGS
        *
        CLR.B   RECDF           NO INPUT DATA AVAILABLE
        CLR.B   TRNDF           OUTPUT BUFFER EMPTY
        CLR.B   OIE             INDICATE NO OUTPUT INTERRUPT NEEDED
                                * 6821 READY TO TRANSMIT INITIALLY
```

```
        *
        *INITIALIZE 6821 PIA (PARALLEL INTERFACE)
        *
        CLR.B    PIACRA           ADDRESS DATA DIRECTION REGISTERS
        CLR.B    PIACRB
        CLR.B    PIADDA           MAKE PORT A INPUT
        MOVE.B   #$FF,PIADDB      MAKE PORT B OUTPUT
        MOVE.B   #%00101111,PIACRA
                                  *SET PORT A AS FOLLOWS:
                                  *BITS 7,6 NOT USED
                                  *BIT 5 = 1 TO MAKE CA2 OUTPUT
                                  *BIT 4 = 0 TO MAKE CA2 A PULSE
                                  *BIT 3 = 1 TO MAKE CA2 A BRIEF INPUT
                                  *  ACKNOWLEDGE
                                  *BIT 2 = 1 TO ADDRESS DATA REGISTER
                                  *BIT 1 = 1 TO MAKE CA1 ACTIVE LOW-TO-
                                  *  HIGH
                                  *BIT 0 = 1 TO ENABLE CA1 INTERRUPTS
        MOVE.B   #%00100111,PIACRB
                                  *SET PORT B AS FOLLOWS:
                                  *BITS 7, 6 NOT USED
                                  *BIT 5 = 1 TO MAKE CB2 OUTPUT
                                  *BIT 4 = 0 TO MAKE CB2 A PULSE
                                  *BIT 3 = 0 TO MAKE CB2 A LONG OUTPUT
                                  *  BUFFER FULL
                                  *BIT 2 = 1 TO ADDRESS DATA REGISTER
                                  *BIT 1 = 1 TO MAKE CB1 ACTIVE LOW-TO-
                                  *  HIGH
                                  *BIT 0 = 1 TO ENABLE CB1 INTERRUPTS
        RTE                       RESTORE STATUS (THIS RESTORES THE
                                  * STATE OF THE INTERRUPT MASKS WHEN INIT
                                  * WAS CALLED)

*
*INTERRUPT MANAGER
*DETERMINES WHETHER INPUT OR OUTPUT INTERRUPT OCCURRED
*
IOSRVC
        *
        *INPUT INTERRUPT FLAG IS BIT 7 OF CONTROL REGISTER A
        *OUTPUT INTERRUPT FLAG IS BIT 7 OF CONTROL REGISTER B
        *
        TST.B    PIACRA           CHECK FOR INPUT INTERRUPT
        BMI.S    RDHDLR           BRANCH IF INPUT INTERRUPT
        TST.B    PIACRB           CHECK FOR OUTPUT INTERRUPT
        BMI.S    WRHDLR           BRANCH IF OUTPUT INTERRUPT
        MOVE.L   NEXTSR,-(SP)     INTERRUPT IS FROM ANOTHER SOURCE
        RTS

*
*INPUT (READ) INTERRUPT HANDLER
*
RDHDLR
        MOVE.B   PIADRA,RECDAT    READ DATA FROM 6821 PIA
                                  * AND SAVE IT IN INPUT BUFFER
        MOVE.B   #$FF,RECDF       INDICATE CHARACTER AVAILABLE
```

```
        BRA.S   IOSREXIT        EXIT

*
*OUTPUT (WRITE) INTERRUPT HANDLER
*
WRHDLR
        TST.B   TRNDF           TEST DATA AVAILABLE FLAG
        BEQ.S   NODATA          JUMP IF NO DATA TO TRANSMIT
        JSR     OUTDAT          SEND DATA TO 6821 PIA
        BRA.S   IOSREXIT        EXIT
*
*IF AN OUTPUT INTERRUPT OCCURS WHEN NO DATA IS AVAILABLE,
* WE MUST CLEAR IT (IN THE 6821) TO AVOID AN ENDLESS LOOP.  LATER,
* WHEN A CHARACTER BECOMES AVAILABLE, WE NEED TO KNOW THAT AN
* OUTPUT INTERRUPT HAS OCCURRED WITHOUT BEING SERVICED.  THE KEY
* TO DOING THIS IS THE OUTPUT INTERRUPT EXPECTED FLAG OIE.  THIS FLAG IS
* CLEARED WHEN AN OUTPUT INTERRUPT HAS OCCURRED BUT HAS NOT BEEN
* SERVICED.  IT IS ALSO CLEARED INITIALLY SINCE THE 6821 PIA STARTS
* OUT READY.  OIE IS SET WHENEVER DATA IS ACTUALLY SENT TO THE PIA.
* THUS THE OUTPUT ROUTINE OUTCH CAN CHECK OIE TO DETERMINE WHETHER
* TO SEND THE DATA IMMEDIATELY OR WAIT FOR AN OUTPUT INTERRUPT.
*THE PROBLEM IS THAT AN OUTPUT DEVICE MAY REQUEST SERVICE BEFORE
* THE COMPUTER HAS ANYTHING TO SEND (UNLIKE AN INPUT DEVICE THAT
* HAS DATA WHEN IT REQUESTS SERVICE).  THE OIE FLAG SOLVES THE
* PROBLEM OF AN UNSERVICED OUTPUT INTERRUPT ASSERTING ITSELF
* REPEATEDLY, WHILE STILL ENSURING THE RECOGNITION OF OUTPUT
* INTERRUPTS.
*
NODATA
        TST.B   PIADRB          READ PORT B DATA REGISTER TO CLEAR
                                * INTERRUPT
        CLR     OIE             DO NOT EXPECT AN INTERRUPT

IOSREXIT
        RTE                     SINGLE EXIT FROM INTERRUPT SERVICE
                                * ROUTINE


*************************************
*ROUTINE: OUTDAT
*PURPOSE: SEND CHARACTER TO 6821 PIA
*ENTRY: TRNDAT = CHARACTER TO SEND
*EXIT: NONE
*REGISTERS USED: CCR
*************************************

OUTDAT
        MOVE.B  TRNDAT,PIADRB   GET DATA FROM OUTPUT BUFFER
                                * AND SEND IT TO 6821 PIA
        CLR     TRNDF           INDICATE OUTPUT BUFFER EMPTY
        MOVE.B  #$FF,OIE        INDICATE OUTPUT INTERRUPT EXPECTED
                                * OIE = FF HEX
        RTS
```

```
*DATA SECTION

NEXTSR  DS.L    1               ADDRESS OF NEXT INTERRUPT SERVICE
                                *  ROUTINE
RECDAT  DS.B    1               RECEIVE DATA
RECDF   DS.B    1               RECEIVE DATA FLAG (0 = NO DATA,
                                *  FF = DATA)
TRNDAT  DS.B    1               TRANSMIT DATA
TRNDF   DS.B    1               TRANSMIT DATA FLAG
                                *  (0 = BUFFER EMPTY, FF = BUFFER FULL)
OIE     DS.B    1               OUTPUT INTERRUPT EXPECTED
                                *  (0 = INTERRUPT OCCURRED WITHOUT
                                *  BEING SERVICED, FF = INTERRUPT
                                *  SERVICED)
*
*       SAMPLE EXECUTION:
*
*CHARACTER EQUATES
*
ESCAPE  EQU     $1B             ASCII ESCAPE CHARACTER
TESTCH  EQU     'A'             TEST CHARACTER = A

SC9B
        MOVE.L  #0,-(SP)        PUT 68000 IN SUPERVISOR MODE
        MOVE.W  #$20,-(SP)
        TRAP    #1
        MOVE.L  2(SP),USERSP    SAVE ORIGINAL STACK POINTER
        ADDQ.L  #6,SP           REMOVE GEMDOS PARAMETERS FROM STACK
        JSR     INIT            INITIALIZE 6821 PIA, INTERRUPT SYSTEM
        MOVE    #INTENB,SR      ENABLE INTERRUPTS
        *
        *SIMPLE EXAMPLE - READ AND ECHO CHARACTERS
        * UNTIL AN ESC IS RECEIVED
        *
LOOP
        JSR     INCH            READ CHARACTER
        MOVE.W  D0,D1           SAVE CHARACTER
        JSR     OUTCH           ECHO CHARACTER
        CMP.B   #ESCAPE,D1      IS CHARACTER AN ESCAPE?
        BNE.S   LOOP            STAY IN LOOP IF NOT
        *
        *AN ASYNCHRONOUS EXAMPLE
        * OUTPUT "A" TO CONSOLE CONTINUOUSLY BUT ALSO LOOK AT
        * INPUT SIDE, READING AND ECHOING INPUT CHARACTERS.
        *
ASYNLP
        *OUTPUT AN "A" IF OUTPUT IS NOT BUSY
        JSR     OUTST           IS OUTPUT BUSY?
        BCS.S   ASYNLP          BRANCH (WAIT) IF IT IS
        MOVE.B  #TESTCH,D0
        JSR     OUTCH           OUTPUT TEST CHARACTER
        *
        *CHECK INPUT PORT
        *ECHO CHARACTER IF ONE IS AVAILABLE
        *EXIT ON ESCAPE CHARACTER
        *
```

```
        JSR     INST            IS INPUT DATA AVAILABLE?
        BCS.S   ASYNLP          BRANCH IF NOT (SEND ANOTHER "A")
        JSR     INCH            GET CHARACTER
        CMP.B   #ESCAPE,DO      IS IT AN ESCAPE?
        BEQ.S   DONE            BRANCH IF IT IS
        JSR     OUTCH           ELSE ECHO CHARACTER
        BRA.S   ASYNLP          AND CONTINUE

DONE
        MOVE.L  USERSP,-(SP)    RESTORE 68000 TO USER MODE
        MOVE.W  #$20,-(SP)
        TRAP    #1
        ADDQ.L  #6,SP           REMOVE GEMDOS PARAMETERS FROM STACK
        BRA.S   SC9B            REPEAT TEST

USERSP  DS.L    1               STORAGE FOR USER'S STACK POINTER

        END
```

9C Buffered interrupt-driven input/output using a 6850 ACIA (SINTB)

Performs interrupt-driven input and output using a 6850 ACIA and multiple-character buffers. Consists of the following subroutines:

1. INCH reads a character from the input buffer.

2. INST reports whether the input buffer is empty.

3. OUTCH writes a character into the output buffer.

4. OUTST reports whether the output buffer is full.

5. INIT initializes the buffers, the interrupt system, and the 6850 ACIA.

6. IOSRVC determines which interrupt occurred and services ACIA input or output interrupts.

Procedures

1. INCH waits for a character to become available, gets the character from the head of the input buffer, moves the head of the buffer up one position, and decreases the input buffer counter by 1.

2. INST clears Carry if the input buffer counter is 0 and sets it otherwise.

3. OUTCH waits until there is space in the output buffer (i.e. until the output buffer is not full), stores the character at the tail of the buffer, moves the tail up one position, and increases the output buffer counter by 1.

4. OUTST sets Carry if the output buffer counter is equal to the buffer's length (i.e. if the output buffer is full) and clears Carry otherwise.

5. INIT makes the buffer counters 0 and sets all buffer pointers to the buffers' base addresses. It then resets the 6850 ACIA and sets its operating mode by loading its control register. It initializes the ACIA with input interrupts enabled and output interrupts disabled. See Subroutine 8F for more details about initializing 6850 ACIAs. INIT also clears the output interrupt expected flag, indicating that the ACIA is ready to transmit data, although it cannot cause an output interrupt.

6. IOSRVC examines the ACIA's status register to identify an input interrupt (bit 0 = 1), an output interrupt (bit 1 = 1), or an interrupt from some other device. If the input interrupt occurred, the program reads a character from the 6850 ACIA. If there is room in the input buffer, it stores the character at the tail of the buffer, moves the tail up one position, and increases the input buffer counter by 1. If the buffer is full, it simply discards the character.

If the output interrupt occurred, the program determines whether output data is available. If not, it simply disables the output interrupt (so it will not interrupt repeatedly) and clears the Output Interrupt Expected flag. The flag tells the main program that the ACIA is ready even though it cannot cause an interrupt. If there is data in the output buffer, the program obtains a character from the buffer's head, sends it to the ACIA, moves the head up one position, and reduces the output buffer counter by 1. It then enables both input and output interrupts and sets the Output Interrupt Expected flag (in case that flag had been cleared earlier).

The new problem with multiple-character buffers is how to manage queues. The main program must read the data in the order in which the input interrupt service routine receives it. Similarly, the output interrupt service routine must send the data in the order in which the main program stores it. Thus we have the following requirements for handling input:

1. The main program must know whether the input buffer is empty.

2. If the input buffer is not empty, the main program must know where the oldest character is (that is, the first one received).

3. The input interrupt service routine must know whether the input buffer is full.

4. If the input buffer is not full, the input interrupt service routine must know where the next empty place is (i.e. where it should store the new character).

The output interrupt service routine and the main program have similar requirements for the output buffer, although the roles of sender and receiver are reversed.

We meet requirements 1 and 3 by maintaining a counter ICNT. INIT initializes ICNT to 0, the interrupt service routine adds 1 to it whenever it receives a character (assuming the buffer is not full), and the main program subtracts 1 from it whenever it removes a character from the buffer. Thus the main program can determine whether the input buffer is empty by checking if ICNT is 0. Similarly, the interrupt service routine can determine whether the input buffer is full by checking if ICNT is equal to the size of the buffer.

We meet requirements 2 and 4 by maintaining two pointers, IHEAD and ITAIL, defined as follows:

1. ITAIL is the address of the next empty location in the input buffer.
2. IHEAD is the address of the oldest character in the input buffer.

INIT initializes IHEAD and ITAIL to the base address of the input buffer. When the interrupt service routine reads a character, it puts it in the buffer at ITAIL and moves ITAIL up one position (assuming that the buffer is not full). When the main program reads a character, it removes it from the buffer at IHEAD and moves IHEAD up one position. Thus IHEAD 'chases' ITAIL across the buffer with the service routine entering characters at one end (the tail) while the main program removes them from the other end (the head).

The occupied part of the buffer thus could start and end anywhere. If either IHEAD or ITAIL reaches the physical end of the buffer, we simply set it back to the base address. Thus we allow wraparound on the buffer; i.e. the occupied part of the buffer could start near the end (say, at byte #195 of a 200-byte buffer) and continue back past the beginning (say, to byte #10). Then IHEAD would be BASE+194, ITAIL would be BASE+9, and the buffer would contain 15 characters occupying addresses BASE+194 through BASE+199 and BASE through BASE+8.

Entry conditions

1. INCH: none
2. INST: none
3. OUTCH: character to transmit in low byte of register D0
4. OUTST: none
5. INIT: none

Exit conditions

1. INCH: character in low byte of register D0
2. INST: Carry = 0 if input buffer is empty, 1 if a character is available

3. OUTCH: none
4. OUTST: Carry = 0 if output buffer is not full, 1 if it is full
5. INIT: none

Registers used

1. INCH: A0, CCR, D0
2. INST: CCR, D0
3. OUTCH: A0, CCR, D0, D1
4. OUTST: CCR, D0
5. INIT: A0, CCR

Execution time

1. INCH: approximately 263 cycles if a character is available
2. INST: 56 cycles if data is available; 42 cycles if not
3. OUTCH: approximately 310 cycles if the output buffer is not full and an output interrupt is expected; approximately 247 more cycles if no output interrupt is expected.
4. OUTST: 56 cycles
5. INIT: 336 cycles
6. IOSRVC: 351 cycles to service an input interrupt; 471 cycles to service an output interrupt; 212 cycles to determine the interrupt is from another device. These times all include the CPU's interrupt response time (44 cycles).

Note The approximations come from variations in how long it takes to obtain status and update the buffer pointers with wraparound.

Program size 410 bytes

Data memory required 20 bytes anywhere in RAM for the heads and tails of the input and output buffers (4 bytes starting at addresses

IHEAD, ITAIL, OHEAD, and OTAIL, respectively), the number of characters in the buffers (2 bytes at addresses ICNT and OCNT), and the Output Interrupt Expected flag (address OIE). An extra byte is wasted to retain word alignment. This does not include the actual input and output buffers. The input buffer starts at address IBUF and its size is IBSZ; the output buffer starts at address OBUF and its size is OBSZ.

```
*       Title               Interrupt input and output using a 6850 ACIA
*                           and multiple character buffers.
*       Name:               SINTB
*
*       Purpose:            This program consists of 5 subroutines that
*                           perform interrupt driven input and output using
*                           a 6850 ACIA.
*
*                           INCH
*                             Read a character.
*                           INST
*                             Report input status (whether input buffer
*                             is empty).
*                           OUTCH
*                             Write a character.
*                           OUTST
*                             Report output status (whether output buffer
*                             is full).
*                           INIT
*                             Initialize 6850 ACIA and interrupt system.
*
*       Entry:              INCH
*                             No parameters.
*                           INST
*                             No parameters.
*                           OUTCH
*                             Character to transmit in low byte of
*                                register D0.
*                           OUTST
*                             No parameters.
*                           INIT
*                             No parameters.
*
*       Exit:               INCH
*                             Character in low byte of register D0.
*                           INST
*                             Carry = 0 if input buffer is empty,
*                             1 if character is available.
*                           OUTCH
*                             No parameters
*                           OUTST
*                             Carry = 0 if output buffer is not
*                             full, 1 if it is full.
*                           INIT
*                             No parameters.
*
*       Registers Used: INCH
```

```
*                       A0,CCR,D0
*                     INST
*                       CCR,D0
*                     OUTCH
*                       A0,CCR,D0,D1
*                     OUTST
*                       CCR,D0
*                     INIT
*                       A0,CCR
*
*       Time:         INCH
*                       Approximately 263 cycles if a character is
*                       available
*                     INST
*                       56 cycles if input data is available, 42
*                       cycles if not
*                     OUTCH
*                       Approximately 310 cycles if output buffer is
*                       not full and output interrupt is expected.
*                     OUTST
*                       56 cycles
*                     INIT
*                       336 cycles
*                     IOSRVC
*                       212 cycles minimum if the interrupt is not ours
*                       351 cycles to service an input interrupt
*                       471 cycles to service an output interrupt
*                       These include the processor's interrupt
*                       response time (44 cycles).
*
*       Size:         Program 410 bytes
*                     Data     20 bytes plus size of buffers
*
*       Buffers:      The routines assume two buffers starting at
*                     address IBUF and OBUF.  The lengths of the
*                     buffers in bytes are IBSZ and OBSZ.  For the
*                     input buffer, IHEAD is the address of the
*                     oldest character (the next one the main
*                     program should read), ITAIL is the address of
*                     the next empty element (the next one the service
*                     routine should fill), and ICNT is the number of
*                     bytes currently filled with characters.  For the
*                     output buffer, OHEAD is the address of the
*                     character (the next one the service routine
*                     should send), OTAIL is the address of the next
*                     empty element (the next one the main program
*                     should fill), and OCNT is the number of bytes
*                     currently filled with characters.
*
*       Note:         Wraparound is provided on both buffers, so that
*                     the currently filled area may start anywhere
*                     and extend through the end of the buffer and
*                     back to the beginning.  For example, if the
*                     output buffer is 40 hex bytes long, the section
*                     filled with characters could extend from OBUF
*                     +32H (OHEAD) through OBUF+10H (OTAIL-1).  That
```

```
*                           is, there are 19H filled bytes occupying
*                           addresses OBUF+32H through OBUF+10H.  The buffer
*                           thus looks like a television picture with the
*                           vertical hold skewed, so that the frame starts
*                           above the bottom of the screen, leaves off at
*                           the top, and continues at the bottom.

*
*6850 ACIA (UART) EQUATES
*ARBITRARY 6850 ACIA MEMORY ADDRESSES (ATARI ST MIDI PORT)
*
ACIA    EQU     $FFFFC04        6850 ACIA BASE ADDRESS
ACIASR  EQU     ACIA            6850 ACIA STATUS REGISTER
ACIACR  EQU     ACIA            6850 ACIA CONTROL REGISTER
ACIADR  EQU     ACIA+2          6850 ACIA DATA REGISTER
*
*ATARI 520ST INTERRUPT VECTOR
*
INTVEC  EQU     $0118           VECTOR TO INTERRUPT SERVICE ROUTINE
                                * (USER INTERRUPT VECTOR 6)
*
*INTERRUPT ENABLE/DISABLE EQUATES
*
INTDIS  EQU     $2700           STATUS REGISTER VALUE TO DISABLE
                                * ALL INTERRUPTS IN SUPERVISOR MODE
INTENB  EQU     $2000           STATUS REGISTER VALUE TO ENABLE
                                * ALL INTERRUPTS IN SUPERVISOR MODE


*
*READ CHARACTER FROM INPUT BUFFER
*
INCH
        JSR     INST            GET INPUT STATUS
        BCC.S   INCH            BRANCH (WAIT) IF NO CHARACTER AVAILABLE
        MOVE.W  SR,-(SP)        SAVE STATUS REGISTER (PARTICULARLY
                                * INTERRUPT MASK)
        MOVE.W  #INTDIS,SR      DISABLE INTERRUPTS WHILE WORKING WITH
                                * BUFFER POINTER AND COUNT
        SUBQ.W  #1,ICNT         REDUCE INPUT BUFFER COUNT BY 1
        MOVEA.L IHEAD,A0        GET CHARACTER FROM HEAD OF INPUT BUFFER
        MOVE.B  (A0),D0
        JSR     INCIPTR         MOVE HEAD POINTER UP 1 WITH WRAPAROUND
        MOVE.L  A0,IHEAD
        RTE                     RETURN, RESTORING STATUS REGISTER

*
*RETURN INPUT STATUS (CARRY = 1 IF INPUT DATA AVAILABLE)
*
INST
        TST.W   ICNT            TEST INPUT BUFFER COUNT (AND CLEAR
                                * CARRY)
        BEQ.S   EXINST          BRANCH (EXIT) IF BUFFER EMPTY
        MOVE    #1,CCR          SET CARRY TO INDICATE DATA AVAILABLE
EXINST
        RTS                     RETURN, CARRY INDICATES WHETHER DATA
                                * IS AVAILABLE
```

```
*
*WRITE A CHARACTER INTO OUTPUT BUFFER
*
OUTCH
        MOVE.W  D0,D1           SAVE CHARACTER TO WRITE

        *WAIT UNTIL OUTPUT BUFFER NOT FULL, STORE NEXT CHARACTER
WAITOC
        JSR     OUTST           GET OUTPUT STATUS
        BCS.S   WAITOC          BRANCH (WAIT) IF OUTPUT BUFFER FULL
        MOVE.W  SR,-(SP)        SAVE STATUS REGISTER (PARTICULARLY
                                * INTERRUPT MASK)
        MOVE.W  #INTDIS,SR      DISABLE INTERRUPTS WHILE WORKING WITH
                                * BUFFER POINTER AND COUNT
        ADDQ.W  #1,OCNT         INCREASE OUTPUT BUFFER COUNT BY 1
        MOVEA.L OTAIL,A0        POINT AT NEXT EMPTY BYTE IN BUFFER
        MOVE.W  D1,(A0)         GET CHARACTER AND STORE IT
                                *  AT TAIL OF BUFFER
        JSR     INCOPTR         MOVE TAIL POINTER UP 1
        MOVE.L  A0,OTAIL
        MOVE.W  (SP)+,SR        RESTORE STATUS REGISTER
        TST.B   OIE             TEST OUTPUT INTERRUPT EXPECTED FLAG
        BNE.S   EXWAIT          BRANCH IF OUTPUT INTERRUPT EXPECTED
        JSR     OUTDAT          OUTPUT CHARACTER IMMEDIATELY IF
                                * OUTPUT INTERRUPT NOT EXPECTED
EXWAIT
        RTS


*
*OUTPUT STATUS (CARRY = 1 IF OUTPUT BUFFER FULL)
*
OUTST
        CMPI.W  #SZOBUF,OCNT    IS OUTPUT BUFFER FULL?
                                *NOTE THAT THIS COMPARISON SETS CARRY
                                * IF OUTPUT BUFFER IS NOT FULL AND
                                * CLEARS IT IF OUTPUT BUFFER IS FULL
                                *OCNT IS NEVER LARGER THAN SZOBUF
        EORI.B  #1,CCR          INVERT CARRY, SO IT IS CLEARED IF OUTPUT
                                * BUFFER IS NOT FULL AND SET IF IT IS.
        RTS

*
*INITIALIZE 6850 ACIA, INTERRUPT SYSTEM
*
INIT
        *
        *DISABLE INTERRUPTS DURING INITIALIZATION BUT SAVE
        *  PREVIOUS VALUE OF INTERRUPT MASK
        *
        MOVE.W  SR,-(SP)        SAVE CURRENT STATUS (PARTICULARLY
                                * INTERRUPT MASK)
        MOVE.W  #INTDIS,SR      DISABLE INTERRUPTS DURING
                                * INITIALIZATION
        *
        *INITIALIZE ATARI 520 ST INTERRUPT VECTOR
```

```
        *
        MOVE.L   INTVEC,NEXTSR    GET CURRENT INTERRUPT VECTOR AND SAVE
                                  * IT AS ADDRESS OF NEXT SERVICE ROUTINE
        MOVE.L   #IOSRVC,INTVEC   GET ADDRESS OF OUR SERVICE ROUTINE
                                  * AND SAVE IT AS INTERRUPT VECTOR
        *
        *INITIALIZE BUFFER COUNTERS AND POINTERS, INTERRUPT FLAG
        *
        CLR.B    ICNT             INPUT BUFFER EMPTY
        CLR.B    OCNT             OUTPUT BUFFER EMPTY
        CLR.B    OIE              INDICATE NO OUTPUT INTERRUPT EXPECTED
        LEA      IBUF,A0          INPUT HEAD/TAIL POINT TO BASE
        MOVE.L   A0,IHEAD           ADDRESS OF INPUT BUFFER
        MOVE.L   A0,ITAIL
        LEA      OBUF,A0          OUTPUT HEAD/TAIL POINT TO BASE
        MOVE.L   A0,OHEAD           ADDRESS OF OUTPUT BUFFER
        MOVE.L   A0,OTAIL
        *
        *INITIALIZE 6850 ACIA
        *
        MOVE.B   #%00000011,ACIACR MASTER RESET 6850 ACIA (NOTE IT
                                  * HAS NO RESET INPUT)
        MOVE.B   #%10010001,ACIACR SET ACIA OPERATING MODE
                                  *BIT 7 = 1 TO ENABLE INPUT INTERRUPTS
                                  *BITS 6,5 = 0 TO DISABLE OUTPUT
                                  * INTERRUPTS
                                  *BITS 4,3,2 = 100 FOR 8 DATA BITS,
                                  *  2 STOP BITS, NO PARITY
                                  *BITS 1,0 = 01 FOR DIVIDE BY 16 CLOCK
                                  *  MODE
        RTE                       RESTORE STATUS AND EXIT (THIS RESTORES
                                  *  THE VALUE OF THE INTERRUPT MASKS WHEN
                                  *  INIT WAS CALLED)


*
*INPUT/OUTPUT INTERRUPT SERVICE ROUTINE
*
IOSRVC
        *
        *GET ACIA STATUS: BIT 0 = 1 IF AN INPUT INTERRUPT,
        *  BIT 1 = 1 IF AN OUTPUT INTERRUPT
        *
        MOVEM.L A0/D0-D1,-(SP)  SAVE REGISTERS
        MOVE.B   ACIASR,D0        GET ACIA STATUS
        LSR.B    #1,D0            EXAMINE RECEIVE INTERRUPT FLAG
        BCS.S    RDHDLR           BRANCH IF AN INPUT INTERRUPT
        LSR.B    #1,D0            EXAMINE TRANSMIT INTERRUPT FLAG
        BCS.S    WRHDLR           BRANCH IF AN OUTPUT INTERRUPT
        *
        *INTERRUPT WAS NOT OURS, TRY NEXT SOURCE
        *
        MOVEM.L (SP)+,A0/D0-D1   RESTORE REGISTERS
        MOVE.L   NEXTSR,-(SP)     NOT THIS ACIA, EXAMINE NEXT INTERRUPT
        RTS
*
```

```
*SERVICE INPUT INTERRUPTS
*
RDHDLR
        MOVE.B  ACIADR,D0       READ DATA FROM ACIA
        CMPI.W  #SZIBUF,ICNT    ANY ROOM IN INPUT BUFFER?
        BEQ.S   IOSREXIT        BRANCH (EXIT) IF NO ROOM IN INPUT BUFFER
        ADDQ.W  #1,ICNT         INCREMENT INPUT BUFFER COUNT
        MOVEA.L ITAIL,A0        STORE CHARACTER AT TAIL OF INPUT BUFFER
        MOVE.B  D0,(A0)
        JSR     INCIPTR         INCREMENT TAIL POINTER WITH WRAPAROUND
        MOVE.L  A0,ITAIL
        BRA.S   IOSREXIT        EXIT

*
*OUTPUT (WRITE) INTERRUPT HANDLER
*
WRHDLR
        TST.W   OCNT            TEST OUTPUT BUFFER COUNT
        BEQ.S   NODATA          BRANCH IF NO DATA TO TRANSMIT
        JSR     OUTDAT          ELSE OUTPUT DATA TO 6850 ACIA
        BRA.S   IOSREXIT
*
*IF AN OUTPUT INTERRUPT OCCURS WHEN NO DATA IS AVAILABLE,
* WE MUST DISABLE IT TO AVOID AN ENDLESS LOOP. WHEN THE NEXT CHARACTER
* IS READY, IT MUST BE SENT IMMEDIATELY SINCE NO INTERRUPT WILL
* OCCUR.  THIS STATE IN WHICH AN OUTPUT INTERRUPT HAS OCCURRED
* BUT HAS NOT BEEN SERVICED IS INDICATED BY CLEARING OIE (OUTPUT
* INTERRUPT EXPECTED FLAG).
*
NODATA
        MOVE.B  #%10010001,ACIACR  ESTABLISH ACIA OPERATING MODE WITH
                                   * OUTPUT INTERRUPTS DISABLED
        CLR     OIE                DO NOT EXPECT AN INTERRUPT
*
*SINGLE RETURN POINT FROM I/O INTERRUPT SERVICE ROUTINE
*
IOSREXIT
        MOVEM.L (A7)+,A0/D0-D1  RESTORE REGISTERS
        RTE

****************************************
*ROUTINE: OUTDAT
*PURPOSE: SEND CHARACTER TO 6850 ACIA FROM THE OUTPUT BUFFER
*ENTRY: A0 CONTAINS THE ADDRESS OF THE CHARACTER TO SEND
*EXIT: NONE
*REGISTERS USED: A0,CCR,D0
****************************************

OUTDAT
        MOVE.B  ACIASR,D0
        ANDI.B  #%00000010,D0   IS ACIA OUTPUT REGISTER EMPTY?
        BEQ.S   OUTDAT          BRANCH (WAIT) IF REGISTER NOT EMPTY
        MOVEA.L OHEAD,A0        GET HEAD OF OUTPUT BUFFER
        MOVE.B  (A0),ACIADR     GET CHARACTER FROM HEAD OF BUFFER
                                * AND SEND IT TO ACIA
```

```
        JSR     INCOPTR             INCREMENT POINTER WITH WRAPAROUND
        MOVE.L  A0,OHEAD            RETURN BUFFER HEAD POINTER TO MEMORY
        SUBQ.W  #1,OCNT             DECREMENT OUTPUT BUFFER COUNTER
        MOVE.B  #%10110001,ACIACR ENABLE 6850 INPUT AND OUTPUT
                                    * INTERRUPTS
                                    * 8 DATA BITS, 2 STOP BITS, DIVIDE BY
                                    * 16 CLOCK
        MOVE.B  #$FF,OIE            INDICATE OUTPUT INTERRUPTS ENABLED
        RTS

****************************************
*ROUTINE: INCIPTR
*PURPOSE: INCREMENT POINTER INTO INPUT
*       BUFFER WITH WRAPAROUND
*ENTRY: A0 = POINTER
*EXIT: A0 = POINTER INCREMENTED WITH WRAPAROUND
*REGISTERS USED: A0,CCR
****************************************

INCIPTR
        ADDQ.L  #1,A0               INCREMENT POINTER BY 1
        CMPA.L  #EIBUF,A0           COMPARE POINTER, END OF BUFFER
        BNE.S   RETINC              BRANCH IF NOT EQUAL
        LEA     IBUF,A0             IF EQUAL, SET POINTER BACK TO BASE OF
                                    * BUFFER
RETINC
        RTS


****************************************
*ROUTINE: INCOPTR
*PURPOSE: INCREMENT POINTER INTO OUTPUT
*       BUFFER WITH WRAPAROUND
*ENTRY: A0 = POINTER
*EXIT: A0 = POINTER INCREMENTED WITH WRAPAROUND
*REGISTERS USED: A0,CCR
****************************************

INCOPTR
        ADDQ.L  #1,A0               INCREMENT POINTER BY 1
        CMPA.L  #EOBUF,A0           COMPARE POINTER, END OF BUFFER
        BNE.S   RETONC              BRANCH IF NOT EQUAL
        LEA     OBUF,A0             IF EQUAL, SET POINTER BACK TO BASE OF
                                    * BUFFER
RETONC
        RTS


*DATA SECTION
IHEAD   DS.L    1                   POINTER TO OLDEST CHARACTER IN INPUT
                                    * BUFFER (NEXT CHARACTER TO READ)
ITAIL   DS.L    1                   POINTER TO NEWEST CHARACTER IN INPUT
                                    * BUFFER (LAST CHARACTER READ)
ICNT    DS.W    1                   NUMBER OF CHARACTERS IN INPUT BUFFER
OHEAD   DS.L    1                   POINTER TO OLDEST CHARACTER IN OUTPUT
                                    * BUFFER (LAST CHARACTER WRITTEN)
```

```
OTAIL   DS.L    1               POINTER TO NEWEST CHARACTER IN OUTPUT
                                * BUFFER (NEXT CHARACTER TO SEND)
OCNT    DS.W    1               NUMBER OF CHARACTERS IN OUTPUT BUFFER
SZIBUF  EQU     10              SIZE OF INPUT BUFFER
IBUF    DS.B    SZIBUF          INPUT BUFFER
EIBUF   EQU     $               END OF INPUT BUFFER
SZOBUF  EQU     10              SIZE OF OUTPUT BUFFER
OBUF    DS,B    SZOBUF          OUTPUT BUFFER
EOBUF   EQU     $               END OF OUTPUT BUFFER
OIE     DS.B    1               OUTPUT INTERRUPT EXPECTED
                                * ( 0 = NO INTERRUPT EXPECTED,
                                *   FF = INTERRUPT EXPECTED)
        DS.B    1               UNUSED BYTE FOR WORD-ALIGNMENT
NEXTSR  DS.L    1               ADDRESS OF NEXT INTERRUPT SERVICE
                                *  ROUTINE
*
*       SAMPLE EXECUTION:
*
*CHARACTER EQUATES
ESCAPE  EQU     $1B             ASCII ESCAPE CHARACTER
TESTCH  EQU     'A'             TEST CHARACTER = A

SC9C
        MOVE.L  #0,-(SP)        PUT 68000 IN SUPERVISOR MODE
        MOVE.W  #$20,-(SP)
        TRAP    #1
        MOVE.L  2(SP),USERSP    SAVE ORIGINAL STACK POINTER
        ADDQ.L  #6,SP           REMOVE GEMDOS PARAMETERS FROM STACK
        JSR     INIT            INITIALIZE 6850 ACIA, INTERRUPT SYSTEM
        *
        *SIMPLE EXAMPLE - READ AND ECHO CHARACTERS
        * UNTIL AN ESC IS RECEIVED
        *
LOOP
        JSR     INCH            READ CHARACTER
        MOVE.B  D0,D1           SAVE CHARACTER
        JSR     OUTCH           ECHO CHARACTER
        CMPI.B  #ESCAPE,D1      IS CHARACTER AN ESCAPE?
        BNE.S   LOOP            STAY IN LOOP IF NOT
        *
        *AN ASYNCHRONOUS EXAMPLE
        * OUTPUT "A" TO CONSOLE CONTINUOUSLY BUT ALSO LOOK AT
        * INPUT SIDE, READING AND ECHOING ANY INPUT CHARACTERS.
ASYNLP
        *OUTPUT AN "A" IF OUTPUT IS NOT BUSY
        JSR     OUTST           IS OUTPUT BUSY?
        BCS.S   ASYNLP          JUMP IF IT IS
        MOVE.B  #TESTCH,D0
        JSR     OUTCH           OUTPUT CHARACTER
        *
        *CHECK INPUT PORT
        *ECHO CHARACTER IF ONE IS AVAILABLE
        *EXIT ON ESCAPE CHARACTER
        *
        JSR     INST            IS INPUT DATA AVAILABLE?
        BCS.S   ASYNLP          JUMP IF NOT (SEND ANOTHER "A")
```

```
        JSR      INCH                 GET CHARACTER
        CMPI.B   #ESCAPE,D0           IS IT AN ESCAPE CHARACTER?
        BEQ.S    DONE                 BRANCH IF IT IS
        JSR      OUTCH                ELSE ECHO CHARACTER
        BRA.S    ASYNLP               AND CONTINUE
DONE
        MOVE.L   USERSP,-(SP)         RESTORE 68000 TO USER MODE
        MOVE.W   #$20,-(SP)
        TRAP     #1
        ADDQ.L   #6,SP                REMOVE GEMDOS PARAMETERS FROM STACK
        BRA.S    SC9C                 REPEAT TEST

USERSP  DS.L     1                    STORAGE FOR USER'S STACK POINTER

        END
```

9D Real-time clock and calendar (CLOCK)

Maintains a time-of-day 24-hour clock and a calendar based on a real-time clock interrupt. The interrupt is generated from a timer in a 68901 Multifunction Peripheral (MFP). Consists of the following subroutines:

1. CLOCK returns the base address of the clock variables.

2. ICLK initializes the clock interrupt and the clock variables.

3. CLKINT updates the clock after each interrupt (assumed to be spaced one tick apart).

Procedure

1. CLOCK loads the base address of the clock variables into register A0. The clock variables are stored in the following order (lowest address first): ticks, seconds, minutes, hours, days, months, more significant byte of year, less significant byte of year.

2. ICLK initializes the 68901 MFP's timer, the interrupt system, and the clock variables. The arbitrary starting time is 00:00.00 (12 a.m.) on 1 January 1980. A real application would clearly require outside intervention to load or change the clock.

3. CLKINT reduces the remaining tick count by 1 and updates the rest of the clock variables if necessary. Of course, the number of seconds and minutes must be less than 60, and the number of hours must be less than 24. The day of the month must be less than or equal to the last day for the current month; an array of the last days of each month begins at address LASTDY.

If the month is February (i.e. month 2), the program checks whether the current year is a leap year. This involves determining if the two least significant bits of memory location YEAR are both 0s. If the current year is a leap year, the last day of February is the 29th, not the 28th.

The month number may not exceed 12 (December) or a carry to the year number is necessary. The program must reinitialize the variables properly when carries occur; i.e. TICK to DTICK; seconds, minutes, and hours to 0; day and month to 1 (meaning the first day and January, respectively).

Entry conditions

1. CLOCK: none
2. ICLK: none
3. CLKINT: none

Exit conditions

1. CLOCK: base address of clock variables in register A0
2. ICLK: none
3. CLKINT: none

Examples

These examples assume that the tick rate is DTICK Hz (less than 256 Hz — typical values would be 60 Hz, 100 Hz, or 200 Hz) and that the clock and calendar are saved in memory locations

TICK	number of ticks remaining before a carry occurs, counted down from DTICK
SEC	seconds (1—59)
MIN	minutes (0—59)
HOUR	hour of day (0—23)
DAY	day of month (1—28, 29, 30, or 31, depending on month)
MONTH	month of year (1—12 for January—December)
YEAR and YEAR+1	current year

1. Starting values are 7 March 1987, 11:59.59 p.m. and 1 tick left. That is:

(TICK) = 1
(SEC) = 59
(MIN) = 59
(HOUR) = 23
(DAY) = 07
(MONTH) = 03
(YEAR and YEAR+1) = 1987

Result (after the tick): 8 March 1987, 12:00.00 a.m. and DTICK ticks. That is:

(TICK) = DTICK
(SEC) = 0
(MIN) = 0
(HOUR) = 0
(DAY) = 08
(MONTH) = 03
(YEAR and YEAR+1) = 1987

2. Starting values are 31 Dec. 1987, 11:59.59 p.m. and 1 tick left. That is:

(TICK) = 1
(SEC) = 59
(MIN) = 59
(HOUR) = 23
(DAY) = 31
(MONTH) = 12
(YEAR and YEAR+1) = 1987

Result (after the tick): 1 Jan. 1988, 12:00.00 a.m. and DTICK ticks. That is,

(TICK) = DTICK
(SEC) = 0
(MIN) = 0
(HOUR) = 0
(DAY) = 1
(MONTH) = 1
(YEAR and YEAR+1) = 1988

Registers used

1. CLOCK: A0, CCR
2. ICLK: A0, CCR, D0
3. CLKINT: none

Execution time

1. CLOCK: 28 cycles

2. ICLK: 361 cycles

3. CLKINT: 202 cycles if only TICK must be decremented, 645 cycles maximum if changing to a new year. These times include the CPU's interrupt response time (44 cycles).

Program size 302 bytes

Data memory required 8 bytes anywhere in RAM for the clock variables (starting at address CLKVAR).

```
*       Title           Real time clock and calendar
*       Name:           CLOCK
*
*       Purpose:        This program maintains a time of day 24 hour
*                       clock and a calendar based on a real time clock
*                       interrupt from a 68901 Multifunction Peripheral
*
*                       CLOCK
*                         Returns base address of clock variables
*                       ICLK
*                         Initializes 68901 MFP and clock interrupt
*
*       Entry:          CLOCK
*                         None
*                       ICLK
*                         None
*
*       Exit:           CLOCK
*                         Register A0 = Base address of time variables
*                       ICLK
*                         None
*
*       Registers Used: CLOCK
*                         A0,CCR
*                       ICLK
*                         A0,CCR,D0
*
*       Time:           CLOCK
*                         28 cycles
*                       ICLCK
*                         361 cycles
*                       CLKINT
*                         If decrementing tick only, 202 cycles
*                         Maximum if changing to a new year, 645
*                         cycles
*                         These include the processor's interrupt
*                         response time (44 cycles).
*
*       Size:           Program 302 bytes
*                       Data      8 bytes
*
*  68901 MULTIFUNCTION PERIPHERAL (MFP)
*
```

```
*  INITIALIZE TIMER A OF 68901 MFP AS 200 HZ DELAY TIMER
*    FOR USE IN TIME-OF-DAY CLOCK.
*  TIMER GENERATES INTERRUPT AT END OF EACH 5 MS INTERVAL (EVERY
*    CYCLE)
*  WE ASSUME A 2.4576 MHZ CLOCK INTO THE 68901 (AS IN THE ATARI
*    ST), SO THAT A COUNTER VALUE OF 192 TOGETHER WITH A DIVIDE
*    BY 64 PRESCALER IS NEEDED TO GENERATE THE 200 HZ REAL-TIME
*    CLOCK

*
*    68901 MULTIFUNCTION PERIPHERAL (MFP) ADDRESSES
*
MFP      EQU     $FFFFFA00      68901 MFP BASE ADDRESS
MFPGPIR EQU      MFP            68901 GENERAL-PURPOSE I/O REGISTER
MFPAER   EQU     MFP+2          68901 ACTIVE EDGE REGISTER
MFPDDR   EQU     MFP+4          68901 DATA DIRECTION REGISTER
MFPIERA EQU      MFP+6          68901 INTERRUPT ENABLE REGISTER A
MFPIERB EQU      MFP+8          68901 INTERRUPT ENABLE REGISTER B
MFPIPRA EQU      MFP+$0A        68901 INTERRUPT PENDING REGISTER A
MFPIPRB EQU      MFP+$0C        68901 INTERRUPT PENDING REGISTER B
MFPISRA EQU      MFP+$0E        68901 INTERRUPT IN-SERVICE REGISTER A
MFPISRB EQU      MFP+$10        68901 INTERRUPT IN-SERVICE REGISTER B
MFPIMRA EQU      MFP+$12        68901 INTERRUPT MASK REGISTER A
MFPIMRB EQU      MFP+$14        68901 INTERRUPT MASK REGISTER B
MFPVR    EQU     MFP+$16        68901 VECTOR REGISTER
MFPTACR EQU      MFP+$18        68901 TIMER A CONTROL REGISTER
MFPTBCR EQU      MFP+$1A        68901 TIMER B CONTROL REGISTER
MFPTCDCR EQU     MFP+$1C        68901 TIMERS C,D CONTROL REGISTER
MFPTADR EQU      MFP+$1E        68901 TIMER A DATA REGISTER
MFPTBDR EQU      MFP+$20        68901 TIMER B DATA REGISTER
MFPTCDR EQU      MFP+$22        68901 TIMER C DATA REGISTER
MFPTDDR EQU      MFP+$24        68901 TIMER D DATA REGISTER
MFPSCR   EQU     MFP+$26        68901 SYNCHRONOUS CHARACTER REGISTER
MFPUCR   EQU     MFP+$28        68901 USART CONTROL REGISTER
MFPRSR   EQU     MFP+$2A        68901 RECEIVER STATUS REGISTER
MFPTSR   EQU     MFP+$2C        68901 TRANSMITTER STATUS REGISTER
MFPUDR   EQU     MFP+$2E        68901 USART DATA REGISTER


*
*DEFAULT TICK VALUE (200 HZ REAL-TIME CLOCK)
*
DTICK    EQU     200            DEFAULT TICK VALUE

*
*TIMER A INTERRUPT VECTOR LOCATION (ATARI ST)
*
TAIVEC   EQU     $134           TIMER A INTERRUPT VECTOR

*CLOCK VARIABLE INDEXES
TCKIDX   EQU     0              INDEX TO TICK
SECIDX   EQU     1              INDEX TO SECOND
MINIDX   EQU     2              INDEX TO MINUTE
HRIDX    EQU     3              INDEX TO HOUR
DAYIDX   EQU     4              INDEX TO DAY
MTHIDX   EQU     5              INDEX TO MONTH
YRIDX    EQU     6              INDEX TO YEAR
```

```
*RETURN BASE ADDRESS OF CLOCK VARIABLES
CLOCK
        LEA     CLKVAR,A0       GET BASE ADDRESS OF CLOCK VARIABLES
        RTS

*
*INITIALIZE 68901 MFP TIMER A TO PRODUCE REGULAR CLOCK INTERRUPTS
* EVERY 5 MILLISECONDS
*
ICLK
        BCLR    #5,MFPIERA      DISABLE TIMER A INTERRUPTS
        MOVE.L  #CLKINT,TAIVEC  INSTALL INTERRUPT SERVICE ROUTINE
        MOVE.B  #%00010000,MFPTACR RESET TIMER A
*
*2.4567 MHZ SYSTEM CLOCK / 64 = 38,400 HZ PRESCALED CLOCK
*38,400 HZ PRESCALED CLOCK / 192 = 200 HZ INTERRUPT FREQUENCY
*
        MOVE.B  #192,MFPTADR    192 PRESCALED TICKS PER INTERRUPT
        MOVE.B  #%00000101,MFPTACR
                                *BITS 7-5 UNUSED
                                *BIT 4 = 0 TO NOT RESET TAO
                                *BITS 3-0 = 0101 FOR DELAY MODE,
                                * DIVIDE BY 64 PRESCALER

*
*INITIALIZE CLOCK VARIABLES TO ARBITRARY VALUE
*JANUARY 1, 1980 00:00.00 (12 A.M.)
*A REAL CLOCK WOULD NEED OUTSIDE INTERVENTION
* TO SET OR CHANGE VALUES
*
        LEA     TICK,A0
        MOVE.B  #DTICK,(A0)     INITIALIZE TICKS
        CLR.B   SECIDX(A0)      SECOND = 0
        CLR.B   MINIDX(A0)      MINUTE = 0
        CLR.B   HRIDX(A0)       HOUR = 0
        MOVE.B  #1,DAYIDX(A0)   DAY = 1 (FIRST)
        MOVE.B  #1,MTHIDX(A0)   MONTH = 1 (JANUARY)
        MOVE.W  #1980,YRIDX(A0) YEAR = 1980
        BCLR    #5,MFPIPRA      CLEAR ANY PENDING TIMER A INTERRUPT
        BCLR    #5,MFPISRA      ACKNOWLEDGE ANY PENDING TIMER A
                                * INTERRUPT
        BCLR    #5,MFPIMRA      UNMASK TIMER A INTERRUPT
        BCLR    #5,MFPIERA      ENABLE TIMER A INTERRUPT
        RTS                     ASSUME A GENERAL STARTUP ROUTINE
                                * INITIALIZES THE CPU INTERRUPT MASK

*
*SERVICE CLOCK INTERRUPT
*
CLKINT
        MOVEM.L A0/D0-D1,-(SP)  SAVE REGISTERS
        LEA     CLKVAR,A0
        SUBQ.B  #1,TCKIDX(A0)   SUBTRACT 1 FROM TICK COUNT
        BNE.S   EXITCLK         JUMP IF TICK COUNT NOT ZERO
        MOVE.B  #DTICK,TCKIDX(A0)  SET TICK COUNT BACK TO DEFAULT

        *INCREMENT SECONDS
```

```
        ADDQ.B  #1,SECIDX(A0)   INCREMENT TO NEXT SECOND
        CMPI.B  #60,SECIDX(A0)  SECONDS = 60?
        BCS.S   EXITCLK         EXIT IF LESS THAN 60 SECONDS
        CLR.B   SECIDX(A0)      ELSE SECONDS = 0

        *INCREMENT MINUTES
        ADDQ.B  #1,MINIDX(A0)   INCREMENT TO NEXT MINUTE
        CMPI.B  #60,MINIDX(A0)  MINUTES = 60?
        BCS.S   EXITCLK         EXIT IF LESS THAN 60 MINUTES
        CLR.B   MINIDX(A0)      ELSE MINUTES = 0

        *INCREMENT HOUR
        ADDQ.B  #1,HRIDX(A0)    INCREMENT TO NEXT HOUR
        CMPI.B  #24,HRIDX(A0)   HOURS = 24?
        BCS.S   EXITCLK         EXIT IF LESS THAN 24 HOURS
        CLR.B   HRIDX(A0)       ELSE HOUR = 0

        *INCREMENT DAY
        CLR.W   D0              EXTEND MONTH TO 16 BITS
        MOVE.B  MTHIDX(A0),D0   GET CURRENT MONTH
        MOVE.B  DAYIDX(A0),D1   GET DAY OF MONTH
        LEA     LASTDY,A1
        CMP.B   -1(A1,D0.W),D1  IS IT LAST DAY?
        BCC.S   CHKMTH          IF SO, CHECK MONTH AND YEAR
        ADDQ.B  #1,DAYIDX(A0)   OTHERWISE, INCREMENT DAY
        BRA     EXITCLK         AND EXIT
        *
        *DETERMINE IF THIS IS END OF FEBRUARY IN A LEAP
        * YEAR (YEAR DIVISIBLE BY 4)
        *
CHKMTH
        CMPI.B  #2,D0           IS THIS FEBRUARY?
        BNE.S   INCMTH          JUMP IF NOT, INCREMENT MONTH
        MOVE.W  YRIDX(A0),D1    IS IT A LEAP YEAR?
        ANDI.W  #%00000011,D1
        BNE.S   INCMTH          BRANCH IF NOT LEAP YEAR
        *
        *FEBRUARY OF A LEAP YEAR HAS 29 DAYS, NOT 28 DAYS
        *
        ADDQ.B  #1,DAYIDX(A0)   INCREMENT DAY
        CMPI.B  #29,DAYIDX(A0)
        BEQ.S   EXITCLK         EXIT IF NOT 1ST OF MARCH (FEBRUARY
                                * 29TH IS VALID, BUT FEB 30TH IS NOT)

        *INCREMENT MONTH
INCMTH
        MOVE.B  #1,DAYIDX(A0)   DAY = 1
        ADDQ.B  #1,MTHIDX(A0)   INCREMENT MONTH
        CMPI.B  #12,D0          WAS OLD MONTH DECEMBER?
        BCS.S   EXITCLK         BRANCH (EXIT) IF NOT DECEMBER
        MOVE.B  #1,MTHIDX(A0)   ELSE CHANGE MONTH TO 1 (JANUARY)

        *INCREMENT YEAR
        ADDQ.W  #1,YRIDX(A0)    ADD 1 TO YEAR

EXITCLK
```

```
        *RESTORE REGISTERS AND EXIT
        MOVEM.L (SP)+,A0/D0-D1  RESTORE REGISTERS
        RTE                     RETURN

*ARRAY OF LAST DAYS OF EACH MONTH
LASTDY
        DC.B    31              JANUARY
        DC.B    28              FEBRUARY (EXCEPT LEAP YEARS)
        DC.B    31              MARCH
        DC.B    30              APRIL
        DC.B    31              MAY
        DC.B    30              JUNE
        DC.B    31              JULY
        DC.B    31              AUGUST
        DC.B    30              SEPTEMBER
        DC.B    31              OCTOBER
        DC.B    30              NOVEMBER
        DC.B    31              DECEMBER

*CLOCK VARIABLES
CLKVAR
TICK    DS.B    1               TICKS LEFT IN CURRENT SECOND
SEC     DS.B    1               SECONDS
MIN     DS.B    1               MINUTES
HOUR    DS.B    1               HOURS
DAY     DS.B    1               DAY (1 TO NUMBER OF DAYS IN A MONTH)
MONTH   DS.B    1               MONTH 1=JANUARY .. 12=DECEMBER
YEAR    DS.W    1               YEAR

*
*       SAMPLE EXECUTION
*

SC9D
        MOVE.L  #0,-(SP)        PUT 68000 IN SUPERVISOR MODE
        MOVE.W  #$20,-(SP)
        TRAP    #1
        MOVE.L  2(SP),USERSP    SAVE ORIGINAL STACK POINTER
        ADDQ.L  #6,SP           REMOVE GEMDOS PARAMETERS FROM STACK
        JSR     ICLK            INITIALIZE CLOCK
        MOVE.L  USERSP,-(SP)    RESTORE 68000 TO USER MODE
        MOVE.W  #$20,-(SP)
        TRAP    #1
        ADDQ.L  #6,SP           REMOVE GEMDOS PARAMETERS FROM STACK
        *
        *INITIALIZE CLOCK TO 2/7/87 14:00:00 (2 PM, FEB. 7, 1987)
        *
        JSR     CLOCK           A0 = ADDRESS OF CLOCK VARIABLES
        CLR.B   SECIDX(A0)      SECONDS = 0
        CLR.B   MINIDX(A0)      MINUTES = 0
        MOVE.B  #14,HRIDX(A0)   HOUR = 14 (2 PM)
        MOVE.B  #7,DAYIDX(A0)   DAY = 7
        MOVE.B  #2,MTHIDX(A0)   MONTH = 2 (FEBRUARY)
        MOVE.W  #1987,YRIDX(A0) YEAR = 1987
        *
        *WAIT FOR CLOCK TO BE 2/7/87 14:01:20 (2:01.20 PM, FEB. 7, 1987)
```

```
        *
        *NOTE: MUST BE CAREFUL TO EXIT IF CLOCK IS ACCIDENTALLY
        * SET AHEAD.  IF WE CHECK ONLY FOR EQUALITY, WE MIGHT NEVER
        * FIND IT.  THUS WE HAVE >= IN TESTS BELOW, NOT JUST =.
        *
        *WAIT FOR YEAR >= TARGET YEAR
        JSR     CLOCK           A0 = BASE ADDRESS OF CLOCK VARIABLES
        MOVE.W  TYEAR,D0        D0 = YEAR TO WAIT FOR
WAITYR:
        *COMPARE CURRENT YEAR AND TARGET YEAR
        CMP.W   YRIDX(A0),D0
        BHI.S   WAITYR          BRANCH IF YEAR NOT >= TARGET YEAR
        *
        *WAIT FOR REST OF TIME UNITS TO BE GREATER THAN OR EQUAL
        *  TO TARGET VALUES
        *
        MOVEA.L #TARGET,A1      POINT TO TARGET VALUES
        LEA     SECIDX(A0),A0   POINT TO FIRST SOURCE VALUE
        MOVE.W  NTUNIT,D1       NUMBER OF TIME UNITS TO COMPARE
        SUBQ.W  #1,D1           REDUCE COUNT BY 1 FOR DBRA LOOP
        *
        *WAIT FOR TIME TO BE GREATER THAN OR EQUAL TO TARGET
        *
WTUNIT
        MOVE.B  (A1,D1.W),D0    GET TARGET TIME UNIT
        CMP.B   (A0,D1.W),D0    COMPARE TO CURRENT TIME UNIT
        BHI.S   WTUNIT          BRANCH IF TIME UNIT NOT >= TARGET VALUE
        DBRA    D1,WTUNIT       CONTINUE UNTIL ALL UNITS CHECKED
        *
        *DONE
        *
HERE
        BRA.S   HERE            IT IS NOW TIME OR LATER

*
*TARGET TIME - 2/7/87, 14:01:20 (2:01.20 PM, FEB. 7, 1987)
*
TYEAR   DC.W    1987            TARGET YEAR
NTUNIT  DC.B    5               NUMBER OF TIME UNITS IN COMPARISON
TARGET  DC.B    20,1,14,7,2     TARGET TIME (SEC,MIN,HR,DAY,MONTH)

USERSP  DS.L    1               STORAGE FOR USER'S STACK POINTER

        END
```

A 68000 Instruction set summary

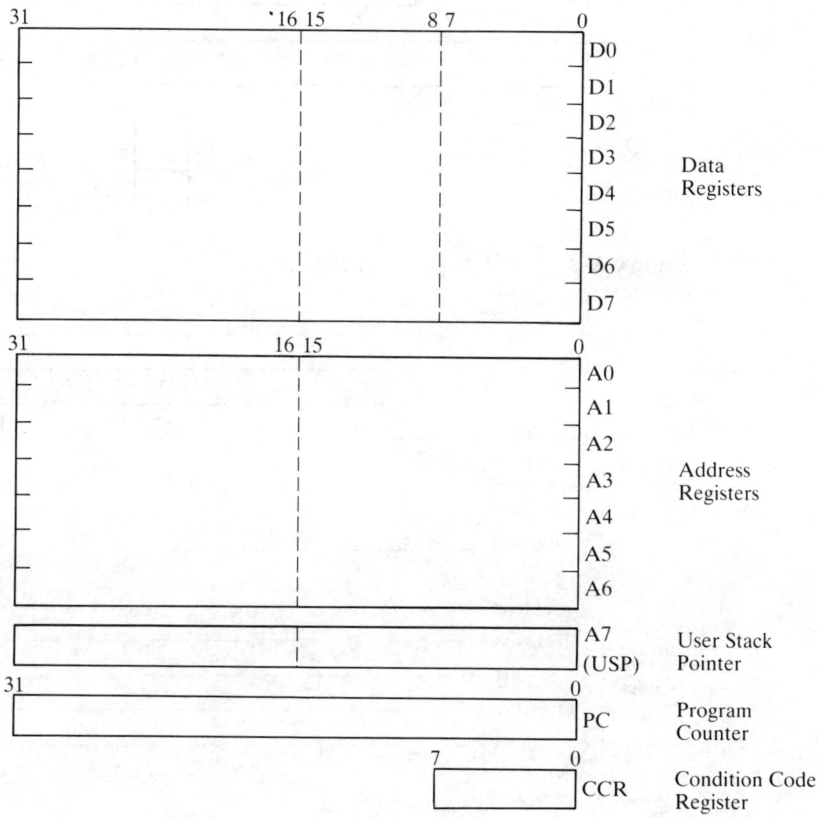

Figure A-1 68000 user registers.

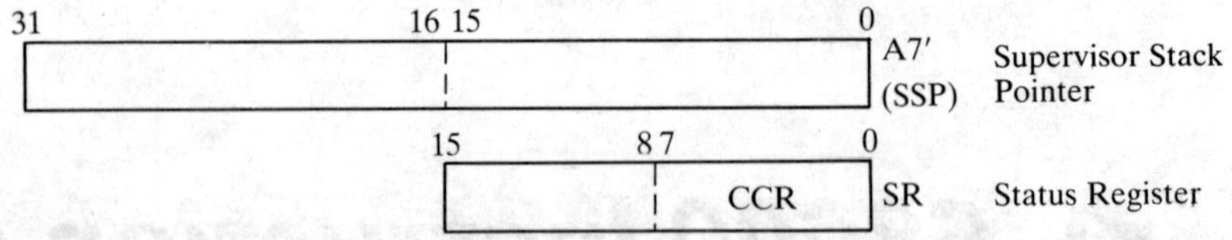

Figure A-2 68000 supervisor registers.

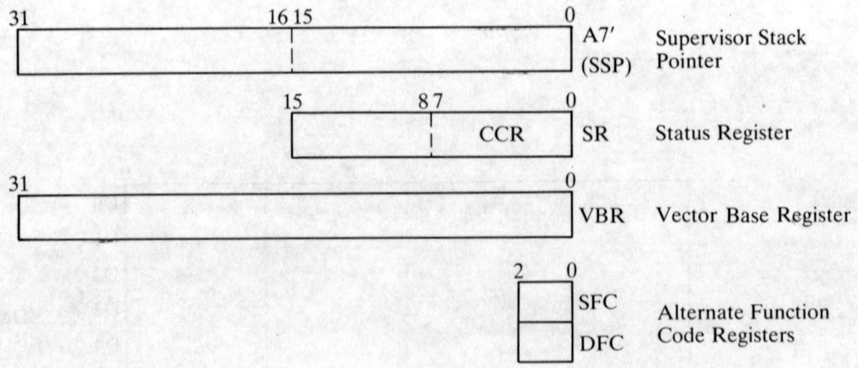

Figure A-3 68010 supervisor registers.

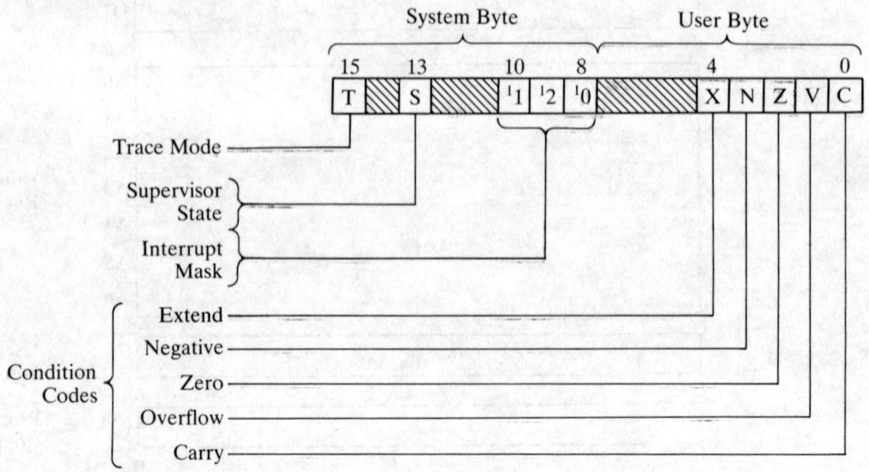

Figure A-4 68000 status register.

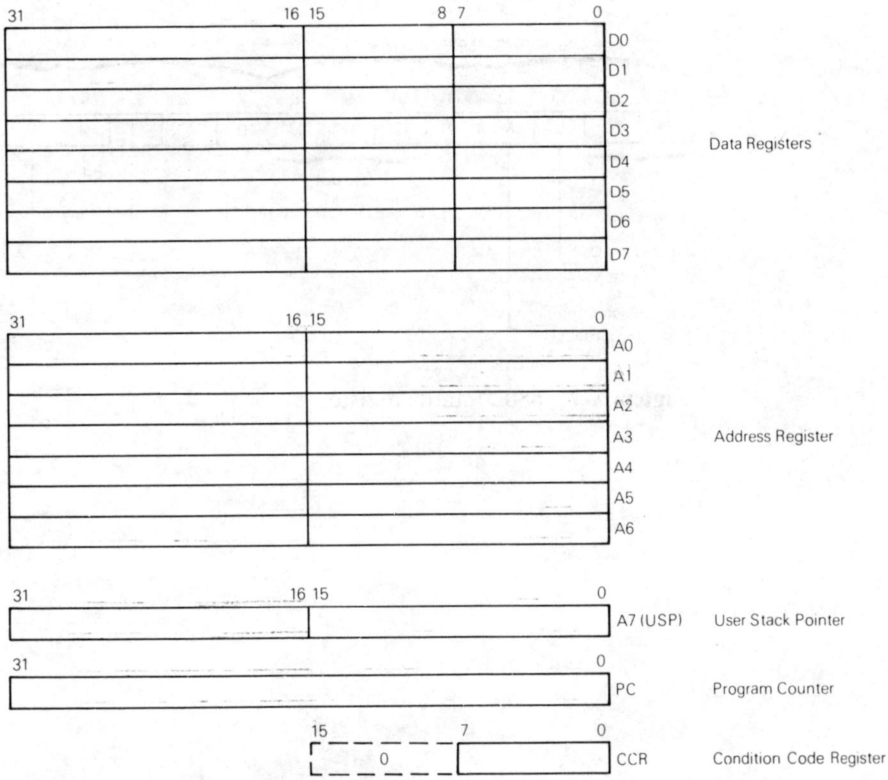

Figure A-5 68020 user registers.

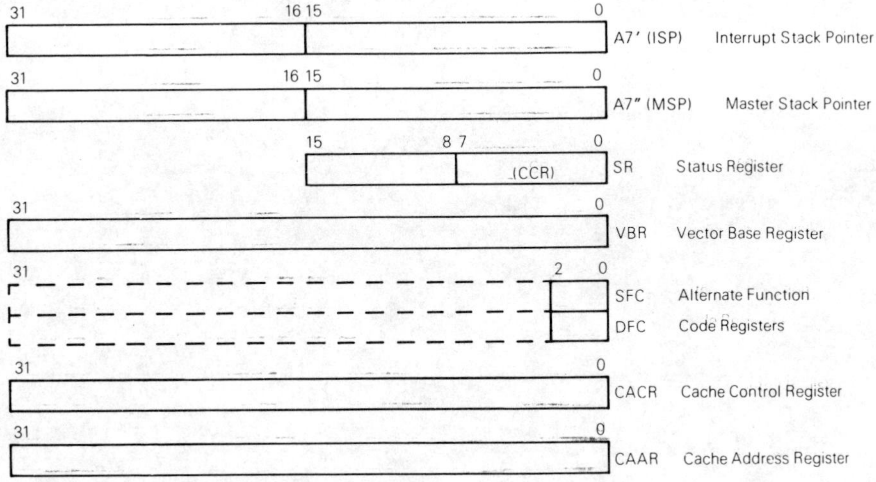

Figure A-6 68020 supervisor registers.

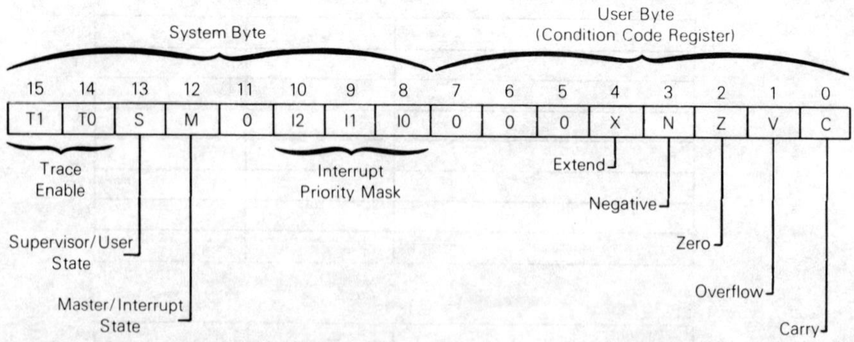

Figure A-7 68020 status register.

Table A-1 (pages 370 to 375) contains a summary of the 68000 instruction set. The shorthand for flag (condition code) settings is:

0,1 Specific values
* Affected according to the result
- Not affected
U Undefined

Table A-2 describes the condition code computations in more detail. Table A-3 explains the addressing modes, Table A-4 lists the conditional tests, Table A-5 contains the assignment of exception vectors, and Table A-6 lists the timing requirements for exception processing. Tables A-7 through A-9 summarize the 68000's instruction set, addressing modes, and coprocessor interface.

Table A-1 Instruction set summary (reprinted courtesy of Motorola Inc., MOS Integrated Circuits Division, Austin, TX

Addressing Mode

Mnemonic Operation	Size	Addr. Mode		Dn		An		(An)		(An)+		(An)		d(An)		d(An, Xi)		Abs.W		Abs.L		d(PC)		d(PC, Xi)		s = Immed d = SR/CC		Opcode Bit Pattern 1111 11 5432 1098 7654 3210	Boolean	Condition Codes X N Z V C
				#	~	#	~	#	~	#	~	#	~	#	~	#	~	#	~	#	~	#	~	#	~	#	~			
ABCD	B	s-Dn	d-	2	6																							1100 RRR1 0000 0rrr	d10+s10+X→d	* U * U *
Add Digits		s- -(An)	d-									2	19															1100 RRR1 0000 1rrr		
ADD	B/W	s-Dn	d-			ADDA		2	13	2	13	2	15	4	17	4	19	4	17	6	21							1101 DDD0 SSEE EEEE	d+Dn→d	* * * * *
Add		d-Dn	s-	2	4	2*	4	2	8	2	8	2	10	4	12	4	14	4	12	6	16	4	12	4	14	4	8	1101 DDD1 SSee eeee	Dn+s→Dn	
Binary	L	s-Dn	d-			ADDA		2	22	2	22	2	24	4	26	4	28	4	26	6	30							1101 DDD0 1OEE EEEE	d+Dn→d	
		d-Dn	s-	2	8	2	8	2	14	2	14	2	16	4	18	4	20	4	18	6	22	4	18	4	20	6	14	1101 DDD1 1Oee eeee	Dn+s→Dn	
ADDA	W	d-An	s-	2	8	2	8	2	12	2	12	2	14	4	16	4	18	4	16	6	20	4	16	4	18	4	12	1101 AAA0 11ee eeee	An+s→An	- - - - -
Add Address	L	d-An	s-	2	8	2	8	2	14	2	14	2	16	4	18	4	20	4	18	6	22	4	18	4	20	6	14	1101 AAA1 11ee eeee		
ADDI	B/W	s-Imm	d-	4	8	ADDA		4	17	4	17	4	19	6	21	6	23	6	21	8	25							0000 0110 SSEE EEEE	d+#→d	* * * * *
Add Immed	L	s-Imm	d-	6	16	ADDA		6	30	6	30	6	32	8	34	8	36	8	34	10	38									
ADDQ	B/W	s-Imm3	d-	2	4	2*	4	2	13	2	13	2	15	4	17	4	19	4	17	6	21							0101 QQQ0 SSEE EEEE	d+#→d	* * * * *
Add Quick	L	s-Imm3	d-	2	8	2	8	2	22	2	22	2	24	4	26	4	28	4	26	6	30									
ADDX	B/W	s-Dn	d-	2	4																							1101 RRR1 SS00 0rrr	d+s+X→d	* * * * *
Add Multi-		s- -(An)	d-									2	19															1101 RRR1 SS00 1rrr		
precision	L	s-Dn	d-	2	8																							1101 RRR1 1000 0rrr		
		s- -(An)	d-									2	32															1101 RRR1 1000 1rrr		
AND	B/W	s-Dn	d-					2	13	2	13	2	15	4	17	4	19	4	17	6	21							1100 DDD1 SSEE EEEE	d <and> Dn→d	- * * 0 0
Logical And		d-Dn	s-	2	4			2	8	2	8	2	10	4	12	4	14	4	12	6	16	4	12	4	14	4	8	1100 DDD0 SSee eeee	Dn <and> s→Dn	
	L	s-Dn	d-					2	22	2	22	2	24	4	26	4	28	4	26	6	30							1100 DDD1 1OEE EEEE	d <and> Dn→d	
		d-Dn	s-	2	8			2	14	2	14	2	16	4	18	4	20	4	18	6	22	4	18	4	20	6	14	1100 DDD0 1Oee eeee	Dn <and> s→Dn	
ANDI	B/W	s-Imm	d-	4	8			4	17	4	17	4	19	6	21	6	23	6	21	8	25					4	20	0000 0010 SSEE EEEE	d <and> #→d	- * * 0 0
And Immed.	L	s-Imm	d-	6	16			6	30	6	30	6	32	8	34	8	36	8	34	10	38									
ASL, ASR	B/W	count-Dn	d-	2	6+2n																							1110 rrrf SS10 0DDD		
Arithmetic		count-#1-8	d-	2	6+2n																							1110 QQQf SS00 0DDD	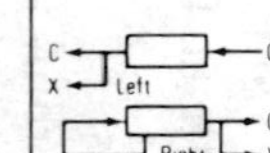	* * * * *
Shift	L	count-Dn	d-	2	8+2n																							1110 rrrf 1010 0DDD		
		count-#1-8	d-	2	8+2n																							1110 QQQf 1000 0DDD		
Memory	W	count-1	d-					2*	13	2*	13	2*	15	4*	17	4*	19	4*	17	6*	21							1110 000f 11EE EEEE		
BCHG	B	bit#-Dn	d-					2	13	2	13	2	15	4	17	4	19	4	17	6	21							0000 rrr1 01EE EEEE	~(bit)# of d→Z,	- - * - -
Test and		bit#-Imm	d-					4	17	4	17	4	19	6	21	6	23	6	21	8	25							0000 1000 01EE EEEE	~(bit)# of d→	
Change	L	bit#-Dn	d-	2	<8																							0000 rrr1 01EE EEEE	(bit)# of d	
		bit#-Imm	d-	4	<12																							0000 1000 01EE EEEE		
BCLR	B	bit#-Dn	d-					2	13	2	13	2	15	4	17	4	19	4	17	6	21							0000 rrr1 10EE EEEE		
Test and		bit#-Imm	d-					4	17	4	17	4	19	6	21	6	23	6	21	8	25							0000 1000 10EE EEEE	~(bit)# of d→Z,	- - * - -
Clear	L	bit#-Dn	d-	2	<10																							0000 rrr1 10EE EEEE	0→(bit)# of d	
		bit#-Imm	d-	4	<14																							0000 1000 10EE EEEE		
BSET	B	bit#-Dn	d-					2	13	2	13	2	15	4	17	4	19	4	17	6	21							0000 rrr1 11EE EEEE	~(bit)# of d→Z,	- - * - -
Test and		bit#-Imm	d-					4	17	4	17	4	19	6	21	6	23	6	21	8	25							0000 1000 11EE EEEE	1→(bit)# of d	
Set	L	bit#-Dn	d-	2	<8																							0000 rrr1 11EE EEEE		
		bit#-Imm	d-	4	<12																							0000 1000 11EE EEEE		
BTST	B	bit#-Dn	d-					2	8	2	8	2	10	4	12	4	14	4	12	6	16							0000 rrr1 00EE EEEE	~(bit)# of d→Z	- - * - -
Bit Test		bit#-Imm	d-					4	12	4	12	4	14	6	16	6	18	6	16	8	20							0000 1000 00EE EEEE		
	L	bit#-Dn	d-	2	<6																							0000 rrr1 00EE EEEE		
		bit#-Imm	d-	4	<10																							0000 1000 00EE EEEE		
CHK	W				<43	←trap→			<47		<47		<49		<51		<53		<51		<55		<51		<53		<47	0100 DDD1 10ee eeee	If Dn < 0, or	- * U U U
Check Reg-		d-Dn	s-	2				2		2		2		4		4		4		6		4		4		4			Dn > (bound),	
ister Against		(bound)			8'	←no→			12'		12'		14'		16'		18'		16'		20'		16'		18'		12'		then trap	
Bounds						trap																								
CLR	B/W		d-	2	4			2	13	2	13	2	15	4	17	4	19	4	17	6	21							0100 0010 SSEE EEEE	0→d	- 0 1 0 0
Clear Operand	L		d-	2	6			2	22	2	22	2	24	4	26	4	28	4	26	6	30									

Addressing Mode

Mnemonic Operation	Size	Addr. Mode		Dn #	Dn ~	An #	An ~	(An) #	(An) ~	(An)+ #	(An)+ ~	-(An) #	-(An) ~	d(An) #	d(An) ~	d(An, Xi) #	d(An, Xi) ~	Abs.W #	Abs.W ~	Abs.L #	Abs.L ~	d(PC) #	d(PC) ~	d(PC, Xi) #	d(PC, Xi) ~	s = Immed d = SR/CC #	s = Immed d = SR/CC ~	Opcode Bit Pattern 1111 11 5432 1098 7654 3210	Boolean	Condition Codes X N Z V C
CMP	B/W	d-Dn	s-	2	4	2*	4	2	8	2	8	2	10	4	12	4	14	4	12	6	16	4	12	4	14	4	8	1011 DDD0 SSee eeee	Dn-s	– * * * *
Compare	L	d-Dn	s-	2	6	2	6	2	14	2	14	2	16	4	18	4	20	4	18	6	22	4	18	4	20	6	14			
Binary																														
CMPA	W	d-An	s-	2	6	2	6	2	10	2	10	2	12	4	14	4	16	4	12	6	18	4	14	4	16	4	10	1011 AAA0 11ee eeee	An-s	– * * * *
Compare	L	d-An	s-	2	6	2	6	2	14	2	14	2	16	4	18	4	20	4	18	6	22	4	18	4	20	6	14	1011 AAA1 11ee eeee		
Address																														
CMPI	B/W	s-Imm	d-	4	8	CMPA		4	12	4	12	4	14	6	16	6	18	6	16	8	20							0000 1100 SSEE EEEE	d-#	– * * * *
Compare Imm.	L	s-Imm	d-	6	14	CMPA		6	20	6	20	6	22	8	24	8	26	8	24	10	28									
CMPM	B/W	s-(An)+	d-							2	12																	1011 RRR1 SS00 1rrr	d-s	– * * * *
Compare	L	s-(An)+	d-							2	20																			
Memory																														
DIVS	W	d-Dn	s-	2	< 158			2	< 162	2	< 162	2	< 164	4	< 166	4	< 168	4	< 166	6	< 170	4	< 166	4	< 168	4	< 162	1000 DDD1 11ee eeee	Dn32/s16→ Dn(r:q)	– * * * 0
Divide Signed																														
DIVU	W	d-Dn	s-	2	< 140			2	< 144	2	< 144	2	< 146	4	< 148	4	< 150	4	< 148	6	< 152	4	< 148	4	< 150	4	< 144	1000 DDD0 11ee eeee	Dn32/s16→ Dn(r:q)	– * * * 0
Divide Unsigned																														
EOR	B/W	s-Dn	d-	2	4			2	13	2	13	2	15	4	17	4	19	4	17	6	21							1011 rrr1 SSEE EEEE	d ⊕ Dn→d	– * * 0 0
Exclusive OR	L	s-Dn	d-	2	8			2	22	2	22	2	24	4	26	4	28	4	26	6	30									
Logical																														
EORI	B/W	s-Imm	d-	4	8			4	17	4	17	4	19	6	21	6	23	6	21	8	25					4	20	0000 1010 SSEE EEEE	d ⊕ # → d	– * * 0 0
Exclusive OR	L	s-Imm	d-	6	16			6	30	6	30	6	32	8	34	8	36	8	34	10	38									
Immediate																														
EXG	L	s-Dn	d-	2	6	2	6																					1100 DDD1 0100 0DDD	s↔d	– – – – –
Exchange		s-An	d-	2	6	2	6																					1100 AAA1 0100 1AAA		
Registers																												1100 DDD1 1000 1AAA		
EXT	W		d-	2	4																							0100 1000 1000 0DDD	bit 7→bit 8-15	
Sign Extend	L		d-	2	4																							0100 1000 1100 0DDD	bit 15→bit 16-31	– * * 0 0
LEA	L	d-An	s-					2	4					4	8	4	12	4	8	6	12	4	8	4	12			0100 AAA1 11ee eeee	s→An	– – – – –
Load Effective Address																														
LINK		disp-Imm	s-			4	18																					0100 1110 0101 0AAA	An→-(SP) SP→An SP+disp→SP	– – – – –
Link and Allocate																														

*Word only
< Maximum value

Opcode Bit Pattern Key

A: Address Register #
C: Test Condition
D: Data Register #
e: Source Effective Address
E: Destination Effective Address
f: Direction; 0-Right, 1-Left
M: Destination EA Mode
P: Displacement
Q: Quick Immediate Data
r: Source Register
R: Destination Register
S: Size; 00-B, 01-W, 10-L, 11-Another Operation
V: Vector #

Addressing Mode

Mnemonic Operation	Size	Addr. Mode	Dn		An		(An)		(An)+		-(An)		d(An)		d(An, Xi)		Abs.W		Abs.L		d(PC)		d(PC, Xi)		s=Immed d=SR/CC		Opcode Bit Pattern 1111 11 5432 1098 7654 3210	Boolean	Condition Codes X N Z V C
			#	~	#	~	#	~	#	~	#	~	#	~	#	~	#	~	#	~	#	~	#	~	#	~			
LSL, LSR	B/W	count-Dn d-	2	6+2n																							1110 rrr[illegible] SS10 1DDD	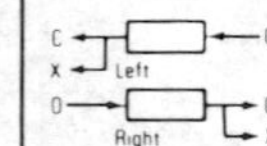	• • • 0 •
Logical Shift		count-#1 8 d-	2	6+2n																							1110 [illegible] SS00 1DDD		
	L	count-Dn d-	2	8+2n																							1110 [illegible] 1010 1DDD		
		count-#1 8 d-	2	8+2n																							1110 [illegible] 1000 1DDD		
Memory	W	count-1 d-					2*	13	2*	13	2*	15	4*	17	4*	19	4*	17	6*	21							111[illegible] [illegible] 11EE EEEE		
MOVE	B/W	s-Dn d-	2	4	MOVEA		2	9	2	9	2	9	4	13	4	15	4	13	6	17							00SS RRRM MMee eeee	s→d	– • • 0 0
Move Data		s-An s-	2	4	MOVEA		2	9	2	9	2	9	4	13	4	15	4	13	6	17									
		s-(An) d-	2	8	MOVEA		2	13	2	13	2	13	4	17	4	19	4	17	6	21									
		s-(An)+ d-	2	8	MOVEA		2	13	2	13	2	13	4	17	4	19	4	17	6	21									
		s- -(An) d-	2	10	MOVEA		2	15	2	15	2	15	4	19	4	21	4	19	6	23									
		s-d(An) d-	4	12	MOVEA		4	17	4	17	4	17	6	21	6	23	6	21	8	25									
		s-d(An,X) d-	4	14	MOVEA		4	19	4	19	4	19	6	23	6	25	6	23	8	27									
		s-Abs.W d-	4	12	MOVEA		4	17	4	17	4	17	6	21	6	23	6	21	8	25									
		s-Abs.L d-	6	16	MOVEA		6	21	4	21	6	21	8	25	8	27	8	25	10	29									
		s-d(PC) d-	4	12	MOVEA		4	17	4	17	4	17	6	21	6	23	6	21	8	25									
		s-d(PC,X) d-	4	14	MOVEA		4	19	4	19	4	19	6	3	6	5	6	3	8	27									
		s-Imm d-	4	8	MOVEA		4	13	4	13	4	13	6	17	6	19	6	17	8	21									
	L	s-Dn d-	2	4	MOVEA		2	14	2	14	2	13	4	18	4	20	4	18	6	22									
		s-An d-	2	4	MOVEA		2	14	2	14	2	13	4	18	4	20	4	18	6	22									
		s-(An) d-	2	12	MOVEA		2	22	2	22	2	22	4	26	4	28	4	26	6	30									
		s-(An)+ d-	2	12	MOVEA		2	22	2	22	2	22	4	26	4	28	4	26	6	30									
		s- -(An) d-	2	14	MOVEA		2	24	2	24	2	24	4	28	4	30	4	28	6	32									
		s-d(An) d-	4	16	MOVEA		4	26	4	26	4	26	6	30	6	32	6	30	8	34									
		s-d(An,X) d-	4	18	MOVEA		4	28	4	28	4	28	6	32	6	34	6	32	8	36									
		s-Abs.W d-	4	16	MOVEA		4	26	4	26	4	26	6	30	6	32	6	30	8	34									
		s-Abs.L d-	6	20	MOVEA		6	30	4	30	6	30	8	34	8	36	8	34	10	38									
		s-d(PC) d-	4	16	MOVEA		4	26	4	26	4	26	6	30	6	32	6	30	8	34									
		s-d(PC,X) d-	4	18	MOVEA		4	28	4	28	4	28	6	32	6	34	6	32	8	36									
		s-Imm d-	6	12	MOVEA		6	22	6	22	6	22	8	26	8	28	8	26	10	30									
MOVE Move to Condition Codes	W	d-CCR s-	2	12			2	16	2	16	2	18	4	20	4	22	4	20	6	24	4	20	4	22	4	16	0100 0100 11ee eeee	s→CCR	• • • • •
MOVE Move to/from Status Reg.	W	d-SR s-	2	12			2	16	2	16	2	18	4	20	4	22	4	20	6	24	4	20	4	22	4	16	0100 0110 11ee eeee	s→SR	• • • • •
		s-SR d-	2	6			2	13	2	13	2	15	4	17	4	19	4	17	6	21							0100 0000 11EE EEEE	SR→d	– – – – –
MOVE Move to/from User SP (A7)	L	s-USP d-			2	4																					0100 1110 0110 1AAA	USP→An	– – – – –
		o-USP s-			2	4																					0100 1110 0110 0AAA	An→USP	
MOVEA	W	d-An s-	2	4	2	4	2	8	2	8	2	10	4	12	4	14	4	12	6	16	4	12	4	14	4	8	0001 AAA0 01ee eeee	s→An	– – – – –
Move Address	L	d-An s-	2	4	2	4	2	12	2	12	2	14	4	16	4	18	4	16	6	20	4	16	4	18	6	12	0010 AAA0 01ee eeee		
MOVEM	W	s-Xn d-					4	8+5n			4	8+5n	6	12+5n	6	14+5n	6	12+5n	8	16+5n							0100 1000 10EE EEEE a7 a0 d7 d0↑	Xn→d	– – – – –
Move Multiple Registers		d-Xn s-					4	12+4n	4	12+4n			6	16+4n	6	18+4n	6	16+4n	8	20+4n	6	16+4n	6	18+4n			0100 1100 10ee eeee a7 a0 d7 d0	s→Xn	
	L	s-Xn d-					4	8+10n			4	8+10n	6	12+10n	6	14+10n	6	12+10n	8	16+10n							0100 1000 11EE EEEE a7 a0 d7 d0↑	Xn→d	
		d-Xn s-					4	12+8n	4	12+8n			6	16+8n	6	18+8n	6	16+8n	8	20+8n	6	16+8n	6	18+8n			0100 1100 11ee eeee a7 a0 d7 d0	s→Xn	

Addressing Mode

Mnemonic Operation	Size	Addr. Mode	Dn #	Dn ~	An #	An ~	(An) #	(An) ~	(An)+ #	(An)+ ~	-(An) #	-(An) ~	d(An) #	d(An) ~	d(An, Xi) #	d(An, Xi) ~	Abs.W #	Abs.W ~	Abs.L #	Abs.L ~	d(PC) #	d(PC) ~	d(PC, Xi) #	d(PC, Xi) ~	s=Immed d=SR/CC #	s=Immed d=SR/CC ~	Opcode Bit Pattern 1111 11 5432 1098 7654 3210	Boolean	Condition Codes X N Z V C
MOVEP	W	s-Dn d-											4	18													0000 DDD1 1000 1AAA	Dn→d by bytes	– – – – –
Move		s-d(An) d-	4	16																							0000 DDD1 0000 1AAA	s→Dn by bytes	
Peripheral	L	s-Dn d-											4	28													0000 DDD1 1100 1AAA	Dn→d by bytes	
		s-d(An) d-	4	24																							0000 DDD1 0100 1AAA	s→Dn by bytes	
MOVEQ	L	s-Imm8 d-	2	4																							0111 DDD0 QQQQ QQQQ	#→Dn	– * * 0 0
Move Quick																													
MULS	W	d-Dn s-	2	< 70			2	< 74	2	< 74	2	< 76	4	< 78	4	< 80	4	< 78	6	< 82	4	< 78	4	< 80	4	< 74	1100 DDD1 11ee eeee	Dn×s→Dn	– * * 0 0
Multiply Signed																													
MULU	W	d-Dn s-	2	< 70			2	< 74	2	< 74	2	< 76	4	< 78	4	< 80	4	< 78	6	< 82	4	< 78	4	< 80	4	< 74	1100 DDD0 11ee eeee	Dn×s→Dn	– * * 0 0
Multiply Unsigned																													
NBCD	B	d-	2	6			2	13	2	13	2	15	4	17	4	19	4	17	6	21							0100 1000 00EE EEEE	0-d10-X→d	* U * U *
Negate Digit																													
NEG	B/W	d-	2	4			2	13	2	13	2	15	4	17	4	19	4	17	6	21							0100 0100 SSEE EEEE	0-d→d	* * * * *
Negate Binary	L	d-	2	6			2	22	2	22	2	24	4	26	4	28	4	26	6	30									
NEGX	B/W	d-	2	4			2	13	2	13	2	15	4	17	4	19	4	17	6	21							0100 0000 SSEE EEEE	0-d-X→d	* * * * *
Negate Multi-precision	L	d-	2	6			2	22	2	22	2	24	4	26	4	28	4	26	6	30									
NOT	B/W	d-	2	4			2	13	2	13	2	15	4	17	4	19	4	17	6	21							0100 0110 SSEE EEEE	'd→d	– * * 0 0
Logical Complement	L	d-	2	6			2	22	2	22	2	24	4	26	4	28	4	26	6	30									
OR	B/W	s-Dn d-					2	13	2	13	2	15	4	17	4	19	4	17	6	21							1000 DDD1 SSEE EEEE	d< or >Dn→d	– * * 0 0
Inclusive OR		d-Dn s-	2	4			2	8	2	8	2	10	4	12	4	14	4	12	6	16	4	12	4	14	4	8	1000 DDD0 SSee eeee	Dn< or >s→Dn	
Logical	L	s-Dn d-					2	22	2	22	2	24	4	26	4	28	4	26	6	30							1000 DDD1 10EE EEEE	d< or >Dn→d	
		d-Dn s-	2	8			2	14	2	14	2	16	4	18	4	20	4	18	6	22	4	18	4	20	6	14	1000 DDD0 10ee eeee	Dn< or >s→Dn	
ORI	B/W	s-Imm d-	4	8			4	17	4	17	4	19	6	21	6	23	6	21	8	25					4	20	0000 0000 SSEE EEEE	d< or >#→d	– * * 0 0
OR Immediate	L	s-Imm d-	6	16			6	30	6	30	6	32	8	34	8	36	8	34	10	38									
PEA	L	s-					2	14					4	18	4	22	4	18	6	22	4	18	4	22			0100 1000 01ee eeee	s→-(SP)	– – – – –
Push Effective Address																													
ROR, ROL	B/W	count-Dn d-	2	6+2n																							1110 rrrf SS11 1DDD	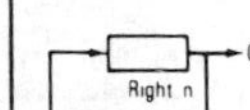	– * * 0 0
Rotate		count-#1-8 d-	2	6+2n																									
without X	L	count-Dn d-	2	8+2n																							1110 QQQf SS01 1DDD	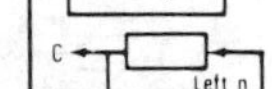	
		count-#1-8 d-	2	8+2n																							1110 rrrf 1011 1DDD		
	W	count-1 d-					2*	13	2*	13	2*	15	4*	17	4*	19	4*	17	6*	21							1110 QQQf 1001 1DDD		
Memory																											1110 011f 11FE EEEE		

†Note: for PRE-DECREMENT mode, register mask d0 d7 a0 a7

*Word only

< Maximum value

Opcode Bit Pattern Key

A:	Address Register #	e:	Source Effective Address	M:	Destination EA Mode	r:	Source Register	V:	Vector #
C:	Test Condition	E:	Destination Effective Address	P:	Displacement	R:	Destination Register		
D:	Data Register #	f:	Direction; 0-Right, 1-Left	Q:	Quick Immediate Data	S:	Size; 00-B, 01-W, 10-L, 11-Another Operation		

Addressing Mode

Mnemonic Operation	Size	Addr Mode		Dn		An		(An)		(An)+		-(An)		d(An)		d(An, Xi)		Abs.W		Abs.L		d(PC)		d(PC, Xi)		s = Immed d = SR/CC		Opcode Bit Pattern 1111 11 5432 1098 7654 3210	Boolean	Condition Codes
				#	~	#	~	#	~	#	~	#	~	#	~	#	~	#	~	#	~	#	~	#	~	#	~			X N Z V C
ROXR, ROXL	E/W	count-Dn	d-	2	6+2n																							1110 rrrf SS11 0DDD	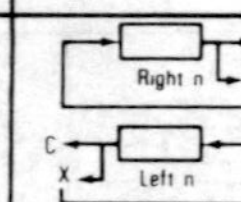	• • • 0 •
Rotate		count-#1-8	d-	2	6+2n																							1110 QQQf SS01 0DDD		
through X	L	count-Dn	d-	2	8+2n																							1110 rrrf 1011 0DDD		
		count-#1-8	d-	2	8+2n																							1110 QQQf 1001 0DDD		
Memory	W	count-1	d-					2*	13	2*	13	2*	15	4*	17	4*	19	4*	17	6*	21							1110 010f 11EE EEEE		
SBCD	B	s-Dn	d-	2	6																							1000 RRR1 0000 0rrr		
Subtract		s--(An)	d-									2	19															1000 RRR1 0000 1rrr	d10-s10-X→d	• U • U •
digits																														
Scc	B	cc	d-	2	6/4'			2	13	2	13	2	15	4	17	4	19	4	17	6	21							0101 CCCC 11EE EEEE	If cc true, 1's→d	- - - - -
Set																													Else, 0's→d	
Conditionally																														
SUB	B/W	s-Dn	d-			SUBA		2	13	2	13	2	15	4	17	4	19	4	17	6	21							1001 DDD1 SSEE EEEE	d-Dn→d	• • • • •
Subtract		d-Dn	s-	2	4	2*	4	2	8	2	8	2	10	4	12	4	14	4	12	6	16	4	12	4	14	4	8	1001 DDD0 SSee eeee	Dn-s→Dn	
Binary	L	s-Dn	d-			SUBA		2	22	2	22	2	24	4	26	4	28	4	26	6	30							1001 DDD1 10EE EEEE	d-Dn→d	
		d-Dn	s-	2	8	2	8	2	14	2	14	2	16	4	18	4	20	4	18	6	22	4	18	4	20	6	14	1001 DDD0 10ee eeee	Dn-s→Dn	
SUBA	W	d-An	s-	2	8	2	8	2	12	2	12	2	14	4	16	4	18	4	16	6	20	4	16	4	18	4	12	1001 AAA0 11ee eeee	An-s→An	- - - - -
Subtract	L	d-An	s-	2	8	2	8	2	14	2	14	2	16	4	18	4	20	4	18	6	22	4	18	4	20	6	14	1001 AAA1 11ee eeee		
Address																														
SUBI	B/W	s-Imm	d-	4	8	SUBA		4	17	4	17	4	19	6	21	6	23	6	21	8	25							0000 0100 SSEE EEEE	d-#→d	• • • • •
Subtract	L	s-Imm	d-	6	16	SUBA		6	26	6	26	6	32	8	34	8	36	8	34	10	38									
Immediate																														
SUBQ	B/W	s-Imm3	d-	2	4	2*	4	2	13	2	13	2	15	4	17	4	19	4	17	6	21							0101 QQQ1 SSEE EEEE	d-#→d	• • • • •
Subtract	L	s-Imm3	d-	2	8	2	8	2	18	2	18	2	24	4	26	4	28	4	26	6	30									
Quick																														
SUBX	B/W	s-Dn	d-	2	4																							1001 RRR1 SS00 0rrr	d-s-X→d	• • • • •
Subtract		s--(An)	d-									2	19															1001 RRR1 SS00 1rrr		
Multiprecision	L	s-Dn	d-	2	8																							1001 RRR1 1000 0rrr		
		s--(An)	d-									2	32															1001 RRR1 1000 1rrr		
SWAP	W		d-	2	4																							0100 1000 0100 0DDD	Dn[31:16]↔Dn[15:0]	- • • 0 0
Swap Regis-																														
ter Halves																														
TAS	B		d-	2	4			2	15	2	15	2	17	4	19	4	21	4	19	6	23							0100 1010 11EE EEEE	test d→cc	- • • 0 0
Test and Set																													1→bit 7 of d	
Operand																														
TST	B/W		d-	2	4			2	8	2	8	2	10	4	12	4	14	4	12	6	16							0100 1010 SSEE EEEE	test d→cc	- • • 0 0
Test	L		d-	2	4			2	12	2	12	2	14	4	16	4	18	4	16	6	20									
UNLK						2	12																					0100 1110 0101 1AAA	An→SP, (SP)+→An	- - - - -
Unlink																														
Program Control Instructions																														
Bcc	B	disp-																							bra taken	2	10	0110 CCCC PPPP PPPP	if cc true, PC+disp→PC	- - - - -
Branch	W	disp-																							bra not taken	2	8'			
Conditionally																									bra taken	4	10			
																									bra not taken	4	14'			
BRA	B	disp-																								2	10	0110 0000 PPPP PPPP	PC+disp→PC	- - - - -
Branch	W	disp-																								4	10			
Always																														

Mnemonic Operation	Size	Addr Mode	Dn #	Dn ~	An #	An ~	(An) #	(An) ~	(An)+ #	(An)+ ~	-(An) #	-(An) ~	d(An) #	d(An) ~	d(An, Xi) #	d(An, Xi) ~	Abs.W #	Abs.W ~	Abs.L #	Abs.L ~	d(PC) #	d(PC) ~	d(PC, Xi) #	d(PC, Xi) ~	s d Immed SR/CC #	s d Immed SR/CC ~	Opcode Bit Pattern 1111 11 5432 1098 7654 3210	Boolean	Condition Codes X N Z V C
BSR Branch to Subroutine	B W	disp- disp-																							2 4	20 20	0110 0001 PPPP PPPP	PC → -(SP), PC+disp → PC	- - - - -
DBcc Decrement Counter, & Branch Until Condition True or Count = -1	W	disp-Imm counter-	4	10 12' 14'	cc: false / true / false		Counter: ≠ -1 / ≠ -1 / expired		Branch: yes / no / no																		0101 CCCC 1100 1DDD	If cc false, Dn-1 → Dn & if Dn ≠ -1, PC+disp → PC Else, NOP	- - - - -
JMP Jump to		d-					2	8					4	10	4	14	4	10	6	12	4	10	4	14			0100 1110 11EE EEEE	d → PC	- - - - -
JSR Jump to Subroutine		d-					2	18					4	20	4	24	4	20	6	22	4	20	4	24			0100 1110 10EE EEEE	PC → -(SP), d → PC	- - - - -
NOP No Operation			2	4																							0100 1110 0111 0001	none	- - - - -
RESET Reset External Devices			2	132																							0100 1110 0111 0000	assert RESET pin	- - - - -
RTE Return from Exception			2	20																							0100 1110 0111 0011	(SP)+ → SR, (SP)+ → PC	• • • • •
RTR Return from Subroutine/ Restore CC			2	20																							0100 1110 0111 0111	(SP)+ → CC, (SP)+ → PC	• • • • •
RTS Return from Subroutine			2	16																							0100 1110 0111 0101	(SP)+ → PC	- - - - -
STOP Load SR/Stop																									4	4	0100 1110 0111 0010	# → SR, Wait for Interrupt	• • • • •
TRAP Trap			2	37																							0100 1110 0100 VVVV	PC → -(SSP), SR → -(SSP), (Vector) → PC	- - - - -
TRAPV Trap if Overflow Set			2	37 4	Trap taken Trap not taken																						0100 1110 0111 0110	If V=1, then PC → -(SSP), SR → -(SSP), (TRAPV vector) → PC, else, NOP	- - - - -

*Word only

< Maximum value

Opcode Bit Pattern Key

A:	Address Register #	e:	Source Effective Address	M:	Destination EA Mode	r:	Source Register	V:	Vector #
C:	Test Condition	E:	Destination Effective Address	P:	Displacement	R:	Destination Register		
D:	Data Register #	f:	Direction; 0=Right, 1=Left	Q:	Quick Immediate Data	S:	Size; 00=B, 01=W, 10=L, 11=Another Operation		

Table A-2 68000 condition code computations (reprinted courtesy of Motorola Inc., MOS Integrated Circuits Division, Austin, TX)

Condition Code Computations

Operations	X	N	Z	V	C	Special Definition
ABCD	•	U	?	U	?	C - Decimal Carry $Z - Z \bullet \overline{Rm} \bullet \ldots \bullet \overline{R0}$
ADD, ADDI, ADDQ	•	•	•	?	?	$V - Sm \bullet Dm \bullet \overline{Rm} + \overline{Sm} \bullet \overline{Dm} \bullet Rm$ $C - Sm \bullet Dm + \overline{Rm} \bullet Dm + Sm \bullet \overline{Rm}$
ADDX	•	•	?	?	?	$V - Sm \bullet Dm \bullet \overline{Rm} + \overline{Sm} \bullet \overline{Dm} \bullet Rm$ $C - Sm \bullet Dm + \overline{Rm} \bullet Dm + Sm \bullet \overline{Rm}$ $Z - Z \bullet \overline{Rm} \bullet \ldots \bullet \overline{R0}$
AND, ANDI, EOR, EORI, MOVEQ, MOVE, OR, ORI, CLR, EXT, NOT, TAS, TST	–	•	•	0	0	
CHK	–	•	U	U	U	
SUB, SUBI SUBQ	•	•	•	?	?	$V - \overline{Sm} \bullet Dm \bullet \overline{Rm} + Sm \bullet \overline{Dm} \bullet Rm$ $C - Sm \bullet \overline{Dm} + Rm \bullet \overline{Dm} + Sm \bullet Rm$
SUBX	•	•	?	?	?	$V - \overline{Sm} \bullet Dm \bullet \overline{Rm} + Sm \bullet \overline{Dm} \bullet Rm$ $C - Sm \bullet \overline{Dm} + Rm \bullet \overline{Dm} + Sm \bullet Rm$ $Z - Z \bullet \overline{Rm} \bullet \ldots \bullet \overline{R0}$
CMP, CMPI, CMPM	–	•	•	?	?	$V - \overline{Sm} \bullet Dm \bullet \overline{Rm} + Sm \bullet \overline{Dm} \bullet Rm$ $C - Sm \bullet \overline{Dm} + Rm \bullet \overline{Dm} + Sm \bullet Rm$
DIVS, DIVU	–	•	•	?	0	V - Division Overflow
MULS, MULU	–	•	•	0	0	
SBCD, NBCD	•	U	?	U	?	C - Decimal Borrow $Z - Z \bullet \overline{Rm} \bullet \ldots \bullet \overline{R0}$
NEG	•	•	•	?	?	$V - Dm \bullet Rm$, $C - Dm + Rm$
NEGX	•	•	?	?	?	$V - Dm \bullet Rm$, $C - Dm + Rm$ $Z - Z \bullet \overline{Rm} \bullet \ldots \bullet \overline{R0}$
BTST, BCHG, BSET, BCLR	–	–	?	–	–	$Z - \overline{Dn}$
ASL	•	•	•	?	?	$V - Dm \bullet (\overline{D_{m-1}} + \ldots + \overline{D_{m-r}})$ $+ \overline{Dm} \bullet (D_{m-1} + \ldots + D_{m-r})$ $C - D_{m-r+1}$
ASL (r - 0)	–	•	•	0	0	
LSL, ROXL	•	•	•	0	?	$C - D_{m-r+1}$
LSR (r - 0)	–	•	•	0	0	
ROXL (r - 0)	–	•	•	0	?	C - X
ROL	–	•	•	0	?	$C - D_{m-r+1}$
ROL (r - 0)	–	•	•	0	0	
ASR, LSR, ROXR	•	•	•	0	?	$C - D_{r-1}$
ASR, LSR (r - 0)	–	•	•	0	0	
ROXR (r - 0)	–	•	•	0	?	C - X
ROR	–	•	•	0	?	$C - D_{r-1}$
ROR (r - 0)	–	•	•	0	0	

Table A-3 68000 addressing mode summary (reprinted courtesy of Motorola Inc., MOS Integrated Circuits Division, Austin, TX)

Single-Effective-Address-Instruction Operation Word – General Format

15	14	13	12	11	10	9	8	7	6	5	4	3	2	1	0
X	X	X	X	X	X	X	X	X	X	Effective Address Mode			Effective Address Register		

Effective Addressing Mode Categories

Type	Mode	Register	Generation	Assembler Syntax
Data Register Direct	000	reg. no.	EA - Dn	Dn
Address Register Direct	001	reg. no.	EA - An	An
Register Indirect	010	reg. no.	EA - (An)	(An)
Postincrement Register Indirect	011	reg. no.	EA - (An), An — An + N	(An) +
Predecrement Register Indirect	100	reg. no	An — An - N, EA - (An)	- (An)
Register Indirect With Offset	101	reg. no.	EA - (An) + d16	d(An)
Indexed Register Indirect With Offset	110	reg. no.	EA - (An) + (Xn) + d8	d(An, Xn)
Absolute Short	111	000	EA - (Next Word)	xxx
Absolute Long	111	001	EA - (Next Two Words)	xxxxxx
Relative With Offset	111	010	EA - (PC) + 16	PC relative
Relative With Index and Offset	111	011	EA - (PC) + (Xn) + d8	PC relative + Xn
Immediate	111	100	Data - Next Word(s)	#xxx
Quick Immediate	–	–	Inherent Data	–
Implied Register	–	–	EA - SR, USP, SP, PC	–

Notes:
EA - Effective Address
An - Address Register
Dn - Data Register
Xn - Address or Data Register used as Index Register
SR - Status Register
PC - Program Counter
d8 - Eight-bit Offset (displacement)
d16 - Sixteen-bit Offset (displacement)
N - 1 for Byte, 2 for Words and 4 for Long Words
( ) - Contents of
 - Replaces

Table A-4 68000 conditional tests (reprinted courtesy of Motorola Inc., MOS Integrated Circuits Division, Austin, TX)

Conditional Tests

Mnemonic	Condition	Encoding	Test
T	true	0000	1
F	false	0001	0
HI	high	0010	C•Z
LS	low or same	0011	C + Z
CC	carry clear	0100	C
CS	carry set	0101	C
NE	not equal	0110	Z
EQ	equal	0111	Z
VC	overflow clear	1000	V
VS	overflow set	1001	V
PL	plus	1010	N
MI	minus	1011	N
GE	greater or equal	1100	N•V + N•V
LT	less than	1101	N•V + N•V
GT	greater than	1110	N•V•Z + N•V•Z
LE	less or equal	1111	Z + N•V + N•V

Table A-5 68000 exception vector assignments (reprinted courtesy of Motorola Inc., MOS Integrated Circuits Division, Austin, TX)

Exception Vector Assignment

Vector Number(s)	Address Dec	Hex	Space	Assignment
0	0	000	SP	Reset: Initial SSP
–	4	004	SP	Reset: Initial PC
2	8	008	SD	Bus Error
3	12	00C	SD	Address Error
4	16	010	SD	Illegal Instruction
5	20	014	SD	Zero Divide
6	24	018	SD	CHK Instruction
7	28	01C	SD	TRAPV Instruction
8	32	020	SD	Privilege Violation
9	36	024	SD	Trace
10	40	028	SD	Line 1010 Emulator
11	44	02C	SD	Line 1111 Emulator
12*	48	030	SD	(Unassigned, reserved)
13*	52	034	SD	(Unassigned, reserved)
14*	56	038	SD	(Unassigned, reserved)
15	60	03C	SD	Uninitialized Interrupt Vector
16-23*	64	04C	SD	(Unassigned, reserved)
	95	05F		–
24	96	060	SD	Spurious Interrupt
25	100	064	SD	Level 1 Interrupt Autovector
26	104	068	SD	Level 2 Interrupt Autovector
27	108	06C	SD	level 3 Interrupt Autovector
28	112	070	SD	Level 4 Interrupt Autovector
29	116	074	SD	Level 5 Interrupt Autovector
30	120	078	SD	Level 6 Interrupt Autovector
31	124	07C	SD	Level 7 Interrupt Autovector
32-47	128	080	SD	TRAP Instruction Vectors
	191	0BF		–
48-63*	192	0C0	SD	(Unassigned, reserved)
	255	0FF		–
64-255	256	100	SD	User Interrupt Vectors
	1023	3FF		–

*Vector numbers 12, 13, 14, 16 through 23 and 48 through 63 are reserved for future enhancements by Motorola. No user peripheral devices should be assigned these numbers.

Table A-6 68000 exception processing timing requirements (reprinted courtesy of Motorola Inc., MOS Integrated Circuits Division, Austin, TX)

Exception Processing Clock Periods

Exception	Periods
Address Error	57
Bus Error	57
Interrupt	47
Illegal Instruction	37
Privileged Instruction	37
Trace	37

*The interrupt acknowledge bus cycle is assumed to take four external clock periods

Mnemonic	Description
ABCD	Add Decimal with Extend
ADD	Add
ADDA	Add Address
ADDI	Add Immediate
ADDQ	Add Quick
ADDX	Add with Extend
AND	Logical AND
ANDI	Logical AND Immediate
ASL, ASR	Arithmetic Shift Left and Right
Bcc	Branch Conditionally
BCHG	Test Bit and Change
BCLR	Test Bit and Clear
BFCHG	Test Bit Field and Change
BFCLR	Test Bit Field and Clear
BFEXTS	Signed Bit Field Extract
BFEXTU	Unsigned Bit Field Extract
BFFFO	Bit Field Find First One
BFINS	Bit Field Insert
BFSET	Test Bit Field and Set
BFTST	Test Bit Field
BRA	Branch
BSET	Test Bit and Set
BSR	Branch to Subroutine
BTST	Test Bit
CALLM	Call Module
CAS	Compare and Swap Operands
CAS2	Compare and Swap Dual Operands
CHK	Check Register Against Bound
CHK2	Check Register Against Upper and Lower Bounds
CLR	Clear
CMP	Compare
CMPA	Compare Address
CMPI	Compare Immediate
CMPM	Compare Memory to Memory
CMP2	Compare Register Against Upper and Lower Bounds
DBcc	Test Condition, Decrement and Branch
DIVS, DIVSL	Signed Divide
DIVU, DIVUL	Unsigned Divide
EOR	Logical Exclusive OR
EORI	Logical Exclusive OR Immediate
EXG	Exchange Registers
EXT	Sign Extend
JMP	Jump
JSR	Jump to Subroutine
LEA	Load Effective Address
LINK	Link and Allocate
LSL, LSR	Logical Shift Left and Right
MOVE	Move
MOVEA	Move Address
MOVE CCR	Move Condition Code Register
MOVE SR	Move Status Register
MOVE USP	Move User Stack Pointer
MOVEC	Move Control Register
MOVEM	Move Multiple Registers
MOVEP	Move Peripheral
MOVEQ	Move Quick
MOVES	Move Alternate Address Space
MULS	Signed Multiply
MULU	Unsigned Multiply
NBCD	Negate Decimal with Extend
NEG	Negate
NEGX	Negate with Extend
NOP	No Operation
NOT	Logical Complement
OR	Logical Inclusive OR
ORI	Logical OR Immediate
PACK	Pack BCD
PEA	Push Effective Address
RESET	Reset External Devices
ROL, ROR	Rotate Left and Right
ROXL, ROXR	Rotate with Extend Left and Right
RTD	Return and Deallocate
RTE	Return from Exception
RTM	Return from Module
RTR	Return and Restore Conditon Codes
RTS	Return from Subroutine
SBCD	Subtract Decimal with Extend
Scc	Set Conditionally
STOP	Stop
SUB	Subtract
SUBA	Subtract Address
SUBI	Subtract Immediate
SUBQ	Subtract Quick
SUBX	Subtract with Extend
SWAP	Swap Register Words
TAS	Test Operand and Set
TRAP	Trap
TRAPcc	Trap Conditionally
TRAPV	Trap on Overflow
TST	Test Operand
UNLK	Unlink
UNPK	Unpack BCD
COPROCESSOR INSTRUCTIONS	
cpBcc	Branch Conditionally
cpDBcc	Test Coprocessor Condition, Decrement, and Branch
cpGEN	Coprocessor General Instruction
cpRESTORE	Restore Internal State of Coprocessor
cpSAVE	Save Internal State of Coprocessor
cpScc	Set Conditionally
cpTRAPcc	Trap Conditionally

Table A-7 68020 instruction set summary (reprinted courtesy of Motorola Inc., MOS Integrated Circuits Division, Austin, TX)

Table A-8 68020 addressing mode summary (reprinted courtesy of Motorola Inc., MOS Integrated Circuits Division, Austin, TX)

Addressing Modes	Syntax
Register Direct	
Data Register Direct	Dn
Address Register Direct	An
Register Indirect	
Address Register Indirect	(An)
Address Register Indirect with Postincrement	(An)+
Address Register Indirect with Predecrement	–(An)
Address Register Indirect with Displacement	(d_{16},An)
Register Indirect with Index	
Address Register Indirect with Index (8-Bit Displacement)	(d_8,An,Xn)
Address Register Indirect with Index (Base Displacement)	(bd,An,Xn)
Memory Indirect	
Memory Indirect Post-Indexed	([bd,An],Xn,od)
Memory Indirect Pre-Indexed	([bd,An,Xn],od)
Program Counter Indirect with Displacement	(d_{16},PC)
Program Counter Indirect with Index	
PC Indirect with Index (8-Bit Displacement)	(d_8,PC,Xn)
PC Indirect with Index (Base Displacement)	(bd,PC,Xn)
Program Counter Memory Indirect	
PC Memory Indirect Post-Indexed	([bd,PC],Xn,od)
PC Memory Indirect Pre-Indexed	([bd,PC,Xn],od)
Absolute	
Absolute Short	xxx.W
Absolute Long	xxx.L
Immediate	#<data>

NOTES:

Dn = Data Register, D0-D7
An = Address Register, A0-A7
d_8, d_{16} = A twos-complement, or sign-extended displacement; added as part of the effective address calculation; size is 8 or 16 bits (d_{16} and d_8 are 16- and 8-bit displacements); when omitted, assemblers use a value of zero.
Xn = Address or data register used as an index register; form is Xn.SIZE*SCALE, where SIZE is .W or .L (indicates index register size) and SCALE is 1, 2, 4, or 8 (index register is multiplied by SCALE); use of SIZE and/or SCALE is optional.
bd = A twos-complement base displacement; when present, size can be 16 or 32 bits.
od = Outer displacement, added as part of effective address calculation after any memory indirection; use is optional with a size of 16 or 32 bits.
PC = Program Counter
<data> = Immediate value of 8, 16, or 32 bits
( ) = Effective address
[ ] = Use as indirect address to long word address.

Table A-9 68020 coprocessor registers (reprinted courtesy of Motorola Inc., MOS Integrated Circuits Division, Austin, TX)

Register	Function	Read/Write
Response*	Requests Action from CPU	Read
Control*	CPU Directed Control	Write
Save*	Initiate Save of Internal State	Read
Restore*	Initiate Restore of Internal State	R/W
Operation Word	Current Coprocessor Instruction	Write
Command Word*	Coprocessor Specific Command	Write
Condition Word*	Condition to be Evaluated	Write
Operand*	32-Bit Operand	R/W
Register Selector	Specifies CPU Register or Mask	Read
Instruction Address	Pointer to Coprocessor Instruction	R/W
Operand Address	Pointer to Coprocessor Operand	R/W

*Registers must be implemented in order for each of the instruction types to be implemented.

Table A-10 68020 coprocessor primitives (reprinted courtesy of Motorola Inc., MOS Integrated Circuits Division, Austin, TX)

Primitives
Processor Synchronization Busy from Previous Instruction Busy with Current Instruction Proceed with Next Instruction, If No Trace Proceed with Next Instruction, If Trace Enabled Proceed with Execution, Condition True/False
Instruction Manipulation Tranfer Operation Word Transfer Words from Instruction Stream
Exception Handling Take Privilege Violation if S Bit Not Set Take Pre-Instruction Exception Take Mid-Instruction Exception Take Post-Instruction Exception
General Operand Transfer Evaulate and Pass <ea> Evaluate <ea> and Transfer Data Write to Previously Evaluated <ea> Take Address and Transfer Data Transfer to/from Top of Stack
Register Transfer Transfer CPU Register Transfer CPU Control Register Transfer Multiple CPU Registers Transfer Multiple Coprocessor Registers Transfer CPU SR and/or PC

B Programming reference for the 6820 peripheral interface adapter (PIA)

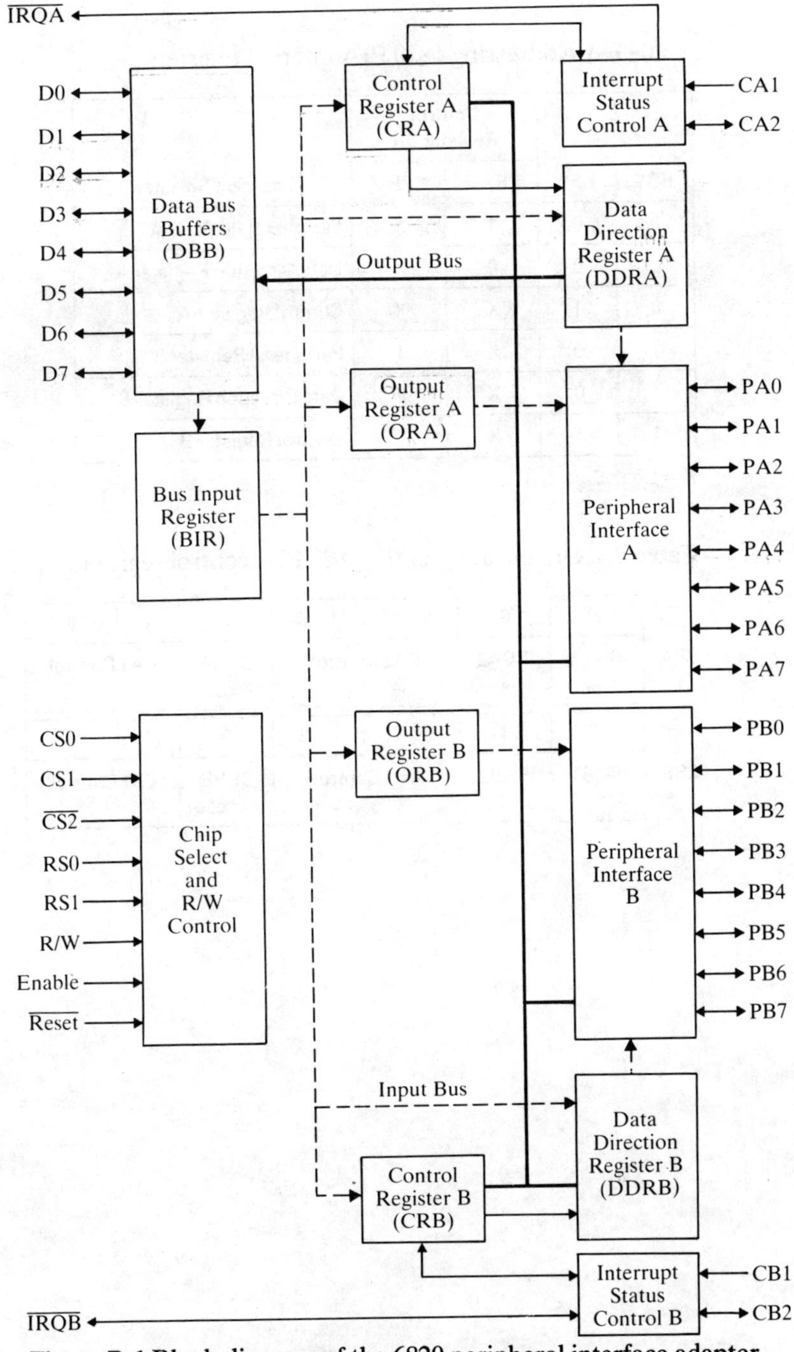

Figure B-1 Block diagram of the 6820 peripheral interface adapter.

Table B-1 Addressing 6820 PIA internal registers

		Control Register Bit		
RS1	**RS0**	**CRA-2**	**CRB-2**	**Location Selected**
0	0	1	X	Peripheral Register A
0	0	0	X	Data Direction Register A
0	1	X	X	Control Register A
1	0	X	1	Peripheral Register B
1	0	X	0	Data Direction Register B
1	1	X	X	Control Register B

X = Don't Care

Table B-2 Organization of the 6820 PIA control registers

	7	6	5	4	3	2	1	0
CRA	IRQA1	IRQA2	CA2 Control			DDRA Access	CA1 Control	
	7	6	5	4	3	2	1	0
CRB	IRQB1	IRQB2	CB2 Control			DDRB Access	CB1 Control	

Table B-3 Control of 6820 PIA interrupt inputs CA1 and CB1

CRA-1 (CRB-1)	CRA-0 (CRB-0)	Interrupt Input CA1 (CB1)	Interrupt Flag CRA-7 (CRB-7)	MPU Interrupt Request $\overline{IRQA}$ ($\overline{IRQB}$)
0	0	↓ Active	Set high on ↓ of CA1 (CB1)	Disabled – $\overline{IRQ}$ remains high
0	1	↓ Active	Set high on ↓ of CA1 (CB1)	Goes low when the interrupt flag bit CRA-7 (CRB-7) goes high
1	0	↑ Active	Set high on ↑ of CA1 (CB1)	Disabled – $\overline{IRQ}$ remains high
1	1	↑ Active	Set high on ↑ of CA1 (CB1)	Goes low when the interrupt flag bit CRA-7 (CRB-7) goes high

Notes: 1. ↑ indicates positive transition (low to high)
2. ↓ indicates negative transition (high to low)
3. The interrupt flag bit CRA-7 is cleared by an MPU Read of the A Data Register, and CRB-7 is cleared by an MPU Read of the B Data Register.
4. If CRA-0 (CRB-0) is low when an interrupt occurs (interrupt disabled) and is later brought high, $\overline{IRQA}$ ($\overline{IRQB}$) occurs after CRA-0 (CRB-0) is written to a "one"

Table B-4 Control of 6820 PIA interrupt inputs CA2 and CB2 [CRA5 (CRB5) is low]

CRA-5 (CRB-5)	CRA-4 (CRB-4)	CRA-3 (CRA-3)	Interrupt Input CA2 (CB2)	Interrupt Flag CRA-6 (CRB-6)	MPU Interrupt Request $\overline{IRQA}$ ($\overline{IRQB}$)
0	0	0	↓ Active	Set high on ↓ of CA2 (CB1)	Disabled – $\overline{IRQ}$ remains high
0	0	1	↓ Active	Set high on ↓ of CA2 (CB2)	Goes low when the interrupt flag bit CRA-6 (CRB-6) goes high
0	1	0	↑ Active	Set high on ↑ of CA2 (CB2)	Disabled – $\overline{IRQ}$ remains high
0	1	1	↑ Active	Set high on ↑ of CA2 (CB2)	Goes low when the interrupt flag bit CRA-6 (CRB-6) goes high

Notes: 1. ↑ indicates positive transition (low to high)
2. ↓ indicates negative transition (high to low)
3. The interrupt flag bit CRA-6 is cleared by an MPU Read of the A Data Register, and CRB-6 is cleared by an MPU Read of the B Data Register.
4. If CRA-3 (CRB-3) is low when an interrupt occurs (interrupt disabled) and is later brought high, $\overline{IRQA}$ ($\overline{IRQB}$) occurs after CRA-3 (CRB-3) is written to a "one"

Table B-5 Control of 6820 PIA CB2 output line (CRB5 is high)

CRA-5	CRA-4	CRA-3	CA2 Cleared	CA2 Set
1	0	0	Low on negative transition of E after an MPU Read "A" Data operation.	High when the interrupt flag bit CRA-7 is set by an active transition of the CA1 signal.
1	0	1	Low on negative transition of E after an MPU Read "A" Data operation.	High on the negative edge of the first "E" pulse which occurs during a deselect.
1	1	0	Low when CRA-3 goes low as a result of an MPU Write to Control Register "A".	Always low as long as CRA-3 is low. Will go high on an MPU Write to Control Register "A" that changes CRA-3 to "one".
1	1	1	Always high as long as CRA-3 is high. Will be cleared on an MPU Write to Control Register "A" that clears CRA-3 to a "zero".	High when CRA-3 goes high as a result of an MPU Write to Control Register "A".

Table B-6 Control of 6820 PIA CA2 output line (CRA5 is high)

CRB-5	CRB-4	CRB-3	CB2 Cleared	CB2 Set
1	0	0	Low on positive transition of the first E pulse following and MPU Write "B" Data Register operation.	High when the interrupt flag bit CRB-7 is set by an active transition of the CB1 signal.
1	0	1	Low on the positive transition of the first E pulse after an MPU Write "B" Data Register operation.	High on the positive edge of the first "E" pulse following an "E" pulse which occured while the part was deselected.
1	1	0	Low when CRB-3 goes low as a result of an MPU Write in Control Register "B".	Always low as long as CRB-3 is low. Will go high on an MPU Write in Control Register "B" that changes CRB-3 to "one".
1	1	1	Always high as long as CRB-3 is high. Will be cleared on an MPU Write Control Register "B" results in clearing CRB-3 to "zero".	High when CRB-3 goes high as a result of an MPU Write into Control Register "B".

C ASCII character set

LSD	MSD	0 000	1 001	2 010	3 011	4 100	5 101	6 110	7 111
0	0000	NUL	DLE	SP	0	@	P	`	p
1	0001	SOH	DC1	!	1	A	Q	a	q
2	0010	STX	DC2	”	2	B	R	b	r
3	0011	ETX	DC3	#	3	C	S	c	s
4	0100	EOT	DC4	$	4	D	T	d	t
5	0101	ENQ	NAK	%	5	E	U	e	u
6	0110	ACK	SYN	&	6	F	V	f	v
7	0111	BEL	ETB	’	7	G	W	g	w
8	1000	BS	CAN	(	8	H	X	h	x
9	1001	HT	EM	)	9	I	Y	i	y
A	1010	LF	SUB	*	:	J	Z	j	z
B	1011	VT	ESC	+	;	K	[	k	}
C	1100	FF	FS	,	<	L	\	l	¦
D	1101	CR	GS	−	=	M	]	m	{
E	1110	SO	RS	•	>	N	^	n	~
F	1111	SI	US	/	?	O	_	o	DEL

Note On most computers, one can enter a non-printable ASCII character (i.e. those below 20 hex) by pressing the CONTROL (CTRL) key and the key corresponding to the character 40 hex higher. For example, one can enter an ETX (03) character by pressing CTRL and C (43 hex). See Table 8-1 for the equivalences.

D 68881 instruction set summary*

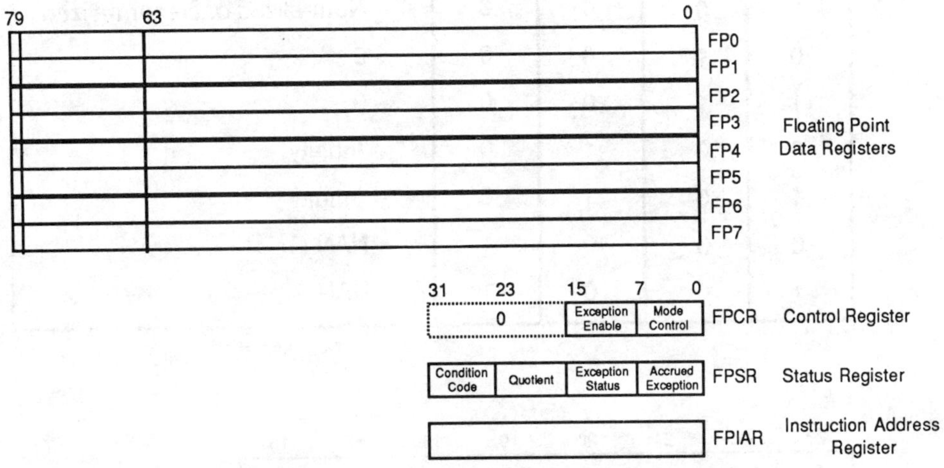

Figure D-1 68881 internal register organization.

*Reprinted courtesy of Motorola Inc., MOS Integrated Circuits Division, Austin, TX

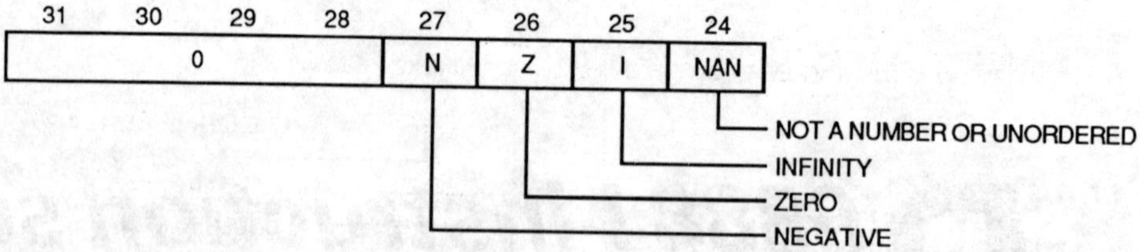

Figure D-2 68881 condition code byte (bits 24–31 of the floating point status register).

Table D-1 68881 condition codes as a function of result data type.

N	Z	I	NAN	Result Data Type
0	0	0	0	+ Normalized or Denormalized
1	0	0	0	– Normalized or Denormalized
0	1	0	0	+ 0
1	1	0	0	– 0
0	0	1	0	+ Infinity
1	0	1	0	– Infinity
0	0	0	1	+ NAN
1	0	0	1	– NAN

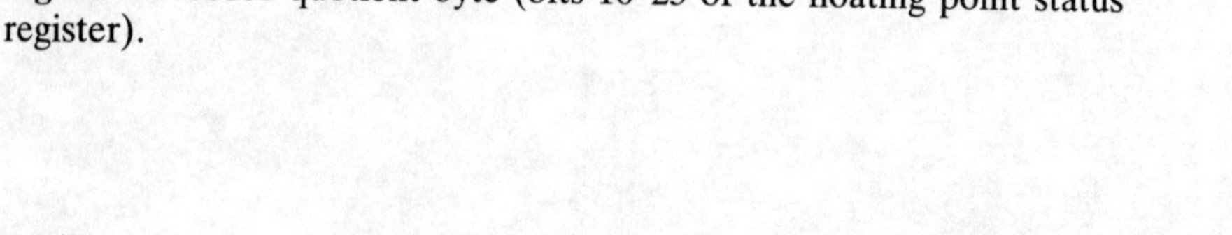

Figure D-3 68881 quotient byte (bits 16–23 of the floating point status register).

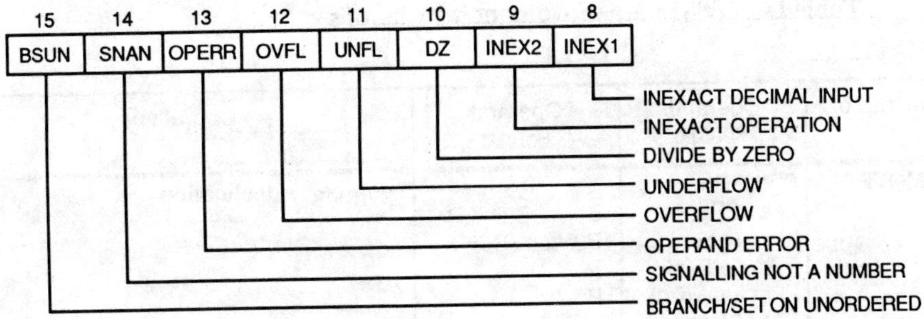

Figure D-4 68881 exception status byte (bits 8–15 of the floating point status register).

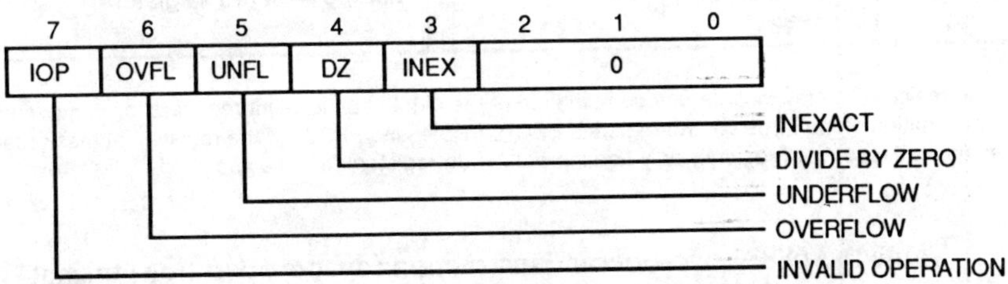

Figure D-5 68881 accrued exception byte (bits 0–7 of the floating point status register).

Table D-2 68881 data movement instructions

Instruction	Operand Syntax	Operand Format	Operation
FMOVE	FPm,FPn	X	source → destination
	<ea>,FPn	B,W,L,S,D,X,P	
	FPm,<ea>	B,W,L,S,D,X	
	FPm,<ea>{#k}	P	
	FPm,<ea>{Dn}	P	
	<ea>,FPcr	L	
	FPcr,<ea>	L	
FMOVECR	#ccc,FPn	X	ROM constant → FPn
FMOVEM	<ea>,<list>[1]	L,X	listed registers → destination
	<ea>,Dn	X	
	<list>[1],<ea>	L,X	source → listed registers
	Dn,<ea>	X	

NOTE:

The register list may include any combination of the eight floating-point registers, or it may contain any combination of the three control registers FPCR, FPSR, and FPIAR. If the register list mask resides in a main processor data register, only floating-point data registers may be specified.

Table D-3 68881 two-operand instruction (dyadic operation) format

Instruction	Operand Syntax	Operand Format	Operation
F<dop>	<ea>,FPn	B,W,L,S,D,X,P	FPn <function> source → FPn
	FPm,FPn	X	

NOTE: <dop> is any one of the dyadic operation specifiers.

Table D-4 68881 two-operand instructions (dyadic operations)

Instruction	Function
FADD	add
FCMP	compare
FDIV	divide
FMOD	modulo remainder
FMUL	multiply
FREM	IEEE remainder
FSCALE	scale exponent
FSGLDIV	single precision divide
FSGLMUL	single precision multiply
FSUB	subtract

Table D-5 68881 one-operand instruction (monadic operation) format

Instruction	Operand Syntax	Operand Format	Operation
F<mop>	<ea>,FPn	B,W,L,S,D,X,P	source → function → FPn
	FPm,FPn	X	
	FPn	X	FPn → function → FPn

NOTE: <mop> is any one of the monadic operations specifiers.

Table D-6 68881 one-operand instructions (monadic operations)

Instruction	Function
FABS	absolute value
FACOS	arc cosine
FASIN	arc sine
FATAN	arc tangent
FATANH	hyperbolic arc tangent
FCOS	cosine
FCOSH	hyperbolic cosine
FETOX	e^x
FETOXM1	$e^x - 1$
FGETEXP	extract exponent
FGETMAN	extract mantissa
FINT	extract integer part
FINTRZ	extract integer part, rounded-to-zero
FLOGN	ln(x)
FLOGNP1	ln(x+1)
FLOG10	$\log_{10}(x)$
FLOG2	$\log_2(x)$
FNEG	negate
FSIN	sine
FSINH	hyperbolic sine
FSQRT	square root
FTAN	tangent
FTANH	hyperbolic tangent
FTENTOX	10^x
FTWOTOX	2^x

Table D-7 68881 one-operand dual instruction (dual monadic operation) format

Instruction	Operand Syntax	Operand Format	Operation
FSINCOS	<ea>,FPc:FPs FPm,FPc:FPs	B,W,L,S,D,X,P X	SIN(source) → FPs; COS(source) → FPc

Table D-8 68881 program control instructions

Instruction	Operand Syntax	Operand Size or Format	Operation
FBcc	<label>	W,L	if condition true, then PC + d → PC
FDBcc	Dn,<label>	W	if condition true, then no operation; else Dn − 1 → Dn; if Dn ≠ −1 then PC + d → PC
FNOP	none	none	no operation
FScc	<ea>	B	if condition true, then 1's → destination else 0's → destination
FTST	<ea> FPn	B,W,L,S,D,X,P X	set FPSR condition codes

Table D-9 68881 conditional test mnemonics

Exception on Unordered

GE	greater than or equal
GL	greater than or less than
GLE	greater than or less than or equal
GT	greater than
LE	less than or equal
LT	less than
NGE	not (greater than or equal)
NGL	not (greater than or less than)
NGLE	not (greater than or less than or equal)
NGT	not greater than
NLE	not (less than or equal)
NLT	not less than
SEQ	signalling equal
SNE	signalling not equal
SF	signalling always false
ST	signalling always true

No Exception on Unordered

OGE	ordered greater than or equal
OGL	ordered greater than or less than
OR	ordered
OGT	ordered greater than
OLE	ordered less than or equal
OLT	ordered less than
UGE	unordered or greater than or equal
UEQ	unordered or equal
UN	unordered
UGT	unordered or greater than
ULE	unordered or less than or equal
ULT	unordered or less than
EQ	equal
NE	not equal
F	always false
T	always true

Table D-10 68881 system control instructions

Instruction	Operand Syntax	Operand Size	Operation
FRESTORE	<ea>	none	state frame → internal registers
FSAVE	<ea>	none	internal registers → state frame
FTRAPcc	none #xxx	none W,L	if condition true, then take exception